Critical Mappings

Of Arturo Islas's Fictions

Bilingual Press/Editorial Bilingüe

Publisher
  Gary D. Keller

Executive Editor
  Karen S. Van Hooft

Associate Editors
  Adriana M. Brady
  Brian Ellis Cassity
  Amy K. Phillips
  Linda St. George Thurston

Address:
  Bilingual Press
  Hispanic Research Center
  Arizona State University
  PO Box 875303
  Tempe, Arizona 85287-5303
  (480) 965-3867

Critical Mappings

of Arturo Islas's Fictions

Edited by Frederick Luis Aldama

Bilingual Press/Editorial Bilingüe
Tempe, Arizona

© 2008 by Bilingual Press/Editorial Bilingüe

All rights reserved. No part of this publication may be reproduced or transmitted in any form or by any means, electronic or mechanical, including photocopy, recording, or any information storage and retrieval system, without permission in writing from the publisher, except in the case of brief quotations embodied in critical articles and reviews.

ISBN-13 978-1-931010-31-3
ISBN-10 1-931010-31-5

Library of Congress Cataloging-in-Publication Data

Critical mappings of Arturo Islas's fictions / Frederick Luis Aldama, editor.
    p. cm.
    Includes bibliographical references.
    ISBN 1-931010-31-5
    1. Islas, Arturo, 1938—Criticism and interpretation. 2. Mexican Americans in literature.   I. Aldama, Frederick Luis, 1969-

PS3559.S44Z53 2004
813'.54—dc22

2004054545

PRINTED IN THE UNITED STATES OF AMERICA

Front cover art: The Eye Contemplates Death (1998) by Daniel Martín Díaz
Cover and interior design by John Wincek, Aerocraft Charter Art Service

ACKNOWLEDGMENTS

The editor wishes to thank the following persons and publications for permission to reprint material appearing in this volume:

Nepantla, for Aldama, Frederick Luis, "Ethnoqueer Re-Archi*tex*turing of Metropolitan Space." *Nepantla,* vol. 1, no. 3 (2000), 581-604.

Bilingual Review Press, for Gonzales-Berry, Erlinda, "Sensuality, Repression, and Death in Arturo Islas's *The Rain God.*" *Bilingual Review/Revista Bilingüe,* vol. 12, no. 3 (Sept.-Dec. 1985), 258-61.

Duke University Press, for Saldívar, José David, "The Hybridity of Culture in Arturo Islas's *The Rain God.*" *The Dialectics of Our America.* Durham: Duke University Press, 1991.

Duke University Press, for Sánchez, Rosaura, "Ideological Discourses in Arturo Islas's *The Rain God.*" *Criticism in the Borderlands: Studies in Chicano Literature, Culture, and Ideology.* Héctor Calderón and José David Saldívar, eds. Durham: Duke University Press, 1991, 114-26.

American Literature, for Sánchez, Marta E., "Arturo Islas's *The Rain God*: an Alternative Tradition." *American Literature*, vol. 62, no. 2 (June 1990), 284-304.

LIT: Literature Interpretation Theory, for Rice, David, "Sinners Among Angels, or Family History and the Ethnic Narrator in Arturo Islas's *The Rain God* and *Migrant Souls.*" *LIT: Literature Interpretation Theory*, vol. 11, no. 2 (Summer 2000), 169-97.

Stanford Center for Chicano Research, for Rosaldo, Renato, "Race and the Borderlands in Arturo Islas's *Migrant Souls.*" Stanford Center for Chicano Research Working Paper Series no. 37, 1992.

Stanford University Libraries, for selected letters and one essay from the Arturo Islas Papers.

TABLE OF CONTENTS

Introduction ix

Islas's Early Fiction

BENDING CHICANO IDENTITY AND EXPERIENCE
in Arturo Islas's Early Borderland Short Stories
Frederick Luis Aldama 3

The Rain God

SENSUALITY, REPRESSION, AND DEATH
in Arturo Islas's *The Rain God*
Erlinda Gonzales-Berry 15

THE HYBRIDITY OF CULTURE in Arturo Islas's *The Rain God*
José David Saldívar 21

ARTURO ISLAS'S *THE RAIN GOD:* An Alternative Tradition
Marta E. Sánchez 39

IDEOLOGICAL DISCOURSES in Arturo Islas's *The Rain God*
Rosaura Sánchez 61

AWASH IN A VALLEY OF TEARS:
The Dialectics of Generation in Arturo Islas's *The Rain God*
John Honerkamp 77

THE MONSTROUS PSEUDOPREGNANT BODY
as Border Crossing Metaphor in *The Rain God*
Vivian Nun Halloran 91

ANOTHER CLOSET IN THE HOUSE OF ANGELS:
The Denial of Identity in *The Rain God*
David N. Ybarra 103

OUT OF PERSONHOOD, OUT OF PRINT:
Cultural Censorship from Harriet Wilson to Arturo Islas
Karen E. H. Skinazi 115

WAYS OF APPROACHING *THE RAIN GOD* in the Classroom
Frederick Luis Aldama 139

Migrant Souls and The Rain God

SINNERS AMONG ANGELS, OR
FAMILY HISTORY AND THE ETHNIC NARRATOR
in Arturo Islas's *The Rain God* and *Migrant Souls*
David Rice 161

"EL CONTRABANDO DE EL PASO": Islas and Geographies of Knowing
Theresa Meléndez 193

MAKE A RUN FROM THE BORDERLANDS:
Arturo Islas's *The Rain God* and *Migrant Souls*
and the Need to Escape Homophobic Masternarratives
Michael Hardin 219

Migrant Souls

RACE AND THE BORDERLANDS in Arturo Islas's *Migrant Souls*
Renato Rosaldo 243

"THE CREATIVE DEFORMATION THAT IS PLOT":
Arturo Islas, Cultural Authenticity, and Ethno/biography
Rosemary Weatherston 251

La Mollie and the King of Tears

ETHNOQUEER RE-ARCHI*TEXT*URING of Metropolitan Space
Frederick Luis Aldama 289

FROM EL PASO TO DEL SAPO: Intersections of Biography and Fiction
Mimi Gladstein 315

Interview

FACTS AND FICTIONS: A Last Interview with Arturo Islas
Héctor Torres 339

Chronology of Major Events 355
Works Cited 361
Contributors 375

introduction

As the title already suggests, the seventeen essays and the interview collected in *Critical Mappings of Arturo Islas's Fictions* focus on Islas's significant contribution to Chicano/a letters. These essays variously explore his early short stories written in the late 1950s and early 1960s now collected in one volume, *Arturo Islas: The Uncollected Works* (2003), to his three published novels, *The Rain God* (1984), *Migrant Souls* (1990), and the posthumously published *La Mollie and the King of Tears* (1996). Each essay—including one that is strictly pedagogical—variously explores how Islas wraps time/space and language around characters as they move through and experience their borderland worlds.

In the mid- to late-1950s, when Islas was a young Stanford undergraduate at coming to terms with his own identity, he first began to perceive of himself as a writer that would texture the experience and identities of Chicanos/as living on borders of race, ethnicity, class, gender, and sexual orientation. While Islas was drawn to the short story form, writing longer narratives would become his true passion. He came of age as a novelist during a period when the voices of the "pioneers" (see Bruce-Novoa, *Chicano Authors* 30) of Chicano/a literature were finally being heard. Indeed, it was in the wake of the civil rights struggles and the heightened visibility of *la causa* as a result of the ever more popular support gained by *el movimiento* that they appeared. They included fiction writers such as Ron Arias, Rolando Hinojosa-Smith, Estela Portillo Trambley, Bernice Zamora, Ernesto Galarza, Rudolfo A. Anaya, Aristeo Brito, and Isabella Ríos. Their work covered a wide range of storytelling styles and resorted to themes aimed at highlighting *la causa* by, among other things, giving texture to the experiences of migrant workers, depicting the alienation and estrangement of urban Chicanos and Chicanas, and celebrating the symbolic reclamation of the Southwest (Aztlán) by positively evoking a Nahuatl spiritual tradition and an Amerindian heritage.

However, by the mid-1970s, when Arturo Islas began to write *The Rain God*, which as a work in progress he had entitled "Día de los muertos/Day of the Dead," many authors like him and Luis Leal were already growing weary of "Aztlán" as the only model sanctioned for Chicano/a artistic expression. Two years before embarking on the writing of "Día de los muertos" (1975-1976), Islas pointed this out in the journal *Miquiztli: A Journal of Arte, Poesía, Cuento, y Canto*: "More often than not, much of the fiction we do have is document, and sometimes not very well written document. Much of what is passed off as literature is a compendium of folklore, religious superstition, and recipes for tortillas. All well and good, but it is not literature" (Aldama, *Dancing with Ghosts* 27). While writing "Día de los muertos," Islas revisited and studied the work of many different authors and their craft. His influences evinced in this period not only hailed from both north and south of the U.S.-Mexico border and several South American countries (including García Márquez's magic realism and Faulkner's dynastic gothic epics), but also from the East and beyond. At one point, he considered that the standards that should be used to judge him as a writer should be those called upon to assess his peers not just from the United States and Latin America, but also from England, Russia, France, and Spain. He imagined himself a novelist working alongside all those authors he felt attracted to—all of them writing "novels at once in a circular room" (cited in Aldama's *Dancing with Ghosts* 48). As such, he did not see himself as a writer confined by a single type of influence or circumscribed by national literary canons; on the contrary, he actively studied the craft of Cervantes's *mise-en-abyme* and other self-reflexivity devices, as well as his particular brand of picaresque narration, Flaubert's carefully devised art of allusion and *mot précis* stylistics, Proust's radical renovation of realism in narrative and most innovative use of temporality as the central organizing principle of his opus magnum, Forster's queer thematic and aesthetics, Stendhal's subtle art of character creation, Conrad's impressionistic technique, and Turgenev's patrilineal epic form. He studied such different writers—along with others—while seeking the voice that would allow him to create a novel capable of exploding all barriers limiting the narrative expression of the full Chicano/a experience. As his pen flowed, he both affirmed Chicano cultural heritage—using bilingual technique and bicultural image and form—and also radically complicated the literary terrain with the introduction of his queer Chicano protagonist. (Though John Rechy's queer Chicano protagonist appeared over a decade earlier in *City of Night*, Rechy nearly erased the "Chicano" cultural element in this novel.)

Needless to say, Islas had an extremely difficult time finding a publisher. His aim to radicalize the Chicano literary topography of his time by using a temporally experimental technique to tell the story of a queer Chicano, and by including in his narration a large amount of words and phrases in Spanish, was met with nearly a decade of rejection letters that did little to hide their homophobia and racism. (See José David Saldívar's "The Hybridity of Culture in Arturo Islas's *The Rain God*.") In spite of the great gains in the political arena as far as the queer and brown civil and other rights were concerned, the publishing world was clearly still being run by editors that had not yet acknowledged this or were too afraid to take certain commercial risks.

By the time Islas finally managed to find a publisher in 1984 (the Palo Alto-based Alexandrian Press), some deep changes were starting to take place—at least among the independent publishers. For example, Aunt Lute had already published in 1981—and to notable acclaim—the lesbian feminist-charged woman-of-color-voiced poems, short stories, and essays collected in *This Bridge Called My Back*. And, in 1983, Pat Mora, Alma Gómez, and Mariana Romo-Carmona's *Cuentos: Stories by Latinas* made visible Chicana and Latina (Nuyorican and Cuban émigré) short story writers who sought to break a long-imposed silence surrounding sexuality—especially Latina lesbianism. The writings in both collections explored a number of storytelling techniques and used a mixture of Spanish and English to complexly refigure a traditional Chicano/a and Latino/a literary landscape dominated by heteronormative narratives. However, as far as gay Chicano narratives were concerned, Islas was still working against resistant currents—even within the smaller presses.

When Islas published *The Rain God* in October 1984, he had toned down the queer voice, transformed his earlier first-person narrative to that of a third person, and subtracted much of its bilingualism. But this did not delete the presence of a commanding bicultural, bilingual queer borderland subjectivity. The novel was an instant success—so much so that the distribution capabilities of Alexandrian Press soon became largely insufficient to supply the demand. (Later, because of this, Islas acquired the paperback rights and eventually sold them to Avon.) When Islas's *The Rain God* entered the book marketplace, other post-1960s "second-wave" authors were just being published, among them Mary Helen Ponce (*Taking Control*), Helena María Viramontes (*The Moths and Other Stories*), Ana Castillo (*The Mixquiahuala Letters*), Sandra Cisneros (*Woman Hollering Creek*), and Denise Chávez, to name a few. And *The Rain God* coincided with the arrival of other so-identified "multicultural" writers such as John Edgar Wideman, Leslie Marmon Silko, Louise Erdrich, Maxine Hong Kingston, Alice Walker, and Toni Morrison, who employed a number of storytelling modes and genres to explore otherwise unnarrated stories of the African American, Asian American, and Native American experience. (Such attention to writers like Islas, Walker, Kingston, and so on resulted in the very heated "culture war debates" at universities across the nation. At Stanford, Islas helped to engineer the radical reformation of Stanford's Western Culture Program, which led the curriculum committee to accept the inclusion of works by women and minority writers; it also led to a visit by then secretary of education William Bennett, who went to Stanford to defend the Western canon.)

Six months after *The Rain God* received the Border Regional Library Association Award in 1986, Islas set out to write his second novel, *La Mollie and the King of Tears*, a narrative fiction that moved him away from the more autobiographical approach he had used in his first novel. When Islas first sat down to pound out

La Mollie, he imagined it not as a sequel to *The Rain God* but as a "picaresque novel" (his words) set in San Francisco that would stand alone. Islas had always been interested in the Spanish-born picaresque tradition and in its various transnational manifestations, including the Mexican ones (he had studied the tradition formally as a graduate student at Stanford in the 1960s). He found the voice he needed for his narrative—that of the *pachuco* Louie Mendoza—and wrote a draft of the novel in less than a year. After several revisions and rewrites, Islas was ready to send it out. Again, he received nothing but rejection after rejection, including from the very press—University of New Mexico—that ended up posthumously publishing the novel in 1996.

The late 1980s was a period in which Islas's life was emotionally very unsteady. He wanted to pursue his craft as a novelist, but publishers were not interested in his work, and in January 1988 he received the news that he was HIV positive. Though he kept writing, much of it served mainly to channel his huge pendulum swings of emotions, moving from deep depression brought on by his overwhelming awareness of looming death to the euphoria and even ecstasy over his coming into his own as a writer—*The Rain God*'s popularity and the continuous pouring out of *La Mollie and the King of Tears*.

In spite of the physical and emotional setbacks, Islas's determination to continue to write and publish novels went unflinching. However, it was not until the well-known agent Sandra Djikstra (Amy Tan's and Maxine Hong Kingston's representative) took him under her wing that the tides shifted for the better. With Dijkstra at the helm, he found a New York publisher (Avon) to publish a mass-marketed paperback version of *The Rain God* and another (William Morrow) to buy his sequel, *Migrant Souls*.

Writing, rewriting, and finely sculpting *Migrant Souls* into a novel took longer than Islas had expected—and his impatient editor wished—but this constant work served as a pressure release valve, a clear proof of his vitality, and a way to escape and overcome feelings of being a very ill person and a sexual pariah. Writing allowed him to appease those demons that would, he wrote in his journal, "eat my brains w/out mercy" (Aldama,

Dancing with Ghosts 60). His hard work had paid off. On January 11, 1990, Islas received his first copy of *Migrant Souls* from William Morrow. By the end of the month, 6,000 copies of *Migrant Souls* had hit Bay Area bookstore shelves. The novel sold out within a month, taking it to the top of the *San Francisco Chronicle*'s best-seller list. The seal of approval given by famous writers such as Denise Levertov and Adrienne Rich, who wrote blurbs for the novel's dust jacket, was confirmed by the generally favorable critical praise. For example, in a review for the *El Paso Times*, Mimi Gladstein wrote, "Islas is an insightful writer: his characters ring with the authenticity born of a keen insight into the working of the human heart in conflict with itself. *Migrant Souls* is a compelling novel written in a way that both instructs and moves the reader" (Gladstein 27). For those familiar with Chicano/a letters, Islas's *Migrant Souls* had broken new ground: it was hailed as one of the most powerful Chicano/a novels to radically contest those pure (Spanish) and impure (mestizo) colonialist ideologies that many within the Chicano/a community internalized and continued to perpetuate.

This period of efflorescence coincided with the appearance of many of the first scholarly analyses of Islas's work. In *Critical Mappings* I include some of them, written by Renato Rosaldo, Marta Sánchez, and Rosaura Sánchez. In "Race and the Borderlands," Renato Rosaldo identifies the powerful presence of a critique of internalized colonialism within the Chicano/a community in *Migrant Souls*. Rosaldo also situates the novel within a large discussion of ethnicity ("difference") within a U.S. nation-state based on racial exclusionary practices. For Rosaldo, Islas complicates the traditional Anglo-Other racial binary in the narrativization of a *mestizaje* subjectivity; as such, *Migrant Souls* destabilizes exclusionary master narratives of nation—European as purity/Mexican-Chicano as impurity—to embrace a more comprehensive and inclusive citizenship paradigm.

Also included here is Erlinda Gonzales-Berry's seminal review essay on *The Rain God* that was published in 1985. In "Sensuality, Repression, and Death in Arturo Islas's *The Rain God*," Gonzales-Berry identifies the bridge function of the narration that creates in-between spaces (saint and sinner as well as life and death) that open up new possibilities for the protagonist Miguel Chico to experience a less oppressive present and future. This essay was followed by the much deeper analyses published in the early 1990s by José David Saldívar, Marta Sánchez, and Rosaura Sánchez.

In "The Hybridity of Culture in Arturo Islas's *The Rain God*," Saldívar shows the social prejudices and materialist conventions that prevailed in the New York publishing scene. The New York publishing gatekeepers published Antonio Villarreal and Víctor Villaseñor not because they were better writers, but because they adhered to a safe, up-by-the-bootstraps migrant formula; they chose not to publish Islas's novels because of his experimental and queer-gazed narrative—especially as seen in "Día de los muertos." Saldívar's exploration of what he identifies as the "extradiscursive" context of Islas's attempt to break into mainstream publishing speaks to larger issues of which "ethnic" voices are allowed to be heard and how these ultimately constitute a simplistic and reductive "ethnic" American literary canon.

Marta Sánchez's essay, "Arturo Islas's *The Rain God*: an Alternative Tradition," enlarges the scope of the American literary canon in her nuanced analysis of the content and form of *The Rain God*. As such she shows how Islas's use of a variety of narrative techniques (self-reflexive narration, for example) gives voice to the otherwise voiceless and educates Anglophonic, monolingual readers to be more culturally sensitive and aware. Thus she writes that Islas "transforms the liability of 'otherness' into the asset of narrative device" to highlight the "minority" writer's role of mediator between cultures. She also points out how such a narrative that focuses on the lives of Chicano/a characters inhabiting borderland spaces radically sets this novel apart from others that make up the canon.

In "Ideological Discourses in Arturo Islas's *The Rain God*," Rosaura Sánchez explores the procedures and approaches that allow the novel to represent and complicate identity and experiences within a United States-Mexico geopolitical borderland. Here, too, she powerfully explores the issue of heterosexism and heteronormativity within such male-dominated areas. In a deconstructionist move, Rosaura Sánchez finally contends that the novel's resistance "does not formulate a distinctive alternative but merely opposes what it, ironically, affirms." With this in mind, she powerfully shows that Félix's queer preferences do not de facto negate patriarchal structures: both in his role as an "authoritarian husband with a wife *and* four children at home" and also in his relations with men in which he takes advantage of his "position of power." As Sánchez indicates, the image of the desert aptly captures the novel's "deconstructive and reconstructive strategies" whereby the text simultaneously reconstructs cultural practices and ideologies while deconstructing such structures "to reveal their contradictions."

Building on and complicating further these early interpretations of *The Rain God* are essays by John Honerkamp, Vivian Nun Halloran, David Ybarra, and Karen E. H. Skinazi. In Honerkamp's "Awash in a Valley of Tears: The Dialectics of Generation in Arturo Islas's *The Rain God*," Mamá Chona's asceticism and the carnality she ascribes to her children and grandchildren is fully explored. For Honerkamp, the Angel family's inhabitation of a borderland cultural and geopolitical space is defined by the overwhelming subtextual presence of religious belief systems. Specifically, Honerkamp does not simply dismiss Mamá Chona's religious fanaticism and internalizing of racist paradigms, but explores her asceticism as a complex expression of identity. For example, he writes, "Her repudiation of her body is not merely a renunciation of the flesh or a disavowal of pleasure. It is better described paradoxically as the promotion of a body whose agency and maintenance are ensured in that body's privation." Her absolute negation of a bodily presence, then, is more than her desire to ascend to that place of purity embodied by the Virgin Mary; it is a "reconstruction of her life narrative as a story of Christian abnegation and self-containment—a story of the reclamation of spiritual, sexual, and racial purity—[that] fails because her alienness resists suppression."

In "The Monstrous Pseudo-Pregnant Body as Border-Crossing Metaphor in *The Rain God*" Vivian Nun Halloran also focuses on the body. Here, however, she explores Islas's use of the trope of the monstrous pregnant body as the "site of the abject as well as the embodiment of the border identity that defines Mexican Americans." In her careful analysis, the condition of Mamá Chona's uterus and Miguel Chico's ileostomy and colostomy becomes an "uncanny instance of border crossing, which blurs the boundaries between inside and outside." Halloran provocatively suggests that "by invoking the pregnant male and/or post-menopausal body itself as both monstrous and, literally, as a monster who haunts both characters in their moments of delirium, Islas critiques the Angel family's negative view of reproduction and their fear of the permanence of immigration." Finally, Halloran's "monstrous body" becomes an expression of the characters' inability to claim a Chicano identity as a way to negotiate life in the borderland.

David N. Ybarra turns to a highly nuanced reading of *The Rain God* to suggest that it is the queer Chicano subject that, like the Chicana feminist-lesbian recuperated figure of La Llorona, has the power to intervene and resist otherwise gender and sexuality restrictive codes of conduct within the Chicano community. Here, Ybarra further enhances our understanding of Miguel Chico by exploring how an "in-the-closet" queer identity can work powerfully as an "absent presence" to "deconstruct the myths the Angel family have fashioned of and for themselves."

Expanding on Saldívar's analysis of the social and material conventions that confine Chicano/a writers, Karen E. H. Skinazi offers an incisive comparative examination of texts by Arturo Islas and the African American nineteenth-century writer Harriet Wilson. Though separated by a century and hailing from different ethnic literary traditions, in "Out of Personhood, Out of Print: Cultural Censorship from Harriet Wilson to Arturo Islas," Skinazi identifies a common ground: Harriet Wilson wrote *Our Nig* (1859) during a time when black writers could find a publisher only if their work belonged to the slave narrative genre, and Arturo Islas's unpublished and published novels were also systematically rejected by publishing houses because of their texturing of a gay Chicano subjectivity: "Just as Islas's novels of gays and Mexicans fail to fit the standards of Chicano and minority literature, so too did Wilson's tale of Northern Aggression fail to fit the standard of Southern slave narratives." However, as Skinazi writes, "Both *did* publish their works, but only by subverting their 'dangerous' ideas." Here she formulates what she calls a "triangulation of identity, or *triple-consciousness*," to discuss Islas's and Wilson's invention of a "new Other" that is less than desired by agents, publishers, and critics. For Skinazi, although Arturo Islas and Harriet Wilson attempted to revise their various manuscripts to conform to normative cultural expectations, they ultimately did not erase the presence of a "third consciousness." As such, she concludes, their work continues to "break down the fortifications of minority literature's constructed uniformity."

To wrap up these essays that focus on Islas's *The Rain God*, I include a pedagogically oriented essay, "Ways of Approaching *The Rain God* in the Classroom." Here I offer suggestions for teaching the text in a classroom, which include discussion of dominant themes and possible close readings.

In the next section, "*Migrant Souls* and *The Rain God*," I include comparative scholarly essays by David Rice, Theresa Meléndez, and Michael Hardin that focus on the Angel family novels. In "Sinners Among Angels, or Family History and the Ethnic Narrator in Arturo Islas's *The Rain God* and *Migrant Souls*," David Rice provides an intra- and inter-textual analysis that deepens our understanding of characters such as Miguel Chico and Josie Salazar, who look beyond the borders of Del Sapo—though not to the mainstream—for a sense of self. For example, Rice reads Miguel Chico's illness—and his monstrous dream—not as a way to mask his queer sexuality, but as his coming into a complicated sexually and culturally hybrid vision of himself. Thus, Rice states, "Just as he allowed the monster of ethnic contradiction to embrace him and possess him, he must himself embrace that monster in return; he must accept the contradictions inherent in his ethnicity if he is ever to make sense of his identity or his family's story." Rice then turns to an analysis of narrative form and to how the narratives in both books represent one long continuous narration that ends with the celebration of the "hybrid-ethnic figure."

Theresa Meléndez explores the concept of *contrabando* to frame her analysis in the aptly titled "*El Contrabando de El Paso*: Islas and Geographies of Knowing." For Meléndez, Islas's Angel family novels represent conflict and resistance within a reimagined El Paso spatiality. To read the novels is to read El Paso's multiple layers of political and cultural history. Here the Angel family's relationships are marked by racial tension, conflict, poverty, and violence. The river becomes the image in the novel of El Paso's fractured urban space as well as the image of possibility and the expression of new confluences of form. After tracing the literary figuration of the borderlands from Cabeza de Vaca's *Relación* (1542), John Rechy's short story "El Paso del Norte" through to contemporary poets such as Benjamin Sáenz and Ricardo Sánchez—and using the theories of Henri Lefebvre and Edward Soja on the economics of space—Meléndez shows Islas's use of five topoi—mountains, river, desert, *mexicanidad*, and the body—to continue and complicate a tradition of writing that opens eyes to how "geography informs power relations in a place marked by race and class struggles since its entrance into the Western imaginary."

Michael Hardin's essay "Make a Run from the Borderlands: Arturo Islas's *The Rain God* and *Migrant Souls* and the Need to Escape Homophobic Masternarratives" is also attuned to the intersection of space and body. After discussing the queer and lesbian writings of Richard Rodriguez's *Days of Obligation*, Anzaldúa's *Borderlands*, and John Rechy's *City of Night*, Hardin explores how Islas's Angel family novels exist within a tradition of borderland narratives that queer U.S. and Mexican heteronormative cultural and national paradigms, but do so from a distant remove. Namely, it is because these writers move to urban centers like San Francisco and Los Angeles so that they can invent story worlds that complicate United States-Mexico borderland spaces.

In the section "Migrant Souls," I include the already mentioned essay by Renato Rosaldo ("Race and the Borderlands in Arturo Islas's *Migrant Souls*") and an essay by Rosemary

Weatherston titled "The Creative Deformation That Is Plot: Arturo Islas, Cultural Authenticity, and Ethno/biography." Unlike Rosaldo's essay that focuses on how *Migrant Souls* destabilizes "naturalized" narratives of racial purity and national belonging, Weatherston explores the conflictive role of the ethnic writer: Islas as both the voice of a community and one who seeks to sidestep readings of his novel as ethnography. Here Weatherston carefully delineates the social and academic contexts and conditions that lead readers to consume the ethnic novel as "ethno-biography"; she then demonstrates how *Migrant Souls* resists such a delimiting ethnographic reading. As she sums up, "rather than subsuming issues of intrapersonal and intragroup variations under a stable, homogenous model of cultural difference, the novel, in fact, formally and thematically depicts culture and difference in terms of contradiction, mediation, and change. Chicano ethnic identity becomes significant in *Migrant Souls* not as inheritable cultural property or descriptive literary content, but as a shifting, mediated process." Weatherston proposes that we refrain from approaching a novel like *Migrant Souls* in terms of an assumed truth-telling content, for such an approach plays into reductive models of representing Chicano/a culture and considers that it should be read instead in terms of how the novel educates its readers to identify a more fluid and complexly layered ethnic identity and experience.

In the last section of this book, I include essays that focus on Islas's posthumously published *La Mollie and the King of Tears*. In my essay "Ethnoqueer Re-Archi*tex*turing of Metropolitan Space" I explore how Islas—and Richard Rodriguez—invent "autoethnographic" texts that sidestep old-school us/them models for understanding the formation of the queer Chicano self within metropolitan spaces. Both Islas and Rodriguez turn to the metropolis to invent "coexisting subjects that multiply inhabit palimpsestic city spaces that enfold race, sexuality, class, and gender." Here I explore Islas's radical shift in narrative style and characterization from *The Rain God*, showing how his straight-identified narrator/protagonist comes into a *bent* revisioning of straight/queer self that dedifferentiates Chicano subjectivity.

Following this, I include Mimi Gladstein's autobiographically informed essay "From El Paso to Del Sapo: Intersections of Biography and Fiction." Gladstein uses *La Mollie and the King of Tears* as a springboard to explore Islas's blurring of the boundaries between biographical fact and narrative fiction in all his novels in order to make room for the texturing of many characters and selves.

I conclude this work with Héctor Torres's interview: "Facts and Fictions: A Last Interview with Arturo Islas." This was the last interview with Arturo Islas before he died at his home in Palo Alto on February 15, 1991. Here Islas speaks about his life, Chicano/a literature generally, and the art of crafting fiction.

Critical Mappings aims to enliven and enrich our understanding of Arturo Islas's creative œuvre. The many scholarly essays provide various new and vital wedges into the complex story worlds presented in his short stories and novels that have helped clear a space for the expression of a complex Chicano/a identity and experience within our contemporary American literary canon.

Frederick Luis Aldama

ISLAS'S
EARLY
FICTION

BENDING CHICANO IDENTITY AND EXPERIENCE
in Arturo Islas's Early Borderland Short Stories

Frederick Luis Aldama

Since the hard-won publication of his novel *The Rain God* in 1984, the late Arturo Islas has secured a central place in Chicano/a letters today. Of course, there is much more to Islas as a writer than *The Rain God*. There are his other novels: the darkly lyrical borderscaped *Migrant Souls* and his posthumously published rapid-fire *caló*-narrated, urban-set *La Mollie and the King of Tears*. There are his short stories and poems that use style and narrative technique to play with linear time and fictionalize storyworld spaces that texture a complex array of Chicano/a identity and experience. Though Islas's visibility as a central figure in Chicano/a letters was delayed because of the deep-seated prejudices in the New York publishing circles—*The Rain God* met thirty-plus rejections based on its "too ethnic" content—his sense of himself as a border-themed Chicano writer dates to his days as an undergraduate at Stanford in the late 1950s. (See also Aldama, *Dancing with Ghosts*.) Islas turned from a career as a neurosurgeon to commit himself to writing about the experiences of Chicanos/as learning to negotiate borders between nations, races, genders— even sexualities. While Islas tried his hand at poetry during this early period, it was the short story form that he gravitated toward to creatively recover his identity as a Chicano informed by nascent same-sex feelings and desires. Islas's early fictional worlds not only cycle through acts of re-covering (making disappear) and recovering (making appear by narrating, remembering, and forgetting), but also identify those Chicano/a subjects that inhabit a constant state of "recovery" and desire for health and life as they feel disease in a xenophobic, heterosexist Euro-American mainstream and macho Chicano world. (These early short stories appear along with a large corpus of poems and analytic essays I recovered in the edited volume *Arturo Islas: The Uncollected Works*.)

Islas's act of recovering his Chicano identity through short story writing is especially loaded. Such acts extend beyond his choice to become a writer who reflects and complicates Chicano/a experience and identity. His writing functioned as a vital resource that helped him recover from a variety of deathly diseases: after the polio virus attacked Islas at age eight and left him with a lifelong limp, he immersed himself in writing—a skill he carefully honed as a writer and the editor of the undergraduate literary journal *Sequoia*, and which was shaped under the tutelage of Yvor Winters and Hortense Calisher as an undergraduate and graduate student at Stanford. After an ileostomy at age thirty-one, he channeled his estrangement from his body—a post-operative body in which his anus had been replaced with a plastic tube that connected his stomach to what he called his "shit bag"—into his poetry, short stories, and novels. Later, he would race against impending death from HIV-related pneumonia by *recovering* more of his semi-autobiographical character, Miguel Ángel, in the writing of *Migrant Souls*, the sequel to *The Rain God*. Finally, then, Islas's acts of recovery in his early short stories are some of the early manifestations of what would become a lifelong commitment to exploring the ever-changing and complex landscape of Chicano/a experience and identity.

Borderland Bodies and Texts

Islas was born in El Paso, Texas, on May 25, 1938. His birth corresponded with Mexican President Lázaro Cárdenas's push to define the United States-Mexico border as a free-zone space for corporate development. As Islas grew up on the El Paso-Juárez border, he experienced the contradictory tensions of capital first hand: the huge prosperity of an Anglo elite along with the simultaneous impoverishment of what was growing into a Mexican majority. While the racial and class geopolitical rifts were felt by Islas because of his family's bilingual privilege and position north of the Mexican border, in the 1940s Islas also experienced the contradictions of capitalism at home. Even though the U.S. and

Mexican governments began to regulate the movement of brown bodies across the Stanton Street and Santa Fe bridges to control flows of labor and ensure maximum profit, Islas could move across the border freely. His father's fluency in English and Spanish opened doors into the El Paso police department, where he first worked as a patrolman and then later as a detective and officer. He became one of the appendages to a panoptic surveillance system on the border and within the differently racially classed neighborhoods in El Paso. Moreover, the family could use their dollars to hire lower-wage earning mestiza labor to help look after Islas and his two younger brothers, Mario and Louie. As Islas grew older, he became increasingly aware of his family's participation and uncritical reproduction of economic exchanges that guaranteed the growth of an asymmetric capitalism along the border. He became increasingly aware of his own need to critique the formation of this economically exploitive borderland that turned a dollar by using, abusing, then turning into garbage *mexicano/a* subjects.

As a late teen and young adult during the 1940s and 1950s, Islas came to identify with a so-called "Greater Mexican" (as José Limón uses the term) geopolitical sensibility—a sense of self being stretched between nations and cultures as long as the length of the border; a sense of self acutely aware of the borders that divided neighborhoods in El Paso and that divided Chicanos/as north from *mexicanos* south of the border. For Islas, home was filled with contradictions and divisions. When he began to study and write fiction formally at Stanford, he gave thematic presence and complex narrative texture to the contradictions felt at home and to those racial and economic tensions that were ripping bodies apart within a very real borderland space.

His early short stories revolve around the border as well as experiment with narrative technique (point of view and tempo, for example) to destabilize boundaries that traditionally divide forms (essay from story or serious realism from comedy, for example). In response to his family's participation in the economic division of brown peoples, while in graduate school at Stanford he wrote a piece titled "Dear Arturo" (1962) that craftily shifts between essayistic, autobiographical, and fictional styles. He invents a narrating self that crystallizes a conflicted relationship between an older- and newer-generation Mexican-identified border dweller. At one point the new-generation identified narrator critiques the old generation's internalizing of a Spanish (coded as pure) versus Mexican (coded as impure) paradigm that, ironically, reveals itself only during times of familial intimacy. On one occasion, he informs, "the only moments my grandmother became real to me were those times when she—the well-educated Mexican aristocratic lady—would weep because she had to wash the dishes because it was the maid's day off. She taught me to be polite and courteous, which I learned quickly because those qualities endeared me to everyone, except my father" (Aldama, *Arturo Islas: The Uncollected Works* 36). By fictionalizing experience of this whiteness-as-civilized and darkness-as-primitive located within the space of home (something he continued in his writing of *The Rain God*, where he displaces his self into the third-person characterization of Miguel Ángel), Islas turns his critique of his family's reproduction of hierarchies of difference into a more universal borderland setting. In another hybrid-genre piece entitled "An Existential Document" (1958), Islas continued to fuse fiction and fact to formulate a critique not so much against the racist Euro-Anglo communities in El Paso, but against those Chicano families like his own whose internalized racism reproduced deep schisms within the brown community. At one point, he writes in this essayistic story that he will "see if poverty breeds sanctity" (32) by crossing over to the other side against the wishes of his family ("they cannot see why I bother with those people"), experiencing as a U.S.-formed brown body (bilingual and with the privilege of a dollar income) those geopolitically informed racial and social contradictions as an enhanced reality in Juárez.

Short Story and the Decolonial Imaginary

In several of Islas's more traditionally structured short stories (those characterized by a straightforward chronology and the presence of the grand epiphany), he adds issues of gender and sexuality into his texturing of U.S./Mexico border subjectivity. Islas does not always mix genre and narrative technique to destabilize the reader's understanding of colonizing borders. He often uses the straightforward short story narrative form with its linear plot and character arcs to detail the possible transgression of sexual, racial, social, and gendered boundaries. For example, in his short story "A Boy with the Eyes of a Fawn" (1957), Islas manipulates the content of that identified as a subordinate genre (traditionally the short story has been identified as a more primitive, childlike narrative to the more civilized and mature genre of the novel) to frame brown voices of subversion and resistance. Here, Islas packs in metaphors and motifs that gravitate around vision and the eyes—veils, glasses, windows, and optical instruments—to emphasize not just those characters who have internalized oppressive master-narrative frames such as Catholicism, but also to reflect the way in which the story aims to de-form such frames. Here, Islas employs the story form to give agency and empowerment to the experiences of the gendered outlaw—the prostitute Teresa—who uses the ideological lens of Catholicism as a vehicle to make known a mestiza feminist subjectivity. And, in the story "Poor Little Lamb" (1957), Islas invents a seemingly straightforward story about the life of Miguel Chávez that becomes a complex coming-of-age narrative of a young Chicano defying the will of his father and coming to terms with a non-macho male identity. Miguel's father seeks to quash any non-macho coded behavior: He writes, "His father was ashamed of him, complaining that his firstborn—and a Chávez at that—was a brat" (21). Alienated from his macho father because he refuses to fit into a restrictive male role, Miguel learns to clear a space for his own rebirth as a non-macho by coming into a critical consciousness of an oppressive patriarchal ideology at work within the home and beyond. Moreover, the struggle between son (non-macho) and father (macho) becomes a metonym for the struggle between a disenfranchised U.S./Mexico borderland subject and an Anglo elite community. As the story unfolds, such constructed hierarchies of class (*casta*) difference are destabilized when Miguel Chávez chooses to reach beyond the confines of home with all of its concomitant ideological baggage. He reaches out to the women in his community and chooses to become a doctor (who employs both Western and mestizo medicines) working for the community. Islas's character Miguel Chávez, then, comes to represent a new generation of brown male subject that breaks with traditionally restrictive patriarchal roles and also chooses to cast aside a *casta* ideology that divides brown borderland communities. As Chávez clears the space for a new hybrid subjectivity (coded as feminine and masculine as well as non-*indio* and *indio*), he comes into that place where the body and spirit exist as one and transcend national, cultural, and social ideologies that otherwise restrict experience and identity.

Islas was very much interested in writing stories about new generations of Chicanos/as that could balance the premodern and modern, community and individuality, and Mexican and U.S. culture. In 1957 Islas wrote the short story "Clara Mendoza," which focused on three Chicana characters who variously renegotiate a borderland governed by a brown, macho patriarchy heavily invested in maintaining racial, gendered, and social hierarchies of difference. The three sisters, Clara, Luisa, and Arabella Mendoza, live in an unidentified border town. They exist at the socioeconomic margins, working for just enough money to survive as taco vendors at the local bullfight arena. Islas's story shows that the sisters become harshly divisive when they fall into the trap of desiring according to the traditional axis of heterosexuality: each dreams of catching the ur-macho matador, Miguel. (It is not coincidental that Islas chooses the name "Miguel"; he used this name in all his fictions to identify male characters that were intellectually powerful and spiritually grounded. Miguel is the protagonist in *The Rain God* and *Migrant Souls* and appears as a minor character in the *La Mollie and the King of Tears,* for example.) The story also has two of the sisters ultimately choosing not to participate in this divisive game and form a strong bond of collective survival. Again, Islas creates a short story that is largely symbolic. As the narrator describes the stadium crowd's "olés" growing louder and louder and how this crowd begins to shape into a threatening "mob," Clara and Luisa come into a sense of solidarity as women (24). Here, the narrator juxtaposes the crowd with the women to emphasize the connection between the working class and gender oppression: both become a threat to an elite-identified (Euro-

Spanish) nation-state identity. (Notably, bullfights were banned in Mexico during Spanish colonial rule for fear of the galvanization and revolt of the mestizo peoples.) The narrator's detailing of the geometric lines of attack and retreat that take place within a pre-defined space of the arena begins to weigh heavily with symbolism as read against the two sisters' struggle to survive within the boundaries that restrict their lives. The narrator describes the bullfight as a performance—"a kind of ridiculous and grotesque dance"—that reflects the story's construction of gender as performance, but a performance that has the power to overturn restrictive gendered roles (28). Throughout the narrator's description of the bullfight, the word "across" appears eighteen times, foregrounding the sisters' move away from a past that restricts and into a present that emancipates in their newly established solidarity. Finally, the story's denouement arrives as Clara and Luisa resist performing predetermined gendered roles, choosing not to function as bodily sites to reproduce matadors (male warrior-heroes) to promote a gender-oppressive Mexican patriarchal ideology.

When the reader encounters the other sister, Arabella, constructions of class and gender as they inform and de-form subjectivity crystallize. When the narrator describes Clara and Luisa in terms of their working-class position, he characterizes (negatively) Arabella with more upwardly mobile, urban/modern attributes. Arabella stands in sharp contrast to her sisters. She performs her gender to an exaggerated degree, internalizing the illusion that she will make it out of her oppressive conditions by performing a U.S.-styled femininity to catch her matador. While Luisa and Clara are presented without makeup and with dark, curly hair, the narrator describes Arabella as fully decked out with a "glossy black purse" and white-framed modern sunglasses, with lips aglow in "orange-colored lipstick," smoking U.S.-brand cigarettes, and with straightened, "dyed-red hair" (24). Arabella has internalized the heteronormative codes by turning herself into the image-object of woman for male consumption: the narrator comments at one point that she was "willing to do things you did not mention to anyone" (26). Islas ends the story with Arabella's tragic demise and Clara's delighting not in the illusion of romancing the matador, but in the memory of her "beautiful Mama with the olive-colored eyes." Islas invests Clara and Luisa with the power of collective gendered resistance to the ideological codes that see women as objects (saints and/or whores) to be consumed and exploited within their patriarchal borderland world.

In a radical move toward destabilizing ethnosexualized spaces, Islas wrote the short story "The Submarine" (1957), which follows twelve hours in the life of Art, a college boy who returns home to the border. Here, Islas mixes fiction with autobiographical fact to destabilize sexual borders. Here I mean not just the easy pronominal transposition of the biographical "Arturo" with that of his protagonist "Art," but the biographical facts of Arturo's struggle with his own sexuality during the late 1950s at Stanford. On this strictly segregated coed campus Islas found himself surrounded by young men. The draconian rule on campus that policed borders between the male and female populations ironically made for a same-sex male environment that opened Islas's feelings and sexual desires for men. By the time Islas turned to the writing of "The Submarine" and gave flesh to the character Art's experiences in a fictionalized El Paso-Juárez borderland, he was a senior at Stanford who had already formed strong homoerotic bonds with many of his male friends. His unrequited love for the men in his life would become visible only obliquely and in fictional form; as with many of his generation, to articulate his love and desire for a man would mean becoming a social outcast—a sinful outlaw. Of course, even with those male "friends" who reciprocated his love—as fictionalized here in his characterization of J. D., for example—they would fear the consequences and reject his love. Short stories like "The Submarine" provided a way for Islas to understand same-sex desire and love that he was unable to explore and nurture within a homophobic, sexually surveillanced 1950s reality. The writing of such stories often gave him an outlet to understand his feelings of self-mutilation and even suicide. In this short story, Islas's Chicano-identified Art is home from college for the holiday. However, Islas breaks with the tradition of the "scholarship boy" returning home to feel a deep estrangement from family and instead follows the complex emotions that surround Art's brief exploration of a same-sexual desire for his friend J. D. The story begins with Art crossing over from El Paso into Juárez to meet up with some former high-school friends; more importantly, as we discover, this crossing over allows him the opportunity to meet up with his love interest, the straight J. D. Here, we discover too that Art is only interested in indulging in alcohol not to get the women (like the other "normal" boys, he explains), but rather to become more intimate with an alcohol-imbibing J. D. And, as the story progresses and the two become more and more inebriated, those traditional boundaries of heterosexuality begin to blur. Here, the fictionalized space of Juárez opens up the possibility for transgressive sexual love and desire. Finally, however, this fictionalized journey of his character's same-sex encounter expresses what Arturo could not do at Stanford; it also complicates the traditional imagining of the Mexican borderland as that space of white heterosexual exploitation of brown bodies. Here, the borderland space opens up the possibility of transracial same-sex love between a U.S. born and raised brown-identified character, Art, and that of a white-identified character, J. D. Islas reminds us that such expressions of racial and sexual transgressive love can exist only on paper. The narrator does not romanticize Juárez as a site of same-sex jouissance, reminding its readers after Art and J. D.'s drunken night of intimacy of a restrictive reality. For example, once Art and J. D. stumble back across the Santa Fe bridge back to the U.S. side, they wake up with deep shame: "We cried. We sat down on his mother's geraniums and cried. We stayed there for about two hours until everything started to clear up and the sky got all pink and the goddamn birds started making a racket. I told J. D. to go to bed before his mother woke up and saw us. Now, I wish she had seen us." He ends the story not on an queer utopic upbeat, but describing Art's disappointment when at the end of his adventure, "J. D. got up and ruined everything by shaking my hand" (19). With the shake of hands back on the U.S. side, the heteronormative and the brown vs. white racial dichotomy spring quickly into place.

After his undergraduate days at Stanford, Islas continued to use the short story form to explore his racial and sexual identity.

He continued to hone his story writing skills not just for himself, but to present for larger audiences other imaginative possibilities of existing as a queer Chicano in a homophobic and xenophobic world. For example, in the 1970s Islas wrote the stories "Tía Chucha" (the seed of what later became his novel *The Rain God*), "The Dead," and "The Reasons Mirror," to name a few that more explicitly detailed the complex intersections of race, gender, and sexuality than did his late 1950s stories. In such borderland spaces, Islas invented young and old, straight and bent, male and female characters who struggle to de-form oppressive borders that restrict identity. In these stories, too, Islas's narrators and characters explore critically the Chicano/a community's internalizing of racist and heterosexist values; he becomes more critical of how members of the Chicano/a community undermine the efforts of self-affirmation and resistance in their desire to attain the American dream. For example, Tía Chucha is such a character whose fantasy of living the middle-class dream comes crashing down when her insistence on upholding the myth of success and her own pure Spanish bloodline leads to her tragic demise. And Islas's short stories not only probe deeply and critically characters who internalize those hierarchies of racial difference, but they also continue to explore the complexity of a queer Chicano subjectivity.

These readings are meant to be suggestive—not exhaustive. Clearly this is just the beginning of a discussion that sheds light on Islas as a writer who did not appear *ab ovo* in the 1980s as a Chicano writer, but whose commitment to texturing the complex identity of the Chicano (queer) experience has been long in the making. Islas's early borderland short stories both critique existing national, sexual, racial and gendered paradigms as well as offer new imaginary terrains that crack open doors to the suggestion of new relational possibilities. Islas's use of the more experimental and formal short story frame, then, uses the traditionally marginalized narrative space of this genre to situate his characters within imagined borderlands where they explore various movements across sexual, gendered, and racial borderlines.

The Rain God

SENSUALITY, REPRESSION, AND DEATH
in Arturo Islas's *The Rain God*

Erlinda Gonzales-Berry

On the cover of his first novel, Arturo Islas announces that *The Rain God* is a tale of the desert. It is indeed that. It is also a tale of sensuality (indulged in by the "sinners" of the Ángel family) and repression (embraced and imposed on others by the "otherworld" Angels). Moreover, it is a tale of the great taboo that mediates between the inhabited space of the former and the desired space of the latter. It is therefore fitting that the novel should begin and end with a discussion of death.

The first chapter, "Judgment Day," describes the intense sense of violation and alienation experienced by the protagonist, Miguel "Chico" Ángel, as he recuperates from a brush with death (abdominal surgery) that leaves him permanently attached to an elimination appliance. After his recovery, Miguel Chico continues to be assaulted by a sense of discontinuity that fuels a desire to return to his geographical and familial roots. A photo of himself and his grandmother, Mamá Chona, fleeing "from this world to the next" (4)—an apt metaphor for the border reality depicted in the novel—serves as the gateway to a remembered past.

In that photograph Mamá Chona holds Miguel Chico's hand tightly, much as she does in the final scene of the novel when she embarks on her passage from this "valley of tears" (179) to her cherished Christian heaven. Miguel Chico, however, is no longer a child; having fled years ago from the desert and the bosom of his family, and having become one of its sinners ("Because he was still not married and seldom visited them in the desert, they suspected that he, too, belonged on the list of sinners" [4], he is finally able to make a public gesture announcing the end of Mamá Chona's lifelong hold: "Let go of my hand, Mamá Chona. I don't want to die" [180]). The discourse here must be read not as a desire on the part of Miguel Chico to be mortal, but rather as his rejection of Mamá Chona's worldview.

It is not fortuitous that Mamá Chona's last name is Ángel. Actually, that is her dead husband's name; the symbolic nature of her own family name, Olmeca, is indeed ironic. A dyed-in-the-wool snob who denies her indigenous provenance and a staunch believer in the superior quality of the afterlife, she takes the Ángel name seriously—so seriously, in fact, that toward the end of her life she manages to expel her womb, thus "justifying" her claim to immaculate conception. This incident is most appropriate for a woman who "denied the existence of all parts of the body below the neck" (164). Perennially donning mourning clothes and protecting her skin from the vital rays of the sun, the proud matriarch instills in her clan a strong sense of Catholic sin, guilt, and repression of all things associated with the body. In fact, Miguel Chico, in the post-surgery recovery room, appraises his situation in the following manner: "Without this pain, he would have possessed for the first time in his life that consciousness his grandmother and the Catholic Church he had renounced had taught him was the highest form of existence: pure, bodiless intellect. No shit, no piss, no blood—a perfect astronaut" (8).

Mamá Chona's worldview is irrefutably linked to death. Reducing the moral realm to a "desert of thorns and ashes" (173) and a "world of brutes and fools" (9), she sublimates her sensual inclinations and lives her life in expectation of death. When death finally arrives she announces happily, "I know the life awaiting me will be much, much better" (179). Her progeny, however, rebel against the great taboo, and, instead, respond to the call of Eros, the call of life. The oldest daughter, Mema, disobeys her family and runs off with the father of her illegitimate son. Miguel Grande engages in a scandalous affair with his *comadre* Lola, the community temptress and evil woman who refuses to abide by cultural rules that dictate gender-specific behavior. Grandson Antonio refuses to march to the rhythm of his tyrannical mother's whip, responding to her domination with suicide. Mamá Chona's sister Cuca has lived "in sin" with old Mr. Davis "for as long as any of them, even his oldest cousins, could remember" (144). Félix, the most sensitive and gentle of all the Angels, cannot resist the lure of youthful male beauty, and Miguel Chico flees the repressive hold of the clan's matriarch and the suspicious inquiries of his alienated father in order to make a life of his own choosing, a life that scorns traditional heterosexual marriage. On her deathbed Mamá Chona makes one last attempt to influence her grandson with the agonizing plea "*La familia*" (180), which he chooses to ignore.

While the "otherworld" Angels respect Mamá Chona's way and demonstrate respect and temerity vis-à-vis the great taboo, the sinners relish life, push it to its limits, not infrequently testing death itself. In the case of Félix, death responds with violence and fury, striking its fatal blow through the feet of a young soldier who does not appreciate his advances. Antonio's thirst for life leads to suicide by drowning in a desert lake, and Lola's ego is the cause of her husband's death.

Miguel Chico's initiation into the world of sensuality, under the tutelage of the family's Mexican nanny, comes early in life:

> When he was very young, Maria made him laugh by putting her eyes very close to his face and saying in her uneducated Spanish, 'Do you want to eat my raisin eyes?' He pretended to take bites out of her eyelids. She drew back and said, 'Now it's my turn. I like your chocolate eyes. They look very tasty and I'm going to eat them!' She licked the lashes of his deeply set eyes and Miguel Chico screamed with pleasure. (13)

María, however, "gets religion"; her *joie de vivre* is replaced by a vision of fire and brimstone, and she spends the rest of her life awaiting Armageddon. Eventually, the sensual feelings aroused in Miguel Chico by her presence and her relentless sermons about the end of the world lead him to associate love and death: "In that instant, smelling her hair and feeling her voice of truth moist on his ear, love and death came together for Miguel Chico and he was not from then on able to think of one apart from the other" (19).

How does Miguel Chico extricate himself from the miasma of guilt and terror? Though his liberation is not completed for many years, it begins at the scene of his grandmother's death. Mamá

Chona is redeemed in her last moments and Miguel Chico profits from her redemption as new vistas and possibilities open up that will eventually allow him to tame the beast within. Shortly before her death, the Ángel matriarch has a vision in which she sees wild roses amidst a proliferation of desert weeds (resonances of Tepeyac do not escape the reader familiar with Mexican legend). Just as Mamá Chona is about to depart to Christian paradise, the Rain God visits her room. We can surmise that he extends her an invitation to his heaven. Subsequently, when, in the spirit of magic realism, she is carried off by her dead son Félix, it seems appropriate to view him as an angel from Tlalocan (the fact that as a child he performed ritual dances after it rained in the desert provides the clue) summoned by Tlaloc to accompany Encarnación Olmeca to her rightful resting place, thereby allowing her to appropriate her true identity and to reverse the lie she lived on earth.

Years after his grandmother's death, Miguel Chico returns to the desert. While there, he visits his cousin JoEl who, still trapped in guilt and grief over his father's death, seeks the continuity of death through drugs. Haunted by the memory of his lost cousin, Miguel Chico dreams of a monster who assaults him and urges him to jump off a bridge. As he jumps, Miguel Chico grabs the monster and they both plunge toward the sea. Floating through space, Miguel feels "the pleasure of the avenged and an overwhelming relief" (160). René Girard in *Violence and the Sacred* observes that the double, which not infrequently assumes the form of a monster, "retains the concept of an antagonist, exterior to the subject.... The subject watches the monster take shape within him and outside him simultaneously" (165). There is in Miguel's dream a sense of possession by a double. His monstrous double could well represent a symbolic metamorphosis of his appliance, a reminder of his illness and his own impending death, which is at once alien and a part of him. Girard further observes that when the self is possessed by a monster, the phenomenon can appear as "sickness, cure, or both at once" (166). If we read the monster as the transformation of the emblematic appliance and as a projection of Miguel Chico's fear of death, then his possession represents both his illness *and* his cure, for upon awakening from the nightmare, only Miguel Chico survives; the monster vanishes into the abyss, taking Miguel's fear with him.

It follows that upon awakening, Miguel Chico sits at his desk to record the dream, thus engaging in the final stage of his exorcism. It is at this point that the reader realizes that the protagonist, author, and narrator are one, and Miguel Chico's liberation is brought to closure: "He needed very much to make peace with his dead . . . so they would stop haunting him. He would feed them words and make his candied skulls out of paper. He looked, once again, at that old photograph of himself and Mamá Chona" (160). The impulse to write this desert tale is thus born from a need to make peace *and* a desire to pay homage to his dead. The words of the novel's epigraph (a Neruda poem about death) and the final line of a poem by Nezahualcoyotl, the latter sent to Miguel Chico by his Aunt Mema, make explicit this desire. As a rhetorical device, the Nezahualcoyotl poem allows the narrator/author to explore the possible meaning(s) of death.

Much of Aztec poetry demonstrates a querying stance vis-à-vis the mysteries of life and death. In fact, Miguel León-Portilla argues that in the writings of the *tlamatinime* (wise men) one can discern three lines of thinking: (1) there is no afterlife: "For only here on earth / shall the fragrant flowers last and the songs which are our bliss / enjoy them now!"; (2) there is an afterlife: "where perhaps there is only suffering"; (3) perhaps there is an afterlife and, if so, it is a happy one: "Indeed one must go elsewhere; beyond, happiness exists" (132-3).

Certainly there was no unanimity among the Aztec thinkers. In *The Rain God*, the Chicano *tlamatini* assumes a stance similar to that of the Aztec philosophers. On the one hand he promotes the notion of an afterlife when he summons the Rain God to Mamá Chona's deathbed and when he quotes a poem that suggests the cosmic continuity implicit in death:

> Rivers, rivulets, fountains and waters flow,
> but never return to their joyful beginnings;
> anxiously they hasten on to the vast realms
> of the Rain God. (162)

Nezahualcoyotl's poem is riddled with the same ambiguity that marks much of Aztec metaphysical poetry. While natural phenomena flow into the ultraterrestrial domain of the gods, no mention is made of a similar human destiny. In fact, humans seem doomed to remain but "pestilential dust" on earth. However, in the final line Nezahualcoyotl expresses the modern notion that immortality is created by human discourse: "Nothing recalls them but the written page" (162).

Irrespective of what the fictitious author actually believes regarding the "ultimate" meaning of death, what matters here is that the act of writing has liberated him from fear of death and allowed him to give his loved ones, both saints and sinners, a resting place in flower and song. Despite this very satisfying resolution, one cannot help but wonder what form the author/protagonist's life will take in the aftermath of his exorcism, for the text is devoid of even a vague glimpse of the future. While it is true that a strong emotional link is established between the young Miguel Chico and the Ángel clan, the author/narrator remains emotionally detached, intellectually aloof, and disturbingly reticent about his life. As such, one is left with the feeling that the text somehow closes in on itself, burying Miguel Chico alongside Mamá Chona and all the other dead Angels.

THE HYBRIDITY OF CULTURE
in Arturo Islas's *The Rain God*

José David Saldívar

In recent years critical interest in the theorizing of ethnic, Third World, and "minor" literature has increased. For the most part, however, this new writing has tended not to emphasize what Charles Newman in *The Post-Modern Aura* calls "the new agencies of production, transmission, and administration of knowledge as dominant cultural institutions," (185) according to which the distinctions between minor and major work are posited. This is the case with William Boelhower's *Through A Glass Darkly: Ethnic Semiosis in American Literature,* whose first chapter, "A Modest Ethnic Proposal," valuably traces, with the help of Henry James, the identity crisis of Americans and concludes that "everybody in America is willy-nilly an ethnic subject" (33). Throughout his study, however, Boelhower defers analysis of the canon's ideological function and blurs the opposition that continually haunts his work, namely, the collapsing of a radically minor literature into one that seeks a major function. Likewise, Werner Sollors declares in *The Invention of Ethnicity* that ethnicity is an invention, a cultural construction. To be sure, Sollors's analysis of U.S. mainstream and minority discourses has a structuralist slant, for even if Puritan and minority discourses differ in their application, he claims they are the same in their grammar. Puritan and what he calls "non-WASP" discourses all find redemption in representing themselves as outside, radical dissent.

To produce an adequate understanding of ethnic, minor, or Third World writing, it is necessary to understand the criteria that determine the constitution of a canon at every juncture and to grasp those criteria in relation to the ideological forms that legitimate domination at any given time. Arnold Krupat's *The Voice in the Margin* goes a long way toward engaging this issue. What Krupat effectively demonstrates is how Anglo-American New Critics consistently chose to privilege texts "that could accommodate the wider context of international—or at least of Western—literature." In other words, Anglo-American New Critics, for Krupat, defined international literature as independent of all socio-temporal determinant—as if one actually could read globally (and timelessly), passing directly to the highest levels of generalization (linguistic, philosophical), by passing the mean and ordinary local—as if rhetoric were a matter of figures and of no occasions" (183).

Indeed, rhetoric and literary history are more than a matter of figures or tropes. Rather, literary history tells us how writers' works are packaged, distributed, sold, or censored in the postmodern marketplace. This chapter contests Boelhower's and Sollors's poststructuralist generalizations about ethnic literature by discussing the editorial deliberations of some mainline editors and reviewers (male and female) who read Arturo Islas's *The Rain God* within an Anglocentric monocultural matrix, thereby refusing to see his magical narrative as a novel with a difference. To put it in Krupat's terms, *The Rain God* reveals the local and ordinary but accommodates its own cosmopolitan critical context. A study of the editors' and reviewers' reading practices will reveal the complex ideological calculations and negotiations of one part of the Anglo-American middle class as it attempts to define itself within the already established taste hierarchy. (See also Pierre Bourdieu's *Distinction: A Social Critique of the Judgement of Taste.*) By tracing some deliberations of the editors who read Islas's novel in manuscript, we can learn something of the taste and ideological and ethnic assumptions of those who, in Richard Ohmann's words, control "the gate, deciding not only what cultural creations will be formally produced but also which among those will be distributed in an urgent or attractive way" (202).

New York publishers who read *The Rain God* in manuscript largely directed their attention to Islas's Chicano background and the ethnic cultural gaze in his work. This narrow view overlooked the complex literary and cross-cultural influences from both

North America and Latin America that shape his writing. Put differently, white middle-class editors refused to consider his narrative as part of the hemisphere's trans-American traditions.

In a letter from Frances McCullough, senior editor at Harper & Row, on December 30, 1975, to John Meyers, Islas's agent, Ms. McCullough made this comment: "I think what's wrong with the characters is tha[t] they are so busy conveying a cultural message that they have no time to be real people. This is true also of the plot; whatever happens has a heavy cultural message but you don't feel its weight in terms of the people's lives" (Letter from Frances McCullough). This characteristic reading of Islas's fiction precisely addresses the problem that Chicano and Chicana writers are confronted with in New York: the ethnic, "cultural message" label imposed on them by mainline editors draws simplistic attention to their "otherness," while their place in U.S. society and the relation of their work to global literature tends to be undervalued.

The temptation to examine Islas's work only for its "insider" Chicano cultural message has been considerable. Two examples are enough to show the shortcomings of this approach. A reviewer for the *San Francisco Chronicle*, Raymond Mungo, suggested that the Chicano essence of *The Rain God* is the author's "striving for the key to some Castañedan, soulful mystery in the lives of these [Chicano] people" (5). Likewise, Carol Fowler used similar racial criteria in her 1985 review for the *Contra Costa Times*, claiming that Islas's Chicano characters "seem" to have "a sense of clannishness stronger than Anglo families." The suggestion that his work reflects some aboriginal "soulful mystery" or some "clannishness" betrays an insufficient understanding of the background to his writings. Such critical stances lead to an unbalanced and restricted view of his importance as an American writer with a difference and give rise to pernicious stereotypes.

In the introduction to *"Race," Writing, and Difference*, Henry Louis Gates, Jr. has convincingly argued that the trope of "race" is an important concern of many U.S. writers and thus demands our critical attention (120). And since Chicano and Chicana identities are shaped in the tension between cultures—U.S. and Mexican—they embrace elements from different backgrounds. In other words, Islas does not work in an artistic vacuum. He is free to incorporate what he chooses from outside his immediate "Latino" cultural sphere.

The value of Islas's *The Rain God* lies not in the author's depiction of traditions alien to American readers but in the specific way he bridges the gap between North American and Latin American cultures and unites, like Shange, literary and transnational traditions. The "ethnic" label used by New York editors therefore detracts from these qualities.

Islas's personal background and his academic interest in American literatures—he was a professor of English at Stanford University and had served as visiting professor of creative writing at the University of Texas, El Paso—explain why his work is marked by cross-cultural hybridization. Yvor Winters and Wallace Stegner, two of his Stanford mentors, and such writers as William Faulkner, Wallace Stevens, Maxine Hong Kingston, Juan Rulfo, and Gabriel García Márquez have left their mark on his double voiced writing. He used his own experience of migration to create an ideal of himself out of his Mexican and American background, his knowledge of "New World" Amerindian cultures, his experiences in postcontemporary American society, and his study of classic American literatures. All of these factors must be considered when assessing his fiction.

Another reason editors were incapable of acknowledging the true character of his novel was their fear that *The Rain God* would be bought by only a limited number of Chicano readers. Henry William Griffin, a senior editor at Macmillan, put it this way in an April 5, 1976, letter to Bob Cornfield, Islas's agent at the time: "Interesting, very interesting indeed, but I'm afraid our sales force would be very hard put to sell a thousand copies" (Letter to Robert Cornfield). Seven years after its publication by Alexandrian Press, *The Rain God* had sold approximately ten thousand copies. (Computer Curriculum Corporation of Palo Alto was the first northern California corporation to lend support to literature. Alexandrian Press was established as its division to publish a few novels of "genuine merit" each year.) One can only imagine how many copies might have been sold if the book had been published, distributed, and marketed with understanding by the mainline "big boys" in New York.

Comments such as Mr. Griffin's led Islas to remark in an interview with Eileen Walsh for Stanford's *Campus Report* that "the constant observation from New York was that publishers felt there was no audience for this work—no market. And market is really the word because it means money." Although Islas did not deny that his novel was about Chicanos and Chicanas who live in a Southwestern border town, he said over and over again that "it was not intended solely for a Chicano audience" (Walsh). But after eight years of struggle with unresponsive New York publishing houses (he submitted his novel to more than twenty), he gave up trying to convince them that his story about the Ángel family would have "universal" appeal, remarking to Howard J. Taylor of the *San Francisco Sunday Examiner & Chronicle* that, "I finally decided to stop banging my head against the wall" (2).

To his credit, Islas claimed that his comments were not "sour grapes." But he did point out that people he went to school with at Stanford, who later became editors in New York, consistently ignored Chicano and Chicana writers: "I know that world. I went to Stanford with a lot of the [people] who are editors, and it's a very circumspect and provincial world; they publish their own" (Walsh).

Certainly, Islas was not the only Chicano writer to be angry and distressed at traditional U.S. publishers. Rudolfo Anaya, professor of English at the University of New Mexico and author of the best-selling *Bless Me, Ultima*, says that "a lot of Chicano writers have been out there for fifteen or twenty years, producing good work, getting nominated for National Book Awards and recognition around the world. But they can't get New York publishers even to look [at their work]. It makes me wonder if the system is fair. [. . .] We've been waiting for our turn and it hasn't come" (Taylor 2).

Brad Chambers, director of the New York Council for Interracial Books for Children, agrees with Islas's and Anaya's criticisms. He calls Chicano writers' lack of access to New York publishers "shocking and shameful," and he argues that "a lot of it is based on the fact that publishing houses are based in the

Northeast and there is very little awareness of Mexican-American, Chicano [and Chicana] realities" (Taylor). To support his claim, Chambers points to a creative writing contest that his council conducted for more than a decade as an attempt to bring unpublished African American, Chicano, Puerto Rican, Asian American, and Native American writers to the attention of major publishers. "In 10 years, not a single winner in the Chicano category was picked up by a major house and published," he says. He emphasizes, however, "it worked for winners of every other category. It did not work for Chicanos. And several were really quality work" (2). In other words, those who create subjects privileging the WASP, Eastern, male outlook have primary claim to attention in the U.S. literary canon. Those who attend to African American, Native American, and Puerto Rican subjects come next, Chambers suggests. A distant last are works attentive to Chicano and Chicana subjects.

Finally, Al McDonald, who has described himself as the only senior African American editor "in all of New York," said this about the "brown barrier" in the New York publishing world: the problems Chicanos and Chicanas face with major houses are symptomatic of American publishing, an "insular" business that breeds a "homogeneity among editors" and often "ghettoizes" minority discourses. He gives this advice: "The trick is not to publish a book that's black or Chicano but a book that everybody should read for its literary value, its honesty, its power" (Taylor 2). But Islas's *The Rain God* was not picked up by a major publisher precisely because its so-called "brown" cultural elements are what attracted most of the attention of editors.

So far we have examined how the dominant institutional practices caused Islas's *The Rain God* to be rejected as an American novel with a difference. To show specifically how New York publishers influence Chicano texts and determine which images of the Chicano and Chicana will appear in them, let me examine how these institutional practices produced, in an exploitative manner, two novels by and about Chicanos: José Antonio Villarreal's *Pocho* and Victor (under the name "Edmundo") Villaseñor's *Macho!*

As the title suggests, *Pocho* is Villarreal's attempt to write about the "*pocho*" (an Americanized Mexican) experience in

California. In so doing, the author (unwittingly) projects a stereotypical view. The opening scenes of the novel, for example, as Evangelina Enríquez has pointed out, introduce us to Juan Rubio, an arrogant, callous *macho* who has been a soldier in Pancho Villa's army and has now returned to Juárez. (See also editors Alfredo Mirandé and Evangelina Enríquez's *La Chicana: The Mexican-American Woman*.) He enters a cantina complete with a mariachi band playing sentimental ballads and a young girl dancing a *tapatío* on a tabletop. Juan takes a fancy to the señorita and orders her to sit and drink with him. She obeys nervously, for she knows that her lover is nearby. Juan, however, kills the boyfriend and literally pulls the señorita out of the saloon and into a hotel room. She dutifully removes his boots, and after their lovemaking tells him that he does not even know her name. "'¿Qué quieres?' She spoke in the familiar. In a cantina, as in bed, courtesy was nonexistent" (Villarreal 2).

As we gather from this scene, *Pocho* is marked by the protagonist's cliché Mexican male values. An ex-revolutionary, he leaves Mexico and becomes a farmworker in California. While struggling to exist in the United States, he tries to retain his Mexican cultural values in the rearing of his family. Richard Rubio, Juan's son and the *pocho* in the family, experiences the novel's basic tensions: either assert an Americanized individuality, or succumb to the burden of machismo and cultural nationalism imposed on him by his father and his community.

In much the same way, Victor ("Edmundo") Villaseñor's *Macho!*, hailed by Bantam Books as "the first great Chicano novel"—although by 1973 "greater" Chicano novels such as Tomás Rivera's "*. . . y no se lo tragó la tierra*" and Rolando Hinojosa's *Estampas del Valle* had already been published by Chicano presses—confirmed popular views of the Chicano family that had made *Pocho* the first Chicano novel to be published by a major New York house. *Macho!* focuses on one year in the life of Roberto García, a Tarascan Indian boy from Michoacán who is forced to cover for his father's poor work in the fields. As with a principal character in *Pocho*, the father in *Macho!* is a misogynist and a drunk. The novel stresses the isolation and "backwardness" of the protagonist's village, where strict obedience to old customs makes the atmosphere suffocating for the younger generation. After a night's brawl in a cantina, Roberto, seeking material wealth, emigrates to the United States, following the example of the norteño Juan Aguilar. In the United States, Roberto becomes acquainted with César Chávez, the Chicano labor leader. But Roberto is uninterested in Chávez's causes, since he is primarily concerned about his parents and his family's suffering in Mexico.

Macho! thus describes the young field hand's disillusionment with life as a migrant farmworker in the United States. (See Charles Tatum's *Chicano Literature*.) Roberto has several negative encounters as a worker: he is cheated by a Mexican *coyote* (labor contractor) who breaks his promise to obtain legal status for Roberto; he is humiliated by immigration officers when he crosses the border; he is initiated into the endless cycle of dawn-to-dusk work in the California fields.

Clearly, Roberto García, like Juan Rubio in *Pocho*, is a one-dimensional character: he blindly follows the cult of machismo, which Villaseñor posits as the essence of the Mexican's value system. One example will suffice to point out the author's limited understanding: "Roberto got the first whore of his life, and then the next morning he felt bad and went to church and lit three candles and prayed a long time, but by afternoon with a few beers and money in his pocket it was all much better inside his soul, and he went back to the cantina with the woman" (Villaseñor 85). As this representative passage shows, Villaseñor's language, a poor Hemingway imitation at best, is stiff and awkward. Throughout the novel, his Chicano and Chicana characters sound like Hollywood stereotypes.

This brings us back to the original question about Arturo Islas's *The Rain God*. Why were Villarreal's and Villaseñor's Chicano novels published by major New York houses and Islas's refused? Can we say that Villarreal's and Villaseñor's books were simply better written? Or can we best answer if we shift from the purely "literary" to an extra-discursive examination of definitions, assumptions, and criteria used to determine the values of "ethnic" American texts?

The rejection of *The Rain God* by New York publishers can best be explained, first, by acknowledging that the novel does not stereotype Islas's Chicano and Chicana characters. More significantly, it did not conform to the editors' ideas about ethnic American literature's intrinsic "themes." It did not indulge in determinism, survival, the immigrant experience, and violence as Villarreal's and Villaseñor's texts did. Unfortunately, these so-called ethnic themes are still part of reality as defined by the ruling ideological apparatus. Briefly, Villarreal and Villaseñor were writing according to New York editors' standards about certain U.S. ethnic themes—social maladjustment, the individual and his environment, the pathological character of the Chicano family, illegals, violence, and criminal behavior—that dominant cultural practices define as worthy and "universal." Thus, it was Villarreal's and Villaseñor's ability to produce cultural objects whose effect and function generated a popular American mythology and cultural view of Mexicans and Chicanos that made *Pocho* and *Macho!* the first Chicano novels to be published in New York.

To show how Islas's work can be read as a direct refutation of the New York publishing world's view of Chicano literary and cultural practices as well as of a narrow U.S. sense of literary and historical "tradition," the following sections draw upon Islas's letters and interviews to trace the classical Anglo-American and Latin American literary backgrounds of *The Rain God*. In other words, Islas dissents from the consensus ideology of classic American literature that projects a totalizing cultural homogeneity onto the vast and diversified body of literature. (For a historical analysis of the consensus ideology in classic American literature, see Sacvan Bercovitch's "The Rites of Assent: Rhetoric, Ritual, and the Ideology of American Consensus.")

Two statements by Islas in a letter to his agent are particularly pertinent to an initial understanding of *The Rain God*. He suggests that his novel is in the U.S. Southern tradition of Faulkner's classic *Absalom, Absalom!*: "I am chronicling," he writes, "the life of a historical creature who happened to live at a time when he was taught to hate what he perceived himself to be" (Letter to Robert Cornfield). In the same letter Islas elaborates:

"[Miguel Chico is] my Quentin Compson; he would say in exactly the same tone Quentin uses at the end of *Absalom*, 'I don't hate Mexicans! I don't hate Anglos! I don't hate gays!'" (Letter to Robert Cornfield).

In *The Mind of the South*, W. J. Cash notes of U.S. Southern writers—and Islas, like García Márquez and Fuentes, stresses an affinity with them: "[they are] romantics of the appalling," who only hate the South "with the exasperated hate of a lover who cannot persuade the object of his affections to his desire," much as "Narcissus, growing at length analytical, might have suddenly begun to hate his image in a pool" (386-87). Presumably, what Islas wants us to see is that his central consciousness, Miguel Chico, like Faulkner's Quentin Compson, comes under Cash's definition. There is every reason to see, at least on a first reading, the novel as a compressed exploration of Miguel Chico's narcissistic hatred and resentment. Put differently, Miguel Chico exemplifies what Nietzsche identifies in *The Genealogy of Morals* as a form of profound *ressentiment* in intellectuals. He suffers in a "psychological" sense from the destructive envy of the have-nots for the haves.

Seen in this light, Islas would have readers center the novel's interest on Miguel Chico. Those who do so, he believes, will see the primary importance he places on the contemplative mind and its exploratory, interpretive acts. Hence, early in the novel he describes the protagonist as its central consciousness:

> He, Miguel Chico, was the family analyst, interested in the past for psychological, not historical reasons ... he preferred to ignore facts in favor of motives, which were always and endlessly open to question and interpretation... [He] wanted to look at motives and at people from an earthly, rather than otherworldly, point of view. (*Rain God* 28)

Clearly, the hero's central consciousness is the fixed point of view from which readers overhear the various generations of the Ángel family. It follows that instead of attempting to give readers an "ethnic cultural message," as many editors in New York narrowly claimed, Islas's Chicano narrative is in the long tradition of psychologically complex novels, for *The Rain God* constantly draws attention to its ideas and labyrinthine methods. The central task of Miguel Chico as "family analyst" therefore is clear: to penetrate and attempt to see below the surface of things and so arrive at psychological judgments. Like a bookish Henry James character, he is "affected with a certain high lucidity" (qtd. in Donadio: 122). For Islas, his character becomes not simply exceptionally intelligent and sensitive with a "value intrinsic," but, as in James's best work, "a compositional resource" of the highest order. From the point of view of structure, Islas obviously places Miguel Chico and the play of his impressions and reactions at the book's center to make for a unity and intensity of focus that could not be easily achieved by other means. But his interest in such a character clearly extends beyond his structural use, for, like Henry James before him, he sees the "large lucid reflector" as no less than "the most polished of possible mirrors of the subject" (122).

As a consequence of this method, the novelist seems to withdraw from the action, allowing his intense perceiver to discover the subject for himself and in the process reveal it to the reader. Miguel Chico's function is to create the story from its particulars by gradually perceiving the full significance of events in which he is involved. A word of qualification about Miguel Chico is in order here, for like John Marcher in James's classic tale "The Beast in the Jungle," in which Marcher spends most of his time staring his fate (in the person of May Bartram) in the face and failing to get the point precisely because it is so apparent, Miguel Chico often tends to (mis)read experience. Miguel Chico, Islas writes, "was still seeing people, including himself, as books. He wanted to edit them, correct them, make them behave differently. And so he continued to read them as if they were invented by someone else, and he failed to take into account their separate realities, their differences from himself. When people told him of their lives, or when he thought about his own in the way that is not thinking but a kind of reverie outside time, a part of him listened with care. Another part fidgeted, thought about something else or went blank, and wondered why once again he was being offered such secrets to examine" (*Rain God* 26). In *The Rain God*, as in James's fiction, failure to get the point that directly confronts one is often a matter of life and death.

Another source of difficulty for early mainline reviewers and readers was Islas's use of chronological dislocation—the free, wandering flow of mind, back and forth in time, over names and events known to the narrator but not to us on a first reading. Early reviewers, like the editors at major publishing houses, were baffled by these techniques in Islas's art. "The first 78 pages," Raymond Mungo wrote in the *San Francisco Chronicle*, "seemed to me nothing more than a long introduction to the scores of characters in the novel, in which each is described but not given enough depth or color to be believable. The net effect is one of wholesale confusion as the reader tries to memorize dozens of names and figure out their relationships in this fictional middleclass Mexican-American family" (5). Capable of such remarks, the reviewer seems never to have read a Faulkner or García Márquez novel!

Additionally, the work of Wallace Stevens, Yvor Winters, and Wallace Stegner probably has most affected Islas's preoccupation in *The Rain God* with morality, postsymbolist technique, male utopias, and death. During his undergraduate and graduate studies in English and American literature at Stanford, Winters and Stegner undoubtedly were his most important artistic and scholarly influences. The full extent of his indebtedness to Winters can be appreciated only if we recall the most basic of Winters's powerful literary theories. Winters, as Terry Comito explains in his book *In Defense of Winters*, was concerned with a moral evaluation of literature. In Winters's view, literary works of art enable people to come to a rational and emotional understanding of the human condition and allow writers to make moral judgments. Above all, writers are to avoid producing obscure and confused works of art.

Islas profited immensely from Winters's great dictum stated in his essay "Poetic Styles, Old and New": "It ought to be possible to employ our sensory experience [. . .] in an efficient way, not as ornament, and with no sacrifice of rational intelligence" (71). In this regard, central to Islas's *The Rain God* is what Winters termed "controlled associationism," or a "postsymbolist method." This Wintersian technique is to establish a theme or introduce an abstract idea in conceptual terms. Such a rational framework is then entwined with sharp sensory details. The controlled association of abstract theme with imagery charges images with meaning. For Winters and, by extension, for Islas, the writer's moral attitude is defined not only by the logical content of the work, but by the writer's emotional reaction to its ideas.

Many of Islas's literary preferences—his interest in anti-romantic American literature, or his deep admiration for Stevens—were first induced by Winters. Stevens's influence on *The Rain God* has not been noted by either his mainline or his brown "inside" reviewers and critics. Briefly, Stevens's entire poetic enterprise can be seen, points out Daniel Hoffman in his essay "Poetry: After Modernism," as a heroic and brilliant attack against the emptiness of "heaven," where "the death of one god is the death of all" (442). For Stevens, the withering away of traditional religion leaves the poet-artist of the twentieth century with only the impoverished earth and what Stevens termed "the gaiety of language." This is one of *The Rain God*'s central issues.

Specifically, Stevens's classic poem "Sunday Morning" informs much of Islas's thinking about traditional religion, for the poem as Stevens said in one of his letters "was simply an expression of paganism" (qtd. in Hoffman: 442). Like "Sunday Morning," *The Rain God* mounts a counter-rhetoric against the words of idealism (*holy, divinity, lord, Jesus, soul*) by bringing those words into his Chicano narrative and to the Southwest desert: *freedom* is rain, *soul* is sexual passion, the *lord* is the Amerindian Tlaloc (the rain god), and angels are well-built young men.

Stevens's "Sunday Morning," moreover, argues in provocatively erotic language, what Frank Lentricchia refers to as "gutsy, wet, blooming passion," that the Christian myth has outlived its usefulness, for just as Jove stayed inhuman in the clouds only until he could move among us, so did a later God-myth go unrealized until "our blood" mingled with Christ's at Bethlehem and the shepherds discerned it in a star (156). Today, Stevens contends, the myth of Christ is as obsolete as the myth of Jove. Like Stevens, Islas argues in *The Rain God* that we are unable to look beyond the human for our gods. Thus, he suggests, even the gods need human flesh.

In short, Islas, like Stevens, gives his idealist readers a lesson: we must avoid abstraction, fixed principles, and closed systems.

Throughout *The Rain God* he challenges the legitimacy of universals, repeatedly offsetting images of hollow spiritual categories with wet, blooming imagery of a vibrant sexual world. To be sure, Islas, like Stevens, replaces what he sees as the desolate Christian mythology with one of his own: he inverts the procedure of Christianity in which people reach toward paradise in humble supplication. Naked in the desert, gay Uncle Félix, the rain dancer, in a male utopian vision chants not to paradise but from paradise, not in supplication but in triumph, projecting himself from the center of the world, not from its margins.

At the same time, Islas supplements Stevens's "pagan view" by interpolating an indigenous brown poem by the great Amerindian King Nezahualcoyotl:

> All the earth is a grave and nothing escapes it;
> nothing is so perfect that it does not descend
> to its tomb.
> Rivers, rivulets, fountains and waters flow,
> but never return to their joyful beginnings;
> anxiously they hasten on to the vast realms
> of the Rain God.
> As they widen their banks, they also fashion
> the sad urn of their burial.
> Filled are the bowels of the earth
> with pestilential dust once flesh and bones,
> once animate bodies of men who sat upon thrones,
> decided cases, presided in council,
> commanded armies, conquered provinces,
> possessed treasure, destroyed temples,
> exulted in their pride, majesty, fortune,
> praise and power.
> Vanished are these glories, just as the fearful smoke
> vanishes that belches forth from the infernal fires
> of Popocatepetl.
> Nothing recalls them but the written page. (*Rain God* 162)

In the Amerindian view, men and women hold an insignificant place in the world. The very world in which people make their brief struggle is seen as no more than an ephemeral shape, one experiment among others, and like them doomed to catastrophe. King Nezahualcoyotl's poem, like *The Rain God*, is haunted by the idea of death as total annihilation. For Nezahualcoyotl and Islas, religion and the art that expresses religion crush men and women with the harshness of a fate beyond their control.

Last, Islas owes something to Stegner, his dissertation advisor at Stanford. Like Stegner, he yearns for the day when the American West will have not only writers but all the infrastructure of literary life—a book publishing industry, a range of literary and critical magazines, and a reviewing corps not enslaved by East Coast opinions, support organizations such as PEN, and all the rest. Thematically, *The Rain God*, like the best of Stegner's narratives about the American West, takes life from the memory of formative events in a specific landscape characterized by migration. For them, the American West is an arid country, and aridity enforces space, which in turn enforces mobility and travel. In contradistinction to the settled communities of New England and the Midwest, the oasis space of the American West, they claim, does something to vision. It makes the country itself formidable and ever-present, and in the words of Stegner "it tends to make humans as migratory as antelope" ("The New Literary Frontier" E3). It is therefore true to say that Islas belongs to that large family of U.S. writers—from Willa Cather to N. Scott Momaday—whose works have been defined by motion and desire. Both Stegner and Islas ransack their memories, submitting them back to a special place and to the unforgettable time of childhood, followed by their achieving adulthood and deciding to become writers.

Similarly, Islas's autobiographical impulse in *The Rain God* owes much to Stegner's influence, for both writers deal with youth, initiation, and disillusionment. If Islas's affinity for Stevens was induced by Winters, his affinity for Cather was initiated by Stegner. Lines of kinship can be drawn between *The Rain God* and *My Antonia*. Presumably, Islas read Stegner's essay "Willa Cather, My Antonia," in which he argued that Cather discovered her true voice when she began to write about the region and people she knew best. Then, Stegner avers, she wrote "spontaneously because she was tapping both memory and affection" (145).

A significant technical device that Islas draws from Cather and Stegner is the point of view from which *My Antonia* and *Angle of Repose* are told. Each of these writers has in common the use of the narrative mask that enables Jim Burden, Lyman Ward, and Miguel Chico to exercise the author's sensibilities without obvious self-indulgence. In the processes of understanding and commemorating characters such as Antonia or Mamá Chona, the narrators locate themselves.

If Islas belongs among those U.S. writers whose works have been defined by region, his double-voiced novel also has direct lines of kinship to the Latin American new writing by Octavio Paz, Rulfo, and García Márquez. Throughout Islas's desert tale, there are New World-Amerindian qualities that clearly identify the book with the Latin American and, more specifically, the Mexican-Amerindian obsession with death. Islas digs deeply into the reality of his Chicano border culture by showing how the Ángel family fits together in a Mexican cultural pattern.

Foremost in this Amerindian-New World context is the author's assumption that the moment of death does nothing to inhibit communication. This characteristic, an important theme in Rulfo's classic Mexican novel *Pedro Páramo* and in García Márquez's *One Hundred Years of Solitude*, stems from the New World idea of *almas en pena* (souls in torment) that wander the earth even after death. Comprehension of such an unaccustomed reality requires a reading more like the lyrical experiences of poetry than of the dialogical novel. Clues of all kinds are therefore important—repeated images, references to unreal events—not to remake the novel into a realistic experience, but to establish the relationship for a magic realist appreciation of the work.

At the novel's end, for example, Islas writes of Mamá Chona's familiarity with *almas en pena*: "In the daytime, usually before the late afternoon meal, she would ask, 'Where is your father?' The first time she asked, Mema, surprised, told her straight-forwardly that he was dead. Without blinking, Mamá Chona retorted, 'Yes, but why doesn't he come to see me? Where is he?'" (*Rain God* 172). On another occasion, Mamá Chona, like Úrsula Buendía in *One Hundred Years of Solitude*, matter-of-factly reveals to Mema that she has visited with her dead husband, Carlos: "I saw your father today. He was with that woman Josefina. They came to see me together, can you imagine? I knew he was seeing a great deal of her, but it was shameless of him to bring her here when there are children in the house. I will not forgive him for that" (172).

Mamá Chona, to be sure, is not the novel's only character conversant with the Amerindian spiritual world. Nina, Miguel Chico's godmother, also is intimate with the supernatural: "The otherworldly side of her," Islas writes, "came to the surface before her son's death, and she explored it with the care and precision she used to prepare the annual income tax accounts of various business firms in town" (33). Like the best magic realist writers, Islas often turns his back on realism. But it is important to note how, like García Márquez, he extends a magic realist situation to the edge of comedy and parody:

> It was not until she discovered the spirit world that Nina began to recognize that death might not exist as she imagined it in her terror. At the bi-weekly séances in the basement of her friends' Mexican food restaurant, her nose itching from the Aqua Velva they sprinkled into the air to induce serenity, Nina gradually became aware of two women waving at her from a strange and unknown region. They were about the same age and Nina saw with joy that one of the women was her sister Antonia, who had died in her late twenties. The other woman was her mother, who at twenty-nine had died giving birth to Nina. (34)

The comical "signifyin[g]" distortion of reality at the séance—induced by the sprinkling of aftershave in the air—conveys an absurd and humorous effect. Indeed, this humorous critique of the magic realist tradition informs much of this comic-tragic novel. For example, when Juanita, Nina's sister, begins attending Nina's "classes in mind control," Islas "signifies" on García Márquez's fantastic world in *One Hundred Years of Solitude*, where one character literally ascends to heaven. As in García Márquez's writing, Islas's prose style is usually plain and exact, and easily leaps into the comical and exuberant. However, Nina's séance is accurately described, and with a wonderful, inventive touch his desert tale in the end is always brought back to ordinary experience.

As his title suggests (the rain god is Tlaloc in Amerindian religion), Islas's novel is preoccupied with the Amerindian beginnings of Chicano culture in the United States. Originally "Día de los Muertos/Day of the Dead," the book challenges American literature's very concept of "tradition" and deconstructs the one-dimensional (linear) view of history on which it is often predicated. Freed from strictly national U.S. genealogical imperatives, tradition in Islas's sense of the Americas can be perceived as a system of affinities independent of racial, ethnic, national, or linguistic criteria. The author thus combines historical with literary revision by demonstrating the impact of what M. M. Bakhtin identified as hybridization on literary production in *The Dialogic Imagination*, specifically on questions of American literary canonization. Translating cultural interaction into an exchange of literary forms, Islas, like Ntozake Shange and Rolando Hinojosa, invalidates distinctions and proposes his own distinctive U.S.-Amerindian mythology of writing.

ARTURO ISLAS'S *THE RAIN GOD:*
An Alternative Tradition

Marta E. Sánchez

Chicano author Arturo Islas's *The Rain God, A Desert Tale* belongs to a contemporary tradition of autobiographical fiction by Latino men and women that has emerged from working-class Hispanophone communities such as Chicano and Puerto Rican. In their search to define different "American" identities, Chicano and Chicana authors recall an earlier tradition of American immigrant authors who, at the turn of the century, found themselves on the other side of the dominant ethnic identity, namely, the Western European, Anglo-Saxon, or Nordic English-speaking American. This generation of "others" whose families immigrated from southern and eastern, not northern or western, Europe formulated a literary tradition in the 1930s different from the modernism of T. S. Eliot and Ezra Pound (Klein 13-18).

However, important differences must be noted when viewing contemporary Chicano and U.S. Puerto Rican authors against the background of this alternative tradition of the 1930s. Chicano and Nuyorican writers belong to a recent literary tradition of immigrant and migrant peoples from countries of non-European origin. Their historical and cultural roots are traced, in part, to nonwestern cultures. It is also important to emphasize that even though Mexican people immigrate, legally and illegally, to this country every day, and even though their immigrant experience has played and continues to play a vital part in the formation of Chicano identities, a substantial amount of the Chicano population is native born.

Taking his inspiration and material from the phenomenon of family, Islas writes a saga of a Mexican American family. The lives of three generations of the Ángel family—grandmother, children, grandchildren—constitute the narrative. The Angels are a binational family, born on both sides of the Texas-Juárez border. Their binational character highlights a unique feature of the Mexican/Chicano community: back-and-forth movement between Mexico and the United States has characterized Mexican and Chicano patterns of settlement for several generations across a permeable two-thousand-mile border.

In this essay I argue that Islas's novel enlarges the scope of "American" literature at levels of both content and form. At the level of content, the author makes Chicanos and Chicanas central in his fictional world, giving voice to those once voiceless in the literary world. At the level of form, he uses narrative strategies that highlight the "minority" writer's role of mediator between cultures. As he writes in a mode that reflects his own bilingual, bicultural heritage, Islas addresses an audience from both Anglophonic and bilingual backgrounds. By "Anglophonic" I refer to those who operate in the English language and who are, for the most part, monolingual. Islas creates bridges of understanding between these sets of readers, but not at the expense of erasing their cultural differences. The novel goes further to instruct Anglophonic, monolingual readers to become self-conscious about the fragility of the presumed centrality of their own culture. By having them see themselves against the background of Mexican/Chicano culture, the novel reveals to them glimpses of their own alterity or "otherness."

Miguel Chico and Self-Conscious Narration

Islas's text is a fictional autobiography because it is, first and foremost, the protagonist's own account of how the Ángel family shaped his self-identity. Yet the novel is not told from a first-person perspective as is, for example, *Los pasos perdidos* by the Cuban Alejo Carpentier, *Bless Me, Ultima* by the Chicano Rudolfo Anaya, or the *Adventures of Huckleberry Finn*. Islas's narrative strategy is to tell his hero's story through the perspective of an omniscient narrator who lacks the precise status of a character. This narrator is self-conscious both about his identity with and difference from the protagonist. He thus reveals that the hero,

Miguel Ángel (also "Miguel Chico" or "Mickie" to his family), is not solely an "object" but also an unintrusive "subject" of narration. This device of creating a gap between narrator and character and yet having them be one and the same is this novel's most important formal feature.

At certain points, the third-person omniscient narrator provides hints that the "he" referred to, or Mickie, is the narrator observing the action and controlling the narration. By the time readers encounter this next passage—"He was still seeing people, including himself, as books. He wanted to edit them, correct them, make them behave differently. And so he continued to read them as if they were invented by someone else. . . . Later he found himself retelling what he had heard, arranging various facts, adding others, reordering time schemes, putting himself in situations and places he had never been in, removing himself from conversations or moments that didn't fit" (*Rain God* 26)—they will know that "he" reverberates to include this narrator, who performs the actions he attributes to Mickie. In "reading," editing, and correcting people, Mickie will tell and write the family secrets—suicide, adultery, homicide, homosexuality, hypocrisy, and drugs—that have long haunted the Ángel family. Both Spanish and English pronunciations of the surname "Ángel" nicely capture the central irony: a book about *la familia Ángel,* "especially its sinners." But these secrets have already been told and written about by the omniscient narrator or Mickie character in the past and writer of the future. The gap closes between narrator and character, and their identity becomes, ironically, the key to their difference. Thus, *The Rain God* is about the formation of the protagonist's "I" with no "I" overtly present at any time.

Islas's technique of creating a gap between narrator and character has a socio-cultural effect because it foregrounds his own self-division and fragmentation. This device highlights his sociocultural situation of being "marginal": he is inside and outside both Mexican/Chicano and the more modern Anglophonic cultures, yet neither completely in one nor the other. He is "different": a dialectical subject who both sustains his subjectivity and challenges it at the same time. Like some of his contemporaries, Islas, as we shall see, transforms the liability of "otherness" into the asset of narrative device.

This self-conscious feature of a narrator who calls attention to himself as both subject and object opens up "new" possibilities for questioning traditional hierarchical relationships within both a Mexican/Chicano culture and a "dominant" literary tradition. This splitting allows Islas a flexibility toward and an ironic distance from his own limitations and blindness, providing him with a method to analyze his estrangement from himself and his native culture. It also relates directly to the different roles the narrator attributes to Mickie but that in actuality he himself performs. The role of family analyst, for example, is performed by the narrator but also relates directly to Mickie's participation in and criticism of Mexican/Chicano culture.

The narrator's other roles of "autobiographer," "novelist," and "indigenous ethnographer" destabilize the hierarchical relationships implicit in some standard literary and anthropological genres, such as the bourgeois autobiography, the modernist novel of identity, and the classical ethnography. Finally, his role as translator opens up the traditional canon, creating possibilities for the inclusion of both Anglophonic and bilingual readers. The two groups are made to "see" each other against the background of one another at the implicit level of audience.

Mickie as Family Analyst: The Unmasking of the Repressed

> His need to give meaning to the accidents of life had become even more intense, and he had not yet begun to laugh at that need. Years earlier, he had started out to be a brain surgeon but had found his pre-med courses lifeless and impossible. Literature had given him another way to examine the mind. He knew he was no poet like his cousin JoEl. . . . He, Miguel Chico, was the family analyst, interested in the past for psychological, not historical, reasons. Like Mama Chona, he preferred to ignore facts in favor of motives, which were always and endlessly open to question and interpretation. (28)

Within a Mexican/Chicano literary tradition, Mickie's function as family analyst is ironic because psychoanalysis is primarily a white, middle-class phenomenon, generally uncharacteristic of Mexican/Chicano culture. Yet Mickie not only sees a therapist in the novel (24), but he functions as an analyst of his own domain. From his position within his family, he observes and reacts; as narrator he judges from the outside. This central device permits him to probe and uncover family secrets, making the text "speak" the unspeakable. The Ángel family has never really become conscious of those repressed forces, human and historical, that have limited and even destroyed it. And so *The Rain God* is Mickie's exorcism of the repressed forces that have ensnared his family for three generations.

These forces relate to issues of sexuality, ethnicity, and social class. As the final chapter ("The Rain God") opens, Mickie has the dream that marks the book's climactic moment, where he confronts the "monster" of his past with his family. Although portrayed as singular in the dream, the "monster" is really a composite of the repressed desires of the different characters, from the matriarch and center of power, Encarnación Olmeca de Ángel (or Mamá Chona), to JoEl (Mickie's deranged and youngest first cousin). Depending upon the character, the meaning of the "monster" shifts. Mickie's confrontation with these demons begins his spiritual odyssey toward liberation from the "distorting influences" of his ancestors.

Importantly, the dream occurs after the operation ("Judgment Day") that physically impoverishes Mickie but saves his life: "he would have to wear a plastic appliance at his side for the rest of his life" (7). The operation and the dream interlink the first and final chapters. They establish connections that create the book's cyclical and nonlinear, as well as its episodic and serial, structure. After his dream, Mickie feels free to bring to consciousness the family secrets. He writes, so to speak, the work that is *The Rain God,* the fruit of the analysis of the dream. The book's central metaphor, "rain god," in part designates the fruit of Mickie's writing, the actual text we have been reading and are just, at the time of the dream, about to complete.[1] His book is an offering to make peace with his dead, a "feast for them so that they will stop haunting him" (160). The manifest content of the dream is this:

> ... the "monster" that had killed her [Mamá Chona] said to him softly, almost kindly, "I am a nice monster. Come into my cave." The two of them were standing on a bridge facing the incoming fog. The monster held Miguel Chico closely from behind and whispered into his ear in a relentless, singsong way, "I am the manipulator and the manipulated." It put its velvet paw in Miguel Chico's hand and forced him to hold it tightly against his gut right below the appliance at his side. "I am the victim and the slayer," the creature continued, "I am . . . the loved and the unloved. I approve and turn away, I am judge and advocate." Miguel Chico wanted to escape but could not. . . . "You are in my cave, and you will do whatever I say." [. . .]
> "Jump!" the monster said with exhilaration, "jump!"
> Miguel Chico felt . . . disgust for the beast . . . "All right," he said, "but I'm taking you with me." He clasped the monster to him . . . and threw both of them backward over the railing and into the fog. As he fell, the awful creature in his arms, Miguel Chico felt the pleasure of the avenged and an overwhelming relief. (159-60)

The fall through the fog and plunge into the sea represents Mickie's decision to break the silence and acknowledge the anguish he has felt about his family for years. The confrontation with the "monster" is the unmasking of the repressed in the narration's present moment, the releasing of the binaries (manipulator-manipulated, slayer-victim, judge-advocate) that structure the tale. The dream empowers Mickie to structure the narrative.

Mickie's grandmother is Mamá Chona, whose "monster" is the repressed sexual pleasure she has denied since the death of her first son. Her system of values embodies the tyranny of the spirit and mind over the psyche's instincts for pleasure. The return of her repressed body is presented in graphic terms in the final chapter just before her death. "She had not left the apartment or bathed for weeks, from the moment she had noticed something unnatural coming out of her womb. 'Another worthless creature,' she said. . . . By not allowing herself to be naked, she had successfully denied the existence of the monster" (174-75). When she is forced to take a bath, her family sees that "The monster between her legs was almost out and Mama Chona was glad that it showed no signs of life" (177). Her uterus, her body, and her children—the unveiled monster—are all merged in Mamá Chona's repressed pleasure. The supremacy of one realm over another in her existence—the spirit and intellect over the body and sex—is one variant of the different hierarchical oppositions that the "monster" incarnates. The rigid values of the Ángel family have reinforced mastery and domination and have condemned its members to repeat for generations the vicious cycle of binaries that the narrator now lays bare through the writing process.

The "monster" also incarnates a slayer-victim relationship between macho heterosexual and homosexual males. The narrator de-centers this traditional sexual hierarchy in the relationship between Mickie and Miguel Grande, his father, who is Mamá Chona's youngest son. The narrator hints that Mickie is, like his Uncle Félix, a gay man. He is unmarried, has no relationships with women, and as a child enjoyed traditionally feminine activities, such as cutting out paper dolls. He enters into deep conflict with Miguel Grande, who lacks a genuine sensitivity for his son's own and different human subjectivity. "Miguel Grande had consistently refused to acknowledge that his son's feelings and needs might be different from his own" (94). Determined to make "a man of the adolescent boy," Miguel Grande forbids his wife, Juanita, a call to the doctor when Mickie is ill and "many children were dying of polio" (94). As a result of his father's unconscionable neglect, Mickie "would have a slight limp for the rest of his life" (95).

Objectified and made "other" by his father all his life, Mickie gets his opportunity for "revenge." Years later, Miguel Grande turns in desperation to his adult son for advice on how best to resolve his marriage to Juanita and his affair with her best friend, Lola. The scene between father and son, with the father squirming, desperate, and on the edge of a nervous breakdown, and the son insisting that "you've got to make a decision, Dad" (97), is an indictment of Miguel Grande's masculine heterosexual identity. Mickie's father had manipulated him in life, but he now manipulates a discourse in his function as narrator that exposes his father's masculine weaknesses and contradictions to an audience. Mickie does not offer the camaraderie that a heterosexual son might give his father, but he is not cruel or nasty to him, either. Through the process of narrating, he "began to taste his father's blood" and to use "the knife as if it had been in his hands forever" (96-97). In a position of power and control over his father-repressor, the son expresses his grievances and finds redress against his father in his writing.

In the first chapter, while "floating" still in his near-dead state before the operation, Mickie thinks of his Uncle Félix, who "had been murdered in such a twilight" (6). In chapter 4, "Rain Dancer," he probes another variant of the manipulator-manipulated relationship that this time relates to Félix's rebellion against Mamá Chona's hierarchical values on race and ethnicity. "In subtle, persistent ways, family members were taught that only the Spanish side of their heritage was worth honoring and preserving; the Indian in them was pagan, servile, instinctive rather than intellectual, and was to be suppressed, its existence denied. Aunt Eduviges, Aunt Jesus Maria, and even Miguel Grande had learned this lesson well, taking to heart their mother's prejudices; Félix and Mema [Félix's sister] would have no part of it" (142). But Félix's unconscious shame and guilt about his ethnicity and race become entangled with his insecurities as a homosexual. The locus of these complex, ambivalent feelings becomes his youngest child and second son, JoEl. "Their arguments never directly confronted the deeper antagonism that had begun to grow between them" (118).

Félix rebels against Mamá Chona's prejudices that Spanish is "better" than Indian, light skin "better" than dark skin, by marrying Angie, a young Mexican American girl he had met in high school who spoke broken English and had very dark skin. Mamá Chona and her family, except Mema, call her the "*india*," a derogatory term implying inferiority of race and social class. Félix is consciously critical of his mother's racial prejudices, but he

An Alternative Tradition

remains driven by subconscious shame about his own ethnicity, as is evident when, during one of his intense arguments with JoEl, he projects his shame and guilt onto him. He vents his anger against JoEl by impugning a school system that teaches its students "to be ashamed of where they come from" (124). JoEl, the son of Félix and Angie, the "*india*," is, according to Félix, ashamed of where he "comes from." Félix rationalizes JoEl's antagonism toward him and Angie by projecting his own shame onto JoEl. Félix has made a "right" choice in opposing the distorting values of Mamá Chona, but has never confronted the guilt he understandably feels for having asserted himself against her authority.

That Félix has not fully confronted what it meant for him to go against his mother's attitudes of racial and ethnic hierarchy is evident in that he was "constantly on the lookout for the shy and fair god who would land safely on the shore at last" (115). This image activates a series of hierarchical oppositions that go back to a remote historical past but are also related to the immediate present of the servicemen's bar, where he awaits sexual gratification. Evoked in this passage is the convergence of Old and New Worlds; the struggles of the non-European Indian peoples of America against the militarily powerful Spaniards of Europe; the supremacy of Christianity over the heathen "other"; man against "savage." These images also evoke hierarchies of ethnicity and sexuality in Félix's contemporary moment: the young Anglo heterosexual soldier, "the fair god," with the older, Chicano, homosexual Félix. For Félix, the shy young soldiers of the base are "his greatest challenge" (135).

But Félix's search for the shy, fair god also has to be read in light of his relationship with JoEl. JoEl is fair, in contrast with his older brother, Roberto, who was "dark-skinned like his mother, very 'Indian,' polite and shy" (119). Through the years, Félix's passions for Angie diminished while a sexual desire for JoEl seemed to emerge and intensify. JoEl replaces Angie in the marriage bed: "When JoEl was ten Felix bought him a bed of his own, but until then they had slept together" (121). Félix's "protective feelings for the child perplexed and disoriented him because they seemed stronger than his desire for his wife" (122). This submerged sexual desire explains Félix's overly protective attitude toward JoEl but not his other three children, two of whom are girls, Lena and Yerma.

Ethnicity, race, and traditional sexuality as repressed forces haunting Félix all come together for him in a tragic way as he sits at the servicemen's bar awaiting the "fair god." As the chapter's scenes alternate between his past and present at the bar, Félix sees "JoEl's eyes floating in the warm darkness of the bar" (118). When the soldier "with light-colored eyes" enters, Félix sees only "the silhouette of a young man in uniform cross the threshold. JoEl's eyes disappeared into the far corner of the room." The innuendoes about Félix sleeping with his son for ten years in Angie's absence from their bed suggest the possibility that Félix might have sexually molested his young son. No explicit mention, though, is ever made of it. However, the intensity of the "demons" that haunt JoEl in his nightmares and the allusions made to him during his father's sexual chase of the "fair god" suggest that Félix's search for a young idealized image of himself is tied directly to repressed sexual desire for his son, as well as to his racial-ethnic insecurities.

Félix unknowingly confronts a racial, sexual bigot in the white heterosexual soldier who not only rejects his sexual advances but murders and disfigures him beyond recognition. He searches for the "fair god" because deep down he is still ensnared by a value system that privileges "light skin" over "dark skin." The whiteness of the god compensates for Félix's internalized feelings of ethnic insecurity. After all, he belongs to that "first large group of Mexicans (or, as their teachers referred to them, 'first generation Americans')" who grew up when hierarchies of race and sex were more fixed than those of Mickie's time (127). The youthful male "god" compensates for Félix's insecurity about his virility. He "had not lost his admiration for masculine beauty. As he grew older that admiration, instead of diminishing as he had expected, had become an obsession for which he sought remedy in simple and careless ways" (116). Repressed ethnicity and an insecurity about his homosexuality are the "monsters" impelling him to search for the white male god "in obscure places on both sides of the river" (115).

These different hierarchical values as represented in Mamá Chona, Miguel Grande, and Félix are part of the cultural legacy that Mickie inherits and confronts. When he undergoes physical pain before and after his operation, Mamá Chona looms large in his memories, perhaps because "he had been schooled by Mama Chona to suffer and, if necessary, to die" (7). We are given his parody of her ideal of pure intellect and spirit. Without the pain that still connected him to his flesh, "he would have possessed for the first time in his life that consciousness his grandmother and the Catholic Church he had renounced had taught him was the highest form of existence: pure, bodiless intellect. No shit, no piss, no blood—a perfect astronaut. 'I'm an angel,' he said inside his mouth to Mama Chona, already dead and buried. 'At last, I am what you taught us to be'" (8). The satire of "I'm an angel," in senses of both the family name and a bodiless spirit, masks the pain Mickie feels now, as a physically impaired human being, and while growing up with his family. From a once desirous homosexual male, he has become "forever a slave to plastic appliances" (7); "He had forgotten what it was like to be able to hold someone, naked, without having a plastic device between them" (25).

Significantly, Mickie's operation directly affects his sexuality. Given the context of his tutelage under Mamá Chona, he could certainly interpret his operation as she would inevitably see it, a punishment for his "sin" of homosexuality. In her world "there were no accidents. Every event was divine retribution or blessing" (164). Mickie, instead, succeeds in finding a more liberating interpretation for his operation and survival: "perhaps he had survived—albeit in an altered form, like a plant onto which has been grafted an altogether different strain of which the smelly rose at his side, that tip of gut that would always require his care and attention, was only a symbol—perhaps he had survived to tell others about Mama Chona.... He could then go on to shape himself, if not completely free of their influence and distortions, at least with some knowledge of them. He believed in the power of knowledge" (28). Mickie refers to his operation precisely as an "accident," therefore seeing life in a different way than Mamá Chona. Like her, he insists on finding a reason to explain it, but it is neither "divine retribution" nor "blessing." Rather, he interprets his "accident" and survival as an opportunity to "tell" his experiences, thus again defying Mamá Chona, who would not have wanted the world to hear the family secrets. Writing about her, Miguel Grande, Félix, and others allows him to escape her net of hierarchical values ("angel-sinner"; "spirit-body"; "pain-pleasure"; "light skin-dark skin"; "Spaniard-Indian") that have ensnared him and the family, allowing him to relive and understand their prejudices, fears, and failures.

By so doing, Mickie composes a "new" self, a composite of flesh and plastic, the grotesque wound from another culture that paradoxically saves his life yet forever separates him from another human being. With an interesting twist, he organicizes this surgical plastic implant by transforming it into a natural phenomenon: "the smelly rose at his side." His metaphor for himself of a plant, "onto which has been grafted an altogether different strain" also describes the text.

To write his text, Islas has appropriated specific modernistic techniques (especially self-conscious narration, but also nonlinear spatial and temporal sequences) and those of psychoanalysis from the dominant culture and has "grafted" them onto Mexican-Chicano culture. He does not turn his back on these techniques, but instead transforms them for his own unique purpose of asserting his "difference" from his two main traditions. By placing these techniques into the different setting of a Chicano novel, Islas ("makes strange")[2] "defamiliarizes" them, removing them from their usual perceptual field and allowing us to "see" them in a new, fresh way. By defamiliarizing the device, he exposes it as artifice, as arbitrary, showing his readers that literary conventions associated with the dominant tradition are neither "fixed" nor "natural." On the contrary, they are subject to movement, alteration, and displacement. In the long run, both Chicano and dominant traditions shape and are shaped by each other, as each tradition helps to transform the destructive forces of the other tradition into creative weapons for the writing of the story.

The Rain God as Transformation of Standard Traditions

Islas's narrative technique transforms his text into an implicit critique of the bourgeois autobiography and modernist novel of identity, or those middle-class texts that offer the "great narrative" of youth, education, and maturation. Usually, the middle-class autobiography has been written by white males who chronicle their lives from birth to the culminating achievement of their public and professional careers. They are the center of the story, with everything and everyone else subordinate to their progressive evolution. The split between narrator and character gives Islas the advantage of permitting the other characters to step into the foreground and speak for themselves. The audience hears the voices of the different characters in the dialogue that is placed within quotation marks: Juanita's voice against her sister Nina's on the issue of parental discipline; Félix's against JoEl's over the latter's freedom to do what he wants; Félix's daughter's insistence on seeking justice for his murder against Miguel Grande's efforts to suppress the embarrassing situation. Mickie does not occupy center stage as he would with a first-person narration, nor does he presume to "speak for" the other characters, a gesture generally associated with a conventional third-person omniscient narrator. Seldom the central focus of our attention, he is often absent or on the periphery of the action. In this sense, the text lacks the cohesive narrative and resists the totalizing system of the bourgeois autobiography, a genre requiring that the protagonist be omnipresent, the center of action.

The Rain God also deviates from the modernist novel of identity, which usually describes a voyage that moves in the direction of, to use Edward Said's terms proposed in *The World, the Text, and the Critic*, the "affiliative order," or an identity with art, institutions, and professional groups (16). James Joyce's *Portrait of the Artist as a Young Man* offers one example. Islas's text, organized into six separate but interlocking tales, like little stories in conversation with one another, reverses the modernist voyage of identity by foregrounding a movement toward the "filiative" order, or an identity with family, nature, native land, and personal relationships based upon sex, love, respect, and obedience.

Those elements that may be ascribed to the "affiliative" order recede into this novel's background. For example, when the story opens, Mickie is a professor at a prestigious university near San Francisco. However, the steps leading to this career goal are not explained or described. As the setting oscillates between the northern California coastline and the southern Texas desert of his family, the novelistic focus is on family. His family is the chief reason that he escapes south Texas; yet it imbues every action and thought of his present life in San Francisco. Separation from family and the impossibility of achieving it is, thus, the novel's major theme.

Mickie's dual identity as both narrator and character suggest a self-consciousness about his privileged position as narrator. From this vantage point, he examines the other characters, his family. From there he turns the tables, now manipulating through the narration the outside, making them "other," or subordinate, to him; in essence, manipulating family members who formerly had manipulated him. On the other hand, he undermines this privileged place by transforming himself into a character, thus becoming one more voice in a novel of multiple voices. He becomes an object as worthy of criticism as any other family member: "In his arrogance, Miguel believed he was finding ways out of [the Catholic guilt that had plagued his parents' generation] through his university education. He had not yet had time to combine learning with experience, however, and he still felt himself superior to those who had brought him up and loved him" (*Rain God* 91). By exposing the narrator's own complicity in family events and undermining his position of someone who is completely "outside," "uninvolved," and "objective," Islas challenges a cornerstone of modernist writing: the author as a detached and disinterested observer.

Mickie's function as character and narrator also gives him a participant-observer status within the text, in both his passive and active dimensions, and this relates to his role as the "indigenous ethnographer" of his family. The image of indigenous ethnographer fits him because he comes to possess important information and documents that are vital for the story of the Ángel family.

Nina and Miguel Grande, for example, turn to him at separate moments for advice about the latter's adulterous affair with Lola. Years after Félix's death, Lena tells him about her actions and feelings at the time of her father's murder.

Mickie's "indigenous informants" also send to him their memorabilia: in San Francisco, he receives a letter from his mother, Juanita, telling him about his childhood nursemaid María's visit to her; later he receives a letter from María herself written in Spanish that Mickie translates into English; his aunt Mema sends him the photograph that frames the novel and also a pre-Hispanic fifteenth-century poem by Nezahualcoyotl, King of Texcoco. The poem, quoted in English in the novel, Mema "thought had been written out in longhand by the first Miguel Angel in whose memory Miguel Chico and his father were named" (161-62). Mickie actively transforms these fragments of memorabilia by threading them together in order to construct the story his family denied for generations.

Like ethnographers who visit foreign tribes, then, Mickie has access to important family information. But unlike classical ethnographers who come from outside the communities they study and write about, he comes from within the "tribe" and is thus implicated in the very "secrets" he reveals to the audience. Islas's linking of Mickie's actions as indigenous ethnographer to both identities of narrator and character suggests a self-conscious portrayal of the subject-object relationship, one called for in recent anthropological writings.[3] The narrator, self-conscious about his position as observer, is not unaware that he is implicated in this discourse about the Ángel family. He does not speak with automatic authority for others, who in the classical anthropological model are defined as objects unable to speak for themselves. The very nature of the identity of indigenous ethnographer, someone simultaneously inside and outside the community, calls attention to the predicament of the subject-observer in the traditional subject-object relationship. The indigenous ethnographer is emblematic of a "new" ethnographic relationship between self and other, where a "new" self cannot entertain an image of itself as unimplicated, as the old one did, but rather must see itself as "other," caught up not only in the representation of cultures but also in the act of being represented. (See also James Clifford's introduction to *Writing Culture*.)

Mickie has the advantage of reviewing the family secrets analytically and critically, without confronting the pain of having lived them. Islas captures a dialectical mixture that highlights his hero's situation as a bicultural product: an "outsider" with the perspective of an "insider" and an "insider" with the perspective of an "outsider."

The Implied Audience, or New "American" Readers

The narrator's multiple functions as family analyst, autobiographer, novelist, and indigenous ethnographer also have relevance for the issue of audience. Islas's narrative strategy of splitting the authorial voice into a narrator and a character, for example, allows him the possibility of attributing the "translation" of the specificities of Chicano culture to an objective narrator, a noncharacter, as opposed to solely having a character do it, which would necessarily be the case in a first-person narration. His strategy puts the stress on the narrative voice, or on the way the content is communicated, rather than on the chain of events that make up the plot. One consequence is that the audience becomes self-conscious of its intercultural and interethnic relationships to the text.

The Rain God aims to create new "American" readers who are aware of and self-conscious about their relationship to other cultures. It presupposes three kinds of readers in its audience: Chicano bilinguals, Anglophonic monolinguals, and nonbilingual Chicanos. Although primarily written in English, the text contains a substantial number of words in Spanish. While some multicultural authors refuse to translate,[4] Islas has his narrator translate the Spanish into English. But note the shape that his translations take. In some cases, the narrator deliberately "mistranslates" in order to put his monolingual, Anglophonic readers in a complicated relationship to the text, creating discomfort within them so as to cause them to reflect about their own culture and their relationship to the culture they are reading about. A few examples illustrate this technique.

When the narrator introduces Mickie's grandmother, he notes, "she instructed everyone in the family to call her 'Mama Grande' or

'Mama Chona' and never, ever to address her as *abuelita*, the Spanish equivalent to granny"[5] (*Rain God* 4). Uninitiated Anglophonic readers may indeed at this point accept the narrator's gloss of "granny" for *abuelita*, allowing themselves to feel at ease in the assurance that cultural barriers will not intrude to interrupt their possession of the text. But the stated equivalence between *abuelita* and "granny" does not fool Spanish-English bilinguals because they know the two words do not convey an identical concept and that the narrator is not stating this equivalence for their sake. In this early contact with a bilingual culture, uninitiated readers might very well continue their reading under the mistaken impression that *abuelita* and "granny" are equivalent terms. In case they do, the narrator provides other opportunities to make them question their mistaken assumptions about cross-cultural communication.

The effect of the narrator's strategy is to bring monolingual readers closer to understanding a bilingual experience. For if Islas permits them to think that they can understand another culture by having it translated entirely into their own language system, he will not really help them to experience a sense of difference. He must challenge them a bit, disorient them, and unsettle their comfortable cultural categories. In this next example, the narrator speaks to his bilingual audience, apologizing to them for not using the Spanish. "Miguel Chico's aunts Jesus Maria and Eduviges left notes for the 'domestics' (the Spanish word *criadas* is harsher)" (15). Couched within this sentence is the assumption that the narrator would like to fulfill his bilingual audience's expectation of *criadas*, but then he explains to them why he cannot. The narrator tells his bilingual audience that he knows the Spanish *criadas* captures better than the English "domestics" the Ángel family's attitude toward "the illiterate riffraff from across the river" (15), but he refuses to use it because it is too "harsh." He prefers the less accurate but softer "domestics," inserting it within quotation marks. At the level of the plot, the narrator informs both groups of readers that he disagrees with the family's harsh attitude toward the undocumented women upon whom they depend. At the level of narrative voice, however, he is letting his Anglophonic readers know that they are not the only audience and that the harsh term *criadas* cannot be translated into English. A certain level of experience is inaccessible to them. Its untranslatability defends this text against being homogenized or essentialized.

There is one word Islas's narrator overtly refuses to translate. Appearing at the beginning and end, *familia* is probably the most important word in the book; in a sense, it is the book. Islas has foregrounded *familia* as the main ideological apparatus of Chicano culture that shapes and conditions the individual's cultural, sexual, racial, and ethnic attitudes. Injurious, it is the primary source of ideological indoctrination, as represented by Mamá Chona. Yet it is also empowering, for without her, there would be no family, no story, and hence no text. "Without me, everything would die" (171), she says toward the end of the book and her life. By the end, monolinguals have grasped the resonances of this word, the different attitudes toward life, death, and history that it conveys to Chicanos and Chicanas, precisely because the narrator has refused to translate it into the English "family."

In a different example, a non-Spanish-speaking nurse mispronounces Mickie's given name while he convalesces in the hospital after his operation. "'Mee-gwell,' sang the nurse, 'wake-up, Meegwell, 'It's Miguel,' he wanted to tell her pointedly, angrily, 'it's Miguel,' but he was unable to speak" (8). The two cultural groups represented here have access to different scriptural and phonetic systems that prevent each one from pronouncing the other's language properly. Islas also portrays Spanish speakers who mispronounce English by transforming English words into their own linguistic sound systems. "Jitterbug" is transformed into "Yitty-bog" (16) and "joke" becomes "yoke" (117). In the example of the nurse's mispronunciation, Chicanos—bilingual and nonbilingual—can identify perfectly with Mickie because they are among those who know what it is to have their names mispronounced by the dominant society. Non-Chicano, monolingual readers cannot really feel this situation, but they learn—through the narrator's mediation—to understand how Mickie feels. Without being able to pronounce his name correctly, they are encouraged to wonder about the desirability of being like this nurse who does not know she is mispronouncing a proper name.

They learn, albeit momentarily, to see themselves as others see them and to be more sympathetic to the hero, but, again, only through the intervention of the narrator.

So far, all these examples have dealt with isolated words or names involving two different languages. Notably, however, the text also includes a passage, involving no Spanish, that makes its audiences self-conscious about their relationship to one another. It is an example of what Michael Fischer, an anthropologist, has referred to as "bifocality" or "reciprocity of perspectives": "seeing others against a background of ourselves, and ourselves against a background of others" (*Writing Culture* 194-233). This particular incident has the effect of making the dual audience self-conscious about the process of reading Chicano literature.

About midway through the text, Juanita tells Nina, her sister, about the best-seller romances she enjoys reading. Juanita's indulging in these romances is a symptom of her repressed sexual life. Even though they are not Chicano romances, she projects herself into their fantasies, which allow her to subconsciously fulfill her repressed sexual desire. She wants Nina to read them too, but Nina, who has more selective tastes, finds these books boring and irrelevant. She does not want to read about Southern belles. "Why don't they write about us?" Nina exclaims. "Who wants to read about Mexicans?" retorts Juanita. "We're not glamorous enough. We just live" (*Rain God* 41).

Juanita's and Nina's ways of "reading" their lives, or the events of the plot, suggest two different kinds of "readers" of literature. Juanita's manner suggests a romantic, naive reader who fully identifies with an author's plots and characters and hence implicitly blends into the undifferentiated, homogeneous audience that they presuppose. Juanita, overly trusting about the events in her marriage, does not see, does not want to see, what goes on between Miguel Grande and Lola. In contrast, Nina's style suggests a more critical, astute "reader" of life and, implicitly, literature, as she focuses on specific incidents involving Miguel Grande and Lola, drawing the correct conclusions about their adulterous behavior.

Within the plot, Nina is involved in "reading" the kind of "text" she would like to read in written form—a novel about "us."

She does not want to read Juanita's Southern belle romances because "they—their authors—do not write about 'us'"—that is, Chicanos and Chicanas. The book that the audience of *The Rain God* is reading is the book Nina would very much like to read. Conscious of her Chicano ethnicity, Nina refuses to read novels that do not include her, even though she has the cultural and linguistic resources to do so. While Juanita has no developed consciousness of ethnic difference, Nina has an excess of it.

In this passage, Chicano and non-Chicano audiences become aware that they are reading about a Chicano character who claims that no one writes about "Mexicans." Chicanos in the audience, no doubt, will identify with Nina as part of the excluded subject matter in American literature. But they, as well as the non-Chicanos, will catch the irony: while Juanita reads Southern belle romances, a non-Chicano audience now reads *The Rain God*, a novel about Mexican-Chicano culture. The lesson for Chicanos is that monolinguals *are* indeed reading about them.

Islas is calling for a reader who represents a fusion, as it were, of certain uncompromised characteristics of both a "Juanita" and a "Nina." He wants Juanita's openness to reading about other cultures but rejects her blindness to her own cultural difference. Similarly, he disapproves of Nina's resistance to reading about cultures other than her own, but desires her critical perspective and her insistence on ethnic difference. The "we" of the audience—bilingual and monolingual Chicanos and non-Chicano monolinguals—represent this "ideal" reader. We *are* reading and, therefore, doing what Nina refuses to do; and we are reading in a way that Juanita does not read, a way that makes us cognizant of cultural difference. Islas has gone out of his way to make his novel accessible to an Anglophonic audience, although by no means so accessible that he neither challenges them nor preserves ethnic characteristics. His text reveals and discloses but also withholds, refusing to speak fully.

Islas has taken creative liberties with the genres of autobiography, novel, and classical ethnography and has offered transformations of their classical models along lines of both content and form. He has worked toward the definition of an alternative tradition that not only critiques these standard models but also enlarges the scope of their implied readership. Within this alternative tradition, Islas foregrounds the text as an assertion of difference, and herein lies its triumph. The text has an assertive character because it shows that difference can be narrativized. *The Rain God* is neither an Anglo-American nor a Mexican text but a *Chicano* text, adhering to and confirming its difference from either of these two traditions.

NOTES

[1] Another meaning of this metaphor is found in the images of rain and fertility that appear throughout. These images, standing in opposition to those of sand and desert, evoke an ambiance of death, sacrifice, and mythic fate reminiscent of the legendary Tlaloc, the Mexican deity of the pre-Hispanic peoples who exacted youthful sacrifices in exchange for the bestowing of the fertile rains. Images of rain, fog, and water exist in a tenuous balance with those of sand, dust, and stones. When the balance is destroyed, as it is with Miguel Grande's adulterous affair or with Félix's brutal murder, the desert moves from the external landscape to invade the minds and hearts of the Ángel family.

[2] I use this term loosely, meaning to "make strange," to designate a process by which a familiar object is made unfamiliar to a culturally specific audience. Defamiliarization is, of course, the English rendition of *ostranenie* developed by Russian formalist Victor Shklovsky.

[3] Many essays collected in James Clifford's *Writing Culture* challenge the traditional notion of ethnography as a privileged discourse by the European subject about non-European cultural objects, in which the Western subject presumes to speak with automatic authority for others defined as unable to speak for themselves.

[4] Islas is different from Reed Way Dasenbrock's (10-19) authors who refuse to translate important words or phrases from their native cultures. But like those authors, he too succeeds in giving readers from different cultures an opportunity to learn about his culture of origin.

[5] Mamá Chona is not at all the archetypal figure of the loving working-class *abuelita* that filled the pages of Chicano literature in the 1960s and 1970s by both men and women.

IDEOLOGICAL DISCOURSES
in Arturo Islas's *The Rain God*

Rosaura Sánchez

Literature is a cultural and semiotic practice. As such it provides through signifying practices an ideological representation of culture, what, to rephrase Lotman and Uspenskii (30), we could call an ideological system of "collective memory and collective consciousness." If, as Lotman and Uspenskii allege, culture evidences "clear-cut divisions into stages that replace one another dynamically" (31), each period making a decisive break with what preceded it, even while repeating or regenerating certain aspects of the culture of the past, then an analysis of the discursive practices in Chicano literature should disclose not only the group's ideological memory but its "lived" experiences of the continuities and discontinuities in its history as well.

The literature of the population of Mexican origin in the United States since 1848 is increasingly being brought to light through continued research into newspapers, journals, and unpublished documents. These new findings enable us to retrace and formulate ideological models textualized in the narratives of two centuries of discourse. With these earlier texts as benchmarks, we will increasingly be able to note not only the ruptures in the discourse but also the links and differences between what was produced in the late nineteenth century and what was produced in the twentieth century. In the most recent stage of literary production, which is the one most studied and best known, several novels have appeared dealing with experiences of occupational and geographical mobility and changing power relations within the family as experienced by a child growing into adulthood. These issues are also central to feminist literature, in particular the works of Chicano female poets, texts that offer additional examples of ideological transformations that are taking place alongside shifts in power relations arising from the questioning of male-dominant cultural practices. But there are other examples of shifts in the collective memory to be explored as yet. A study of both earlier and recent narratives will allow us to track down evolving ideological discursive and cultural practices within the multifaceted Chicano community.

These cultural breaks are a result of internal and external contradictions. Externally the contradictions are multiple and varied. Internally, cultures, as Lenin pointed out, are characterized by both progressive and reactionary elements (80); these ideological contradictions invariably give rise to conflicts, struggles, and shifts, especially when cultural practices are perceived to be forms of exploitation and domination or when they are no longer deemed to be viable given the presence of alternative practices. Such is the case in José Antonio Villarreal's *Pocho* (1959); here the main character, Richard Rubio, rejects his family's patriarchal prescriptions for male children and joins the navy, not for any patriotic reason, but simply to get away from his family, to escape and thus avoid a restrictive situation that suffocates him with expectations of domestic and filial obligations and forces his transformation into what to him is a nonentity, that is, into a steel-mill worker, a family man. Much like his father, who in his youth had set his political and personal allegiance to Pancho Villa above the needs of the family to the point of neglect, the protagonist Richard also feels that his personal goals should take priority. Trapped and confined by those collective bonds that kept him from developing his individuality and from attending the university in order to become a writer, he embraces the anonymity of a military order which, though confining, will free him of family obligations and, if he is not killed, will allow him to work toward his goals. Obviously these middle-class aspirations, while unheard of in his lower-income community, fit in perfectly well with a growing capitalist economy.

Thus Richard does not indict society for his predicament but rather accedes to the dominant ideologies and accepts their definitions of reality. In consenting to his own subordination and making sense of his options, the protagonist attempts to mask and displace what is at odds with the dominant ideologies, but even his passing acknowledgment of social subordination and blatant discrimination against *mexicanos* reveals contradictions and problematic areas. In accepting the myth of individualism, the Chicano of the early 1940s in effect accepted the ideological representations, discourse, and power configurations of entrepreneurial capitalism. Later stages of multinational capitalism with its corporate structure and centralization of capital in core firms would emerge as the dominant form of big business in the United States with World War I (Edwards 69) and become fully consolidated after the 1920s as the economy expanded then and again after 1940 (81). With this shift of control in the firm would come an undermining of previously necessary myths, among them notions of the individualist subject. The novel *Pocho* appears then at the end of an era, while the novel *The Rain God: A Desert Tale* by Arturo Islas, published in 1984, begins in a sense where *Pocho* leaves off, that is, in the decade of the 1940s. It moves, however, not so much within a historical time-space as within a subjective timeless frame in which historical references are blurred and earlier social practices are recalled and mapped out, finally to be expunged from the character's memory, as we shall see.

I read Islas's novel as a literary text made up of a multiplicity of discourses that dialogue with past and present signifying practices in society while at the same time providing a textualization of extradiscursive cultural and social practices. Within this discursive approach all discourse will be viewed as ideological, and experience will be seen to be the product of these ideological practices. The novel—and like it, all texts—is not analyzable in terms of the author's intentions, but as a product of those social and cultural practices and ideological discourses that interact to determine the experiences of the individual who actually writes the work. This network of interacting practices and discourses constitutes the signifying practices that make up the text.

In this analysis, then, ideological practices are said to be discursive and representative of "lived experience," what Louis Althusser calls "the 'representation' of the imaginary relationship of individuals to their real conditions of existence" (162). Here Althusser retains the notion of ideology as illusion, as false consciousness and distortion, not of people's real conditions of existence, but of their relations to those conditions. This imaginary relation of individuals to the real relations in which they live is necessarily complex since an individual is involved in a plurality of relations, assumes a number of positions in society, and interacts with numerous practices of various social institutions, such as family, schools, government, the legal system, media, etc. In fact it is ideology, or more specifically bourgeois ideology, that, like language, is said to constitute or interpellate concrete individuals as subjects (171). The entire notion of the individual subject, as noted earlier, once generally accepted as a given, is today questioned and viewed as a myth, an imaginary representation, which in fact never really existed but was created by bourgeois ideologies. (See Jameson's essay "Postmodernism and Consumer Society.") Current trends assume a decentered subject, a multiple subject, notions which alongside those of the individual autonomous subject are evident in Islas's novel, albeit in a rather fragmented fashion.

It is the Althusserian analysis of ideology as imaginary or unconscious that led to Jameson's notion of the "political unconscious" (see *Political Unconscious* 49). Unfortunately, this notion of the unconscious gives the analysis of ideology a bent that is misleading. Today we can no longer accept idealist notions of deep structures distinct from surface structures, nor can we posit ideology at some hidden or repressed underlying level, for it is manifest at a conscious surface level. Marx's example of the fetishism of commodities (Marx, *Capital* 71) best clarifies the problem arising with hermeneutic notions of levels. The labor time congealed in a commodity may be ignored or negated to the point that value is attributed to the commodity itself as if it were inherently present, but the value determined by the labor is never absent or hidden at some deeper structural level. The value added by labor (Marx, *Grundrisse* 354) is present at the surface level, in the very production of the artifact, waiting only to be deconstructed. In a similar manner ideology is present in the very discourse, in the very signs used for communication (Vološinov 22), and even in the textual surface gaps, lapses, silences, and absences (Althusser 18). Ideology, moreover, cannot be reduced to a functionalist practice that merely ensures the maintenance of the mode of production that gives rise to it, for it is always contradictory and it always harbors countertendencies. For this reason theorists like Callinicos (93) and Hall ("Culture" 340), citing Gramsci, prefer to speak of "ideologies" or a "field of ideology" that bears "'traces' of previous ideological systems and sedimentations." Disjuncture, thus, may arise within ideological hegemony, made up of an alliance of dominant class fractions, to produce counterpractices. The mode of operation of these dominant groups is a complex matter, for, as explained by Hall: "they not only possess the power to coerce but actively organize so as to command and win the consent of the subordinated classes to their continuing sway" ("Culture" 332). Subordinate classes in effect accede to representing their experiences in terms of discursive frameworks set up by the dominant classes; if on the other hand, they refuse to identify with the established definitions of reality and produce counterdiscourses, they face numerous strategies of co-optation, as discussed by Hebdige (*Subculture*) in his work on subcultural styles. As a result, the discourse of opposition can be easily appropriated and incorporated into dominant ideological practices through their reduction to a commodity form or through a redefinition that trivializes, naturalizes, or domesticates what originally may have seemed subversive (94-97).

This essay then will focus on the representation in *The Rain God* of the social practices of three generations of the Ángel family as well as on the ideological discourses used by the characters to represent, interpret, and make sense of their experiences. The older generations will be seen to conform to dominant ideological practices and identify with them, while the younger generations counter specific but limited aspects of parental practices; their counterdiscourses, however, will be seen to be tied to the same formulations and power systems, so that the rejected practice is either simply reversed or replaced by different but analogous power relations. That is the nature of counterdiscourse: it does not formulate a distinctive alternative but merely opposes what it, ironically, affirms.

The novel addresses three important social practices: the patriarchy and all it connotes in terms of family practices and gender roles; ethnic and class prejudices; and, to a lesser extent, religious beliefs. Countering these practices are strategies that contain or restrict problematic events and relations within a limiting framework (Hall, "Culture" 341) wherein individual differences are opposed to family norms and traditions. Among the principal "strategies of containment," to use Jameson's phrase (*Political Unconscious* 53), are resentment, which in time turns into disdain, and deviance or departures from accepted norms, as evidenced in suicide, drug addiction, and homosexuality. Here the affirmation of difference arises not at a collective level but at a strictly individualistic one.

These cultural practices are textualized in six separate segments that make up the novel, with each segment projecting a particular image of the family. The totality of the novel produces a fragmented and discontinuous extended-family portrait that includes three generations of the Ángel family plus the sister-in-law of one family member. Each segment of the novel focuses on one of the households represented in the overall picture and details the crisis of that particular family unit. The fragmented structure is spiral in form, with each segment advancing and retreating in time to cover a period extending from the decade of the 1930s to the present, with two brief references to an earlier period, the Mexican Revolution of 1910 and the year of immigration, 1916. Each segment narrates an episode that contains dialogue between various members of the family, as well as intratextual references to events reiterated from different perspectives in third-person narration; although the segments internally assume a certain chronological framework, there are numerous flashbacks (analepses) and flashforwards (prolepses) within the episodes.

The first segment, "Judgment Day," serves as an introduction to the entire family and juxtaposes the main character's early childhood with his near-death experience in surgery at the age of thirty. It also provides the most vivid image in the novel, that of the main character's colostomy, which forces him to wear an appliance to which a plastic bag, regularly changed, is attached. Twelve years after leaving the desert of his youth, Miguel Chico, a university professor in San Francisco, recalls his family—especially its sinners—as he lies in the hospital recovering from surgery, half-conscious and longing for the desert of his childhood, the place where his aunt Nina fears being buried. His earliest childhood memories are of love, death, religion, and bigotry, evoked along with other subsequent events, not with nostalgia but with resentment; his life-threatening experience would in a sense free him and allow him to deal with his memories, to face up to them, to feel no longer compelled to hide the family's secrets. It is this experience that serves to explain the desert tale, as Miguel Chico is the presumed narrator, although all mentions of the character are in third person as well. The final segment, "The Rain God," ends with the death of the matriarch, Mamá Chona, a scene recalled in the first segment, many years after the fact.

On her deathbed Mamá Chona entrusts the family to Miguel Chico, a burden that he rejects yet still bears. Many years later the grandson would still be looking for a way to stop being haunted by his dead. The novel itself ultimately is the answer; it assumes the form of a collective confession, an act of exorcism, a ritual within which the writer is both confessor and collective sinner. The narrative is thus a cathartic experience, a way of consuming the past, a way of forgetting (Jameson, *Postmodern Condition* xii), as well as of doing penance. The character proposes to tell all the family secrets and in that way to be free of them:

> He needed very much to make peace with his dead, to prepare a feast for them so that they would stop haunting him. He would feed them words and make his candied skulls out of paper. He looked, once again, at that old photograph of himself and Mama Chona. The white daisies in her hat no longer frightened him; now that she was gone, the child in the picture held only a ghost by the hand and was free to tell the family secrets. (*Rain God* 160)

Once narrated, discourse becomes estranged, *ajeno*; in this way the narrator means to be free of this burdensome collective memory, this textual "other" that is a multitextual "inner speech" (Vygotsky 27), in effect the discourse of the living and dead. The novel deals then with a need to exteriorize the private sphere, the family circle from which the character is estranged. In an effort to collect his images of the past, Miguel Chico resolves, like the quoted fifteenth-century king of Texcoco, Nezahualcoyotl, to recall his dead through written discourse: "Nothing recalls them but the written page" (*Rain God* 162).

As noted before, resentment is the major ideological strategy in the novel, but it is not the resentment of subordinated classes against the upper classes but rather that of sons and daughters who reject the authoritarian position of the father and the deleterious effect of the family on its members, a discourse that runs entirely counter to the words of Mamá Chona, who assured her grandchildren that within the family no harm would come to them.

The principal resentment is thus against the patriarchy as constituted in traditional Western society, with its gender roles, power relations, and values. The patriarchal code is particularly explicit in terms of male behavior. A son must not be weak, delicate, or effeminate, but rather strong, independent, aggressive, competitive, and ambitious. Wives are deemed to be subordinate creatures whose principal duties are to reproduce, nurture children, and attend to the various needs of their husbands. The father figure, proudly masculine and dominant, is established as the authority to be unquestionably obeyed. In the novel Miguel Grande, the husband of Juanita and father of Miguel Chico and two other sons, is a policeman, an authoritarian father and husband, and a womanizer. His pernicious influence is countered throughout the novel in various ways. The son, his namesake and first born, Miguel Chico, grows up to be an academic, a bookworm who cares little about bodybuilding and who as a child preferred the company of his mother, grandmother, and the maid, a domestic worker from across the border who enjoyed dressing the child in a skirt and teaching him to dance. When the child is stricken with polio, his father, who does not wish to pamper a sickly son, forbids his mother to take him to the doctor until it is too late and he is, as a result, left with a lifelong limp. Many years later the son's education and economic independence, his professional career as a professor, and his bachelor status allow him to escape the stranglehold of his father's patriarchal standards but not to subvert the power relations altogether. In fact, the son develops such a strong resentment against his father and considers him to be so despicable that he finds that he will never be able to trust another man again (97). Resentment eventually turns to disdain and ultimately to arrogance when the son becomes his father's confessor and feels triumph in the knowledge that his father will never be able to come between him and his mother. For a brief moment, then, the roles are reversed, but they are not undone. Resentment is thus a form of adherence and consent in the end.

Resentment against the patriarchal family structure is tied to the very textualization of the patriarchy in the novel. Years after his grandmother's death and after visiting his drug-addicted cousin in a halfway house, Miguel Chico dreams of being raped by the monster that killed his grandmother. If we recall that her monstrous "abortion" was actually a fallen uterus, it becomes evident that the monster symbolizes the family, the patriarchy; it is a monstrous synthesis of exploiter and exploited, loved and unloved, judge and advocate, and the only way to destroy it is to destroy oneself. The plunge that in the dream the character takes off the bridge with the monster represents his decision to commit suicide with his violator, that is, to end the silence and begin writing the story of his family and thus of himself.

Miguel Chico's rejection of the patriarchal norm has to be viewed in terms of other social practices. In effect, patriarchal discourse is often tied to capitalist ideology in the text and it is not always of male origin. In one case, for example, it is reproduced by a woman, Miguel's aunt and godmother, Nina, whose stubbornness, authoritarian ways, and middle-class patriarchal expectations for her son, Tony, lead to a confrontation between mother and son. Tony's sisters are barely mentioned in the novel; it is the son who represents the family's aspirations and for whom the purchase of a new home is made as an investment, the future sale of which will provide the funds for his college education. The son, on the other hand, resents having to change to a high school in a new neighborhood and scorns his mother's constant interest in making a profit. To protest the move, he threatens to stop studying; moreover he sees no reason to make plans for college when the Vietnam War draft awaits him. After his threats fail to have any effect and he is locked up in his room to force him to do his work, the son determines to counter his family's and, more pointedly his mother's, authoritarianism in a most violent way: he commits suicide.

Another central character in *The Rain God* is Uncle Félix, a contradictory figure, rain dancer, free spirit, and bisexual who seemingly subverts but in fact conforms to patriarchal practices as he governs his home in a typically authoritarian way. The text is ambivalent about Félix, presenting him as a kind and gentle man who is not bigoted like the rest of the Ángel family, while at the same time revealing his seduction of young men and narrating aspects of his life that point to his exploitation of the Mexican workers whom he hires as factory foremen and fondles under the pretext of a necessary medical examination. His death at the hands of a reluctant Anglo "prey" is portrayed as a case of civil rights discrimination against Mexicans when it is covered up by the military personnel at the base where the young man is stationed; it is also said that the dismissal of the case is accepted by Miguel Grande, then concerned with his candidacy for police chief.

Félix's homosexual preferences, however, cannot be seen to negate patriarchal structures, for not only is he an authoritarian husband with a wife and four children at home, but in his relations with men he also assumes the position of power and takes advantage of his subordinates. Resentment of the offspring toward the authority figure also comes into play here as Félix, too, faces the resentment and loss of his son, JoEl, whom he adores but who in time also begins to seek "his own space" by retreating to the printed world of his books and poetry. Once again individualism and the desire to affirm individual differences counter traditional family roles and create father-son conflicts, even though bonds are not entirely severed. In fact JoEl also, like Miguel, will carry the burden of his dead throughout his life; his plunge, however, will be into the oblivion of a drug-induced idiocy.

The women in the novel are true to patriarchal prescription; they are passive, spineless, gentle creatures, except for Nina, Juanita's sister, who is said to be like her authoritarian half-French father, whom she hated. The main character's mother, Juanita, is described as a "selfless angel" who loves her husband dearly and even her best friend, Lola, who would later betray her by becoming her husband's lover. If Lola represents the conniving yet glamorous seductress, the ideal woman is undoubtedly the mother figure as represented by Juanita and Angie, Félix's wife, but this male idealization of women is challenged, if only somewhat, by Juanita's son, who considers his mother masochistic, and is repudiated entirely by Angie's son JoEl, who scorns his mother for putting up with Félix's injustices: "Wordlessly, he let Angie know that she deserved the pain she endured and that she was no better than a worm for letting Felix take advantage of her goodness" (125).

The novel thus captures a generational conflict as it both reconstructs patriarchal images of women as angels or whores and deconstructs them by uncovering the wives' oppression and their subjection to cultural norms. The text, however, deals only with the subordination of women within the home, as it focuses exclusively on the private sphere and neglects the public domain. The chronotope (see Bakhtin, *Dialogic Imagination* 84) of the home as an idyllic refuge for the patriarchal family is thus thoroughly negated and seen instead to be a space wherein tension, oppression, and domination take place. The home is truly the cave where the monster resides.

The novel begins and ends with a portrait of Mamá Chona, the grandmother, the transmitter of patriarchal and capitalist practices and discourses. A woman who had suffered the loss of three children by the time she immigrated to the United States, Mamá Chona lives in constant expectation of suffering and death. A judgmental, pretentious, and proud woman, she ensures the transmission of her class ideology and bigotry, practices that would characterize all but two of her children, Félix and Mena.

The latter also suffers the consequences of patriarchal practices when her illegitimate child is born and she is forced by the family to give him up. In protest Mena crosses the border to live with her man and look for her son. Six years later Mena finds the boy begging in the streets of Juárez and, with the help of Félix, has him brought back to the United States where his grandmother raises him, as if attempting to undo her own deed.

The hypocrisy and snobbery of the Ángel clan are part of a network of contradictions in the family. The two matriarchs, Mamá Chona and Tía Cuca, for example, are in effect poor women with aristocratic airs who consider menial labor beneath them. An earlier situation that had allowed for hired domestic workers in the home had left its ideological traces in the grandmother's discourse long after she had ceased to be able to afford a maid. Her refusal to do her domestic chores because she associates this work with members of the lower working class or undocumented workers, whom she identifies as "Indians," reveals the racist ideology of an ethnic classification system in which class relations are displaced and a chain is created linking illiteracy with paganism and servility with dark skin. Thus Mamá Chona assumes an air of superiority, a class condescension with those she considers her inferiors "the illiterate riffraff from across the river" (*Rain God* 15). Miguel Chico, who resents this snobbery, understands it as a remnant of colonial discourse in women who are obviously of Indian heritage themselves. The grandmother's imaginary representation of her relations to her own conditions of existence serves in fact to hide her actual poverty and mask her Indian features to none but herself. The ideological nature of this perspective is clear to Juanita, who likewise sees through this pretentiousness and notes the meager means of the Ángel family (14–15). On the other hand, this ideology is not unconscious; it assumes concrete manifestation at every turn. Because fair skin is a mark of worth for the Ángel family, Félix, for example, has to marry Angie without his mother's blessing since his wife is considered a "lower-class Mexican," and an "Indian" for being dark complected. Félix's sister best summarizes the inherited discourse:

> She said she did not understand how Angie had even gotten through school. Obviously she belonged to that loathsome group of Indians who were herded through the system, taught to add at least since they refused to learn any language properly, and then let loose among decent people who must put up with their ignorance. Jesus Maria knew that her family was better than such illiterates and she would prove it by going on to college. (128)

After Mamá Chona's children grow up, they attain a lower-middle-class or middle-class status; this can be inferred from the sparse mention made of their means of support, since the public sphere constitutes a notable gap in the narrative. In their conversations, and in the entire novel for that matter, their relation to the dominant class in society is never analyzed or questioned; in fact they are strong proponents of the dominant ideology, consenting, as Hall explains in his analysis of culture ("Culture" 315), to their own subordination. Miguel Grande, as one of the first policemen of Mexican origin in this border Texas town in the desert, is convinced that the "North American dream had worked for him. Only his family reminded him of his roots, and except for his mother he avoided them as much as possible" (*Rain God* 78). Although apparently alienated from his own ethnic group and family, Miguel Grande's best friends are Mexican as well, and he is said to have worked to integrate the police force until more than half are Mexican (76). Strong defenders of the power structure in this country, Miguel Ángel and his buddy, El Compa, are convinced that the United States is the best country in the world; they consider themselves Americans and are totally unaware not only of international affairs, as the narrator points out in reference to the Spanish Civil War (57), but also of their own historical circumstances. It is Félix's daughter Lena, the one who runs around with "lower-class" *mexicanos*, who is glad to find out that Miguel Grande "had not been selected chief, thinking it might force him to understand what life was really like for 'low class' Mexicans in the land that guaranteed justice under the law for all" (88). The loss of this promotion was to be a shock for Miguel Grande, and he is said to have lost faith in "what he's believed in all his life about this country" (91).

While ethnic solidarity and discrimination are not primary issues in the novel, they, along with deviance, are presented as explicit constituents of difference. Class structure, on the other hand, although less visible, is an implicit presupposition, for only it can explain the Ángel resentment toward the lower classes and the family's consent to the dominant ideologies.

The third cultural practice inherited from Mamá Chona is the other side of bigotry: Catholic guilt and a desire for punishment. Although the institution itself—the church—is not represented, its ideology raises its ugly head as its practices are visited even on to the third generation, so that the Ángel grandchildren feel burdened by the sins of their fathers. JoEl seeks relief in drug addiction but it proves to be no escape; we last see him in a halfway house for addicts, a riddle-spouting lunatic. Nina, on the other hand, though Catholic, searches out additional occult practices that eventually allow her to overcome her fear of death. On the other hand, Jesús María, who had married against her mother's wishes, is a shrieking replica of her mother; she attends mass daily and follows her mother's religious norms faithfully, but her hypocritical harangues make her intolerable even to Mamá Chona.

The third generation of the Ángel family continues to evidence vestiges of this practice as well. Miguel Chico, for example, grows up to assume an air of self-righteousness and superiority, thinking himself educated and beyond the plague of guilt and beyond the maid María's distortions of religion, but he too is obsessed with the sins of his fathers and his own. Later, and wiser, like a Foucauldian genealogist, he resigns himself, if not to being totally free of his family's influences and distortions, at least to the illusion of going beyond these practices through his knowledge of them, for "he believed in the power of knowledge" (28). To escape from the power of secrecy, deformation, and mystification, Miguel Chico invokes the privileges and power of knowledge. The narration of the family secrets itself thus becomes a strategy of struggle.

This genealogical analysis focuses, then, on various cultural practices but without discussing their relation to an entire network of social practices that are economic and political in nature, preferring to limit itself strictly to power relations within the family. Consequently, the Ángel family seems to have lived in a vacuum, untouched by World War II, the Korean War, the McCarthyist period, the Vietnam War, the civil rights movement, labor struggles, political struggles, overt racial discrimination, and other forms of class struggles in the United States. It is only by searching through numerous traces of other texts to be found in the novel that we encounter texts of poverty that go beyond Tía Cuca's eccentric lifestyle and allude to an entire population of "low-class" Mexicans in Lena's high school with whom she associates, to the family's consternation. After this rapid mention, however, the text is bracketed and never taken up again. In a similar way we discover that Félix's work as a foreman puts him in a position of *coyote*, recruiting Mexican laborers for the plant. However, it is the men's physical beauty that attracts Félix; their plight beyond this sexual abuse is also bracketed. In a similar fashion we learn that the murder of Mexicans is a routine, casually treated matter in the city while being offered the exceptional case of Félix's murder, which attracts a good deal of attention since the victim is the brother of a candidate for police chief. The family is thus enclosed in a cocoon, a world all its own. Only brief asides, like that of the Catholic president being assassinated, situate the episodes in time. But what is edited out, though absent, is clearly leading to social changes that pit the younger generation against the power positions of the older generations and against the entire family structure, despite provoking pangs of guilt for doing so. The three kinds of social and ideological struggles suggested in the text against the patriarchy; against ethnic, sexual, and class prejudice; and against the teachings of the Catholic Church are cast in a subjective objectivity in defense of the status and primacy of the individual. These serve in this regard as counterdiscourses that, although critical of family relations of power, do not question the larger economic and political structures of power within which they arise.

These struggles take place in the desert, a place of both life and death, the place to which the rain god sends rainstorms as a respite from the hot, dry winds that blow the desert sands. This seemingly lifeless area wherein men toil and die is also a chronotope, a discourse strategy that serves to mirror the lives of the characters and provides the text with a unifying thread that ties various deplorable acts together: suicide, murder, poverty, infirmity, and death. The smell of a rainstorm in the desert is said to be the rain god's covenant with mere mortals, assuring them of the one sure thing in life: death. The desert and its rainstorms thus capture the novel's deconstructive and reconstructive strategies as the text allows a reconstruction of cultural practices and ideologies, collective memories that are subsequently deconstructed to reveal their contradictions. The novel's metaphysical strain serves only as a secondary motif and strategy, itself deconstructed by the novel's cynical discourse. The novel does in fact embrace another ahistorical, theological proposition: Miguel Chico's vision of the writer as god, as transcendental signified of the text, as the purveyor of meaning of a text, as individual subject. But even this ideological discourse allows for its own deconstruction within the text, since the main character and presumed subject of the narration is a fragmented subject; in fact, he sees himself as a "grafted" subject whose symbolic "colostomy" and "severe pruning" allow his discourse to be grafted with a multiplicity of discourses, contradictory in nature and voicing both dominant discourses and counterdiscourses. Although it is again a need to affirm difference and individualism, as in the case of Richard Rubio, that will lead Miguel Chico to leave the desert, it is now a multiplicity of voices that question the experience of subjectivity and individualism and, in a sense, lead him back to the collective.

AWASH IN A VALLEY OF TEARS: The Dialectics of Generation in Arturo Islas's *The Rain God*

John Honerkamp

In the days immediately preceding her death, Mamá Chona, the matriarch of the family whose story is documented in Arturo Islas's *The Rain God: A Desert Tale*, suffers uterine prolapse. As her uterus begins to protrude and blood flows from her uncontrollably, Mamá Chona refuses to bathe or even undress. She imagines the slow expulsion of her womb, which will ultimately mean her death, as the birthing of yet another child, yet another "worthless creature" and "monster" (174-75). Mamá Chona's refusal to acknowledge this "monstrous birth"—to borrow a term John Winthrop uses in his journal to describe the physiological consequences of Anne Hutchinson's banishment from the Massachusetts Bay Colony—is to validate a particular theological position. In a similar context to that of Winthrop's Anne Hutchinson, we encounter Mamá Chona during her last conscious attempt to disown her body and the flow of impurities that has been involuntarily emanating from it throughout her life. Her repudiation of her body is an imposition of class and race distinction, an embrace of the immaculate motherhood venerated by the conquistador ancestors of the Angels, her husband's family. In spite of her maiden name, Olmeca, and her obvious indigenous features, Mamá Chona is imbued with a "snobbery that refused to associate itself with anything Mexican or Indian because it was somehow impure" (*Rain God* 27). Mamá Chona's obsession with spiritual purity is conflated with an obsession with racial purity. Deciding to live more in the afterlife than in this life, she sacrifices her offspring, prone to sexual transgressions because they are products of miscegenation and thus border crossers by birth, for the dead Angels whose identities she can imaginatively contain.

This essay will examine the dialectical relationship in *The Rain God* between Mamá Chona's asceticism and the carnality she ascribes to her children and grandchildren. The history of the Ángel family documented in *The Rain God*, as well as the history of the borderlands documented there, is defined by a struggle over powers of generation in which a narrative informed by Roman Catholic theology competes with one informed by indigenous sources.

Mamá Chona's position in this struggle can be understood by reference to the Foucauldian concept of bio-power. In *The History of Sexuality*, Foucault contends that beginning in the seventeenth century power in the West has manifested itself in regimes designed to maximize life rather than in those designed to take life (123). Foucault calls the form of power that defines modernity "bio-power" and describes it as originating in the bourgeoisie's efforts to legitimate its authority by protecting and strengthening the bodies of its members, by promoting what he calls the "intensification" of the body. The bourgeoisie asserts and maintains its class dominance, following this logic, by arrogating to itself the nobility's claim to a privileged biological status, locating its marker of distinction in superior health rather than particular bloodlines. The bourgeois identity, the emergent modern identity according to Foucault, is constructed then in terms of a self-defined sexuality that must be isolated from the threat of degeneracy lurking in outside contacts. Foucault calls the complex forms—mechanisms, tactics, devices, and representations—in which power constructs sexuality, such as the modern sexuality just described, a "technology of sex." Discipline is, in Foucault's conception, a central feature of the technology of sex that defines bodies, behaviors, and social relations in modern societies; and discipline's most frequent object is the female body.

Foucault's analysis of the technology of bio-power is relevant to *The Rain God*, and is instructive in our understanding of Mamá Chona in two ways. First, Foucault defines a sexuality so pervasive and important that it becomes coterminous with the body. In this formulation, all bodily sensations and pleasures are given a sexual value. Foucault's notion that power becomes exercised almost exclusively in the deployment of sexuality grants an "insidious presence" to a singular, normative sexuality (148). Mamá Chona's repudiation of the body should be seen relative to this belief in the irreducibility of the body and sexuality. Second, the modern social reality Foucault describes, predicated on the formation and validation of a particular class body, demands the denial, segregation, and even elimination of alien bodies. This understanding explains the prominence of racist scientific theories and political practices in the nineteenth and twentieth centuries. (For more on the relationship between nineteenth-century developments in the study of genetics and the emergence of eugenics principles, see Doyle, Birken, and Armstrong.) It also helps explain Mamá Chona's recursion to a discourse of purity and contamination. Mamá Chona's privileging of a European identity, and the veneration of asexual maternity that lies at the center of its religion, needs to be viewed in the context of the affirmation of one body and the elision of others.

I am arguing that Mamá Chona's asceticism must be seen in all of its complexity. Her repudiation of her body is not merely a renunciation of the flesh or a disavowal of pleasure. It is better described paradoxically as the promotion of a body whose agency and maintenance are ensured in that body's privation. A closer look at how Mamá Chona's asceticism is described in the text and how it evolves will make this clear.

Mamá Chona's desire for disembodiment originates in her profound grief following the death of her eldest son Miguel Ángel, namesake of Miguel Chico and his father Miguel Grande. He had been, we are told, the only child born of Mamá Chona's love for her husband. The elder Miguel Ángel is killed at the beginning of the Mexican revolution, the event that compels the family to cross the border to the United States, by a stray bullet in a public square. The source of the bullet is never determined. After Miguel Ángel's burial, Mamá Chona is visited by a delegation of revolutionaries who praise him as a hero. Then she receives a letter from a general of the federal forces that praises her son as a true patriot. Though it is the government's version that is passed down in family lore, Mamá Chona does not care which explanation is given and seems to feel neither version accurate or relevant. Mamá Chona's response is to blame Mexico for its cultural oppositions: she "detested the pomposity of men at war and blamed both pro- and anti-government forces for the murder of her son" and as a result "never forgave Mexico" (*Rain God* 163). Her lifelong attempts to efface her indigenous ancestry may be viewed as an effort to transcend the binary logic, part Spanish and part indigenous, that defines Mexican society and is ultimately responsible, she believes, for her son's death. Migration to the United States seems only to lead to a reimposition of binaries, however, as the new home of the Angels along the United States-Mexico border is marked by a new duality.

Following the death of her first three children, Mamá Chona begins to associate the political environment of her motherland to her status as mother. After the shooting of the first Miguel Ángel and the drowning of his twin sisters presumably while bathing, Mamá Chona decides to resign herself "to Christ and His holy Mother" (164). Mamá Chona's fervent embrace of Roman Catholicism is born of a disgust and rage directed at her children. Her children die, she believes, due to their disobedience. While she had "taught her children to be careful," she thinks, "they died because they would not mind her or what they were doing" (164). Mamá Chona comes to view children as by nature unappreciative of maternal care and therefore a woman's primary cause of suffering. On her deathbed, she confronts the Virgin Mary in murmured monologue:

> Mary, children aren't worth the trouble. Sweet and loving as babies, they turn into monsters who cast you aside and compete with one another to see which of them can cause you the most pain. Your Son alone was worth the trouble, but He made you suffer a great deal. Still, He made you queen of heaven. But my children, mother of God, have not been worth the trouble. (178)

Believing her children have failed her, she is disappointed to discover after a stillbirth that she is still fertile. When her next child, Félix, is born, Mamá Chona reconciles herself to a maternity she associates with the Madonna, a maternity she describes as joyless. She conceives Félix and then Jesús María, Eduviges, Armando, Mema, and Miguel Grande out of duty to husband and church rather than love or pleasure. She imagines that she conceives "the rest immaculately . . . blotting out the act which caused her to become distended like a pig bladder full of air." This blotting out of the erotic she further imagines as her own disembodiment. She comes to deny "the existence of all parts of the body below the neck, with the exception of her hands" (164). Mamá Chona attempts to escape her status as Mexican migrant by becoming an exile from her body. While resigned to her role as producer of new bodies, she disavows her own body because it is tainted with sensuality. As I indicated earlier, Mamá Chona's repudiation of her body indicates the extent to which she has internalized the notion, described in *The History of Sexuality*, that the body and sexuality are irreducible. While Mamá Chona claims disembodiment, she is in actuality emulating the Virgin Mary's embodiment, an embodiment capable of procreation yet purged of sexuality.

Mamá Chona's embrace of Catholicism and virginal motherhood is accompanied by an attempted masking of her body that is also an attempted concealment of her Indian heritage. No matter the temperature, Mamá Chona wears a shawl and a black ankle-length dress in public. She carries an umbrella to protect her skin from the desert sun. No amount of protection from the sun's rays, however, can erase her indigenous features. Her grandson Miguel Chico describes her appearance, imagining her looking at herself in the mirror: "As much as she protected herself from it, the sun still darkened her complexion and no surgery could efface the Indian cheekbones, those small very dark eyes and aquiline nose" (27). The erasure of the alienness of her body requires the complete suppression of that body and the renunciation of the bodies she produces, themselves markers of her indigenousness and thereby destined to be nothing but "lechers." While Mamá Chona affirms a racially pure maternal body by denying alien ones, her status as embodied alien proves difficult to escape. Indeed, Mamá Chona's repression of her and her children's indigenous identity are described in *The Rain God* in terms of fatuity and illusion. The effacement of her indigenous heritage and body may be seen in fact as the first stage in Mamá Chona's descent into a "fairy-tale world" (27), which results ultimately in her crossing a border between sanity and senility. The last months of her life are marked in a sense by a transcendence of borders that is actually an endless blurring of boundaries: she confuses the seasons, mixes up her relatives, and talks more often to her dead husband and dead son Félix than her living relations. Mamá Chona affirms a racially pure body, but in the end that body is denied her.

Mamá Chona's reconstruction of her life narrative as a story of Christian abnegation and self-containment—a story of the reclamation of spiritual, sexual, and racial purity—fails because her alienness resists suppression. Because withholding the paradigm of virgin motherhood amounts to the negation of a negated body, this failure to contain sexuality represents a possible source of political agency. While Foucault's discussion of a modern technology of sex attempts to demonstrate how dominant power in modern societies perpetuates itself in new discourses, social practices, and institutional structures, it also suggests that subversive power in modern societies is most often expressed in sexual terms (terms that the dominant culture attempts to represent as enigmatic and dangerous). In *The Rain God*, subversive power inheres in the countervailing narrative of generation that enfolds Mamá Chona's story of acquired asceticism and salvation.

The narrative of sexual containment that Mamá Chona advances is elided in the novel by a larger narrative of generative ebb and flow. The maternal body, responsible for pollution and suffering in the Mamá Chona narrative, emerges as a source of yearning and vitality. Defying the discourses of sanitation and sanity that seek to contain it, maternity in the subversive narrative is bound only by a logic of flux, the inevitability of boundaries shifting and dissolving. This maternity, the maternity of agricultural mythologies, is associated with the earth. In *The Rain God*, subversive maternity is expressed in terms of the geography of the border region in which the Angels come to live. The relationship between representations of sand and water in the novel defines a system of mutual transgressions, of ontological convergences and divergences in which identities coalesce and bifurcate according to what can best be characterized as biorhythms. The desert-river relationship, which I will suggest is framed in terms of the relationship between mother and child, establishes a paradigm for all human relationships chronicled in *The Rain God*. The powers of generation and syncretism that indigenous myth associates with the border regions, what I am calling subversive maternity, is ultimately available to all bodies and is expressed in all forms of sexuality in the novel.

When the story of Félix's life and murder is introduced, the border region that is the Angels' home is described as a product of geological, meteorological, social, and political forces:

> The border town where Felix spent most of his life is a valley between two mountain ranges in the middle of the southwestern wastes. A wide river, mostly dry except when thunderstorms create flashfloods, separates it from Mexico. Heavy traffic flows from one side of the river to the other, and from the air, national boundaries and differences are indistinguishable. (113)

The river that defines the region, the Rio Grande, is represented here as more a transgressor than container. The river, its course and value a result of temporal and spatial circumstance, imposes indeterminacy rather than categorical distinctions. This passage suggests that to understand the river and those who have lived near it, one must take into account the changing patterns of erosion, weather, commerce, and history that constitute it. With its mountain ridges, wastes, and rhythmic flows, the desert lands through which the river wends is vaguely suggestive of female anatomy. The movement and volume of the river, like those of vaginal flow, are determined by both sudden swells and regular seasonal runoff. The mutual constitution of desert land and river—the river is formed by the land and in return shapes the land—links the two as intimately as mother and child. What is significant about the river is not that it is an obstacle, but that it is the very substance of life and motion.

The irreversible river is also associated with the inevitability of death. When Miguel Chico is recovering from the colostomy that saves his life, his aunt Mema sends him a poem attributed to

Nezahualcoyotl that implicates the river in cycles of life and death. The poem reads in part:

> Rivers, rivulets, fountains and waters flow,
> but never return to their joyful beginnings;
> anxiously they hasten on to the vast realms
> of the Rain God.
> As they widen their banks, they also fashion
> the sad urn of their burial. (162)

Vaginal flows too connote both life and death in *The Rain God*. While still a small child, Miguel Chico comes to believe his mother's discharge of lochia signifies her mortality. After seeing a stain on his mother's undergarment, he is told by his nurse, María, who has recently become a Seventh Day Adventist, his mother will die when the peach tree near him bears fruit. The bright red canna lilies that surround his mother as she walks in her garden merge in his mind with the image of the deep red stain. Miguel Chico is at the same time sexually aroused by the sensation of María's whisper and the smell of her hair. At that moment, "love and death came together for Miguel Chico and he was not from then on able to think of one apart from the other" (19). Miguel Chico continues throughout his life to relate death to a heightening of passion, a deepening of vibrancy. Vaginal discharge and the river that defines the borderlands are deeply associated in *The Rain God* and both carry connotations of life, love, and loss. The flow of bodily fluids and river water are expressive of freedom, of the power ultimately to diverge from even a well-worn past, of the power to make new life.

Like the river, the desert defies containment. While the flow of water, blood, and other bodily fluids in *The Rain God* represents the power to transgress and liberate oneself, the movement of the desert represents a will to merge, to move beyond oneself by integration into someone or something else. The deployment of images of dryness define generative power in *The Rain God* in terms of either an expression of desire or a transcendence at death.

After El Compa dies of a heart attack while fixing a hole in his roof, Miguel Grande finishes the repairs and, we are told, "the desert shifted from the kitchen into [Lola's] heart" (69). El

Compa, the closest friend of Miguel Chico's parents Miguel Grande and Juanita, dies "trying to keep the desert out of [his wife Lola's] kitchen" (64). Every weekend for a year following her discovery of the hole, Lola would tell El Compa that soon the kitchen would be buried under sand. After El Compa dies trying to keep the desert in abeyance, Lola's desire for a man becomes an insatiable thirst, and she and Miguel Grande begin a passionate affair. The desert is identified with a desire, indeed a need, impossible to resist. Miguel Grande becomes obsessed with Lola and believes "his heart would dry up like a scorpion in the sun" without her (75). Far from a representation of barrenness, the desert is figured in the relationship between Miguel Grande and Lola as a thirst that is actually a precondition for life. The desert here becomes a metaphor for the instinct to merge with another human being.

The impulse to merge finds its absolute expression in *The Rain God* in a thematics of drowning. Various Angels either imagine themselves drowning or actually die by being submerged in water or sand. Miguel Chico's godmother Nina has always been terrified by death because she could not bear the idea of being buried in the earth. Nina "knew she would feel the desert trickling down her throat, and that knowledge was unbearable to her" (34). After her son Antony, Miguel Chico's cousin, commits suicide by drowning himself in a smelter lake in an effort to escape the isolation of his new home and his confinement to his room by his mother, she visits his grave and imagines him with the desert in his mouth. This actually provides her some solace, a temporary sense of connection, until Nina decides her son has never been buried there and begins to seek him in the realm of the supernatural. When Miguel Chico's health declines because of an intestinal condition, he "grew thirstier every day" and "longed to return to the desert of his childhood, not to the family but to the place" (5). Lying near death, he tastes the desert in his mouth and remembers Nina's fear of being buried in the desert sand. This triggers in his mind another memory, the murder of his uncle Félix in a twilight world similar to the one he now inhabits. From this near-death experience, Miguel Chico learns to accept death as not only an immersion in the desert landscape but also as an integration into a network of family associations. Death has been rendered a matter of convergence rather than the separation Mamá Chona claims or the loss the death associations of the river suggest.

Like other members of Miguel Chico's family, Félix fears death by asphyxiation. He "detested" the March sandstorms "because they made him feel buried alive" (136). During the period of the sandstorms, he ties a handkerchief around his face to protect himself from the bitter taste of the sand. Félix, does, however, seem capable of transforming the desert environment by summoning rain. When he is a small boy, he runs outside and dances as storm clouds pass and rain begins to fall. Later in life, dying from injuries inflicted by a young serviceman who resents his advances, Félix thinks about his family and parts of his body transmute into elements of the desert that surrounds him. The loose teeth in his mouth feel like stones, then his mouth feels full of the desert. As Félix feels himself falling a great distance, the teeth he has spit on the ground become stepping stones. As he dies, the desert transforms into water and he sinks below its surface. Félix, who has for much of his life searched for youth "on both sides of the river" to satisfy his desires (115), defies sexual, racial, and national boundaries and in so doing transforms his environment. In Uncle Félix's sexual virtuosity, the powers of syncretism and divergence—experienced in the desert as the climatic phenomena of condensation and precipitation—that define subversive maternity come together. His passion makes the desert come alive and thus he is the character most identified with what José David Saldívar calls, in characterizing what opposes "hollow spiritual categories" in *The Rain God*, the "wet, blooming imagery of a vibrant sexual world" ("Hybridity" 167).

By the end of the novel, Félix appears as the incarnation of *The Rain God* of Mesoamerican mythologies. In the moment before Mamá Chona dies, Miguel Chico senses *The Rain God*'s entrance into the room. Félix appears from the shadows, his identity clear to Mamá Chona and seemingly to all her assembled family. For Miguel Chico at least, Félix's status as Ángel family member merges with his status as mythological figure. Félix the rain god takes Mamá Chona in his arms, smelling "like the desert after a rainstorm" (*Rain God* 180).

The Mesoamerican rain god is most commonly known by the Nahuatl name Tlaloc, meaning "of the earth," and is most often depicted wearing a mask with ringed eyes and upper fangs. (For more on Mesoamerican rain mythologies, see Frederiksen, Burgess, and *The Rain of the Earth*.) The name Tlaloc suggests also "that the rain is *for* the earth, where it nourishes crops and moistens the ground" (*The Rain of the Earth*). In western Mesoamerican culture, spirits of rain and earth are closely linked. In many Mesoamerican cultures, the rain god actually inhabits the earth, and the mountain caves where he lives are sites for the ritual sacrifice of children. Capable of causing flooding and drought, he is in all of these cultures conceived as wielding power over both earth and human bodies.

Not long before Félix appears to her, Mamá Chona has a dream in which the Virgin of Guadalupe and then Tlaloc are invoked. Mamá Chona hears and smells passing rainstorms, but no rain falls. She longs to see yucca and ocotillo in bloom, sees the desert sand filled with verbenas and blooming dandelions, and, with the first Miguel Ángel, discovers desert roses similar to those that grow on the hill of Tepeyac, which is the site of the shrine to the Tonantzin, a collective name for the many goddesses that hold power over the earth. These goddesses are embodiments of the various aspects of the Virgin of Guadalupe. (For an analysis of the myths of La Malinche, La Llorona, and the Virgin of Guadalupe, see Pearce.) The reference is to the miraculous appearance of roses in the Virgin of Guadalupe myth. Seeking evidence that the Virgin Mary had visited him, Juan Diego collected the roses growing on the barren Tepeyac hillside where she had appeared. When Juan Diego presented the rose petals to church leaders, the rose petals formed an imprint that is the perfect likeness of the Virgin as Juan Diego had seen her. In Mamá Chona's dream, the myth is reconciled with the myth of the rain god and is revised. Rather than a product of miraculous, spontaneous generation, the roses in the dream are returned to the realm of the organic, to cycles of growth and decay, birth and death, flooding and drought, precipitation and evaporation. The source of the roses is ultimately the rain. As Mamá Chona opens her eyes, the rain is conflated with the weeping of her children. In Aztec mythology, Tlaloc produces rain in proportion to the amount of tears shed by sacrificed children. Mamá Chona's children, whom she has attempted to sacrifice, sustain her on earth and themselves in their mourning and memories. While Mamá Chona says immediately before she dies that she is "happy to leave this valley of tears" (*Rain God* 179) and be with Jesus, she is instead delivered by a Mesoamerican god in the form of her biological son.

The Virgin of Guadalupe, the central figure in the conversion of indigenous Mexicans to Roman Catholicism, is reclaimed in *The Rain God* as a figure of ambiguity and generative power. Mamá Chona, who has long sought incorporation as the Virgin Mary, becomes the Virgin of Guadalupe. When she dies, she is compared to Xochiquetzal, goddess of flowers and wife to Tlaloc. Mamá Chona thus returns at death to her own son in renewed intimacy, as wife to husband. Mamá Chona's association with Xochiquetzal is implied earlier in the novel: as her physical and mental health fail in her later years, she waters her flower beds even in the middle of winter, saying everything would die without her. Mamá Chona's death proves to be both an affirmation of indigenous mythology and a revision of it. In *The Rain God*, a mother's body is sacrificed rather than those of children. What is sacrificed, indeed drowned in the tears of her children, is the negated body of virgin motherhood. True to the syncretism of Mesoamerican culture, Mamá Chona's death proves a transmutation from one form of maternal body into another. Mamá Chona dies to restore eroticism and fertility to the body of the Virgin of Guadalupe.

Mamá Chona's last agonizing plea to Miguel Chico, her cry of "*la familia*," is her appeal for him to recognize this body's availability to him. Such recognition will provide him the store of generative power and source material required to chronicle the Ángel family and ensure its survival. Miguel Chico at the time feels he is the unlikeliest family member to be so entrusted and demands that Mamá Chona release his hand as she passes beyond this world.

When Miguel Chico is in the recovery room following his colostomy, he begins to appreciate the extent to which he has internalized Mamá Chona's Roman Catholic asceticism. Looking at the network of tubes, syringes, and machines that surrounds and supports him, he realizes he has become the embodiment of what his grandmother and her church "had taught him was the highest form of existence: pure, bodiless intellect" (8). Miguel Chico realizes he has achieved the bodily existence to which Mamá Chona had aspired, that of the "perfect astronaut," where there is "no shit, no piss, no blood" (8). In spite of his renunciation of the views of his grandmother and her church, Miguel Chico finds himself occupying the very body, perfectly isolated and contained, Mamá Chona had sought to inhabit. Because of this experience in recovery and the near-death experience before surgery I have already mentioned, Miguel begins to seek outside connections.

Following his visit to his drug-addicted, psychotic cousin JoEl, Miguel Chico has a dream in which he confronts the "monster" that killed Mamá Chona. In this encounter, Miguel Chico addresses his own status as monster, the product of a monstrous birth. Standing together on a bridge in the fog, the monster invites Miguel Chico into his cave and in a riddle identifies himself. The monster, smelling of blood and feces, crowds him so that he must struggle to breathe. Following the monster's command to jump, Miguel Chico fastens himself to the monster and together they fall over a railing. Miguel Chico's ultimate embrace of the monster is an embrace of his own body and an acceptance of his family. It is an acknowledgment of the corporeality, mortality, fertility, and sexuality of his existence. It is an acknowledgment of the flesh from which he came. Miguel Chico's embrace of his own "monstrosity" in this dream suggests a preliminary affirmation of the life-giving power of his body, a body which during his illness had appeared pregnant.

At a moment probably soon after, Miguel Chico defines his role as family chronicler in terms of reproduction:

> And Mama Chona was still very much a part of him. Perhaps, he told himself, watching the first wisps of fog drift in over the garden, perhaps he had survived—albeit in an altered form, like a plant onto which has been grafted an altogether different strain of which the smelly rose at his side, that tip of gut that

would always require his care and attention, was only a symbol—perhaps he had survived to tell others about Mama Chona and people like María. He could then go on to shape himself, if not completely free of their influence and distortions, at least with some knowledge of them. (28)

Miguel Chico imagines himself a hybridized or pruned plant that is an extension, however modified, of the women who have raised him, "the way a seed continues to be a part of a plant after it has assumed its own form which does not at all resemble its origin, but which, nevertheless, is determined by it" (25-26).

Miguel Chico recognizes that he himself can in turn give life. Like the speaker in Neruda's poem "The Heights of Machu Picchu," a portion of which serves as the epigraph of *The Rain God*, Miguel Chico learns that not only are his words his ancestors', but that he literally animates their "dead mouths." Miguel Chico assumes the role of life-giver that Mamá Chona has sought to disavow. Evidence of Miguel Chico's assumption of this role is found in his tending to the flowers he has planted in his garden in San Francisco. Like the flowers Xochiquetzal and Mamá Chona nurtured, these flowers would die without him.

THE MONSTROUS PSEUDOPREGNANT BODY
as Border Crossing Metaphor in *The Rain God*

Vivian Nun Halloran

In *The Rain God,* Arturo Islas uses the trope of the monstrous pregnant body as both the site of the abject as well as the embodiment of the border identity that defines Mexican Americans. The narrator describes the disease-ridden bodies of his two protagonists, Miguel Chico and Mamá Chona, as looking "pregnant" when they are sick—the former with an intestinal disorder and the latter with a fallen uterus. Both characters remain in this in-between state of pseudopregnancy without the possibility of delivering. Outside observers can see the partial presence of an internal organ outside a given character's body, but neither Mamá Chona's uterus nor Miguel Chico's intestines ever fully emerge from the body cavity. This uncanny instance of border crossing, which blurs the boundaries between inside and outside, represents both Mamá Chona's journey north from Méjico to the United States with her children as well as her grandson's continuing identification with his ancestral homeland. The cultural ties that link Mamá Chona and Miguel Chico to each other and to their past are as strong and hard to detect as the ligaments and other mechanisms that hold the viscera together inside the body. By invoking the "pregnant" male and/or postmenopausal body itself as both monstrous and literally, as a monster who haunts both characters in their moments of delirium, Islas critiques the Ángel family's negative view of reproduction and their fear of the permanence of immigration. Mamá Chona's and Miguel Chico's reluctance to link their futures to their American homeland by giving birth to a new generation of Angels also reflects their inability to embrace a "Chicano" ethnic identity. In this context, the family surname, Ángel, suggests an ironic echo of divine agency in both the annunciation to Mary and the virgin birth of Jesus.

The Rain God portrays all of its characters' pregnancies in a negative light. Miguel Chico's maternal grandmother died giving birth to his aunt Nina at the age of twenty-nine. The death of Mamá Chona's first three children in Mexico makes her view her subsequent pregnancies as a punishment she has to endure: "From then on, Mama Chona bore her children out of duty to her husband and the Church" (164). As her motherland, or *madre patria,* Mexico constitutes the unspoken third element in this trinity to which Mamá Chona owes allegiance because she conceives and gives birth to all of her children there. Both the Mexican government and the revolutionaries try to claim Mamá Chona's firstborn as one of their own, calling him "a patriot" and "a hero" respectively because he had the misfortune to be an innocent bystander caught in the crossfire during the Mexican Revolution. She rejects this rhetorical appropriation and "never forgave Mexico for the death of her firstborn" (163) since he died as a direct consequence of the revolution that gave rise (or birth) to the modern Mexican nation state. Mexico also metaphorically consumes Mamá Chona's twin daughters, who accidentally drown in a flood, thus inverting the birth pattern of emerging from the liquid-filled womb of the mother by being forced back into the watery recesses of Mother Earth.

The trauma of her losses is so great that Mamá Chona eventually dissociates herself from both her motherland, by leaving Mexico after her husband's death and immigrating north, and her body, by claiming no agency or involvement in either the planning or conception of her children: "In her mind, she conceived him and the rest immaculately—an attitude which made some of her children think themselves divine—blotting out the act which caused her to become distended like a pig bladder full of air" (164). The narrator here alludes to the immaculate conception incorrectly. The passage implies that Mamá Chona denies that her children were conceived through sexual intercourse. In Catholic doctrine, the term "immaculate conception" refers to Mary's own conception by her mother, Saint Elizabeth, as being free from the blemish of original sin but not occasioned through divine intercession, and not to her conception of Jesus without human agency. Ironically, it is only when she is pregnant that Mamá Chona fully lives up to her given name, "Encarnación" or Incarnation, a not-so-subtle reference to the process through which Jesus became human. Mamá Chona's comparison of her pregnant body to a "pig bladder full of air" is doubly monstrous: first, it likens her body to the internal organ of an animal and her fetus to air. This violation of the natural order, so to speak, implies that Mamá Chona considers pregnancy an anomalous condition or pathology, rather than a normal stage in a woman's life. Thus, as a pregnant woman, Mamá Chona sees herself literally as out of place and her baby as a foreign substance.

The second way in which this description becomes monstrous is by its emphasis on the denatured state of the "pig bladder" as an internal organ imagined completely independent of the animal's body. Since she gives up all claims of controlling both her body and her fertility after the death of her elder three children, Mamá Chona sees her status within patriarchal Mexican society as metonymic: she is valuable as a woman because she has a womb in which to produce the next generation of young Mexicans. By leaving her birthplace after her husband's death, Mamá Chona changes her role from that of *mother* in Mexico to that of *matriarch* in the United States. This same pattern of crossing of internal/external boundaries characterizes the two instances of pseudo-pregnancy in the text, Mamá Chona's and Miguel Chico's, which I will discuss in more detail shortly.

The moniker by which her descendants call her, "*Mamá* Chona," (my emphasis) affirms her symbolic role as founder of the family line even as she downplays the physical aspects of motherhood. In the United States she seizes on the opportunity to fulfill her fantasy of asexual reproduction by adopting her daughter Mema's illegitimate son, Ricardo. Mema herself sets a precedent for reading Mamá Chona as a La Llorona figure. Mema surrenders her own claim of maternal kinship to her illegitimate son to preserve the honor of the family name, yet she also crosses the border into Mexico to find the child she gave up for adoption and bring him back to be raised by her own mother in the United States. Despite the large personal price they pay, both Mema and Mamá Chona each choose to embrace new ethnic identities: Mema that of *mejicana* and Mamá Chona that of Mexican American. As the child, Ricardo is both a pawn in the mother-daughter conflict, but also an unwitting transplant from one culture to another.

The longer she lives in the United States, the more racially prejudiced Mamá Chona becomes. She values those aspects of Mexican culture most closely linked to Spain, like proper pronunciation, Catholic faith, and light skin, more highly than those traits she considers "indigenous" and which the uneducated and illegal workers her children employ to care for the young children exhibit constantly. In an ironic twist of fate, Mamá Chona becomes a La Llorona figure when she suffers from dementia toward the end of her life rather than achieving the status of the virgin mother venerated by the Catholic church, which Mexico inherited from Spain. Mema, who was not allowed to raise her own son, notices that her mother "now woke up in the middle of the night and wandered through the apartment" (171). When asked what she is doing, Mamá Chona replies, "I am looking for my children" (171). By evoking comparisons to this ghostly indigenous Mexican folk figure damned to walk the earth looking for her dead children, Islas further renders motherhood on the Mexican/American borderland dangerous, monstrous, and unnatural. Mema, the character who surrendered her own claim of maternal kinship to her illegitimate son to preserve the honor of the family name, reports her mother's behavior to the rest of the family.

It is little wonder, then, that the novel depicts the outward semblance of pregnancy as an abject pathology. Islas depicts both Mamá Chona's and Miguel Chico's final crisis of consciousness as a battle between themselves and their diseased bodies. In her mental decline, Mamá Chona cannot tell the difference between the past and the present, between her youth in Mexico and old age in the United States. Her final illness, a fallen uterus, becomes the embodiment of her state of mental confusion by blurring the boundary separating the inside and outside. In a horrific parody of the act of birth, Mamá Chona notices something unnatural coming out of her womb. "Another worthless creature," she said to her [dead] husband Jesus who had taken to visiting her, "you ought to be ashamed of yourself." By not allowing herself to be naked, she had successfully denied the existence of the monster. (174-5)

Again, Mamá Chona's denial of her physicality leads her to confuse the issue by using the metaphorical term "womb" to describe her vagina as the site from where her actual uterus is protruding. This euphemism leads her to confuse her condition with pregnancy. Unlike what she has done with her previous, authentic, pregnancies, Mamá Chona asserts herself with regard to this imaginary one by refusing to see it through to its logical conclusion—to give birth. In a marked departure from her submission to husband, church, and nation, Mamá Chona even complains about having to do her duty in carrying yet another child to term and upbraids her (now-dead) husband for his incontinence. She carries out this denial most effectively by refusing to bathe, which prevents her from having to confront the "other" presence within her—that of her protruding uterus. By living in the past, Mamá Chona forfeits the "American" cultural identity that tempered her experience as a Mexican immigrant living in the United States. This temporal displacement has the effect of cementing Mamá Chona's view of herself as a "Mexican," not a "Mexican American" woman.

However, despite her efforts to hide her condition, Mamá Chona's daughter and daughter-in-law take part in yet another parody of the act of birth when they effectively act as midwives and both witness and mediate the emergence of the matriarch's uterus into the world. Eduviges and Juanita usher a reluctant Mamá Chona into the bathroom to bathe her and usher out the male relatives to preserve the matriarch's modesty. This exclusion marks the family bathroom as a gender-segregated place, and it is within this female space that the unnatural border-crossing of Mamá Chona's internal organ into the outside world works simultaneously on two discursive and narrative levels in the novel. The first is Mamá Chona's confirmation of her earlier interpretation of her condition as a stillbirth:

> The monster between her legs was almost out and Mamá Chona was glad that it showed no signs of life. All the better for it. It had not bothered her and she did not understand why everyone else was making such a fuss over it. One should ignore those parts of the body anyway. (177)

Mamá Chona recognizes the effect of her "delivery" has on her female relatives, but persists in viewing the situation in terms of active "labor" not yet completed, thus further occupying an in-between hybrid space: the laboring woman is neither fully pregnant nor yet un-pregnant, but in a transitional stage between both realms of experience. The second discursive level in which Mamá Chona's "delivery" occurs is through Juanita's brief narration. She reports to her husband that Mamá Chona's "uterus is falling out and she's bleeding a lot" (177) and asks him to contact the doctor. This is another key transitional moment in the narrative: it constitutes a translation of experience from the private female realm—where women share the visual proof—to the male realm of the word or logos. Accepting his wife's assessment of his mother's ailment but without seeing for himself, Miguel Grande contacts the doctor, whose "official" status as health worker transcends gender and allows him to examine, diagnose, and treat Mamá Chona. In *Borderlands/La Frontera*, Gloria Anzaldúa discusses a similar instance of a woman facing the spectacle of her denatured uterus in her poem "Matriz sin tumba o 'el baño de la basura ajena'" (136). Both Mamá Chona and the speaker in Anzaldúa's poem deny the medical reality of the gynecological conditions that land them in the hospital. "*Matriz sin tumba*" uses the denatured womb as an illustration of the clash between feminine and patriarchal discourses about the body, whereas Islas's novel portrays it as a metaphor to describe the hybrid and in-between ethnic identity that Mamá Chona claims as a Mexican American. The speaker of Anzaldúa's poem undergoes this uncanny experience by herself in the antiseptic space of an operating room rather than in an intimate and familiar setting surrounded by other women as Mamá Chona does. During her hysterectomy, the speaker watches helplessly as the surgeon unceremoniously discards her uterus into a nearby trash bin. Whereas Mamá Chona considers the organ itself a monster who haunts her, the speaker of Anzaldúa's poem resists the violence of the medical procedure and her surgeon's carelessness in discarding her womb, and thus depicts him as the monster:

> Me siento muy lejana, juzgada por ese buitre en la panza. La bestia noche entra armada con navajas, se me arrima muy cerquita, me manotea, me agujera dos veces, tres veces. Miro que me saca las entrañas que avienta la matriz en la basuramatriz sin tumba. (Anzaldúa 136)

The surgeon becomes the *"buitre,"* or buzzard as well as *"la bestia,"* or the beast. The speaker of this poem interprets the hysterectomy as a violation of her autonomy, sense of self, and cultural traditions that can only be rectified by the performance of a cleansing rite in honor of "Tlazolteotl."

In the poem, the abject arises not from the disease but rather from the contrasting gender, cultural definition, and symbolic value of the uterus. The male assumption that the denatured uterus is disposable appalls the speaker, as do the very medical procedures that save the speaker's life: anesthesia and surgery. In contrast, the speaker celebrates indigenous purification rites through the use of scatological imagery: she dreams about an otherworldly woman ingesting, by turns, feces and the sun itself. Looking for comfort, the speaker searches in the far reaches of ancestral memory for a timeless and idealized indigenous spirituality to counteract the steely coldness of Western medicine and its practitioners. While it challenges male definitions of the female body, "Matriz sin tumba" does not invoke the heterosexual paradigm of reproduction because it never mentions the organ's potential to contain life. What Anzaldúa's poem does is present an instance of physical and cultural border-crossing situated in the sterile environment of the hospital rather than the intimacy of the home. As such, it serves as an interesting point of comparison between the female but home-centered border-crossing experience of Mamá Chona and Miguel Chico's ungendered and sterile hospitalization in *The Rain God*.

Like Anzaldúa's speaker, Miguel Chico's illness and pseudopregnancy takes place in a hospital setting, yet that impersonal state also becomes the very site of his rebirth. While the speaker in "Matriz sin tumba" resents her doctor's indifference to her uterus, a careless doctor actually occasions Miguel Chico's intestinal problems by prescribing a medicine that aggravated a pre-existing condition. Despite this clear instance of malpractice in the novel, Miguel Chico does not express any anger or resentment toward members of the medical community, which bodes well for someone who will need continuous medical care for the rest of his natural life. Although Miguel Chico never considers himself feminized, the narrator introduces the theme of pseudo- or simulated pregnancy through the point of view of doctors. The medical gaze is the agency of objectification in Miguel Chico's case: "The doctors set him down and uncovered him. He weighed ninety-eight pounds and looked pregnant" (*Rain God* 6). The abject arises in this description from the discordant juxtaposition of two contradictory images: an emaciated male figure and the distended abdomen suggested by the reference to pregnancy. A more logical reading of his distended belly would be to describe it according to the pathology of starvation. This juxtaposition suggests a medical assessment of pregnancy as an illness rather than as a natural process not jeopardizing the health of an individual. Applied to the sick male patient, a female metaphor of pregnancy reinforces a cultural definition of masculinity as healthy and femininity as diseased.

Because he does not compare his illness to pregnancy as his grandmother does hers, Miguel Chico does not share in his doctors' experience of the abject. He experiences his male body as abject only after the surgery, when the stoma is in place and he must constantly monitor the transfer of internal bodily fluids, such as blood and feces, to the external receptacle of the plastic colostomy bag. For him, the abject consists in being "forever a slave to plastic appliances" (7), or becoming a "cyborg" in Donna Haraway's terms. The trope of pregnancy entails that of birth and for all its negative connotations, the hospital remains a place of rebirth for Miguel Chico, not of death as it is for both Mamá Chona and the speaker of "Matriz sin tumba." His entry into a new life crosses cultural boundaries much like the surgery from which he is recovering, which intentionally blurred "natural" borders by creating an artificial anus on his side. This second time, Miguel is ushered into consciousness by an English-speaking nurse who continually mispronounces his name:

> Lying on a gurney in the recovery room, Miguel Chico came to life for the second time. Tubes protruded from every opening of his body except his ears, and before he was able to open his eyes, he heard a woman's voice calling his name over and over again in the way that made him wince: "Mee-gwell, Mee-gwell, wake up, Mee-gwell." (7)

Like a newborn, Miguel Chico is powerless to object to this bastardized christening—because of the tubes keeping him alive he cannot express his objection to having his name mispronounced, although he does "wince." He has the uncanny experience of hearing a familiar name, his own, defamiliarized by an Americanized mispronunciation of his Spanish name, which stands in stark contrast to the two distinct appellations by which he is known within his family: either "Miguel Chico" or "Mickie" (3).

As a signifier, "Mee-gwell" connotes only "foreignness," whereas "Miguel Chico" reflects the Spanish heritage of the Mexican culture of which the Ángel family is so proud. Although it sounds American, "Mickey" is the name the family devises to differentiate Miguel Chico from his father Miguel Grande since both share their given name, "Miguel Ángel." Ironically, "Miguel Ángel" was also the name of Mamá Chona's firstborn, whose death changed her view of herself as a wife and mother. Therefore, the English-sounding nickname most appropriately designates his status as an American-born member of the Ángel family as opposed to the two previous Miguel Angels—his father and uncle—who were both born in Mexico. During his recovery, Miguel Chico is as powerless to reject the identity of "foreigner" imposed upon him by the nurse's mispronunciation as he is to assert his masculinity when the doctors perceive him as "pregnant." Like bookends to his hospitalization, these two labels imply an institutionalized reading of the man of color as both feminine and Other. This perception is oddly in keeping with his family's suspicions about Miguel Chico's decisions to move away from the desert and live alone in San Francisco instead of getting married. The Angels cannot decide whether Miguel Chico's behavior is odd because it is more American than Mexican, and thus "foreign," or if it is suspect because it rejects the basic markers of heterosexuality—marriage and children—and therefore marks him as a homosexual Other.

The final manifestation of pseudo-pregnancy in this novel forces Miguel Chico to bridge the gap he feels separates him from his family by embracing the very "monster" that killed his grandmother, Mamá Chona. This confrontation with the personified and monstrous denatured uterus takes place in a dream, yet another in-between, hybrid realm of experience:

> In one of those dreams, the "monster" that had killed her [Mamá Chona] said to him softly, almost kindly, "I am a nice monster. Come into my cave." The two of them were standing on a bridge facing the incoming fog. The monster held Miguel Chico closely from behind and whispered into his ear in a relentless, singsong way, "I am the manipulator and the manipulated." It put its velvet paw in Miguel Chico's hand and forced him to hold it tightly against his gut right below the appliance at his side. "I am the victim and the slayer," the creature continued, "I am what you believe and what you don't believe, I am the loved and the unloved. I approve and turn away, I am judge and advocate." (159)

Perhaps because of its own dual role in Mamá Chona's body as both the container of (future) life and harbinger of (her own) death, the monstrous uterus in Miguel Chico's dream employs a language of paradox. At any rate, the monster in the dream does what Miguel Chico and his grandmother never dare to do in their waking lives: define itself according to its own terms, regardless of the contradictions inherent within those labels. As such, the monster becomes not just multiple and terrifying in its instability, but more importantly, postmodern. Miguel Chico and Mamá Chona are trapped within the narrative of modernity and cannot reimagine themselves outside of the binary framework of experience and subjectivity contained within that discourse.

During their respective illnesses, Miguel Chico and Mamá Chona become living embodiments of the borderland separating Mexico from the United States. Faced with the external protrusion of their internal organs, both characters become literally undone as they grapple with the markers that signal or convey their individual identities and sense of self: their names and their bodies. In her dementia, Mamá Chona vacillates between the nickname she gave herself to avoid being called *"abuelita"* or granny, and her given name, Encarnación Olmeca de Ángel, which marks her as a descendant of the Olmecs, an ancient indigenous culture of eastern Mexico instead of the Spanish identity she claims for herself. Miguel likewise experiences an identity crisis in the hospital, as I discussed earlier, when the American nurse mispronounces his name, thereby objectifying him as a foreign Other and rejecting his status as a fellow American. The simulacrum of pregnancy represented by illness is in itself a metaphor in the novel for each character's inability to claim a Chicano identity as a way to negotiate life in the borderland. Self-chosen as a designator and incorporating both Mexican and American cultures but not fully contained by either adjective, a "Chicano" ethnic identity would give Mamá Chona and Miguel Chico a point of entry into postmodernity and a way to express their hybridity through language. By declaring themselves Chicanos, matriarch and grandson would move beyond the revisionist histories they tell about their family into authorizing or birthing their own subjectivity. Short of taking such a step, Mamá Chona's and Miguel Chico's articulation of their own life and character is reactionary, responding to what others think about them.

ANOTHER CLOSET IN THE HOUSE OF ANGELS:
The Denial of Identity in *The Rain God*

David N. Ybarra

Names and labels have the power to engage the world around us in a collective reality. From the tiniest actions and simplest articles, the use of these things makes them true. It gives them an identity and therefore a sense of comprehension in our lives. Adversely, when something remains unnamed or unidentified it can fail to be true no matter how real its presence.

In the Arturo Islas novel *The Rain God*, homosexuality is a subject neither confronted nor defined within the Ángel family, not unlike entire generations of Mexican and Mexican American people whose lives and expectations continue to be dictated by patriarchal codes of the sexually suppressed Catholic culture in Mexico and beyond the Southwest of the United States. Indeed, Catholicism is more than one's religious denomination; it is a cultural identity for many Mexican Americans as well. In addition to its design of subservient roles for women, the patriarchal oppression of Catholicism denies any sexual orientation, other than heterosexuality as valid, condemning the homosexual nature as a sin one chooses to engage in just as one may choose to engage in gambling or stealing. Homosexual desire is viewed as an unnatural vice or degenerate behavior that at best, may be cured, and at least suppressed for a lifetime.

Rather than define a homosexual presence within the family, which would mean confronting truth, members of the Ángel clan rely on their fear and shame of it to accommodate the illusion that it does not exist in their homes or lives. Homosexuality is a subject so highly guarded that it is a secret even those family members in question keep to themselves. However, it is this single delusion that results in more than social injustice and the revelation of family secrets. For Arturo Islas in *The Rain God*, it becomes a reflective force whose unnamed image begins to deconstruct the myths the Ángel family have fashioned of and for themselves.

Homosexuality is a word that is used once in *The Rain God*. It is a blasphemy not even whispered on the tongue of any member of the Ángel family, but uttered apologetically by the district attorney to Lena during her father's murder investigation: "She sat down facing him as he explained how the evidence convincingly showed that her father was in fact 'excuse me, ma'am' a homosexual and that he had seduced other men, some of whom were willing to testify during a jury trial" (87). The word "homosexual" is so treacherous to the illusions of the Ángel family that it can only be said outside the home by a person not associated on the inside. There are no double meanings or endearing connotations associated with a word as direct as "homosexual." Its absence from the vocabulary of the Angels bares significance in light of other words used openly that suggest homosexuality but doubtfully.

"*Joto*" is a word used by members and friends of the Ángel family, though the weight of its true meaning is deflated in the way that other Spanish names are used within the family without the condemnation of their denotative meanings. The matriarch of the family, Mamá Chona, used "*malcriado*" as "her favorite word for a child, and to be called that by her was the worst form of censure, for it meant that one not only misbehaved, but that one had not been properly brought up. For a member of the Angel family, that was impossible" (160-61). Mamá Chona said it of her favorite son, and "when she called Felix a *malcriado*, she did so with affection" (147).

Lola, the mistress of Miguel Grande, teasingly called the married man a "*sinvergüenza*," even though "literally, it means 'without shame'" (56). She uses the word with the same endearment with which Mamá Chona used *malcriado*, although in the case of *sinvergüenza*, "Lola said it darkly, the way lovers would in an embrace" (56). Another time, Lola tells her husband, El Compa, "Come on, fairy, let's go home" (63), without challenging his masculinity for showing physical and verbal affection toward Miguel Chico. In fact, she "enjoyed teasing him about his affection for other men" (63). Later at the funeral for El Compa, Lola notices "that big *joto* Felix," and confirms, "at least the fairy doesn't care what all these people think about him" (65). "Fairy" is a word that only Lola uses exclusively in *The Rain God*. It is a versatile word from her personal vocabulary that she uses mildly as when she calls Miguel Grande a *sinvergüenza* or his son a "prig" (65).

"Joto" is the strongest of the suggestive names used in the language of the Angels, and though it is supplied with graphic and varied descriptions, it is as evasive as "fairy" or "prig." When Miguel Chico is a little boy, his mother and nursemaid, María, enjoy and encourage his imaginative play and enthusiasm for music by allowing him to play with dolls and dance to music on the radio. María even makes a skirt for the little boy to dance in. When his father returns home, he creates "a terrible scene" in which the boy is forced to apologize for playing with dolls and dancing in a skirt, even though he is clueless as to what he did wrong: "His father said nothing to him but looked at Juanita and accused her of turning their son into a *joto*." The lack of explanation behind Miguel Grande's behavior or the meaning of his special word will be a mystery that his son will "not find out until much later" means "queer" (16).

"Queer" is yet another ambivalent word because it is not truly used or treated in *The Rain God* as a substitute connotation for homosexual. When Félix is beaten to death by the young soldier he has tried to seduce, his pain is "blotted out by a queer painful sensation in his left ear" (137). Queerness is akin to peculiarity in this instance, and could be interpreted as such during an argument between Lola and Miguel Grande when the word appears earlier. The jealous Miguel Grande defends his opinion that "all good dancers are queer" (70), watching Lola dance with another man. His opinion is justified by assuming a stance of macho "distrust of any man who was too handsome or danced too well" (70). Homosexuality is no more implied in this use of the word "queer" than in the one time that the word "gay" appears, when in reflection of Mamá Chona's memory, Miguel Chico remembers "when she was feeling gay, she treated them to comic book versions of the classics" (161).

Miguel Grande's concern about what he calls "the stigma of *jotos*" stems from his childhood relationship with his younger brother, Félix, whose extroverted personality and independent ways both embarrass and appeal to the older Ángel. As a young boy, Félix would dare to dance outside during a rainstorm while his siblings hid inside, fearful of thunder and lightening. He was also known to behave "like a clown, putting on his mother's straw hat, mincing and dancing about in ways that made even Miguel [Grande] laugh" (83). *Joto* is also the word Miguel Grande uses in reference to the joker card during a game of poker (72), confirming the versatility of how lightly the word is used without homosexual implications. According to Miguel Grande, being a *joto* is synonymous with pranks, foolishness, clowning, and dancing for the entertainment of others. In no way is homosexuality implied, although "as they grew older, Felix's behavior embarrassed Miguel Grande, and he hoped that the stigma of being *jotos* would not reach past his brother" (87). A stigma implies a defect or blemish that is typical of a physical abnormality or mental illness, as in chicken pox or leprosy. In Miguel Grande's perception, his brother's mental and/or physical well-being is tainted by "being a *joto*." He feels threatened that his own well-being is at risk, as if there is a danger of some kind of mental or physical contamination. Being a *joto* could be contagious, and his only defense is to recognize its symptoms and combat the behavioral signs that *jotos* possess in order to maintain his own physically and mentally healthy life, no matter how dysfunctional that may be. Sexuality is not once associated in Miguel Grande's ideas about the "stigma of *jotos*," although dancing, clowning, and laughing are. The only apparent stigma (although unnamed) is his own homophobia.

At the time of the well publicized, violent, and scandalous murder of Félix, the young soldier responsible for his death is released on grounds that he "had acted in 'self-defense and understandably,' given the circumstances, and there was no reason to prosecute him" (87). Although no specific year is distinguished at the time of the murder, it is unnecessary since the political and social climate of the later decades in the twentieth century were altogether hostile times for Americans considered racial and sexual minorities, including women. For many Mexican and Mexican Americans today, homosexuality is more than a slight offense against long-established gender codes and cultural assumptions of masculinity. It is also a damnable sin in the eyes of the Catholic Church. The powerful influence of the Catholic Church on Mexican and Mexican Americans does much more than direct and control a specific patriarchal code of beliefs; it forms the blood of a universal cultural identity passed from one generation to the next. Diversity, if not celebrated, has at least been tolerated in most major cities since the Stonewall Riots of 1969. However, in smaller, rural communities across the nation, awareness and education about homosexuality is limited to outdated stereotypes and media myths kept popular by fear and religion. This traditional passing of the torch of ignorance continues. It is possible to conceive that the murder of Félix Ángel, justifiable in the eyes of the law and by rural locale, could have happened anywhere between the 1950s and today in the new millennium.

It is important to recognize how current the events and circumstances in *The Rain God* continue to be, particularly for all Mexican and Chicano/a communities in which traditional gender roles are taught and practiced, and in which patriarchal order strongly remains the cultural backbone of a highly valued social system. Because homosexuality breaks the most basic of these rules, there can be no identity encouraged or accepted in the system. Homosexuality threatens to upset the system, and is kept elusive in Mexican and Mexican American communities. Without visibility as a real presence or identity, homosexuality remains a deviation from the social and religious order of the community, as mysteriously threatening as La Llorona. If the murder of a person known to be homosexual can be justified as an act of "self defense and understandably," then there is no protection on a civil or judicial level of society. In this kind of intolerant environment, homosexual people must at least conceal their nature from family, community, and church in order to function in that society. Homosexual people may conceal their true nature from even themselves in order to survive and maintain sanity. The murder of Félix Ángel sent a message to one and all that homosexuality was a "shame and embarrassment" punishable by death, justifiable by manslaughter (87).

Félix Ángel is a well-known married man with four children who has an "admiration for masculine beauty" that, as time passed, grew into "an obsession for which he sought remedy in simple and careless ways" (116). This "obsession," which is also referred to as "a search for youth" of which he is "constantly on the lookout," is sought at a serviceman's bar and at work by a familiar ruse on unsuspecting new male employees who agree to a mandatory physical examination by Félix as a requirement for fun-time eligibility. His perpetual pursuit of lost youth or masculinity cannot simply be rationalized as an "obsession" with these things, yet they are the reasons Félix assures himself he is "constantly on the lookout for the shy and fair god who would land safely on the shore at last" (116). An obsession implies a mentally motivated desire, not unlike that of his wife, Angie, who is obsessed with painting every room in their home a bright color, or his sister-in-law Juanita's obsession with Hollywood glamour. His love of muscular young men is not the same thing. It is certain that "he had long since stopped wondering why his pursuit of the past led him to young men instead of women" (135), considering the sexually repressive climate of Mexican cultures and communities. The repressive times in which *The Rain God* takes place is not an era lost to the twentieth century, but one that continues today. The rationale Félix uses to "[taste] his own youth once again" (135) is a delusion for the truth about himself that neither he, his family, his community nor his faith can accept; Félix Ángel is a closeted homosexual.

Although the truth of Félix's sexuality and death is turned into a public scandal by the newspapers, the Ángel family, except for Lena, do not allow themselves to confront or talk about the homosexuality they have denied for years. Félix's wife, Angie, firmly refuses "to listen to anything that soiled the memory of her husband" (86). Long before, "without intending it, she stifled her own desires" when their son, JoEl, took precedence in his life, eventually moving her out of the bedroom she shared with Félix so that he and JoEl could sleep together. When Angie confesses her concern in church about the strange sleeping arrangements, she rationalizes, "He's a good man . . . I have my children, my house, enough to eat. What more do I need?' The priest said nothing" (123). Dutifully ignoring her husband's actions and the priest's silence, Angie continues the sexless, separate sleeping arrangements until "her own desire for Felix cooled" and she ages, unfulfilled but able to "[laugh] with the irony of the sexually deprived" (123). Angie does not question or voice indifference over her husband's decision; she simply accepts his choice and the arrangement becomes "normal."

Miguel Grande, well aware of his brother's "obsession," suspects that Félix has only been slightly hurt. He is called in the middle of the night to the emergency room where the lifeless mangled body lies virtually unrecognizable. "Goddammit, Felix, you've got a wife and four kids. When are you going to learn not to fool around with the little boys?" (80), he practices for the speech that will never be delivered to his brother. Miguel Grande is not oblivious to the fact that Félix has not grown out of his "obsession," but nevertheless refuses to confront the contradiction of his brother's life as a married man with children who at the same time is a practicing homosexual. Like the majority of the Angels, "He had never been able to understand Felix's obsession and did not want to" (83). Instead of trying to understand and accept his brother's homosexual nature, which in turn prevents Félix from accepting it himself, Miguel Grande blames his brother's death on deviant foolishness, carelessness, and selfishness. "Felix, you never thought about the rest of us" (83), realizing that all media attention will be focused on the scandalous aspects of the murder, which will play a determining factor in his hope for the job promotion to police chief.

The Ángel family, fearful of the embarrassment and shame an investigation into the death of one of their own would arouse, would rather remain silent and inactive, therefore allowing the delusions about Félix to stay as intact as possible without having to confront a truth that would unravel their own myths about themselves and the Ángel family. When the details behind Félix's death become public, the Angels find a way past accepting facts. " 'The family,' as usual—more concerned with its pride than with justice—had begun to lie to itself about the truth" (85).

Miguel Grande's reaction of shame and frustration (87) to the murder of his brother corresponds with its homosexual implications. Death, shame, and frustration are connected to his perception of homosexuality. Though he, like other members of the family, never call it homosexuality, Miguel Grande believes being a *joto* is a stigmatic obsession of his heterosexual brother. It is specific mental illness that plagues men who are "too handsome or danced too well" (70). By a vision concocted of his own imagining, he justifies his ambivalent assumptions, and "The thought of touching another man in those ways disgusted him, and his knowledge that Felix enjoyed doing such things had created a barrier between them that neither ever made the effort to overcome" (87). To call this a "knowledge" of "such things" is absurd. The "touching" in "those ways" does not clarify any kind of sexual activity. All that is confronted is the thought of touching another man, which disgusts Miguel Grande. Any displays of physical affection are such anathema to this man, that he rejects the touch of his own son attempting a simple non-sexual embrace (93). His "knowledge" of "such things" is not beyond his own insecurity and inflated assumptions about levels of intimacy that he cannot maintain as an emotionally stable father, husband, or brother. The "barrier" it caused between Félix and Miguel Grande that neither attempted to overcome is one of many barriers Miguel Grande has learned to erect around himself against the world, as in the same tradition the Ángel family protect themselves from truth.

The tradition of denial is passed down to Miguel Chico like a family inheritance. The young boy is aware that he is different and "had always felt that his father disliked him for being too delicate, too effeminate" (94). He hears his father scold Juanita for "bringing him up like a girl" and "turning him into a *joto*" (15-16), even though he does not understand why his father is so enraged by his playing, for which he must apologize and promise never to repeat. Miguel Grande does not notice the innocence of his son's actions. He only sees the crossing of gender lines threatening to change his narrow vision of what is mentally and physically appropriate for his son. Perhaps Miguel Grande even sees a young Félix Ángel when he looks at the boy, which angers and frightens him because it forces the man to face a truth he does not want to think about or accept.

His stigma of teaching a child to be a *joto* is such paranoia that Miguel Grande will not even allow himself to be physically touched by the boy, fearful that by showing physical parental affection, he would be steering his son in the direction of homosexuality. The first time Miguel Chico sees Miguel Grande cry is when the latter is packing a suitcase for the trip to the funeral of his brother. The boy attempts to put his arms around his father, but is rejected. "'Don't do that,' his father had said, pushing him away. "Men don't do that with each other. Let me cry by myself. Go away.' The rebuff had hurt him and he had remembered the lesson" (93). The only "lesson" that young Miguel Chico never forgets is the rejection a father has for a son who is "too delicate, too effeminate." Miguel Grande's rejection of Miguel Chico only pushes him closer to Juanita, whose bond he comes to resent: "It was clear to both mother and son that Miguel Grande at his most brutal could not break their intricately woven web of feeling for each other" (94).

When their son complains of bodily pain and failing eyesight, Miguel Grande forbids his wife to take the eight-year-old boy to a doctor, believing he is "only being a brat" and "pretending to be sick so that he wouldn't have to go to school." Despite a polio epidemic killing many children, Miguel Grande sees only a power struggle to take control over their son and argues, "'I'm the head of this family, and you're not calling anybody. I won't have you spoiling him any more'... Juanita did not understand her husband, but she obeyed him" (94-5). Miguel Chico's untreated bout with polio leads to an emergency trip to the hospital (into which he had to be carried), and a permanent limp in one leg. Even though "it pained him to see his son walk" (96), Miguel Grande could not "bring himself to express his regret to Miguel Chico" (95-96). His pride and blind convictions of masculinity stand in the way of allowing for a deserved apology from father to son. Miguel Grande is so determined to "make a man" of his oldest son that he goes as far as to coax his schoolmates to start fights with the boy "so that he might learn to defend himself" (96). Miguel Chico is made to take swimming lessons "with private instructions to the teacher to be harder on him than on the other boys his age" (96). Miguel Grande devises a series of tests of strength and manhood behind his wife's back again and again. When Juanita intervenes to rescue their son, who does not understand that he cannot help disappointing his father, Miguel Grande places the blame for his nature on her. "You've ruined him" (96), he tells Juanita, as if Miguel Chico were the victim of improper parenting.

The possibility that Miguel Chico's homosexuality might be predetermined by nature is an impossibility to his father. He views his son's behavior instead as the result of environmental indifference by the influence of an overprotective mother. He believes that such tendencies can be controlled and overpowered by physical discipline and an intolerant social environment. Homosexuality is then only a matter of gender confusion determined by how a child is raised, the results of which serve as a reflection of parental errors and eternal family shame: "Miguel Grande had consistently refused to acknowledge that his son's feelings and needs might be different from his own, and he had thus failed to help the boy understand life" (94).

By repressing his homosexual nature, enforced by the mental and emotional conditioning to think it shameful to be outwardly sensitive or effeminate, Miguel Chico cannot explore his natural desires or develop his true self: "Miguel Chico ignored his body and became a good student" (96). This was a choice that not only alienated him from the family, but also from himself.

The process of disconnecting progresses as both father and son get older. Their conversations do not go further than Miguel Chico's answers to his father's questions, and any physical communication is "limited to a slap in the face or a bone-crushing hug that lacked affection and had been his father's way of showing that at middle-age he was still physically fit" (96). The "ruining" of his son belongs entirely to Miguel Grande's painful and paranoid parenting techniques for the sake of "making a man" of Miguel Chico.

Another "lesson" Miguel Grande teaches his son is a lack of trust in other men: "Because of his father, Miguel Chico would never trust another man to tell him the truth about anything," even though "He would have preferred a life in which trust rather than suspicion guided his thoughts and actions" (97). Though Miguel Chico does not account for being unmarried, choosing to blame an operation and "let them guess at the rest" (5), he lives in San Francisco and specifically visits Chelsea and Greenwich Village (14), two well-known gay districts of New York. Aside from calling himself "effeminate," "delicate," or "the family analyst" (28), Miguel Chico never identifies himself or confronts identification as a homosexual or *joto*. He claims to "believe in the power of knowledge," though "he preferred to ignore facts in favor of motives" (28). Indeed, Miguel Chico refuses to look "at himself or others truly" (94). Even his uncle Félix, secure in the love from his wife and family, tells himself, "He was not looking for any of them in this boy's mouth. He was looking for something else" (135).

By choosing to closet himself from his homosexuality, Miguel Chico is constantly haunted by guilt and ghosts from his past. His choice to remain closeted is not without valid reason. The murder of his uncle Félix would be a sufficient enough point to understand how frightened and intolerant American and Mexican societies are of homosexuality. Without sanction on a civil, religious, or judicial level, there is no kind of identity a homosexual person can safely express and survive.

There are many excuses that could be rationalized for why one male member of the family stays single and another secretly administers physical examinations to naive muscular men. They might include a passionate pursuit of lost youth, an admiration for muscular beauty, or the stigma of poor parenting. These reasons are given, justified, and rationalized to conform to public and personal codes of acceptability. They are all agreements that there is no homosexual activity in their homes and communities. They are agreements that there are no homosexual identities in the mirror. There are only "family secrets" kept in closets.

Without an identity, homosexuality continues to be defined by fear and imagination. Because it is never confronted but further denied, homosexuality is the myth of the living and truth of the dead. More than a novel, *The Rain God* is the reality of an entire family and community who stay "in the closet" even after the closet comes out of them.

OUT OF PERSONHOOD, OUT OF PRINT:
Cultural Censorship from Harriet Wilson to Arturo Islas

Karen E. H. Skinazi

Dear Arturo,

To answer one question right away: I'd be delighted to represent you as a writer, and this novel of *ours* [emphasis mine]. I see the fine, conscientious work you have done, and I have every admiration for your seriousness, persistence, and talent . . . I have a few suggestions to make about the novel . . .

This book is not convincing as an examination of cultural notions of sexual identity. [. . .] I don't see the necessary connection between the concentration on homosexuality in its neurotic manifestations (cruising, promiscuity, S-M) and the tight family structure of Mexican-Americans in a Texas town. There is so much loving in the latter, so much frenzy of affection, and so little in the former . . .

—Letter from Robert Cornfield, 1978

What happens when a writer's work leaves his hands, and at what point does editing change the written work altogether? I will examine here the way the books of Arturo Islas and Harriet Wilson reflect the pressure to conform to clearly defined cultural limitations. Harriet Wilson, who considered herself a victim of "Northern aggression," was writing at a time when slave narratives were the only acceptable form of African American writing. Arturo Islas, who wanted to deal with the intersection of gay and Chicano identities in his novels, discovered that, in order to publish, he could not. As a result of the zeitgeist, both writers were frustrated in their attempts to educate the public through their fiction about their ways of life. Both *did* publish their works, but only by subverting their "dangerous" ideas. And even then, not one of the books by Wilson or Islas could have been considered a commercial success during the respective authors' lifetimes.

Success, it would seem, rests in fulfilling readers' expectations. Readers of a book marked as Chicano literature are open to following the characters' experiences and explorations of cultural identity, as readers of a book marked as gay literature are open to tracing the characters' forays into issues of sexual identity. A book that negotiates the relationship between sexuality and culture asks much of its readers, perhaps too much, from the standpoint of the publishers. Robert Cornfield, Islas's agent, suggested withdrawing the sexual references and concentrating, instead, on a generational saga. In a letter that established the singular emphasis of Islas's books once and for all, Cornfield concludes:

> To fix the setting and place I think you should have a poetical section of where these people were from (and their backgrounds even before that), why and when they came to the United States. The reader has to do too much sifting this out and then the facts are not complete [. . .] If you do some establishing of place and family biography the reader will be happy indeed. (Cornfield)

What makes a reader happy? Wherein does the juicy story lie, in the words that litter the pages of our books, or the ones that have been swept off? If individuals only wrote about their experiences generally, we could replace the "Chicano" book with an "African American" or "gay" one, as long as each remained focused on its own particular brand of "Otherness"—that favorite academic term—and easily forget which is which. How many books would have to be written before we say, "I've heard this one before"? A glance at the Oprah Book Club list indicates that a novel in which any experience of oppression that is worked out in some (preferably grand) way bodes well for agents and publishers and, it would seem, the reading public at large. Universality means broad readership and broad readership means money. But what about stories that resist universalizing?

When Islas began writing, the few Chicano books that existed could hardly have been called a canon. In a sweep of reflexivity,

Islas addresses this issue in his first published novel, *The Rain God*. Two women, sisters, are discussing the books that they read:

> Juanita, who joined a book club shortly after she married, could never get Nina to read the latest best seller that arrived monthly and which she read immediately. After thumbing through a few of them, Nina judged them boring and "pure trash." Stories about the endless suffering of southern belles left her unmoved.
> "Why don't they write about us?" Nina asked her sister.
> "Who wants to read about Mexicans? We're not glamorous enough. We just live," Juanita answered. (41)

This short anecdote illuminates a number of issues generic to minority literature: the frustration with the lack of representation, the incommensurability of disparate American (in this case, like-gendered) experiences, the anxiety of the minority author caused by his identity-specific subject matter, the refusal to exoticize (or even the insistence on de-exoticizing) the Othered Self.

In *The Nature and Context of Minority Discourse*, Abdul JanMohamed and David Lloyd discuss some of the issues generic to minority literature, concentrating on the surreptitious means by which the dominant culture suppresses minority discourse—from blatant publishing restrictions to a "subtly implicit theoretical perspective that is structurally blind to minority concerns" (6). Yet JanMohamed and Lloyd themselves limit the horizon of possibilities in minority literature when they define the task of minority discourse in the singular. That one task is to determine and display "the common denominators that link the various minority cultures. Cultures designated as minorities have certain shared experiences by virtue of their similar antagonistic relationship to the dominant culture, which seeks to marginalize them all" (1). They seek to efface difference on all levels.

However, the conversation between the two sisters in Islas's text does not only reflect on the concerns of minority literature at large. It also illuminates the specific problem for Chicanos of that time: there were no Chicano stories.

The molding of the Chicano canon occurred largely in the hands of the influential publishing house Tonatiuh-Quinto Sol, which was established in 1967 and "challenged Chicanos to proclaim their cultural uniqueness, encouraged experimentation and innovation, and awarded cash prizes to the authors of distinguished works," according to Raymund A. Paredes ("Evolution" 63). "On the most fundamental level," explains Paredes, "the firm's very existence gave aspiring Chicano writers a sense of self-respect and an assurance that their subject matter was worthy" (63). Paredes lauds Quinto Sol for its support of its people by dint of its existence as well as its ideological rejection of Anglo-American literary models; Quinto Sol did not only publish but also awarded literary prizes to its people, beginning with Tomás Rivera's Spanish . . . *y no se lo tragó la tierra/* . . . *And the Earth Did Not Part* (1971) and Rudolfo A. Anaya's popular English *Bless Me, Ultima* (1972).[1]

Islas's start as a Chicano writing in English was contemporaneous with Anaya's, but the similarities seem to end there. Anaya's first novel, *Bless Me, Ultima,* was published immediately in 1972 and has since served many a course curriculum and graced many a bookshelf. *The Rain God*, on the other hand, was busy receiving a stamp of REJECTION in one publishing house after another before a small press accepted it, much edited, in 1984. Why did Anaya's success come so much more quickly and thoroughly? Islas surely meets Quinto Sol's challenge to proclaim his "cultural uniqueness" and is, without a doubt, experimental and innovative. Perhaps too much so.

The reception of Anaya's *Bless Me, Ultima* says much about readers' expectations. It was labeled "the only true Chicano novel," and "The Great Chicano Novel" (Bradford). The *Los Angeles Times Book Review* pronounced Anaya's novel a "fiesta, a ceremony preserving but reshaping traditions that honor the power within the land and *la raza*, the people." The young boy does not grow up to be just any man, but a man of *la raza*. The *National Catholic Reporter* averred that "Anaya is in the vanguard of a movement to refashion the Chicano identity by writing about it," and *Newsweek* hailed Anaya as the "poet of the Barrio [. . .] the most widely read Mexican-American." (Taken from jacket cover blurbs.) All these fluffy quotations indicate that the book came along perhaps at a time when the Chicano people were "looking for a voice," as if one voice could speak for all, but more certainly when the publishers were ready to cash in on that "voice." Tossing in the buzzwords "*fiesta*," "*la raza*," "Chicano identity," and "the barrio"—is pure gimmick and hype. Islas was not impressed:

> I think it's impossible for any book to express the totality of anyone's human experience. At best it can illuminate a corner of that experience for us in an artful and interesting way; at worst, it can plunge us into further darkness[...] Anaya will have to write a great many more and much better books before I will concede that he recreates our "objective realities, our myths, our legends, our hopes, dreams and frustrations." In short, he is not for me the author of "our total and unfragmented reality." Whatever that means. I suspect that [Herminio] Ríos and [Octavio] Romano were so excited about a book written by a Mexican born in this country that created a world with some literary consistency that they went overboard and made of its author a small god. I resist that kind of excess. I think it's false and misleads potential writers from this perspective into thinking that all they have to do is get one novel published that has enough of the proper ingredients in order to be hailed as the great novelist of the people. Bah! Estan usando la nalga. (Lecture 11)

Islas never wants to be hailed as the greatest novelist of his people nor have his novels hailed as the definitive representation of Chicano culture. For it is the singers of praise, more than the author, who create in their image the god; it is they who increase the potential of plunging readers into "further darkness" (Lecture 11). Islas's first step is to distance himself from the critics, and his second to bring the novel close again, to remember that it is a novel about what he understands best: himself.

This same individualization that sets Islas apart from other minority writers also sets him apart from Chicano writers, which explains Quinto Sol's reaction to his writing (or lack thereof). In "The Promise of Chicano Literature," Raymund A. Paredes sketches a picture of Chicano writers tormented by the outside world and finding sanctuary in their Mexican heritage (32). Luis

Leal and Pepe Barrón, giving an overview of Chicano literature, come to the conclusion that the novels of this canon do not portray a pessimistic attitude, but, instead, an optimistic "affirmation of the Chicano nature" (14). Islas ignored this description, which read hauntingly as prescription. And, as recently as 1994, Antonio Márquez remarked that "Islas has been contentious about certain elements of traditional culture, and he has challenged some assumptions about Chicano/a literature" (12). What is it about a deeply personal and elegiac novel that makes it dangerous? What are the assumptions about and the traditions of Chicano literature, and why does Islas's desire to expose his own secrets make him "contentious" of those traditions?

JanMohamed and Lloyd dismiss the possibilities offered by minority writers who fail to provide a forum for a general solidarity between their literature and that of other differently-marginalized authors, and blindly call for a universalization of minoritization. Quinto Sol's choices indicate that they felt that the establishment of a standard Chicano canon of novels that had a clear, unwavering focus on issues generically Chicano, was deemed necessary before Chicano literature could diversify. We can only wonder whose stories have been forced into silence because they are too complex, have too many parts, involve characters with different needs and desires, or have different ways of defining themselves. It makes me wonder how few books are monoglossic enough to be considered "standard," and how much we lose. Islas fails in his adamant individualization of his multiple marginality to fulfill the demands of minority and Chicano theorists.

All writers have multiple vectors of identity, and those vectors cannot always be the same. Are most authors so untrue to themselves when they pen their characters? What happens when they sit down to write their own stories? Surely not everyone's story is a simple, neat, and linear fairytale.

I wonder what we would find if we could explore the gaps between lived lives and *romans à clef*. I think it would be fascinating to know where the truth must end for the writer. Yet, realistically it is a futile game whose object is to psychoanalyze the dead and buried. If something can be exhumed, it must be material, and for this reason, I want to question the practices of publication, for therein lie the *clefs* to the *romans* of late capitalism. With such *clefs*, we can open new worlds, separate the original art pieces from their commodified forms, and consider the implications of the disparity between the two. We are fortunate indeed that access is available to Islas's original manuscripts. We can interrogate the editing of the corpus of Islas's writing, "American Dreams and Fantasies," divided into published and unpublished (or, unpublishable by the standards of those times) parts and shuffled around to make "the reader [. . .] happy indeed." Islas responded to his agent's changes by saying, "I am not interested in doing a Chicano *Roots*. That crudity 'love' is my territory and I have found it among Mexicans and gays in this country. That's where I cruise" (Letter to Robert Cornfield). And yet, his next line, "However, I am willing to shift some of the material [. . .]" indicated, ultimately, his willingness to concede. At what cost to him and his readers?

Such costs are addressed by Priscilla Wald in her book *Constituting Americans*. Wald attempts to remunerate both readers and writers by exposing if not quite suturing the ruptures that storytellers are forced to create as they edit according to the laws of marketing. She reveals the problematic relationship between a singular, uniform formulation of American personhood and the real people and experiences unable to fit the rigid mold prepared for them. The stories she examines are ones that narrate the nation yet simultaneously ring cacophonously in the apparently monoglossic "We the People." The stories appear "disrupted."

Islas, in his localized way, narrates the nation. The original corpus of Islas's work is entitled "American Dreams and Fantasies." From Mary Antin's novel of eastern European Jewish immigrants, *The Promised Land* (1912), to Gish Jen's novel of Chinese immigrants *Typical American* (1992), writers of American (im)migrant stories throughout the twentieth century bestowed titles upon their books that marked them immediately and integrally as nationally specific. It is precisely this genre of determinedly American novel by a minority that echoes W. E. B. DuBois's notion of *double consciousness*, "an American, a Negro," with a similar tune: "an American, an ethnic" (DuBois 8). The comma or hyphen that separates the two entities marks the gap between the two ways of experiencing the world. It is a disjunction that becomes a physical presence in these stories. Islas's tales can be seen as the updated version of the "hyphenated American." At a time when "An American, A Negro" had become an almost standard starting position for a writer, Islas turned the dichotomy into a triangle: an American, an ethnic, a gay. (See also Werner Sollors's discussion of "out-group" membership and "self-exoticization" in *Beyond Ethnicity*.)

It is impossible to separate one aspect from the rest. For example, Islas's literature is a project of culture-building; yet, it is a building of culture that can only take place within the nation and in relation to it. José David Saldívar's topoanalytic reading of *Migrant Souls* reveals why looking at a "history [. . .] of *spaces* [. . .] from the great strategies of geopolitics to the little tactics of the habitat" can identify "the history of *powers*" (Foucault, in J. Saldívar, *Border Matters* 72). In Islas's writing, the larger world of the United States of America haunts the smaller Chicano world of the borderlands. Saldívar explores the ways in which Chicano identities are entangled with social spaces, from the parlor to the borderland, reading the oppression of the Chicano characters through their compressed spaces (72).

The third corner of the triangle casts its shadow on the other two. While being Chicano sets Islas outside the norms of America, being gay sets him outside those of both America and his own, local Mexican America, and simultaneously ties all sides together, uniting him with his people anew. Gloria Anzaldúa, a borderlands Chicana lesbian who calls homophobia "fear of going home" declares that "[b]eing the supreme crossers of cultures, homosexuals have strong bonds with the queer white, black, Asian, Native American, Latino [. . .] Our role is to link people with each other" (20, 84).

Triangulation of identity, or *triple consciousness*, is the new Other, the newly misunderstood. It highlights the arbitrary nature of conformity, even within ethnic canons wherein *double consciousness* is standard. Triple consciousness in literature is complex—and hence, less than desired by agents, publishers, and critics—in short, by the material world. As such, it continues to be shunned. Shunning the alien, the foreign, the Other is, of course, an old American tactic, wherein censorship is a key strategy. In an essay entitled "Censorship," author Salman Rushdie, renowned victim of the practice, notes some of the consequences:

> [T]he worst, most insidious effect of censorship is that, in the end, it can deaden the imagination of the people. Where there is no debate, it is hard to go on remembering, every day, that there is a suppressed side to every argument. It becomes almost impossible to conceive of what the suppressed things might be. It becomes easy to think that what has been suppressed was valueless, anyway, or so dangerous that it needed to be suppressed. And then the victory of the censor is total. (Rushdie 39)

Even though Islas's books were finally published, fundamental elements of his works have disappeared, been shunned and even been censored. Yet, we ought not be surprised. This experience is embedded in a long, if varying, tradition.

Wald's methodology involves attending to two different kinds of censored or "disrupted" stories: those that appear with lacunae and those that disappear. The latter category cannot include the fully disappeared; what we do have are rediscovered works, such as Hannah Crafts's tale of a "Fugitive Slave, Recently Escaped from North Carolina." Harriet E. Wilson's *Our Nig*, an antebellum tale of Northern oppression, having been out of print for 100 or so years, also falls into this category, and is one of the novels Wald attends to in her study of disrupted texts.[2]

Our Nig's material history is striking for its long-term absence, both in popular culture, and the archives of academe. Most critics today agree that it was suppressed because it was considered a dissident text. Just as Islas's novels of gays and Mexicans fail to fit the standards of Chicano and minority literature, so too did Wilson's tale of Northern aggression fail to fit the standard of Southern slave narratives. I want to investigate this "dissidence" and the consequences of it.

In the narrative, shown by Barbara A. White to be rather autobiographical, Wilson recounts "sketches" from the life of a young "free black," Frado. In the book, Frado is the indentured servant of the white Bellmont family. Frado is mistreated by Mrs. Bellmont and her daughter Mary; befriended on terms so unequal they border on commodification by sons Jack and James;[3] and pitied, though not aided, by Mr. Bellmont and his sister. In history, Wilson, born Harriet Adams c. 1828, was the indentured servant to the Nehemiah Haywards, a family, in composition, quite akin to the fictional Bellmonts (White 22). Mrs. Rebecca Hayward, on whom Wilson is thought to have based Mrs. Bellmont, was descended from an eminent abolitionist family, the Hutchinsons. White quotes a letter from Frederick Douglass to John Hutchinson: "I especially have reason to feel a grateful interest in the whole Hutchinson Family—for you have sung the yokes from the necks and the fetters from the limbs of my race" (White 35). But if the image of the Bellmonts is at all representational of the Haywards/Hutchinsons, Douglass was quite mistaken about the family's desire to liberate his race, indeed.

However, Douglass was not ignorant of the problematic relationship the black community had with the abolitionist one at large, and this difficult relationship is an issue that, according to Wald, is evoked through the discrepancies between his works. How would this intertextual lesson affect Wilson, writing after both *Narrative of the Life of Frederick Douglass, An American Slave* (1845) and *My Bondage and My Freedom* (1855) were published? Wald's discussion of Frederick Douglass's earlier narratives raises questions about the limitations of Wilson's *Our Nig*. It seems that Douglass writes his early slave account, *Narrative,* as an instance of what Wilson calls "humbugs for hungry abolitionists" (128); it is laced with abolitionist rhetoric spun to depict slavery as an expressly moral issue. Wilson declares, "professed abolitionists" went to the "lectures" (her scare quotes) to hear "professed fugitives from slavery who recounted their personal experiences in homely phrase, and awakened the indignation of non-slaveholders against brother Pro" (127). But Douglass, like Wilson, does not tell his story merely to fill a role laid out for him. Critical of abolitionists' "injunctions against his analyses and their attempts to shape his demeanor and choose his words," he eventually chooses an altogether alternative route, and recommends a reinterpretation rather than dissolution of the Constitution (Wald 77). We might ask: If the abolitionists, so troubled by Douglass's gifts, were able to alter his story so radically that, as Wald posits, he had to rewrite it outside of their influence, how could Wilson expect a positive reception of the white audience whose financial support she needed, considering that she openly inveighs against abolitionist hypocrisy? Furthermore, if economic concerns were eminent for Douglass writing *My Bondage and My Freedom* after already becoming an established writer of slave narratives, what would they mean for an unknown writer like Wilson, who was writing as one who had not been a slave but had only fallen under slavery's shadow? As the audience, according to Wald, "expected 'an American slave' and awaited 'a slave narrative,' it was incumbent upon the orator or narrator to provide just that" (80). But Wilson did not.

So when can an author write outside of the limitations set for him? Douglass's second text, we could conclude, more accurately portrays a philosophy and a history of his own reckoning, having been written after his break with Garrison, the abolitionist who guided his career, and having been written after his entry into the literary marketplace. But Wald warns us against such simple conclusions. Despite his freedom from direct Garrisonian influence, Douglass, says Wald, "recognized the importance of his abolitionist sponsors' plot, the story he must tell in accordance with their strategies to captivate audiences in the service of their larger program" (77). Hence, *My Bondage and My Freedom* cannot be read as freely told. It is a text still held in bondage; the constraints of acceptable literary conventions, economic considerations, and fear of alienation of Douglass's audience all continued to play their roles in Douglass's writing. Yet, argues Wald, a self-aware Douglass does offer his readers a text of great literary value. While the bondage of the *slave* has not been altered dramatically in Douglass's second rendition of his life, the bondage of the *text* is acknowledged, subverted, and as such, creates a new possibility for storytelling. Given Wald's depiction of Douglass as a self-conscious writer who subtly but deliberately changes his self-image through an explicit act of revision, we can question Wilson's own use of genre, an unlikely and therefore necessarily self-conscious one. By virtue of her fictionalization, Wilson can weave overt criticism into a novel that is part autobiography, part slave narrative, part sentimental novel, but actually, as Wald points out, is none of these genres.[4] Wilson, in other words, calls attention to the restrictions of northern abolitionists and their rhetoric by adopting and subverting the "master's tools"; she makes this hybrid genre of the novel her own.

Despite her brilliant use of the novel to disguise her criticism, Wilson never becomes the author of a best seller as Harriet Beecher Stowe did with her abolitionist novel that came to define an era by spawning a flurry of response novels such as *Cousin Franck's Household, or Scenes in the Old Dominion; The Planter's Victim; The Autobiography of a Female Slave; Adela, the Octoroon; The Sable Cloud: A Southern Tale with Northern Comments* (Gates, *Figures in Black* 134). In "'This Attempt of Their Sister,'" Eric Gardner argues that because *Our Nig* could not be read as a book about abolition, the book was not accepted by the abolitionist community. Gardner sees a market for an *Our Nig* that preaches Christian values but not one that condemns the Northern oppression of free blacks. Through a comparison of Harriet Beecher Stowe's *Uncle Tom's Cabin* and Harriet Wilson's *Our Nig*, Gardner comes to the conclusion that for the former, the commercial success derives from the fact that in it, "the North is portrayed as a magical land where the protagonists will eventually realize the promise of freedom" (Gardner 243). But is Stowe pandering to her Northern neighbors? And how far north does freedom lie? In parentheses, Gardner adds, "albeit in Canada" (243). Albeit? Gardner's argument fails to be convincing due to two flaws: the Northerners are not drawn as kind friends to the slaves, and the North, meaning north of the Mason-Dixon line in the United States, is not depicted as a land of freedom in Stowe's novel. These differences between *Our Nig* and *Uncle Tom's Cabin* are thus negligible.

Written after the second Fugitive Slave Act (1850), *Uncle Tom's Cabin* reveals a country in which the northern states are implicated in the institution of slavery, and the only white people to treat the African characters as equals are the apolitical Quakers, who "would do the same for the slaveholder as the slave" (224). Tom's owner, St. Clare, tells his northern cousin, "[L]et me see one of you that would take one into your house with you, and take the labor of their conversion on yourselves! No; when it comes to that, they are dirty and disagreeable" (353). Wilson echoes precisely this sentiment: "Watched by kidnappers, maltreated by professed abolitionists, who didn't want slaves at the South, nor niggers in their own houses, North. Faugh! To lodge one; to eat with one; to admit one through the front door; to sit next one; awful!" (Wilson 129). Why would one writer's criticism of Northerners be valid but not another's?

Furthermore, how could Gardner suggest that Stowe's "North" is anything but a separate country, entirely unrelated to the "North" in which Frado resides? Canada is first mentioned in *Uncle Tom's Cabin* in regard to Tom's loyalty: "Some low fellows, they say, said to him, 'Tom, why don't you make tracks for Canada?'" (Stowe 43). Shelby explains that Tom would never leave his slavery for a place of freedom, and through these words, we learn to equate Canada and freedom. It is George who ultimately makes tracks for Canada. He is a character Gardner claims to be for the most part "muted" (an odd and unproven assertion), but in fact one who does not experience Tom's complacent martyrdom (243). George, in fact, is the character who best embodies the American spirit. "I'll fight for my liberty to the last breath I breathe. You say your fathers did it; if it was right for them, it is right for me!" he declares, and with these words, the author, "the little lady who started this great war," offers the rhetoric of inevitability that Abraham Lincoln crystallizes at Gettysburg: "Four score and seven years ago our fathers brought forth on this continent, a new nation, conceived in Liberty, and dedicated to the proposition that all men were created equal" (187). But perhaps in 1852 this country was not yet prepared for an American spirit in a body of African descent, because George, who seeks his liberty, comes to the conclusion that: "I haven't any country, anymore than I have any father. But, I'm going to have one. I don't want anything of *your* country, except to be let alone,—to go peaceably out of it; and when I get to Canada, where the laws will own and protect me, *that* shall be my country" (187). The country's inhabitants, Stowe demonstrates, even its northern ones, are not willing to let him go peaceably; in the North, George's wife reminds her husband, "we are not quite out of danger [. . .] we are not yet in Canada" (285). Northern abolitionism, insists Stowe through the story of the escape and through George's indignant yet unheeded "declaration of independence," is inadequate (298).

Stowe, white but still a woman, cautiously puts her diatribe into a peripheral character (Tom, after all, is our eponymous hero, not George); to be bolder would be to push her luck, indeed. Wilson, black and a woman, probably assumed that she had nothing to lose—realistically, a diatribe that was inked from her pen into any character would not be taken well, were it to be taken at all. She boldly put her criticism into her "I" character—transparently, herself. As for Crafts, black, a woman, and a *fugitive slave*, we cannot know if her diatribe, often tempered with "humbugs for abolitionists" was ever meant to reach the eyes and ears of an audience; we only know that it appears that her book was never published. Whether Crafts feared exposure, missed her market with the impending Civil War, or wrote a publishing impossibility, or all three, no one should be surprised by her failure to become a best-selling author (Crafts lxiv-lxv). In fact, Gates, Jr., calls the publication of Wilson's book a "virtually [. . .] miraculous event" (Crafts lxiii).

Wilson's miracle comes in part through her deployment of "sketches." Despite the transparency of Wilson's "I," the use of a fictional shroud and intentional lacunae hide possibly jarring details. As Wald reminds us, Wilson punctures her own cover in the preface of her book by stating, "I do not pretend to divulge every transaction in my own life" (3). What is significant is the specific content of her missing transactions; she writes, "I have purposely omitted what would most provoke shame in our good anti-slavery friends at home" (3). Despite a reluctance to tell the specific damning stories of Northern abolitionists, she creates a space in her readers' imagination for an infinite number of stories potentially far more damaging than those she retains.

Is it possible that the book was really intended for a black readership, one that could easily fill in the gaps with fact-based knowledge? Surely, she ends her preface with an appeal to her "colored brethren" for their support. However, the financial support she seeks could only come from a white community. Gardner and White argue quite cogently that Wilson's potential audience is necessarily small due to very limited circulation, and as for the black population of Milford, the "1850 Census Population Abstracts show 2,159 people living in Milford; Harriet Wilson was the only black woman, and there were only two black men. In 1860, Milford's population had grown to 2,223, but there were no black residents enumerated by the census" (Gardner 233). In fact, Gardner's detective work reveals that Wilson's readership consisted of white middle-class children who resided in the Milford area. Like *The Rain God*, *Our Nig*, in its published form, had potential for a certain kind of whitewashed universalization, and since many of its unpleasant details were veiled, the subversive side of the book could go unheeded. Frado's gradual acceptance of Christianity and its doctrines makes the book, regardless of Wilson's initial intentions, a good candidate for instruction on moral improvement. According to Gardner, who has examined several of the extant copies, many are "in dilapidated condition, and their scarcity suggests a relatively small print run, or at least that the book was considered by its readers, as well as its printer, an ephemeral product, not to be cherished and preserved" (232). Did someone or some group prevent further circulation of Wilson's *Our Nig*? What are we to make of the fact that *Our Nig* was listed on a 1951 inventory of a library donation from William Lloyd Garrison, Jr., son of the same abolitionist who acted as a mentor to the young Frederick Douglass? Perhaps we could simply conclude that Wilson's position as a poor, black, oppressed woman with little access to Boston literati and abolitionists outside of the family she maligns or the kind of abolitionist movement she censures, could not have reached a population who could, as Margaretta Thorn beseeches, "lend a helping hand" (qtd. in Wilson: 140). Or perhaps it was simply published for a country that little noted nor long remembered her.

A century and a half has gone by and what does the world care to think of now? How is Arturo Islas received? How do we deal with these cultural pioneers? Certainly Islas was far more successful in his life than was Wilson at receiving recognition. It is known by some that in addition to being a pioneer for introducing controversial subject matter in his writing, Islas was the first Chicano in the United States to earn a doctorate in English in 1971 and was Stanford's first tenured Chicano faculty member in 1976. Yet, in a tradition not unlike the Afro-American one that Henry Louis Gates, Jr., describes in which "racial firsts have been heralded loudly and widely, as veritable talismans drawn out to counter racist aspersions," it would seem very likely that Islas and his work would be "heralded loudly and widely" (Gates, *Figures* 138). After Islas struggled to win a 10-year battle to publish his first book, he achieved the brief success of having his second novel published by a New York firm in 1990. Certainly we can imagine that his works are at last appreciated, but that seems not to be the case. That second novel, *Migrant Souls*, published just over a decade ago, is long out of print.

"American Dreams and Fantasies," begun in the early 1970s, appears to have been the original corpus of Islas's works. As far as I can determine, this large chronicle of the Ángel family was subsequently divided into a trilogy from which *The Rain God* and *Migrant Souls* were extracted for publication. They trace the history of the Ángel family from the Mexican Revolution, through the migration from Mexico to El Paso, and into the day-to-day life of the narrator and inheritor of the family legacy, Miguel "Chico" Ángel. The remainder, unpublished and fragmentary, still bearing the original name, "American Dreams and Fantasies," tells a different story—one of sadomasochism, cruising, promiscuity, violence, drugs, suicide—that reveals the secrets of "that generation of 'gays' who are filled with self-hatred for what they are" (Islas, Letter to Robert Cornfield). This is the version that is censored out.

In a vignette in *The Rain God* entitled "Rain Dancer," Islas recounts the story of Miguel Chico's uncle's violent death. The first line reads, "Felix Angel, Mama Chona's oldest son, was murdered by an eighteen-year-old soldier from the South on a cold, dry day in February" (113). The details of the murder are deferred until the end of the chapter. In the bulk of the chapter, Islas delicately explains that Félix is not "a respectable man" (115). He goes to "the serviceman's bar," treats the customers to drinks, and offers young soldiers "a ride" (115).

If unrespectable, Félix is not malicious. He is described as a man looking for love, youth, and beauty. Yet his actions are not innocuous. In charge of hiring young Mexican workers who come to the factory in search of work and American citizenship, Félix finds a convenient forum for sexual harassment. Islas allows the reader to make his/her own judgment of the physical examinations that Félix performs on the worker-hopefuls: "In those brief morning and afternoon encounters, gazing upon such beauty with the wonder and terror of a bride, his only desire was to touch it and hold it in his hands tenderly" (116). The section passes without commentary from the narrator.

Félix's tender desire extends to his young son. One night Félix lifts "JoEl from the cot with great tenderness and took him to their bed" (122) where the boy remained until he was 10 years old. Islas writes that as Félix, his wife, and son slept together frequently, "Felix lost his passion for Angie, and he would wake during the night cradling JoEl on his side of the bed. His protective feelings for the child perplexed and disoriented him because they seemed stronger than his desire for his wife"—who eventually moved into a room of her own (123). Never explicit, Islas suggests that Félix's desires manifest in severely damaging ways. Are we left to decide whether Félix is a man who deserves to be understood or brutally beaten to death? No authorial judgment is forthcoming, only the picture of decline. JoEl slowly loses his mind. In the last narrated conversation between Miguel Chico and JoEl, JoEl is laughing and weeping simultaneously, "I love my father, I love my mother, I love my father, I love my mother" (156).

Can we judge? Are we missing too much information? Unsurprisingly, the published version is simply not the full story Islas had intended to tell, as I discovered, digging up a section in "American Dreams and Fantasies" entitled "Felix." That which was left out is quite significant. The shadowy dark underside of

The Rain God emerges explicitly in the pages that seem destined to rest quietly in a corner of Stanford's Special Collections Library. "Felix" begins:

> The sucking, fucking noises in the corridor, the stench of amyl, the smell of perfumed crotches and abused assholes, piss and leather, semen, sweat and spit and nicotine piercing the nostrils as the throat gags, oh Lord! hear my prayer. In the darkness, one shadow kneels to receive another, crouches to take what comes, tongue or cock, a lick or a fist or a boot or a tube of flesh indiscriminate in this shady grove. There are no kisses here. Prostrate, the prostate is massaged, fingers, hands and phalluses emerge to be licked clean by waiting, tireless, numberless mouths. IammyfatherIammymotherIam[. . .] Love, are you here? (Islas, "Felix" v)

The erasure from the publication is radical. Relationships between the words of a crazed JoEl and those introducing JoEl's father's world of sadomasochism are never drawn. The language of the novel is sterilized. The society of the novel is sterilized.

Criticism about one's culture, as we have seen, is barely acceptable, barely publishable, poorly received. But to add sexuality to the pot, to allow dirty human sexuality to mingle with the other facts of life, also dirty but perhaps less so, also human but within the confines of taste, is too much. P. Gabrielle Foreman, not unlike Wald, searches for "contexts and codes" slipped into *Our Nig* (313). Comparing *Our Nig* to Harriet Jacobs's *Incidents in the Life of a Slave Girl*, Foreman demonstrates the existence of the "unutterable" in both. Sexual abuse, says Foreman, falls into this "terrain of the unspeakable" and therefore the gaps and silences might whisper of precisely this taboo (316). Foreman reads the "shame" in Wilson's preface as indelicacy, the sexually unspeakable (320). One image of Frado's abuse that is particularly startling can be read in terms of muted sexuality:

> Excited by so much indulgence of a dangerous passion, [Mrs. Bellmont] seemed left to unrestrained malice; and snatching a towel, stuffed the mouth of the sufferer, and beat her cruelly. (Wilson 82)

Several times is Frado beaten in this way, with her mouth stuffed. Combined with Foreman's declaration that Mrs. Bellmont is positioned as a "Southern male" (315) and Wilson's picture of "dangerous passion," the reader cannot help but sense Wilson's struggle to depict rape imagery. The "indelicate" details of Wilson's narrative of America remain trapped in this text, which at least, in its cryptic form, is finally accessible today.

As for *The Rain God*'s narrator, Miguel Chico Ángel, there exists a sexuality not subtextual but surrendered. There is no sexuality for this Ángel. He is an "angel," "pure [and] bodiless" without any sexuality (Islas, *Rain God* 8). Islas's only focus appears to be on his culture.

What we are left with, ultimately, is the Chicano *Roots*—the great Chicano saga, in which sexuality is treated as irrelevant. But the cutting room floor can certainly respond to that image of neat unity. A significant section that is cut out occurs near the beginning of *The Rain God*, when Miguel Chico is conversing with a psychiatrist in the hospital. In their discussion, which revolves around his father's rejection of him, Miguel Chico pinpoints the cause as his perceived womanliness. Thus reads the outtake:

> [Psychiatrist]: "Do you think you're womanly?"
> "No."
> "But you are homosexual, aren't you?"
> "That doesn't make me womanly. I don't like men who behave like women. They repel me or make me laugh if they have a sense of irony about what they're doing. I like women who are womanly. I find them very attractive, but I don't feel like sleeping with them."
> "Why don't you feel like sleeping with them?"
> "Are you straight?" [he asks the psychiatrist]
> "Yes."
> "Why don't you feel like sleeping with men?"
> "It seems more natural for me to sleep with women."
> "Well, it seems more natural for me to sleep with men. This is getting us nowhere."
> "I don't agree with you. Maybe you don't like yourself because you're Mexican and homosexual [. . .]." (Islas, "Rain God" ms. 12-13)

The interchange thus ends pointing directly to the problem—Miguel Chico, like Islas, is both Mexican and homosexual, a minority within a minority, and therefore difficult to classify and analyze. With the role of the psychiatrist deleted, so is the issue of sexuality. The story is simplified to one about the problems of a Mexican in America, not a gay Mexican.

Ironically, the published version causes critics to become suspicious of the sexual silence. According to Ricardo L. Ortiz, "For Islas, as for [John] Rechy, nomination becomes a chief tool in accessing the most potent semiotic resources of his cultural environment; indeed, this is one of the rare cases in which Islas's symbolism achieves a kind of Rechean excess" (120). The effect of the novel's "excess" of culture seems to indicate to the reader that it is so encompassing that it occludes any sexuality in Miguel Chico. Perhaps one would conclude that Chicano culture is the cause for the muted treatment of Miguel Chico's homosexuality not only because of its excess but also because of its cultural restrictions. The lack of acceptance of Miguel Chico's uncle's homosexuality demonstrated by the textual omissions as well as the in-text audience reminds the reader that this is not a culture that easily accepts homosexuality in its men. John Rechy's *City of Night* is not considered a Chicano text at all, despite the ethnic origins of its author. According to Juan Bruce-Novoa, it is not because of Rechy's "Anglo" consciousness or lack of Chicano values that he is not accepted, but rather, because of the blatant homosexuality of his characters (201). The pressure to be a "Juan Rubio" of Villarreal lore forces Chicano authors to produce, as Gloria Anzaldúa puts it, "*macho* caricatures of its men" (21). The stories that do not conform are repressed, and Islas is not able to negotiate his characters' sexuality. According to Ortiz, Islas "relegates the sexual histories of his characters to the level of innuendo, to the 'obscene' space off the stage of explicitly narrated events. [. . .] the narrative of Félix Ángel's murder at the hands of a young serviceman he tried to seduce reads almost like a cautionary tale of the grave cost of taking any kind of sexual risk" (118-119). But Ortiz must realize that the reason Félix's murder is reduced to innuendo might not be Islas's prudence at all.

Yet prudence certainly appears to be a quality of Miguel Chico, and as such, he takes no sexual risks. Why? Islas depicts Miguel Chico (the thinly disguised version of himself) as not only the chronicler but also the editor of his family's affairs. Miguel Chico conspicuously plays dual but not always overlapping roles of character and narrator. In *Our Nig*, readers are baffled by the destabilization of pronouns; Frado appears to be both the "I" and the "she" of the text. Is it poor proofreading or an uncertainty in regard to subject positioning that we are encountering? *The Rain God*, too, baffles readers with its narrator/character and Islas, it seems, deters the readers from trying to pin down the source and reliability of the narrative when he describes Miguel Chico's observations of the "world" around him:

> He was still seeing people, including himself, as books. He wanted to edit them, correct them, make them behave differently. And so he continued to read them as if they were invented by someone else, and he failed to take into account their separate realities, their differences from himself. When people told him of their lives [. . .] he found himself retelling what he had heard, arranging various facts, adding others, reordering time schemes, putting himself in situations and places he had never been in, removing himself from conversations or moments that didn't fit. (26)

Wald would argue that Islas is demonstrating his characters' internalization of cultural values in order to explore it, and this moment of self-consciousness reveals the implicit critique. By reordering history, Miguel Chico is implying an inherent fault in the original, and Islas is implying that an "original" as we might imagine it may not exist at all. The reader is reminded that, though "autobiographical," his novel is far more complicated than a straightforward rendition of his life and that "editing" and "correcting" play significant roles in the history of this book.

Islas's revisions are telling, just as Wald shows Douglass's are. In a letter to Ron Arias, author of *The Road to Tamazunchale*, Islas writes of *The Rain God*, "I am sending you a copy of my book. It has been a critical, if not commercial success [. . .] Anyway, the reviews have ranged from California to Philadelphia to Long

Island to Chicago and of course, to Texas. The establishment in Manhattan continues to ignore me and it. They prefer Rodriguez and Santiago, I guess" (Islas, Letter to Arias). This commentary on his novel's reception reappears in *Migrant Souls*, which, of course, was ironically not ignored by Manhattan. In the revision, the comment on marketplace restrictions falls out: "*Tlaloc* [which translates to "rain god"] was an academic, if not commercial, success and its author became known as an ethnic writer. After seeing what the world did to books, he returned humbly to the classroom and to criticism" (210).

Ultimately, a humbled Islas, despite silencing his commentaries on gay self-destruction and the New York publishing industry's cultural exclusions, could not conform enough for Americans or even Mexican Americans. Chicano critics demand novels that add to a monoglossic Chicano literature. Just as John O'Sullivan, founding editor of *Democratic Review*, tried to create a homogeneous American literature by decreeing, "it is only by its literature, that one nation can utter itself and make itself known to the rest of the world," so too do Chicano canonizers seek power in the single voice (qtd. in Wald: 109).

Arturo Islas's Ángel novels exhibit a deep sense of cultural anxiety distinguished by disjunctions and disruptions as they try to fit a mold restricted by a specific cultural identity—Chicano identity—buried within a larger national identity. Islas's negotiation of his sexual orientation with his cultural and national identities is driven to the margins of his compressed space of narration. Through a direct comparison of Islas's published and unpublished works, margins can be read, holes can be filled, and ruptures sutured. This method is not always possible. *Our Nig*, after all, remains in many ways a mystery to us. Yet, discoveries modify and soften that mystery; today we have a holograph by an African American woman contemporaneous with Wilson. It is a great artifact of history that presents observations about the relationships between people black and white, Northern and Southern, male and female, from the perspective of a free black woman. The insights offered in Crafts's book make us take up Wilson's anew; they allow us to compare mediated with unmediated writing, opaque and transparent. *The Bondwoman's Narrative* also adds a new voice to history, and as such, is a reminder that it is our duty to recognize the artificiality of any monoglossia. It is our duty to find places for texts forgotten or ignored because of difference.

Arturo Islas and Harriet Wilson were writers of difference, who attempted, for reasons practical and financial, to conform to clearly defined cultural limitations. Their failure to do so is our boon. Despite hushed receptions, such books continue to exist, and, reader by reader, to break down the fortifications of minority literature's constructed uniformity.

NOTES

[1] Raymund Paredes says *Ultima* is reminiscent of the classic European *künstlerroman*, *Portrait of the Artist as a Young Man* ("Evolution" 67). This statement appears to be said with no irony, yet can only cause us to question the kind of experimentation and innovation expected of the Quinto Sol writers. While *Portrait of the Artist as a Young Man* does deal with postcolonial issues of a minority group, the book had long been considered a classic by the time Anaya was writing. Hence, with such a comparison, Anaya's book appears to fit quite comfortably into the fold of the dominant culture's canonical literature—the very literature Quinto Sol had set out to refute.

[2] It was Henry Louis Gates, Jr., who did the rediscovering of both *Our Nig* by Harriet E. Wilson (1982) and *The Bondwoman's Narrative* by Hannah Crafts (2002). *The Bondwoman's Narrative* is thought to predate *Our Nig*, thus making the former the oldest known novel written by an African American woman and the latter the oldest known novel published by an African American woman. Time and new discoveries might change both of these suppositions. Crafts's novel had not yet been discovered when Priscilla Wald wrote *Constituting Americans*.

[3] I base this statement primarily on the scene in chapter VI in which Frado gives her dog, Fido, her mistress's soiled plate to lick clean before eating off it, having been told she cannot have a plate to herself. Jack relates the story to James and thereby implicates James in the moment of commodification in which, "pulling a bright, silver half-dollar from his pocket, he threw it at Nig, saying, 'There, take that; 'twas worth paying for'" (Wilson 72). Mrs. Bellmont commodifies

Frado in a different way, by speaking of her in terms of the profit she is to the family; e.g. "I'll beat the money out of her, if I can't get her worth any other way" (90). White argues that almost all human interactions in this book can be reduced to economic exchanges: Mag's virginity is a "priceless gem"; she could trade her white skin, a "treasure"; Jane would be a "treasure" as a wife (34).

[4] I think it is important to note that Wilson's book is indeed a novel, with chapter headings, epigraphs, and characters not always directly taken from Wilson's acquaintanceship. In this way it is similar to Crafts's *The Bondwoman's Narrative,* an autobiographical novel that is as generically hybrid as *Our Nig.* Henry Louis Gates, Jr., points out that the former is "an unusual amalgam of conventions from gothic novels, sentimental novels, and the slave narratives" (Gates, Introduction to *Bondswoman's Narrative* xxi). Gates, Jr., reminds us that the novel was not then a form that was common to black women; Wilson was one of the earliest black women to publish a novel. The decision to write a novel then was a conscious one that could not have been free of the "cultural anxiety" of which Wald speaks (Gates, *Figures* 128). Wilson was, at the moment of production, joining the authors who were creating the national literature. Beth Maclay Doriani's essay "Black Womanhood in Nineteenth-Century America: Subversion and Self-Construction in Two Women's Autobiographies" asserts the importance of reading *Our Nig* as an autobiography.

WAYS OF APPROACHING *THE RAIN GOD* in the Classroom

Frederick Luis Aldama

Teaching Arturo Islas's *The Rain God: A Desert Tale* (1984) can follow many different paths. I suggest several here that include discussion of its publication history, its influences, and close readings of the text that focus on its form and content: narrative point of view, style, as well as character, event, and theme.

Background: Born in El Paso, Texas, in 1938, Arturo Islas was raised bilingually and excelled at school. At age nine, he contracted polio, leaving him with a marked limp. This left him self-conscious physically, driving him even more deeply into the world of literature and his studies. Winning a scholarship to attend Stanford in 1956 led him away from his initial desire to study medicine and to pursue a career in writing. As an undergraduate he studied with the writer Hortense Callisher; as a Ph.D. student at Stanford he studied with Yvor Winters and Wallace Stegner. In the study of the craft of fiction, he was greatly influenced by Dostoevsky, García Márquez, Faulkner, and Colette, to name a few.

After completing his Ph.D. in 1971, Islas was given a professorship in Stanford's English department. During this period, Islas turned his hand to writing, and in 1976 he finished a draft of his first novel, "Día de los muertos/Day of the Dead." It was not only to be the book that would grant Islas tenure, but that nearly a decade later would be published as *The Rain God* (1984) with a small Palo Alto-based press.

Beginning with "Día de los muertos/Day of the Dead," Islas became acquainted with the hostile world of publishing. His initial lack of success was not because of a lack of talent on his part, but, as he suspected at the time, because of the novel's content—it follows the life of a queer Chicano protagonist—and narrative experimentation: the novel shifts between a first and third person narrative point of view. In spite of the great gains in queer and brown civil rights in the political arena, the publishing world was still run by editors that were either xenophobic or afraid to take a chance. After Islas sent a draft of the manuscript to Farrar, Straus, and Giroux, he received Roger Straus's reply: "I don't think it is right for us on the basis of this 'taste'" (Letter from Roger Strauss).

In the mid-1970s, New York presses had begun to publish a couple of Chicano and U.S. Puerto Rican authors. However, these were either of the immigrant farm worker (Villaseñor and Galarza, for example) or the urban ghetto (Piri Thomas) variety. In *Dialectics of our America*, José David Saldívar nicely sums up the objective of Victor Villaseñor's *Macho!* and José Antonio Villarreal's *Pocho*, which were written "according to New York editors' standards about certain U.S. ethnic themes—social maladjustment, the individual and his environment, the pathological character of the Chicano family, illegals, violence, and criminal behavior" (112). Islas's novel did not fit either mold. It was focused on a cast of middle-class Chicano characters and a young man's coming to terms with his queer sexuality. "Día de los muertos/Day of the Dead" opens with the following: "Uncle Felix was murdered by an eighteen-year-old soldier from the South on a cold, dry day in February" ("Día de los muertos"), and publishers were not ready for what would follow: a complex exploration of queer sexuality within a Chicano family that begins and ends with death. At the time, not only were there few Latino (Chicano, Puerto Rican, Cuban American) writers published, but even fewer authors were published who focused on themes of queer sexuality.

In spite of the continued onslaught of rejection letters, Islas continued his struggle to publish "Día de los muertos." He invented a consistent narrative in the third person, tightened up the plot, and sculpted characterizations anew. In the new version of "Día de los muertos," the characters spoke less Spanish—and when dialogue did appear in Spanish, Islas made sure that there would be enough context for an English-speaking readership to understand. Islas had also toned down the protagonist's queer sexuality. As such, Miguel Chico's sexual conflicts and relationship traumas move with more subtlety inside and outside of the closet. With all the sculpting and transformation, "Día de los muertos" was close to the shape in which it would appear when published as *The Rain God*.

Soon after *The Rain God* was published by Alexandrian Press on October 8, 1984, it began to receive local critical and popular acclaim. The first print run of 500 hardcover copies sold well enough for Alexandrian Press to print a larger run: 1,500 paperbacks. The paperbacks sold out almost immediately. Word of mouth—friends and colleagues—along with Islas's ruthless self-promotion helped ensure continued sales. By June 1985, *The Rain God* had sold over 3,000 copies. Its success helped the novel travel overseas, and a Dutch press translated and published the novel as *De Regen God* early in 1987. Elated with the novel's overseas success, Islas wrote playfully in his journal that he could not understand a word, but liked the "cover immensely. It captures 'Ants'" (journal February 14, 1987). Since, *The Rain God* has won a Southwestern American Book Award, is taught in high school and college classes alike, and remains one of the best selling titles in Chicano literature.

After giving an overview of the publication history and biographical information, you might choose to **establish the setting** of the novel. The first novel of two, *The Rain God* follows the ins and outs of the Ángel family as they live in an unknown U.S. town on the Texas/Mexico border. The Rio Grande separates the two sides. Although the majority of the narrative takes place in this fictionalized setting, it also briefly moves to San Francisco. We do not get a very good sense of either setting, but we know the Texas setting must be a fairly large town. Miguel Grande, the sheriff, says on page 76, "the force, like the town, was more than half Mexican now . . . The town seemed ready to accept people of Mexican ancestry in positions of power." The town is also growing. On page 46, Nina and Ernesto buy a new house. "The house was one of those new, prefabricated structures that were going up everywhere on the northern and eastern ends of the town. If the economy continued as it had for the last five years, the house would be practically in the middle of town in the next five." Images of the desert abound; otherwise, there is no real sense of the setting.

Then establish the **historical time**: The novel's time frame is also somewhat vague. The narrator mentions JFK's assassination (page 57), the Vietnam War (page 45), the Mexican revolution of 1910-1920 (page 163 and 165), and the Spanish civil war 1936-39 (page 59), though this is clearly a recollection of the distant past. From this scant information, a good guess would be that the novel's protagonist and primary narratorial filter of the events, Miguel Chico, is born in the late 1930s and raised in the 1940s in El Paso; he is an adult in San Francisco in the 1970s and early 1980s. The narrative begins with the mention of a photograph of Miguel and Mamá Chona taken in the early years of World War II (page 3) and then tells us on following page, "Thirty years later . . . at the university hospital," bringing us into the 1970s.

Some points to touch on when discussing that the novel's characters remain largely outside of the events of history would include:

1. The family is untouched by World War II, the Korean War, McCarthyism, and any mention of civil rights and/or labor struggles in the United States at large. The struggles played out between the younger and older generations reflect, in a sense, the social struggles against power taking place on a larger scale nationwide.

2. The lack of temporal, geographic, and personal everyday life—there is an absence of details on what it is like to be a sheriff or professor, for example—makes this a novel less concerned with filling out characters and more with the abstract presentation of event and character. As such, the characters themselves only evolve to the degree that they prove a particular point. The novel becomes, in a sense, a de-realization of reality.

3. The fragmented time structure/temporal motion in the novel is spiral in nature, advancing and retreating in time through a series of organized flashbacks (analepsis) and flash-forwards (prolepsis).

Once the setting is established, provide an overview of the **plot**. The plot is a series of flashbacks; each chapter moves from a more present time frame to a more distant one, so we get a sense of where the characters have come from and where they are going. We are never quite sure of our temporal footing because the flashbacks are interrupted with an unidentified temporal present. Also, the reader is never sure when there is a flashback or a temporal present narrative mood. A brief breakdown of this plot sequencing is as follows:

- "Judgment Day" (chapter one): Miguel Chico is in the hospital for an operation related to an unidentified intestinal illness: "his body was being held together by a network of tubes and syringes" (page 8).
- This allows for the narrator, closely aligned with Miguel Chico, to flash back to his childhood (age 7-9); the death of childhood nursemaid, María, and memories associated with her.
- Flash-forward: Miguel Chico living in San Francisco "a few years after his operation" (20-21). See how much María influences his life and get a sense of passion for literature: "Literature had given him another way to examine the mind" (28).
- "Chile" (chapter two): The Ángel family meal with Juanita and sister Nina and others.
- Flashback to the family's move to the United States and information about their French/Mexican father who worked as a cigar maker and lived in San Francisco in search of work. He loses his first-born child, then moves to New Mexico and later Texas. We get the sense that *machismo* is generational.
- Nina/Ernesto's son Tony drowns.

"Compadres and Comadres" (chapter three): Miguel Grande and Juanita's wedding anniversary.

- Introduction of a new character outside the family, Juanita's best friend, Lola.
- Discover Miguel Grande's affair with Lola.
- Discover that Miguel Grande's brother Félix has been murdered and mutilated in the desert outside the army base. We are not sure yet why. As a result, Miguel Grande is not selected as chief of police: "he lost . . . faith in himself" (91).
- Miguel confesses to Miguel Chico, then Juanita, about his affair.

"Rain Dancer" (chapter four): Félix goes to special place with a soldier, which leads to his murder.

- A flashback gives a sense of Félix's home life; he is a gentle father who dotes on his son, JoEl, and sexually ignores his wife, Angie.
- Flashback to Félix's marriage to Angie. The family is upset because she is dark skinned, *una india*.

"Ants" (chapter five): Meet the outcast older generation family members, Tía Cuca and Mr. Davis, who live together without Mamá Chona's permission; also learn of JoEl's mental breakdown.

"The Rain God" (chapter six): Miguel Chico returns to San Francisco after visiting JoEl.

- flashback to Mamá Chona's death and gathering of family.
- The image of Mamá Chona at the end brings us full circle back to the image at the beginning. She is a great matriarch that contains the family throughout the novel; her image frames the novel.

After carefully delineating the plot with all its flashbacks—and flash-forwards—it would be important to discuss the **rhythm** of the chapters as they unfold. Each chapter varies in terms of page length and can be represented as the following: A (26) B (17)

C (57) D (35) B (15) A (21). The novel winds into its center—Miguel Grande's affair with Lola and the discovery of Félix's mutilated body—then spirals back out through the more subordinate chapters, giving a structure that parallels the protagonist, Miguel Chico's, movement inward—into the center of his past, then out again. The chapters in toto, then, reflect the process of restoration of Miguel Chico's self and of his family. Finally, it is important to emphasize that this is a novel in which all important questions about identity and experience must be examined without looking down the well of the past.

Once the plot is established and it has been explained how this conveys the overall worldview of the narrative, it is time to move into a discussion of the **major themes**. *The Rain God* is a narrative that gives testimony to life that no longer exists. To begin discussing this, read closely the poem by Pablo Neruda in the epigraph as well as the eponymous poem in the last chapter (page 162) by the king of Texcoco. (He was the king of the Chichimeca tribe who was also known as the learned-poet king.) Both poems frame the novel as a narrative that seeks to paradoxically make present the absence of life.

- In *The Rain God* you might want to focus on the lines "All the earth is a grave and nothing escapes it" and "Vanished are these glories [...] / Nothing recalls them but the written page." In Neruda's poem, you might want to focus on "I come to speak through your dead mouths..." and "Hasten to my veins, to my mouth. / Speak through my words and my blood." Then, you might begin to discuss how the writing down of the stories of family acts is a way to preserve a memory of what happened. The dead relatives (mouths) come to life through storytelling.

Once this theme of making present an absence through writing is discussed, it is important to discuss the primary narrative **filtering presence**. While the novel is narrated by a third-person omniscient narrator, the story is filtered through the eyes of the protagonist, Miguel Chico, who is a **writer/professor.** We see the story world as if perched on his shoulder. This is important because Miguel Chico is the one who goes to the university to study literature and write. He is the character endowed with the power to **preserve** through writing the family's story. Some pages to look at closely:

- Page 28: He reads his operation as a "symbol" and "perhaps he had survived to tell others about Mama Chona and people like Maria."
- Page 28: "Years earlier, he had started out to be a brain surgeon but had found his pre-med courses lifeless and impossible. Literature had given him another way to examine the mind. . . ."
- Page 26: "He was still seeing people, including himself, as books. He wanted to edit them . . ."
- Page 27: "He resists the temptation to romanticize his past, recalling Mamá Chona: "'Oh, my dear Miguelito' . . . Sitting at his desk, gazing at the garden, fixing that old photograph forever outside of time and far from where it was taken. . . ."
- Page 96: We learn that his interest in book knowledge starts at an early age and that it also provides a sense of refuge from his family's macho atmosphere. As a result of medical misdiagnosis, as an adult he needs an ileostomy, but still reads this as a symbol. His presence is reduced absolutely to the function of writing stories.
- Page 25: He learns that his body is cut off from the world in a "normal" way and that he replaces his "natural" body with a writing on the body—body as system, as a series of marks that make up his own testimony/story. Also point out here that because writing becomes a surrogate body of sorts, Miguel is ultimately forced to be connected to his body; that he cannot exist completely disembodied.
- Page 4: Miguel Chico is selective as a writer, chronicling stories especially of his family's sinners. Sinners include those who do not participate in heteronormative and/or internalized racist codes of behavior; those that do not participate in patri-

familial codes that ensure reproduction of the capitalist-based system.

- Here, one might also note that the character Ricardo, Mema's illegitimate son, becomes appointed head of the family. Ricardo has internalized codes of containment, those expressed specifically by Mamá Chona, to such a degree that he becomes even more of a "bastard," so to speak; he becomes more rigorous about maintaining family codes of conduct.

Then the discussion can explore Miguel Chico's presence—along with the other characters—within the family and society at large. Namely, in the novel, the more characters **integrate** into the social mainstream, the more they are **estranged** from family. To explore how integration is synonymous with alienation from family in the novel, you might consider looking at the following :

- Page 78: The narrator describes Miguel Grande's desire to integrate himself as perfectly as possible into the power structure: "The North American dream had worked for him. Only his family reminded him of his roots, and except for his mother he avoided them as much as possible." However, the discussion should look at how Miguel Grande's integrationist impulse works only if the facts of his life are suppressed: his macho, heterosexist ways continue unchecked in spite of the discovery of facts: Juanita's discovery of his affair with Lola does not change him because he is so completely a part of the patriarchal system. Instead, the facts are suppressed.
- Page 77: Look at the narrator's comment, "Miguel Grande knew how intransigent the power structure was, but he respected and defended it against Communist ideas like those his son was learning at the university. He bragged about Miguel Chico's abilities and achievements to others and sentimentally believed that his oldest boy was fulfilling his own dreams of a college education—dreams he had never in fact had . . ."

- Also, it is important to discuss that at the same time Miguel Grande promotes the younger generation to fulfill the unrealized dreams of the older generation, he condemns his son for getting an education, pejoratively calling him a communist.

- Page 76: Miguel Grande internalizes the American Dream, anxious to be named chief of police: "By seniority he was entitled to the position and he even allowed himself to feel confident about getting it."

- Page 83: Explores why Miguel Grande reacts to his brother Félix's mutilation with the following: "Felix, you never thought about the rest of us." Here, family is sacrificed for the sake of "making it" socially.

- Page 91: Discuss how Miguel Grande's sense of self-worth is bound up in idea of the American Dream: "And when he didn't get chief of the department he lost a lot of faith in himself."

- Page 119: It is important to explore the concept that the more one is educated, the more one is alienated from family. Note the distance that arises between JoEl and his mother Angie: "She spoke English with a heavy Mexican accent and used it only when she wanted to make 'important' statements . . . After his first year in school JoEl learned to be ashamed of the way his mother abused the language."

- Page 91: Miguel Chico's education gives him the tools to understand his family from a distance: "In his arrogance, Miguel believed he was finding ways out of it through university education. He had not yet had time to combine learning with experience, however, and he still felt himself superior to those who had brought him up and loved him." Here, you might discuss how learning and experience are equated with wisdom and that this exists in tension with the alienation that arises due to his education. At the same time, in order to understand his family better, he requires education—the literacy skills necessary to write the family stories.

Here, you might discuss the catch-22 of the situation: Miguel Chico is alienated from his family in his integration into the social mainstream—his university education—yet must use learned tools to reintegrate into his family through writing.

The discussion might now lead to the theme of **bilingual education** as it is presented in the novel. Some important facts to keep in mind: at least 31.8 million people in the United States speak a language other than English at home. For children attending school, at least one-third of the population speaks a foreign language at home. Bilingualism is largely determined by economics, the funding each state allocates for the institutionalizing of bilingual education in school curricula from kindergarten through the twelfth grade. This is used as a form of discrimination against Chicanos. Until 1971, it was illegal to speak Spanish in a public school building in Texas. In 1973, psychologists at Ellis Island tested thousands of non-English-speaking immigrants exclusively in English and pronounced them retarded. One might also cite the case of a judge in Amarillo, Texas, claiming that a Mexican mother was committing "child abuse" by speaking Spanish to her child at home, for example. Look at the following passages in *The Rain God* to discuss the problem of bilingualism (English/public and Spanish/private):

- Page 141-42: "'Listen to your teachers at school,' Mama Chona told them in Spanish, 'and learn to speak English the way they do. I speak it with an accent, so you must not imitate me. I will teach you how to speak Spanish properly for the family occasions.'"

- Page 142: "Because of them Miguel Chico and his cousins learned to communicate in both languages fluently, a privilege denied the next generation, who began learning to read and write after Tía Cuca was dead and Mama Chona nearly senile."

- Page 142: "[A] truly educated person . . . speaks more than one language fluently."

Finally, it is important to discuss the fact that the novel itself is written largely in English, with only sprinkles of Spanish. Islas's original manuscript of the novel was much more bilingual. However, after receiving rejection after rejection from publishing houses in New York that complained of the excessive presence of Spanish that would alienate audiences, he gradually edited out the Spanish.

As the novel stands, you might discuss how the lack of Spanish reflects Miguel Chico's desire to keep Spanish for his private life—that life to which the reader is ultimately not allowed access. In other words, while he reveals some family secrets, he does not ultimately break the code of silence.

Once the issue of bilingualism is explored, you might lead the class into a discussion of **racial discrimination** in the novel; first, that the racial discrimination that exists in the novel between the mainstream (as represented by Anglos) and Chicanos/Tejanos is very abstractly sketched; it murmurs in the background of the plot:

- Page 127: Félix is kept from taking college preparatory courses.
- Page 77: The narrator describes the first Chicano mayor, who "served competently and without incident, and his only gesture of rebellion was to apply for membership in the town's country club shortly after his election. He was denied official, but given honorary, status in the club."

However, forms of internalized racism within the family have a much stronger presence in the novel. Here, the *criollo* caste system (where skin color determines class standing) is foregrounded. Look at the following passages:

- Page 142: "In subtle, persistent ways, family members were taught that only the Spanish side of their heritage was worth honoring and preserving; the Indian in them was pagan, servile, instinctive rather than intellectual, and was to be suppressed, its existence denied."
- Page 144: "For these visits, Mama Chona wore her formal black dress, put on black gloves, and carried her black umbrella. Puzzled, JoEl asked why she needed the umbrella,

since rain fell only six or seven times a year in torrents that lasted but a few minutes. 'I don't want the sun to burn my skin,' she said. 'It's dark enough already.' JoEl looked closely at her dark, leathery skin but asked no more questions." Here, Mamá Chona suffers the heat of the desert wrapped up in black to preserve a myth of lightness—and therefore the illusion of her aristocratic class standing.

- Page 147: The narrator describes Tía Cuca as "secretly proud of having lighter skin than Mama Chona, and she made certain that the sun never touched her face and hands, the only parts of her any of them ever saw."
- Page 147: "Although they were always poor, the old ladies retained their aristocratic assumptions and remained señoras of the most pretentious sort . . . cleaning house was work for the Indians. . . . Consequently, their homes were dusty . . ."

In a final discussion of the *criollo* myth, one might discuss its grand irony: that the preservation of this myth leads to absolute domestic decay and the absolute decay of the self. It would also be good to discuss the fact that there is no such thing as pure Spanish culture. Spanish people belong to a North African/Sephardic Jewish/Spanish hybrid race and culture. Mention the narrator of Cervantes's *Don Quixote*, who announces that the narrative is a translation of an Arabic story to foreground the long history of cultural admixing between North Africa and Spain. *Don Quixote* is ultimately the product of a Moor and thus not really the adventures of an errant knight, but an attempt to relive a past influenced by the Arabic storytelling tradition. The Arabic philosophers in Spain were also responsible for translating and preserving texts of Greek antiquity that were considered heretical in the church in Europe; the religious purge of the Middle Ages in Europe left the Arabs as the only preservers of the Greek tradition; building on these texts, the Arabs in Spain made up some of the most important philosophers of the Middle Ages. Therefore, they acted as the bridge between Europe and its past.

Following the discussion of how the characters internalize a criollo caste system, a discussion might move on to explore the theme of disintegration. First, you might discuss how the novel's progression is toward disintegration of the family and of the unity of bilingual English/Spanish; as the older generation ceases to exist, bilingualism is no longer present because there is no one left to preserve it. This leads to a sense of disarray in the youngest generation, as seen with JoEl. Also, the instructor might explore how the more characters integrate into society, the more the social cell of the family disintegrates. Here, the degrees of integration are directly tied to the degrees of disintegration of the family and its individuals. In this progression toward decay, you might look at the following passages:

- Page 25: Miguel Chico as the physical embodiment of decay; he is kept alive only because of tubes hanging out of his gut: "It was a weekly ritual which took him an hour, or a little more if the skin around the piece of intestine sticking out from his right side was irritated. Without the appliance and the bags he attached to it and changed periodically throughout each day, he knew he could not live. . . ."

- Page 162. Recalls the poem about the rain god, (notably, acts as the title of the chapter and of the novel itself), which centers on idea of decay: "All the earth is a grave and nothing escapes it . . . Vanished are these glories . . . Nothing recalls them but the written page." Not only does this allude to Ecclesiastes 1:2, "Everything passes all is vanity," but it also foregrounds the novel's dialectic function: as both disintegration and integration, decay and containment. The content of the novel is one of decay/disintegration, but a decay that is ultimately contained by the written page, the novel itself.

- Page 152. "In those moments, JoEl understood infinity for the first time. It was a region without dimensions which registered on one's consciousness in the same way that deaf mutes understand what others are saying to them. It was a timeless space where one is aware of movement without consequence, of a mouth uttering sounds one grasps but does not hear." Explore here JoEl's response to a disintegrating world; he chooses a world of simultaneity. For JoEl, time collapses, emotions conflate (laughing and crying at same time), and manifestations of his being increasingly exist outside of time/space. See also page 155.

Central metaphors that support the theme of decay/disintegration and integration/preservation:

- Page 89: Miguel Chico **recovers** after visiting his family: "The old childhood feelings were then dredged up and he had to be alone for several days after his return to the West Coast. To recover, to rid himself of the desert, he walked on the beach or in the fog." *Recover*: to get well as in health/mental well being; to cover over after uncovering, say a tablecloth; to recollect as in memory; to reattain as a material possession. The family stories are in a sense *recovered*, reattained, and recollected by the page. But, like the omnipresent desert, an image that most characters associate with death, that covers and recovers, certain things disappear and others appear in this ongoing process. The novel recovers stories by re-covering others ultimately in an act of the protagonist Miguel Chico's mental recovery.

Other coverings and recoverings in the novel that might be explored:

- Page 56: "He [El Compa] had decided to make the repairs that day in spite of the heat. His back was better, and he did not want to hear Lola tell him again (as she had every weekend for the past year) that her kitchen would soon be buried under the desert sands if he did not do something about that hole." The desert literally threatens to cover a character's material habitat; it is a stronger than human force.

- Page 148: Tía Cuca and Mr. Davis: "They had found the two old people unable to get up from their beds . . . and because the desert had blocked up the cats' entrance the stench in the place was overwhelming. There were animals and cockroaches everywhere. The sheets were filthy." Physically no longer able to hold the desert back, nature is constantly present as a

suffocating threat. See also page 149: "In the desert, the roof of Tía Cuca's house had been blown away and most of the windows were gone. Inside, everything was covered with sand and the ants were feeding on the carcasses of rodents."

The desert **literally suffocates**:

- On page 118: The desert image prefigures Félix's mutilation/murder in the desert: "Felix felt the cold air of the desert winter as someone came into the bar . . ."
- Page 136: "March sandstorms would begin and the road would be closed. He detested those storms because they made him feel buried alive . . ."
- Page 137: Félix's death: "The kicking continued and he felt great pain in his groin and near his heart. Then his mouth was full of the desert . . ."
- Page 138: "Felix had time to be afraid before he heard his heart stop. The desert exhaled as he sank into the water." The water image here ties into the earlier image of a sandstorm, and also the death of Juanita's sister Nina's son, Antony. On page 48 after Tony has drowned, in actual water, Ernesto, as he gazes into the desert, recalls the image of his son in the "sand before him . . ."
- Page 8: the desert is a simile for Miguel's parched body: "He could not move his lips to ask for water, and from neck to crotch his body felt like dry ice, the desert on a cold, clear day after a snowfall."
- Page 6: "He [Miguel Chico] was allowed only spoonfuls of ice once every two hours and the desert was very much in his mouth, which was parched by drugs . . . those chips of ice fed to him by his brother Raphael were grains of sand scratching down his throat." (The image of dry ice appears again on page 82.)
- Page 152: JoEl is "listening to the sand falling softly on the porch outside, a sound that made him think of veils sliding against each other or of the most delicate knives being sharp-

ened—subtle, beautiful sounds which made him drowsy as he imagined each grain of sand falling."

- Page 153: The desert affects JoEl psychically: "All of his fears and evil dreams merged and he had no voice to cry out against them." It is as if the desert—associated with fear and evil—chokes him up.

The desert is linked also to economics:

- Page 129: Mrs. Ramos's mansion is described as having "a garden filled with flowers. Angie could not believe they were real. 'Imagine,' she said, 'in this desert.'" Here, the desert as a threatening force is linked to economics: Mrs. Ramos has the money to sustain life in an arid climate.

The desert also acts as a metaphor of male codes of conduct, or non-truths:

- Page 90: "Even his mother's [Juanita's] masochistic streak was not that wide—or if it was, she too had been buried by that desert." Given the context, the family's trip to San Francisco motivated by the father's affair with Lola, this desert becomes a metaphor for the familial codes that privilege males' infidelity by covering it over with non-truths.
- Page 97: "Because of his father, Miguel Chico would never trust another man to tell him the truth about anything." (Truth not to be associated with male figures.)

However, such codes of behavior that cover like desert sands to suppress the facts eventually lead to ruptures:

- Page 81: "It was unrecognizable. There was no face, and what looked like a tooth was sticking out behind the left ear. Dried blood and pieces of gravel stuck to the skin. The eyes were swollen shut, bulbous and insectlike. . . . One of the testicles was missing." Ultimate embodiment of male/patriarchal codes: the army, the soldier that murders and mutilates Félix's body; patriarchal code threatened by the intrusion of queerness.

- Page 87: the DA explains to Lena and Miguel Grande he "thought it useless to subject the family to the shame and embarrassment of such an investigation. The young soldier had acted in 'self-defense and understandably,' given the circumstances, and there was no reason to prosecute him."

Here, the instructor may want to refer to Ana Castillo's *Massacre of the Dreamers*, in which she discusses violent *machismo* that is the result of men feeling displaced racially, culturally, and/or because of economic hardships. She writes, "Machismo has divided society in half. It divides the world into the haves and the have-nots, those with material power and those who are rendered powerless. It has divided our behavior into oppositions, our spirituality regards Catholicism in dualistic terms of good and evil, and an economic world politic based on brute might" (82). Castillo, importantly, also discusses why same-sex desire and sexuality is a taboo in economic terms: "That is, the labor force and all its products are commodities to be given value by men and exchanged by men, but men themselves cannot enter into the present system as commodities. Overt homosexuality would disrupt the system in which men are not commodities but agents of commerce and is therefore made a social taboo" (80).

Another important theme to explore is that of the virgin/whore binary opposition in the novel. The novel reconstructs patriarchal images of women as virgins and whores only to uncover (to allow women to recover) their oppression and subjection to the patriarchal system. Here, it would be important to note that before the conquest of the Americas, there existed a more gender fluid worldview of the generative principles of life: The schools of philosophy during the Aztec empire—that included the philosopher-poet king of Texcoco mentioned in *The Rain God*—believed that all life was based on a unified masculine/feminine principle of creation. It was only after the conquest that the female-gendered deities were subordinated to the male. This coincides with the religious colonization that imported the Judeo-Christian image of the fallen seductress Eve and the Virgin

Mary: As a result, Mexican culture grew to mythologize la Virgen de Guadalupe as opposed to la Malintzin (la Malinche and more crudely, "la Chingada," the fucked woman) and betrayer la Llorona. As a result, such iconography is ingrained in Chicano culture: A good woman is "mother," Virgin Mary, docile, and submissive versus Eve, la Malinche, and la Llorona. Look at the following passages:

- Page 75: The narrator describes Miguel Grande's perpetuation of the virgin/whore dialectic: "On one side, his wife and the mother of his sons. On the other, the woman who brought ecstasy to his everyday life."
- Page 99-100: Mother/Juanita/Virgin conflate and we begin to see the generational perpetuation of the myth. "She was unreachable and incorruptible in the same ways as his mother."
- Page 164: "In her [Mamá Chona's] mind, she conceived him and the rest immaculately . . . Mama Chona denied the existence of all parts of the body below the neck, with the exception of her hands."
- Pages 61, 67, 68: The reader sees Lola defined almost exclusively in terms of her body/sexuality and is also, in a sense, the active agent only in her sexual life. Like Eve, la Malintzin, and so on, Lola suffers as a consequence of asserting her will; she also breaks down the female solidarity. Finally, one might discuss how Lola still defines herself in terms of the male gaze, functioning within the system of commodification in the sense that she remains an object of desire.

Finally, such a guide to the teaching of *The Rain God* will also provide the material for writing about paper topics that might revolve around themes of "recovery," gender and religious iconography, racial discrimination (overt and internalized), and bilingualism. For instance, I offered my students the following question to stimulate the writing of analytic papers. Félix's murder and mutilation make for one of the most poignant moments in *The Rain God*. The narrator tells us that the body "was unrecognizable.

There was no face, and what looked like a tooth was sticking out behind the left ear. [. . .] The rest of the body was purple, bloated, and caved in at odd places. One of the testicles was missing" (81). Examine ways in which *The Rain God* puts race, sexuality, gender, and class under a microscope, and consider the effects of these on the women and queer characters as compared with macho characters.

Migrant Souls and The Rain God

SINNERS AMONG ANGELS, OR FAMILY HISTORY AND THE ETHNIC NARRATOR
in Arturo Islas's *The Rain God* and *Migrant Souls*

David Rice

As historical narratives of an extended Mexican American family, Arturo Islas's two novels, *The Rain God* (1984) and *Migrant Souls* (1990), present constructions of Chicano ethnic identities that are based in struggles with family morality and history. Both novels are focused on the conflict between the third-generation Mexican Americans that make up the Ángel family along with the two generations that preceded them in the desert of Del Sapo, Texas. The first of the Mexican American generations is organized around the matriarchal figure of Mamá Chona, with her strong Catholic faith and her insistent prejudice in favor of the family's Spanish blood over its native Indian line. The second generation is comprised of Mamá Chona's children, all of whom recognize her powerful influence and either adhere to it as devotees or live under it with a measure of relatively unthreatening rebellion. By contrast, the third generation struggles most profoundly with Mamá Chona's seemingly pervasive moral authority over the Angels. In *The Rain God*, Miguel Chico is the character that represents the third generation—the generation that begins to seriously question the traditional family matrix; though he has succeeded intellectually and professionally, he is personally and psychologically unable to define himself within either his family or his society until he struggles with the facts and fictions of his family's ethnic heritage. In *Migrant Souls*, Miguel Chico's closest cousin, Josie, is equally embattled by the dominating ideology of the Ángel family. Her mother, Eduviges, and her aunt, Jesus María, uphold the family history and moral code established by their mother, Mamá Chona. Even as a child, Josie rebels against their strict rules and warnings against sin and, as an adult, she marries against their wishes, leaves her small hometown, and returns years later after the marriage has failed. Because of her pattern of infractions against the family ideology, Josie becomes marked as a rebellious Angel, so to speak; she tries to navigate the intersecting roles of her individual identity as a rebel, her responsibility as a mother to her two daughters, and her position as a moral outsider to the Ángel family.

Josie's relationship to Miguel Chico emerges in the second novel and establishes them as partners in crime against the monolith of Angel standards. As *The Rain God* clarifies Miguel Chico's battle with himself and his history through his desire to tell the Angels' story in all its complex truth, *Migrant Souls* deepens our understanding of Miguel Chico's confusion and pain as he empathizes with Josie's very similar struggle with family and heritage. Through the context of both novels, Miguel Chico and Josie come to represent the marginalized members of the third generation of Angels who have sought their identities beyond the borders of Del Sapo. As Mexican Americans who have pursued lives in the America outside their hometown, they recognize themselves as being on the border between the wider world of professional and personal possibility and the ever-present sphere of the Angels in the Texas desert. Mediating this border proves rather tricky, as all of the younger Angels must attempt to preserve a complex individual identity while reconciling themselves to the influence of the Ángel family identity that links them to their past. To further complicate things, their experience with the wider world has led them to question the bigotry and religious authority that pervades their family. As a generation, they find themselves doubly marginalized, both as Mexican Americans in the white-dominated world of the United States and as sinners among the Angels as they fight the ultra-moral mythology of their family with their actual experience as Angels in the real world.

The Rain God represents this process of marginalization and mediation in its attempt to organize a series of memories and revelations into a complex yet coherent history. As the central character of *The Rain God*, Miguel Chico emerges as a primary narrative voice whose liminal position within his family and culture informs the novel's attempt at organizing and reconciling the Ángel heritage and ethnicity. (See also Marta E. Sánchez's essay in this collection in which she discusses how the novel's formal elements also represent Miguel Chico's liminality and hybridity.) By framing the Ángel family's history within Miguel Chico's own search for identity, the novel shows that Miguel Chico's ability to tell his family's history is a necessary step toward understanding his own position as an ethnically fragmented character. As a storyteller, Miguel Chico must resist the polarized ethnic and moral categories of Ángel and sinner that threaten his identity as an individual. If he can find a way to tell his and his family's story so that such limiting categories can be circumvented, then he will have achieved a truer sense of both himself and his family as real, conflicted, and complex ethnic individuals. So, the storyteller's struggle to order his narrative becomes aligned with the ethnic individual's desire for a sense of his or her own history and identity. By telling the story of the Angels, Miguel Chico is able to re-envision both his position as a sinner and the pull of his family's unassailable and impossibly perfect idea of Ángel identity. He becomes a storyteller who envisions and reveals Ángel ethnic identity in its imperfect humanity and worldly complexity.

Because he is continually caught between ethnic standards of ideology, morality, and sexuality, Miguel Chico's liminality between cultural boundaries stands at the heart of his role as an ethnic character and narrator. As a Chicano who has become a successful college professor in San Francisco, Miguel Chico is intellectually and ideologically distanced from his family, who remain rooted in the ways and prejudices of their small hometown just north of the Mexican/American border. He is also morally separated from his family, having rejected both his strict Catholic upbringing and his father's tendencies toward philandering and macho posturing. In addition, Miguel Chico has survived a life-threatening illness that has left him dependent on a colostomy mechanism attached to his side. This creates possibly the most powerful symbol of Miguel Chico's otherness, as he internalizes the fact that his life, and thus his humanity, is dependent upon a machine. To Miguel Chico, this aspect of his body differentiates him on an essential human level. Closely linked to this sign of difference is the fact of Miguel Chico's sexual ambiguity, which stands as his most significant point of distance from his family. His lack of sexual activity due to his colostomy operation, as well as the latent possibility of his homosexuality, places him at odds with his family's standards of Catholic propriety and Chicano male roles.

Miguel Chico is not wholly of the Angels, nor can he ever be completely estranged from them. Even as he reflects upon his family "and especially its sinners," he recognizes that his liminal distance from the family has produced their "contradictory feelings toward him" (4). Despite their pride in his academic and professional achievement, Miguel Chico knows that "[b]ecause he was still not married and seldom visited them in the desert, they suspected that he, too, belonged to the list of sinners" (4). Given such a familial division between Ángel and "sinner," we see that Miguel Chico is not completely identified with either category; he is caught between the two and must mediate between them to find his own positioning in the lists of his family's history.

Miguel Chico's separation and difference from his family splinters his subjectivity and causes him to become utterly isolated from any solid sense of community. By negotiating his own ethnic difference and separation, his narrative is able to achieve partial reconciliation and healing for the Ángel family. As a result, we can recognize Miguel Chico as a transformative figure, a hybrid ethnic whose distance from a pure sense of ethnicity allows him to embrace separate identities simultaneously while prohibiting his ability to inhabit any one ethnic identity altogether. From his position as a hybrid ethnic, Miguel Chico finds the subjective authority to tell his family's story; in the process of his struggle, he is able to reconcile and reintegrate the separate pieces of his family and, thus, his ethnicity. (See also Antonio C. Márquez's article "The Historical Imagination in Arturo Islas's *The Rain God* and *Migrant Souls*.")

As the novel's symbolic mixture of Ángel and sinner, Miguel Chico is singularly able to move between these two typological categories and form a viable and realistically complex ethnic identity. Even as he remains connected to the influence of his family, his struggle to reintegrate his difference from that ethnic identity makes him emblematic of what David Hollinger has termed "postethnicity." According to Hollinger, such a vision of the individual as an ethnic consciousness "recognizes that individuals live in many circles simultaneously and that the actual living of any individual's life entails a shifting division of labor between the several 'wes' of which the individual is a part" (106). Though Miguel Chico often seems alienated from such a seemingly liberating project, his struggle to understand himself in relation to his family is just this sort of exercise; it allows him to embrace complexity and contradiction instead of being crushed under static, monolithic visions of ethnic purity.

The novel's construction of Miguel Chico's subjectivity begins with a recollection of his grandmother, Mamá Chona, and the powerful presence she represents to him. We see him examining a picture of himself and Mamá Chona that hangs above his work space; she is leading the young Miguel Chico down a busy street, and it seems to him that "[t]he camera [had] captured them in flight from this world to the next" (*Rain God* 4). As the staunch Catholic matriarch of the Ángel family, Mamá Chona's gesture of leading the young Miguel Chico to the purity of the "next" world seems appropriate. However, Miguel Chico sees himself as symbolically severed from the ascendant image in the photo. Because of his distance from her influence, the adult Miguel Chico has effectively relinquished her guiding hand and the path to the next world it once promised him. This recognition of Miguel Chico's separation from his grandmother is followed by the pivotal memory of her death scene, which begins and ends the novel's circular narrative. Miguel Chico recalls that his dying grandmother saw him "and said, *la familia*, in an attempt to bring him back into the fold" (5). However, it is clear that her call for Miguel Chico's return to the security of familial identification only intensifies the "lost, uneasy feeling" that marks his levels of separation from "*la familia*" and his Mexican American roots (5). Although he was once a favorite of Mamá Chona, he is now unable to reconcile her strict Catholic morality and ethnic identity with the complexities of his own separation from ethnicity and community. Miguel Chico's distance from his upbringing has allowed him to see the hypocritical imagined purity of ethnicity at the ideological center of "*la familia*." His constant awareness of this hypocrisy in Mamá Chona's Ángel ideology calls into question her power over his marginalized Ángel identity.

Mamá Chona's authority is somewhat diminished by Miguel Chico's worldly experience, but her importance to him remains central to the narrative. Although Miguel Chico feels alienated by Mamá Chona's dying gesture toward him, her last words represent an attempt to pass on important knowledge. By uttering "*la familia*," she is trying to convey her final knowledge of ethnic identity and the importance of family. Although Miguel Chico does not comprehend her meaning at first, his process of memory and understanding throughout the novel ultimately clarifies Mamá Chona's words for him; thus, when her death scene is replayed at the novel's end, Miguel Chico is at last able to recognize that "*la familia*" represents the key to ethnic identity that he seeks. Mamá Chona's final words are a cumulative gesture of her life's wisdom, a desire to transmit her story of the Ángel family as an understanding of ethnic identity. In this way, her dying gesture represents what Walter Benjamin says is the ultimate wisdom of story. He states:

> It is [. . .] characteristic that not only man's knowledge or wisdom, but above all his real life—and this is the stuff that stories are made of—first assumes transmissible form at the moment of his death. Just as a sequence of images is set in motion inside a man as his life comes to an end—unfolding the views of himself under which he has encountered himself without being aware of it—suddenly in his expressions and looks the unforgettable emerges and imparts to everything that concerned him that authority which even the poorest wretch in dying possesses for the living around him. This authority is at the very source of the story. (94)

The obvious difficulty with this formulation is that the complexity of such final wisdom cannot be lucidly translated at the moment of death. Though the gestures and words of the dying might be imbued with a sense of completed understanding, the inchoate nature of their transmission necessarily obscures such wisdom for the hearer. Because of this, Miguel Chico's initial interpretation of Mamá Chona's last words as "an attempt to bring him back into the fold" fills him with a "lost, uneasy feeling" rather than understanding. Still, Mamá Chona's death serves as the impetus for Miguel Chico's narrative search for his own authority as a storyteller. In a way, Miguel Chico must work through the problem posed by Mamá Chona's final words before he can begin to comprehend their importance to his identity. As Antonio Márquez notes, "Mama Chona forms 'the burden of history' that Miguel Chico carries,"[1] and the novel's narrative represents "his struggle as a family member and as a writer/historian to free himself from this burden" (12). Miguel Chico's struggle to understand Mamá Chona's final wisdom is also a process of grappling with history; in this way the novel posits that working through one implies attempting to resolve the other.

By the end of the novel, it is clear that Miguel Chico better understands Mamá Chona's final wisdom as a source for his own storytelling authority; his search for such authority through ethnic identity comes about as he unravels the meaning of *"la familia."* This process further echoes Benjamin's formulations regarding the storyteller. For Benjamin, the wisdom of the dying becomes the source of the living storyteller's authority. He states, "Death is the sanction of everything that the storyteller can tell. He has borrowed his authority from death" (94). Because Miguel Chico's narrative begins and ends with Mamá Chona's death wisdom, her words become a "sanction of" his search for authority and identity through story. By recognizing the significance of *"la familia"* to his ethnic identity, Miguel Chico "borrow[s] his authority" to tell his story from the wisdom of Mamá Chona's death.

Miguel Chico's ultimate understanding of Mamá Chona's dying words requires that he navigate several levels of conflict between himself and his ethnic heritage. One major point of separation for Miguel Chico is based in ideology. For instance, as a Chicano intellectual, Miguel Chico cannot reconcile himself to Mamá Chona's racist and classist beliefs regarding the Mexican domestics who worked for the Ángel family and helped raise Miguel Chico and his siblings. Believing that Mexicans south of the border were "ill educated" and "very bad influences" upon her children and grandchildren, Mamá Chona held the belief "that the Angels were better than the illiterate riff-raff from across the river" (*Rain God* 14-15). Miguel Chico's fondness for María, who was one of the domestics, forces him to struggle with and ultimately question Mamá Chona's adopted class prejudices. When María secretly removes Miguel Chico from the Catholic mass and tries to convert him to Seventh-Day Adventism, we see the effect on the young boy's identity. As she tells him the Biblical story of Satan's fall from grace, Miguel Chico recalls, "He loved hearing about Satan's pride and rebelliousness and secretly admired him" (16). Although Miguel Chico is forcefully retrieved from María's influence and temporarily convinced of her sin against the family, ultimately his fond memories of María reveal that this experience was a starting point for his criticism of Mamá Chona's ideological influence.

Essentially, Mamá Chona's idealized vision of herself and the Angels as ethnically pure is fed by her desire to distance her family from Mexican "Indians." Thus, her racism is incomprehensible to many of the younger Angels, whose experience of the world and their ethnic identity is much more complex. By situating Mamá Chona and her sister, Tía Cuca, as the purveyors of Ángel ideology, the novel reveals that "[t]he snobbery Mama Chona and Tía Cuca displayed in every way possible against the Indian and in favor of the Spanish in the Angels' blood was a constant puzzlement to most of the grandchildren" (142). Miguel Chico especially cannot reconcile Mamá Chona's authoritative influence with her ideological blindness to the truly mixed nature of the Angels' ethnicity. He sees that the rift between her purified vision of the family's ethnicity and the reality of its hybridity is at the heart of his own struggle for ethnic identity. Miguel Chico seeks to distance himself from Mamá Chona's prejudice in order to move toward a more realistic Ángel identity.

Still, attaining and keeping such ideological distance from Mamá Chona is not an easy process for him. Although Miguel Chico has renounced his family's Catholic faith and Mamá Chona's belief in the unassailable strength and unity of the Ángel family, he is unable to replace these things with any definite alternative. As an adult, Miguel Chico is still in a conflicted state regarding María and Mamá Chona. Upon hearing of María's death many years later, Miguel Chico refuses to follow the traditional family rites of the dead; he is, however, unable to find an alternative outlet for his mourning. He does not clearly mourn at all, but instead distances himself from anything that will remind him of *la familia*:

> He did not go to the park that day and did not think very much about Maria or the family in general. He and his therapist had decided that Sundays made him even more melancholy than usual because they were "family" days and he knew that though the park would be filled with all kinds of people, he would find himself drawn to the family groups, especially if there were old people among them. (24)

Miguel Chico must resist his desire to connect to such family groups and "old people" who, like Mamá Chona, represent the seeming wisdom and solid heritage of an extended family. For Miguel Chico, to attempt such a connection would be a search for surrogates, and he would ultimately be unsatisfied by the lack of a genuine familial bond. Instead of the park, Miguel Chico goes to the Laundromat, where "he would be in the company of those people who lived alone in the neighborhood" and who "would not disturb each other except to ask for change and would read their Sunday papers in peace and isolation" (24-25). In his decision to seek company amongst the isolated, Miguel Chico shows that his desire to distance himself from the oppressive and hypocritical elements in his life in "*la familia*" has left him with no alternative source of ethnic identity. He is adrift in a community of strangers because his liminality as an ethnic gives him partial connections to separate groups but no whole identity within any of them.

Indeed, Miguel Chico's hybrid identity has left him in danger of having no stable ethnic identification at all. He is still caught between the opposed influences of María's rebellion and Mamá Chona's orthodoxy, and his suspension between them is indicative of his divided ethnic status.

> In some vastly significant way, he felt he was still a child of these women, an extension of them, the way a seed continues to be a part of a plant after it has assumed its own form which does not at all resemble its origin, but which, nevertheless, is determined by it. He had survived severe pruning and wondered if human beings, unlike plants, can water themselves. (25-26)

By metaphorically comparing himself to a plant, Miguel Chico is able to stress his natural connection to these women as well as his variation from them. Because of the "severe pruning" of his colostomy operation, Miguel Chico's difference from his natural source is taken a step further. His otherness goes beyond the natural result of genetic variety into a vaguely unnatural realm where his very humanity seems cropped and mechanically altered. Miguel Chico's physical survival as a human dependent upon a mechanism creates for him a primary symbol of his hybridity and otherness beyond simple categories of Chicano, Ángel, and physical man. Because of this intense otherness, his desire to "water" himself is the impossible wish to generate an identity from himself and for himself, outside of his partial connections to other identities. His multiple levels of separation from ethnicity and humanity create in him a desire for utter transcendence. Such transcendence is inherently problematic because it is ultimately bound up with death. It is the passage to another, more perfect world promised by Mamá Chona in the photo at the beginning of the novel. However, Miguel Chico does not want to die in order to transcend. He desires a state of suspension in life in which his identity becomes both self-sustaining and self-enclosed.

Obviously, such an easy and complete resolution to Miguel Chico's conflict is impossible, and he is reminded of this fact by the very body that represents this hybridity. Lying in a hospital bed after his colostomy operation, Miguel Chico realizes that his ability to feel pain anchors him to the problematic real world of his conflicts. Because of his pain, he has fallen short of a full transformation into the pure moral category of Ángel that Mamá Chona had set before him: "Without this pain, he would have possessed for the first time in his life that consciousness his grandmother and the Catholic church he had renounced had taught him was the highest form of existence: pure, bodiless intellect. No shit, no piss, no blood—a perfect astronaut" (8). However, like many of his relatives who operate as "sinners" in various ways, Miguel Chico cannot escape the body in the ideal form that Mamá Chona seems to exemplify. Because he is rooted in the pain of his body, he is constantly reminded of his failure to attain the perfected status that Mamá Chona's ideology sets before him. In his failure to become the "perfect astronaut" who is the ethereal ideal of the Angels, he is forcibly reminded of his bodily connection to the sinners.

The novel offers a few characters who represent such sinners and who reveal a historical context of sins against Ángel orthodoxy. Primary among these sinners is Miguel Chico's father, Miguel Grande. He is an adulterer whose wanderings bring shame to his wife, Juanita, and the rest of the family, even though Mamá Chona's favor for him blinds her to his faults. Miguel Chico's memory of him, however, reveals the son's disgust at his father's sins, particularly his long-standing relationship with his mistress, Lola. As a repressed homosexual and Chicano intellectual with a history of frail health, Miguel Chico could not differ more from his father's boorish machismo and lustful wanderings. Miguel Grande, by contrast, sees himself in decidedly misogynist, macho terms: "Any man worthy of the name, Miguel reasoned, must envy the joy and excitement in his heart when he walked into places with a woman on each arm. On one side, his wife and the mother of his sons. On the other, the woman who brought ecstasy to his everyday life" (75). It is quite easy to see how such paternal wisdom was lost on Miguel Chico.

The intense difference between father and son emerges at a number of points in the novel. On one occasion, the young Miguel Chico was riding in a car with his father and Lola and "began to feel sick to his stomach" and "hated the smell of cigarette smoke" as "Lola and his father smoked all the way to her house" (68). It is clear that his sickness is as much a product of his disgust over his father as the smoke. Soon after, he notices that "[t]here was blood in his stool" and his disgust with his father is elided with his later, more serious illness. On another occasion, Miguel Grande ignores his wife's desire to have Miguel Chico checked for polio, and the father's stubbornness leaves his son with "a slight limp for the rest of his life" (95). For Miguel Grande and Juanita, "Their son's illness caused a breach between them that no one, least of all Miguel Chico, knew how to mend" (95). As Miguel Chico's distance from his father increases, his sympathy for his passive mother's situation intensifies his disgust with his father's sins and the hypocrisy he represents within the morally staunch Ángel family.

When his father finally reaches a breaking point in his marriage to Juanita, he is unable to choose easily between her and Lola and feels trapped within the sins of his past. Ironically, he turns to his estranged son for aid, and Miguel Chico is unable to bridge the gap with any gesture of understanding:

> Miguel Grande had consistently refused to acknowledge that his son's feelings and needs might be different from his own, and he had thus failed to help the boy understand life. Because [Miguel Grande] had not looked at himself or others truly, the son could see no way of helping him now. Miguel Chico did not want the responsibility of his father's guilt; he had guilts enough of his own. (94)

Just as Mamá Chona's "perfect astronaut" doesn't help Miguel Chico's ethnic identity, his father's mode of Chicano masculinity is not something Miguel Chico can accept, either. As a sinner, Miguel Grande is as far from Miguel Chico's liminal position as Mamá Chona is at the other extreme. If Miguel Chico is to achieve a position of ethnic authority, he will not be able to rely on a traditional gender role of Chicano manhood as a model. Miguel Chico's hybrid body and marginalized sexuality require alternative models of ethnicity and gender if he is to find a position for himself.

The novel does offer a disturbing precursory model for Miguel Chico's ethnic and sexual identity in the tragic figure of his Uncle Félix. Like Miguel Chico, Félix's life represents the struggle of a bodily sinner within the Ángel family. Although Félix was married and had children, he was nonetheless grouped among the sinners because of the family's hushed knowledge of his homosexuality. The Angels buried their awareness of his clandestine homosexual activity and his wife, Angie, silently ignored Félix's disturbing closeness to their son, JoEl. This latter triad becomes a shocking sign of the Ángel family's tendency to repress knowledge of its sinners:

> As the three of them slept more frequently together, Felix lost his passion for Angie, and he would wake during the night cradling JoEl on his side of the bed. His protective feelings for the child perplexed and disoriented him because they seemed stronger than his desire for his wife. In the beginning, Angie paid no attention and was touched deeply by Felix's love for their son. Slowly, without intending it, she stifled her own desires and lay awake watching her husband and son in their timeless embrace. (122-23)

Félix's incestuous desire for JoEl ultimately manifests itself most clearly in JoEl's later drug abuse and emotional trauma. JoEl lives on as a further manifestation of pain caused by the Ángel family's refusal to acknowledge and deal with its sinners. As for Félix, the Angels lose any opportunity to confront him when he is brutally killed by a young soldier whom he picked up in a bar. Félix's destruction makes some of the Angels hang their heads in grief, but " '[t]he family,' as usual—more concerned with its pride than with justice—had begun to lie to itself about the truth" of Félix's murder (85). Félix's example points out Miguel Chico's own dangerous position as a closeted sinner in the Ángel family. We are told that "Mama Chona's son Felix was not a respectable man," and that, in an effort to satisfy his officially forbidden sexual desire, he was "[c]onstantly on the lookout for the shy and fair god who would land safely on the shore at last" (115). This subtle reference to the legend of Quetzalcoatl as the shy and fair god not only links Félix to ancient and enduring Mexican belief systems outside of Ángel orthodoxy, but it also creates him as a tragic figure when he is killed by the very god he seeks. The connection here is to the legend of Quetzalcoatl, a god who was prompted by the shame of incest into exile from Mexico (Baldwin 9). The legend further posits that native Mexicans awaited the return of their legendary "fair god" and, when the explorer Cortez arrived, they believed him to be Quetzalcoatl (Baldwin 9). However, as history would have it, their mistake made it much easier for Cortez to overrun the native population (Baldwin 9). Félix becomes a kind of symbolic sacrifice; he dies as a native sinner whose cultural and sexual alienation have forced him into the shadows where he meets his doom at the hands of a vicious betrayer.[2]

As characters of complex ethnicity, identity, and sexuality, the "sinners" of the Ángel family become, for Miguel Chico, failed examples of "perfect astronaut[s]"; their struggles with their sinning bodies and Ángel ethnicities give the lie to any notion of a whole ethnic or moral identity. Through his connection to the sinners of the Ángel family, we are made aware that Miguel Chico's hybrid and marginalized status is largely situated within his sexual ambiguity. To his family, Miguel Chico is sexually suspect as an adult male who has yet to marry or have children. To probing questions on this topic, Miguel Chico usually replied, "Well, I had this operation," and he would "stop there, and let them guess at the rest" (*Rain God* 5). Even though he masks his sexuality behind his illness, it is clear that his hybrid body has complicated his vision of himself as a sexual being. He laments that "[h]e had forgotten what it was like to be able to hold someone, naked, without having a plastic device between them" and he wonders "if, on Judgment Day, his body would rise from the grave in its condition before or after the operation" (25). Thus, the colostomy device permanently attached to his side is again representative of Miguel Chico's imperfect hybrid status; his body, like his ethnicity and sexuality, is not simple and whole. Having a tube protruding from his side and the awkward situation of elimination through bags attached to the tube leads Miguel Chico to view his body as partially mechanized and somewhat unnatural. The psychological effects of his medical condition cause him to see himself as sexually undesirable or, at the very least, make him awkward and self-conscious. He cannot escape the pain of this knowledge any more than he can embrace the ethereal perfection of Mamá Chona's "perfect astronaut."

Because it denies him the transcendent completion he desires, Miguel Chico's body becomes the novel's primary symbol of his complex ethnic identity. Remembering the process of his operation becomes a way for Miguel Chico to compare it to the process of extricating himself from "*la familia.*" In the haze of post-operative recovery, Miguel Chico "longed to escape from the drugged and disembodied state of twilight in which he had lived for weeks. His uncle Felix had been murdered in such a twilight" (6). Félix's sexuality complicated the deeply rooted belief system of his family, and he was forced to live and die in a dangerous "twilight" existence without a pure, whole ethnic identity.

Because Miguel Chico has survived his "twilight" state, the pain of his conflicted past and rootless present remains with him, and he must find a way to tell his story and confront his divided identity. Miguel Chico's ultimate awareness of this comes when he visits Félix's son, JoEl, in rehab, years after Félix's brutal murder. Both Miguel Chico and JoEl are allied as "sinners" amongst the Angels, but their similar struggles for identity in the family still fail to unify them. JoEl points out the primary difference between them as Miguel Chico tries to escape the discomfort of a confrontation: "You're afraid of me. You hate the family and it loves you. I love the family and it hates me" (156). As Miguel Chico leaves, JoEl "[began] his litany" of "[m]*alcriado, malcriado, malcriado*, you've been bad, you've been bad, you've been bad" (156). In chanting *malcriado*, JoEl appropriates the term that had been Mamá Chona's "worst form of censure, for it meant that one was not only misbehaved, but that one had not been properly brought up" (161). JoEl's words repudiate them both as sinners and failures in the eyes of the family ideology.

JoEl's words stay with Miguel Chico "like an incantation" that "kept waking him during the night and coloring his dreams in the greys and blacks and dark browns Mama Chona used to wear" (159). Miguel Chico's troubled mind presents him with a dream of the "monster" that had killed Mamá Chona (159). In his dream, Miguel Chico is forced to confront the monster and, by association, Mamá Chona's hold over him. Standing with him on a bridge, the monster whispers to Miguel Chico, "I am the manipulator and the manipulated. [. . .] I am the victim and the slayer, [. . .] I am what you believe and what you don't believe, I am the loved and the unloved. I approve and turn away, I am judge and advocate" (159). Miguel Chico recognizes this series of dichotomies as the division not only of himself, but also of Mamá Chona and the Ángel family as a whole. The monster that killed Mamá Chona is the truth of ethnic disharmony and individual difference and, as Miguel Chico plunges from the bridge in its clutches, he "[feels] the pleasure of the avenged and an overwhelming relief" (160).

His symbolic death in the dream mirrors his route to survival as a hybrid ethnic consciousness. Just as he allowed the "monster" of ethnic contradiction to embrace him and possess him, he must himself embrace that monster in return; he must accept the contradictions inherent in his ethnicity if he is ever to make sense of his identity or his family's story. After the dream, Miguel wants to "make peace with his dead," and when he looks at the old photo of himself and Mamá Chona, he realizes that "[t]he white daisies in her hat no longer frightened him; now that she was gone, the child in the picture held only a ghost by the hand and was free to tell the family secrets" (160). Miguel Chico's renewed vision of the photo represents his completion of the transfer of knowledge that occurred in Mamá Chona's dying words. He is at last able to see the meaning of "*la familia*" as a process of embracing the disparate parts of his family equally; through this realization, he at last has a position of authority from which he can tell the story of the Ángel family in its fullest form.

Once Miguel Chico is empowered to tell his story, the narrative returns to the photograph of Miguel Chico and Mamá Chona and reveals the occasion of the pivotal image. Mamá Chona was taking Miguel Chico to visit his aunts, who are revealed as the main source of Miguel Chico's authority as an ethnic storyteller:

Much of the children's knowledge of the family's history as well as its scandals came from those visits. Miguel Chico learned slowly that his aunts Jesús María and Eduviges exaggerated about the good and bad within the family chronicles, that Mamá Chona preferred not to say much at all about their life in Mexico, and that only his aunt Mema told the truth (161).

The photograph that has haunted Miguel Chico throughout the novel is thus set into motion and the memory it represents moves forward. This process coincides directly with Miguel Chico's transformation from a stifled ethnic voice into an empowered storyteller for his family's heritage and ethnicity. Through his aunts, Miguel Chico not only receives all the gossip and wisdom of the family, but he gets the facts as well. Through Aunt Mema, Miguel Chico is able to understand the true Mamá Chona, the frightened woman who built a fortress of Ángel ideology to protect herself and her family after the Mexican Revolution. Because she lost a child to a sniper during the revolution, Mamá Chona renounced her Mexican heritage. She sought to erase her past in order to isolate and protect her family from future hazard by making them true Angels, who would exist above the scourge of the body and world. However, such isolation cut off the Angels from their true past and, because their ethnic identity was based on Mamá Chona's idealized construction, they were, in truth, rootless. Even the seemingly unassailable Mamá Chona was motivated by failure and fear in her desires for her family. Miguel Chico is thereby able to free himself of a large measure of guilt, recognize the Ángel family in all its bodily sins, and tell his story. The tyranny of the "perfect astronaut" becomes subsumed in the earthbound identity of true, if dirty ethnicity.

The end of the novel provides closure for Miguel Chico's story by amending his earlier recollection of Mamá Chona's death wisdom. Miguel Chico's renewed understanding of the death scene empowers his individual ethnic identity outside of the tyranny of wholeness offered by the ethereal Ángel family ideal. In the novel's closing moments, Miguel Chico's reconciliation with Mamá Chona coincides with Félix's return to her as well, as the latter's ghost appears to the dying matriarch. In this moment of reconciliation between the greatest Ángel and the greatest sinner, "Miguel Chico felt the Rain God come into the room" as a source of salvation for all of them (179). Accompanied by Tlaloc, the Mexican god of rain and lightning, Félix brings the possibility for replenishment and life by offering to reconnect Mamá Chona with the Mexican part of her heritage that she has denied. Félix has been closely aligned to the rain god and the Angels' Indian blood for most of his life. We learn that as a child, "he would run outside and dance when the storm clouds passed over, while his brothers and sisters hid under the bed" (114). Even when he is warned that he might be struck by lightning, Félix defiantly says, "Good, I'll die dancing," and his character is imbued with a sense of true connection to the ancient Indian heritage in his blood (114). The novel aligns Félix's symbolic reintegration into the Ángel family with the native Mexican rain god known as "the provider," who offered or withheld prosperity according to the abundance or scarcity of rain (Miller and Taube 166). Through his vision of Félix's return, Miguel Chico realizes that the family can be saved only if it is reconnected to the past that it represses and denies.[3] Just as it promises a kind of redemption for the Ángel family, the presence of the rain god also represents the novel's central symbol of replenishment and healing for the previously barren landscape of Miguel Chico's ethnic identity. He is finally able to say, "Let go of my hand, Mama Chona, I don't want to die" and she replies, "*la familia*" (180). In her dying wisdom, Mamá Chona assures Miguel Chico that his survival as an ethnic individual depends upon his connection to his whole family, Ángel and sinner alike.

Through its process of reconciling the lives of real people with the ideals of ethnic identification, *The Rain God* becomes what Erlinda Gonzales-Berry calls "a tale of sensuality (indulged in by the 'sinners' of the Ángel family) and repression (embraced and imposed on others by the 'otherworld' Angels)" (258). "Moreover," she states, "it is a tale of the great taboo that mediates between the inhabited space of the former and the desired space of the latter" (258). By imagining the "great taboo" of death as the site where family histories and stories are authorized and knowledge passed on, we can envision how Islas's novel situates storytelling and writing as central to the process of mediation that Gonzales-Berry describes. If the novel's primary problem of ethnicity hinges on the difference between real ethnic people and ideologies of ethnicity, then writing and storytelling become the way out of that gap. Thus, the novel suggests that, as an ethnic individual, Miguel Chico must communicate himself and his heritage in all its aspects. To do so is the only viable way for him to escape the crippling dichotomy of outcast and ethnic zealot, and find a middle ground where a real ethnicity can take hold. Through his final knowledge, Miguel Chico receives his storytelling authority from Mamá Chona's dying wisdom and his narrative finally achieves closure. Miguel Chico's history and identity—his story—*is* his very process of struggle.

In Islas's second novel, *Migrant Souls*, the struggle with history and identity is ongoing, not only for Miguel Chico, but for others of the sinning third generation of Angels. Chief of these in *Migrant Souls* is Josie Salazar. Though her position on the Ángel family tree is located on a branch opposite her cousin, Miguel Chico, she is in many ways a mirror of his own position as a hybrid ethnic and transformative Ángel. She is raised under the authority of Mamá Chona's ideology, but comes to resist it with increasing strength as her awareness of the wider world develops. Although more linear than the circular narrative of *The Rain God*, the narrative of *Migrant Souls* also utilizes memory and temporal shift to juxtapose the elements of Josie's struggle with her developing marginalized Ángel identity. We see her grow from a precocious, skeptical child into a complex woman who leaves her disapproving family and her Texas hometown to pursue marriage and family; when she returns as a divorcée with two daughters, she is forced to recognize her outsider status in the family, even as she maintains her unrepentant individuality against a tide of criticism and resentment from fellow Angels. In Josie's struggle for identity, Miguel Chico's role as confidant and ally comes into play, and both he and Josie must endure a painful process of self-doubt and inner conflict.

The relatively linear progression of *Migrant Souls* allows us to see from the outset of the novel that Josie was born to her role as a sinner against Mamá Chona's pure-blooded Ángel ethnicity. The opening passage of the novel proclaims that "[i]n their mother's eyes, Josie Salazar knew, she and her sister Serena were more like the Indians than the Spanish ladies they were brought up to be" (3). A rebellious child and teenager, Josie shows early signs of her ability to live up to her mother's vision of her. Even as she is indoctrinated into Ángel ideology by Mamá Chona's regular instruction, it is clear that she is restless and bored. On one occasion, Mamá Chona reveals that "[i]t's more difficult for girls to be like angels because they are born wicked in a different way from boys" (14). Instead of being shamed or angered at such a revelation, Josie simply shrugs it off as another piece of tedious litany. She simply thinks of other, less troubling things in order to fight off Mamá Chona's dogma and takes in the tableau of her sisters in the scene with a realist's eye: "She was growing very tired of the old woman's voice and did not like the daffy look on Ofelia's face. Looking away from them, she saw that Serena was just about to fall out of her chair" (15).

Like others of her siblings and cousins in the third generation of Angels, Josie also reveals an early ability to recognize a measure of the racist hypocrisy in Ángel ideology. One Thanksgiving, Josie and Serena insist on having turkey, dressing up like Indians, and "acting out the Pocahontas story and reciting from 'Hiawatha' in a hodgepodge of Indian sentiment" (22). Their mimicry of North American Indians perturbs their father and mother somewhat, and the girls are asked to refrain from wearing their costumes outside for fear that they might be somehow mistaken for Indians and be picked up by immigration (23). The girls' costumes, however harmlessly donned, still align them with a kind of native savagery that is anathema to Ángel ideology. Josie picks up on the true nature of their transgression, and this affords her an opportunity to seriously question the Ángel family's ethnic vision of itself:

> In the first semester of seventh grade, Josie had begun to wonder why being make-believe North American Indians seemed to be all right with their mother. "Maybe it was because those Indians spoke English," Josie said to Serena. Mexican Indians were too close to home and the truth, and the way Eduviges looked at Serena in her art class getup convinced Josie she was on the right track. (24)

What Josie gauges in Eduviges's look of displeasure is the level of transgressive border-crossing she and her sister have achieved. Their dressing up is not only an appropriation of *gringo* stereotypes of North American Indians, but it is also a gesture toward accepting their own Mexican Indian blood, which Ángel ideology seeks to wholly erase. Josie not only realizes the hypocrisy of the Angels' supposedly pure-blooded ethnicity, but she also recognizes her ability to transgress and satisfy her curiosity about the complexities of both the world and herself. Insofar as she is developing her position as a sinner amongst the Angels, Josie is certainly "on the right track."

Like Miguel Chico's narrative search in *The Rain God*, Josie's story is a biographical narrative wrapped in a simultaneously occurring narrative of the Ángel family. Although her tale lacks the circularity of Miguel Chico's story or the central vision of Mamá Chona's deathbed wisdom, Josie's story is nonetheless a compellingly realistic portrait of the struggle of hybridized and worldly ethnicity with a fictionalized pure family ideology and morality. Miguel Chico battles with the nonexistent status of the "perfect astronaut," but Josie has her own version of such an ethereal and impossible figure. While driving back across the border into the United States after an excursion into Mexico for the aforementioned Thanksgiving turkey, "Josie made the mistake of asking her father if they were aliens" (29). Her father's shocked reaction reveals the nerve she has hit: "He looked at Josie very hard and said, 'I do not ever want to hear you use that word in my presence again. About anybody. We are not aliens. We are American citizens of Mexican heritage. We are proud of both countries and have never and will never be that word you just said to me'" (29). Knowing that his skeptical daughter must be aware of the real reason behind his order, Sancho explains further that "'[w]hen people call Mexicans those words, it makes it easier for them to deport or kill them. Aliens come from outer space.' He paused. 'Sort of like your mother's family, the blessed Angels, who think they come from heaven. Don't tell her I said that'" (30). In this revelatory moment, Josie recognizes her father as an ally (albeit a clandestine one) against the monolith of Ángel purity and morality. Until now, Josie had chiefly aligned herself with her sister, Serena, and her cousin, Miguel Chico, but this connection with her father shows that her struggle with Ángel ideology is more than the simple youthful rebellion of one generation against another. The older second generation also struggles with being Angels, even if they do so in hushed tones and with unofficial comment. Sancho might seem to serve the Ángel hierarchy in his loyalty to his wife, sisters-in-law, and mother-in-law, but even he cannot completely internalize Ángel ideology and accept it as a valid, real ethnic identity. In this way, Sancho becomes another model for his daughter's apostasy against the Angels, and Josie embraces it because "[i]n her mind, she, too, suspected that she was an apostate but, like her father, she did not want to be an alien" (32). Josie can accept her apostate status and the potential for marginalization in the Ángel family that it promises her. However, she does not want to become an "alien" ethnic like the more orthodox Angels, with no realistic grounding for her ethnic identity. Nor does she wish to endure discrimination and injustice at the hands of a society and government that is all too able to reject her as a racialized "other." To allow the United States to cast her out as an alien would mean the unjust negation of her actual complex status as an American citizen of Mexican heritage. Her individual identity would be absorbed by a stereotype. Similarly, to allow Ángel orthodoxy to place her into an unreal, perfected Spanish identity would also mean a negation of her complex ethnicity as Indian, Spaniard, and American. Instead of allowing herself to be racialized as pure Spanish Ángel or heathen Indian, she wants to claim her real existence as something of both and, thus, she must embrace apostasy and reject alienation.

As an apostate and sinner tacitly backed by her father, Josie finds her closest ally in her cousin, Miguel Chico. They are connected by not only their contemporaneity and their moral marginality in the family, but also by their sardonic sense of humor and the emotional pain that such humor attempts to mask. The two of them find ways to solidify their bond as outsiders and share their critical attitude toward Ángel morality. In their youth, the two of them "had founded the Order of Saint Wretched so that they might laugh at misery. Passion, betrayal, unrequited love were all offered up to Saint Wretched whenever the cousins found themselves or others once again enthralled by the sins of the flesh" (57). As a satire of Ángel family piety, the Order of Saint Wretched becomes a way for Josie and Miguel Chico to make fun of the blind reverence and unquestioned hypocrisy of their family. She is a saint of physical passion and emotional pain who offers a worldly alternative to the pure, bodiless saints embraced by Ángel orthodoxy. Even as the figure of Saint Wretched symbolically thumbs her nose at her ethereal cohorts, she also represents a real source of comfort to Josie and Miguel Chico. They turn to her with questions and problems that are never voiced or given consideration in the officialdom of Ángel ethnicity and morality. Because she is a saint who accepts offerings pertaining to sins of the flesh, one can imagine the mass of physical and emotional pain that Miguel Chico has offered in his darker, more private moments. Similarly, Josie must have found herself confessing her early sexual curiosity and later physical passion for men, her emotional pain from her divorce, and her frustration with returning home as an outsider in her family. Saint Wretched stands for both Miguel Chico and Josie as a figure who bonds them in their pain and who becomes a silent intermediary to whom they can entrust painful secrets that they cannot fully voice.

Possibly the most powerful secret that Josie and Miguel Chico share is the fact of his closely guarded homosexuality. Though his sexuality can be inferred from scattered details in *The Rain God*, in *Migrant Souls*, his painful struggle with it is brought into higher relief. In fact, Miguel Chico's alliance with Josie becomes one of the few ways that his real sexual identity is expressed within his family. This becomes evident in one episode as he asks Josie frankly about the absence of a man in her life: "Come on, cousin, confess. Where is the man in this picture of distraught, almost middle-aged womanhood?" (119-20). Because "[o]nly he and Serena got away with talking to Josie in this way," we notice both their closeness and the boundary that is crossed when she shoots back, "God, Mickie, you know I have more problems with men than you do" (120). The awkward and somewhat cold silence that follows sparks Josie's revelation that she has reached a powerful boundary in her relationship with Miguel Chico:

It was the first time she had stood in a nonjoking way so near the gate of his secret territory. Years earlier and without having to be told, she had understood that her cousin was a lover of men. Their camaraderie as sinners was born out of that intuitive and unspoken revelation. When she became the only divorced woman in the family, they grew even closer and glowed in each other's company when sitting in the living rooms and dens of their relatives. (120)

Although Josie can sympathize with the general frustration and alienation that her cousin experiences as a sinner, her situation is also very different. She cannot hide her status as a divorced mother with no prospective relationships and, in her family's opinion, a sketchy moral past. Because Miguel Chico has been preceded by Félix's example, he feels the need to closet himself from his family and his hometown. Even when Josie broaches the topic, it is clear to her that their understanding and connection on the subject is to remain silently private.

In fact, this private silence on the topic is maintained throughout most of the novel. In one other instance it becomes visible again, as Miguel Chico confesses his pain over a lost love to his younger brother Gabriel. While the two of them are alone in a room of their aunt's house at Christmas, they are interrupted by their brother, Ricardo, who exemplifies self-assured Ángel orthodoxy. The reader enters the scene with Ricardo, but understands much more than he does about what is overheard. As Ricardo enters, Gabriel advises Miguel Chico to "Let him go in love," as Miguel Chico sits "on the bed with his back to the door, shoulders shaking, head bent in an ugly way, like a hanged man's" (217). Although the context for Gabriel's advice is never clarified, Gabriel's compassion and the depth of Miguel Chico's pain are evident. As Ricardo and Gabriel leave the room, the reader remains with Miguel Chico and is made acutely aware of his agony at that particular moment. As the door closes, we are told that Miguel Chico "surrendered to the devils" who "[i]n matter-of-fact, reasonable voices [. . .] told him he was not a child of the Church or worthy of the family name and that Ricardo should have been his father's firstborn son. Because what they said was true, the demons added, he ought to consider destroying himself" (218). Because this emotional crisis occurs for Miguel Chico late in the narrative of *Migrant Souls*, it seems to serve as a reminder of the fact that his struggle as a marginalized hybrid ethnic, as displayed in *The Rain God*, is far from over; in fact, it seems as if Miguel Chico's struggle with sexual and ethnic identity, like others of his generation of Angels, will never be fully resolved. That seems to be one of the lessons of *Migrant Souls,* as it presents no circular narrative or promise of great reconciliation or resolution. Its clear, fairly linear narrative simply shows the continuation of an ongoing struggle for identity among the younger generation of Angels. Ethnic identity becomes for them something that is continually fought for even though it is never perfectly achieved. It remains fluid according to the shifting cultural contexts of the people who claim it as a way of understanding themselves as individuals in the world.

For many of the younger Angels, education has become one way that they have attempted to get a hold on the shifting borders of their cosmopolitan ethnic identities. This becomes most prominent in the novel as the family gathers for Christmas and all of the younger generation has returned home and been reminded of their marginalized and unstable ethnic position within the family. Jesús María scolds the younger Angels by commenting that she and her generation had to sacrifice their own opportunity so that their sons, daughters, nieces, and nephews could go to college. Furthermore, she reveals her disappointment at the result of such sacrifice as she declares, "[c]ollege was supposed to help you, not ruin you" (146). Jesús María's son, Rudy, who is a lawyer in Washington DC, later provides a kind of response to the older Angels as he humorously comments, "I think the main reason we all went away to school was to learn how to explain that generation to itself," to which Jesús María replies, "We know perfectly well who we are. It's you who don't know that we are all God's children, even if you don't believe" (160-61). This family dispute provides a beginning for one of the novel's most poignant revelations about the complex and irresolvable battle between the Spanish and Indian components of Ángel identity. Rudy's skills as a lawyer prompt him to issue a somewhat drunken, yet still honestly lucid critique of Ángel identity.

> "The truth is," he began very quietly, "we don't know what we are because we don't know where we are. And where are we?" he asked in a louder tone. "Just like our souls are between heaven and earth, so are we in between two countries completely different from each other. We are the Children of the Border." His speech was beginning to sound like a *corrido* played and sung by *mariachis*. All were mesmerized. (164-65)

As his voice takes on the impassioned pitch of the Mexican *corrido*, Rudy proclaims the reality of Ángel existence in both a geographic and an ethnic borderland. He declares of his family, "[w]e are on the border between a land that has forgotten us and another land that does not understand us," and then asks the question that haunts the Angels' third generation, "So what are we educated wetbacks and migrant souls to do?" (165). Despite Rudy's education and prominent position, he is only able to come up with a comically improbable solution to his question as he says, "Let's keep the border and give both lands back to the Indians!" (165). Rather than propose any real solution or healing for the Angels' pain of marginalization on all its levels, Rudy only diffuses the difficult topic he has raised with a vaudevillian gesture: "Rudy's toast was greeted with a roar of laughter and applause from some, nervous titters and sorrowful looks from others, and shrieks of delight from the children when he staged a pratfall and spilled beer on his creamy shirt. Before he sat down, Rudy made the sign of the cross over them" (165). In the end, he can only assuage his pain and resolve the potential for conflict with the kind of satire that Saint Wretched represents for Josie and Miguel Chico. Certainly the laughter and satirical gestures measure some sort of catharsis, but no real ideological resolution seems to be forthcoming for the divided members of the family.

The primary difference between Islas's two novels lies in the distinct way each novel's structure reflects the process of striving to resolve fragmented ethnic identities. Instead of offering a final scene of possible redemption or closure to the Ángel family history, as *The Rain God* does, *Migrant Souls* suggests that the struggle simply goes on for those who choose to engage their ethnic complexities. Through Josie's narrative, we realize that neither cosmopolite education nor attempting to order or articulate one's history will ultimately make that history any more logical or manageable.[4] Josie is much more stoic in her ethnic struggle than Miguel Chico is in his. Her attempts to order or control her life center on raising her daughters and defending herself from the family's attacks with her skeptical attitude and biting wit. In a memory of her return to Del Sapo with her two girls, we see a fine example of the way that Josie has prepared her daughters to withstand Ángel orthodoxy just as she did as a girl. They approach the desert and, "[a]s the landscape changed from a wet green to a dry beige, Josie made them memorize all the names of the Ángel family and explained in what ways they were related. She also gave them their first lesson in Mama Chona's rules of perfection" (197). When the girls protest that no one could possibly achieve such ideal standards, Josie assures them that they need only feign perfection to satisfy the Ángel elders. However, Josie makes sure that her girls know that she is their source for more realistic values.

> "If you tell me the truth, no matter what it is, I'll stand by you. If you don't, I won't know what to do. There are some things you're going to have to figure out for yourselves. Just remember that life—"
>
> "We know," Hannah said, and then, as if reciting a lesson, "life is not fair and almost nothing makes sense. Be kind to others and tell the truth to those you love." (198)

This pragmatic moral is a distilled version of Josie's own life lessons in preserving one's sanity and identity in a confusing and contradictory world. With this gesture, Josie attempts to save her daughters from the kind of self-doubt and alienation that she has experienced as a sinner in the Ángel family. She is, in effect, making realists out of her girls so that they do not buy into the impossible ideals and hypocritical contradictions of dogmatic Ángel ideology. They are learning to play both sides of the ideological border convincingly while preserving their real identities somewhere within the gray area of the borderland.

In *Migrant Souls*, the wisdom imparted is altogether of a more pragmatic nature compared to the mystical, dreamlike revelations that surrounded Mamá Chona's death wisdom in *The Rain God*. If *The Rain God* is a process of translating the impossibly complex wisdom of Benjamin's storyteller, then *Migrant Souls* is about learning to live with the imperfect and often confusingly contradictory bits of life wisdom that are imparted by one's fellow survivors. This kind of imperfect, but still encouraging wisdom reaches Miguel Chico in a way that is less mystical than Mamá Chona's final wisdom, yet it is somehow more human. At the close of *Migrant Souls*, Miguel Chico is gripped with the same sort of emotional and physical crisis that characterized his struggle in *The Rain God*. As he rides with his family in a car and looks out upon the Christmas decorations in the town, he once again begins to connect his feelings of emotional pain and alienation with the physical and psychological anguish of his illness. In a scene of holiday peace and joy, Miguel Chico's pain is all the more amplified. We are once again led into his confusion: "Miguel Chico's throat began to ache. Who are these strangers? What are they celebrating? Who is this God? He could not feel himself breathe or hear the beating of his heart" (243). This sense of being overwhelmed and constricted by the seemingly unbridgeable ideological distance between him and his family brings to mind a frightening past experience with a spinal anesthetic in an operation. He recalls that "[h]e was told that when the medication reached his chest, he would not be able to feel himself breathe and that he need not be afraid," and "[a] pleasant numbing began in his toes and crept dreamily and methodically from muscle to muscle, joint to joint, like hundreds of razor blades chopping up his nervous system. When it embraced his ribs, Miguel Chico became panic-stricken and begged with his eyes to be put under completely" (243). Once again, Miguel Chico finds himself desiring death as a way of escaping the awful confines of his existence. Only now he is not aspiring to the ideal state of the "perfect astronaut"; he is simply looking for ultimate release through death—"driven by a desire to be anywhere except in this world. His eyes saw nothing" (243-44).

The narrative of *Migrant Souls* does not seek to match Miguel Chico's heightened sense of struggle with any kind of grand specter of family mythology or recovered history. No ancient gods or Ángel forbears appear to him now. Instead he is offered the kind of advice that Saint Wretched might give or that Josie might use to educate her daughters in the real ways of Ángel identity. This time, however, the advice is given by Jesús María, who reveals herself as a source of unexpected empathy for Miguel Chico's obvious sorrow. As Miguel Chico walks his aunt home later in the evening, she leaves him not with the wisdom of the dying, but with the wisdom of a survivor: " 'Mickie, I want you to remember what I'm going to tell you,' she said in the Angel manner of imparting wisdom by mocking it. She looked at him without pity. 'God squeezes our throats occasionally, but he does not strangle us' " (244). As Miguel Chico bids her good-bye and promises to pass on her wisdom about God to Josie and her daughters, we are left with the sense that some sort of connection has been made between these generations of Angels. Jesús María has been able to reach down from Mamá Chona's ethereal orthodoxy and offer Miguel Chico a kind of theological wisdom that encourages him. To envision a God who "squeezes our throats occasionally" but never kills us is to see the struggle of the world as a natural process—a controlled test that is part of the grand design. One's identity, ethnic or otherwise, is not blessed or punished by a judge from on high, but is instead periodically tested, like faith, for its strength.

In her advice, Jesús María assures Miguel Chico that this test, too, shall pass and that she recognizes the struggle for ethnic identity that he and Josie are engaged in. By speaking in a manner of "imparting wisdom by mocking it," Jesús María is communicating with Miguel Chico in a way that he and Josie might readily understand. Jesús María's advice is given in a tone akin to that of Saint Wretched; and like the invented icon, Jesús María is recognizing as valid the sins of the flesh and passionate struggles that come with being human. This newly revised angle on God is based in reality and pragmatism and subverts the previously dichotomous iconography of Mamá Chona's Ángel ideology. Jesús María's parting advice serves as encouragement to further struggle, not as a deathbed summons. It is not the wisdom of finality and wrapping up the family story; instead it allows us to see the story as ongoing. The lesson for Josie and Miguel Chico is that their roles as ethnic identities and narrators of family history are rooted in the very process of surviving and going on.

In this way, it is useful to recognize Islas's two novels as an exploration into the possible ways of imagining and ordering ethnic identity within one's familial and cultural history. *The Rain God* proposes a more circular narrative ordering of Ángel family history with a spiritually revelatory scene of reconciliation at the end. A solid sense of ethnic identity, the novel seems to suggest, lies in grappling with the facts and fictions of one's history and being able to sort out those facts into a more or less coherent personal and historical narrative. However, *Migrant Souls* suggests that such an ordering of identity and family history does not ultimately withstand the vagaries of time and change. *Migrant Souls* offers a corrective to *The Rain God*'s notion of a narratively ordered history and identity. What we see in the latter book is the fact that fluidity and adaptability to change mark the true transformative, hybrid-ethnic figure. One must always be able to embrace separate parts of one's heritage and experience, while still maintaining an ideological center in truthful and loving relationships with those closest to us. Even if the ideology of "*la familia*" proves too burdensome a source of identity, ultimately one might still find imperfect fragments of wisdom that encourage to one to forge ahead in the ever-complex and unresolved narrative of ethnic identity.

NOTES

[1] Here, Márquez refers to Alfred J. MacAdam's article "Carlos Fuentes: The Burden of History." Márquez notes MacAdam's observation that the "burden of history" provides the impetus behind a good number of Latin American novelists. He states that, "In [. . .] examining historical consciousness in Latin American literature, Alfred J. MacAdam makes this observation: 'Writing has now become the

means by which Latin America can learn to live with its ghosts, learn from them and use the burden of history instead of being crushed by it' ([MacAdam] 562)" (Márquez 3).

² In an interesting twist to the Quetzalcoatl legend, one form of Quetzalcoatl, named Ehecatl, is the god of wind who "was credited with 'sweeping the way' for the Tlaloque, the gods of rain and lightning" (Miller and Taube 84). In this way, one could read a symbolic relationship between the destruction of Félix at the hands of his "fair god" and this aspect of Quetzalcoatl as one who prepares the way for the coming of the rain god. When Félix's spirit returns to Mamá Chona with the rain god, such a process seems to have been completed.

³ Throughout the novel, there are a few references to the desert that surrounds the Angels' hometown and creeps into their homes and lives. The dry, barren element of desert sand certainly emphasizes the Angels' struggle for survival in a somewhat inhospitable environment. Most of the more orthodox Angels dread the invasion of the sand upon the supposed purity of their lives. Miguel Chico's godmother, Nina, is quite afraid that at her death she will still "feel the desert trickling down her throat" even after she is buried (*Rain God* 34). However, the encroaching desert also represents a cultural barrenness at the heart of Ángel ideology as it seeks to bury the native Mexican part of its blood and heritage. Félix is representative of the Angels' native Mexican heritage through his connection to the rain god. Even as Félix is beaten and left to die in the desert, he is described in his last moments as surrounded by water, and when he died "the desert exhaled as he sank into the water." Because of his connection to the ancient myth of the rain god, Félix is allowed to die a death by water so that he might find comfort in Tlaloc's realm of Tlalocan (Miller and Taube 167).

⁴ There is a rather interesting scene in *Migrant Souls* that makes a direct reference to Miguel Chico's desire to organize, understand, and ultimately write his family history in *The Rain God*. While visiting with Josie and her girls, Miguel Chico is given the following critique of his writing, which could be read as an overall critique of the project of *The Rain God* as an effort to reconcile and encapsulate family history and ethnic identity.

> "You have to stop writing about our perfectly happy family," Josie said. "The older generation does not approve. They think you're telling their terrible secrets to the world and they don't like it [. . .]."

"Some of the younger generation don't like it either," Rebecca said. "Grandmother told us that Ricardo read the whole book out loud to Alicia and that they both found it very upsetting, especially him." She sipped a pink and green margarita and gave him a beatific smile.

"Well, we knew Ricardo wouldn't like it," Josie said. "It's just envy. I keep telling them it's all fiction and they keep wanting to believe every word. They should be glad I didn't write that book. I'm not as nice as you are, cousin. I would have told the truth."

Miguel Chico's novel had been written during a sabbatical leave when he decided to make fiction instead of criticize it. A modest, semi-autobiographical work, it was published by a small California press that quickly went out of business. *Tlaloc* [The rain god] was an academic, if not commercial, success and its author became known as an ethnic writer. After seeing what the world did to books, he returned humbly to the classroom and to criticism. (209-210)

While this passage tacitly recognizes Miguel Chico's failure to successfully translate his ethnic history and identity neatly to the page (and thus the failure of *The Rain God* to achieve such an overly idealized goal), it also proclaims something of the project at hand in *Migrant Souls*: specifically, the way that Josie's realistic memory and narrative seeks to deal with family history and identity in all its tangles and irresolvable conflicts. One imagines that her biography would be more of a tell-all with none of the aspirations to organize and resolve ethnic identity for its readers. At the very least, we see yet again that Miguel Chico's struggle with his history and identity has yet to be resolved, much as *The Rain God* suggested that it might have been.

"EL CONTRABANDO DE EL PASO":
Islas and Geographies of Knowing

Theresa Meléndez

I

In the Texas-Mexican oral tradition, the corrido "El contrabando de El Paso" (c. 1920s) is a well-known border story of the fate of a smuggler who is apprehended in El Paso for having trafficked in illegal goods across "*el charco seco*," the Rio Grande River. Américo Paredes describes the figure of the smuggler as "an extension of the hero of intercultural conflict" (43) for Mexican border communities. The actions of border patrolmen, many from the ranks of the hated Texas Rangers, were notorious for their insulting and violent behavior against Mexicans on both sides of the river. The act of friends and relatives crossing the border with supplies was commonplace, and when Anglo law captured or attacked smugglers, it was seen as the continuance of a long tradition of violence against the Mexican. Paredes continues, "When the river became a dividing line instead of a focus for normal activity, it broke apart an area that had once been a unified homeland" (43). Given the historical ambiguity of the border for Chicanas/os and more specifically for Arturo Islas, I find the phrase "contrabando de El Paso" an appropriate metaphor to underline Islas's positioning of conflict and resistance, located within a critical spatial imaginary that is the city of El Paso, Texas. To read his works, especially *The Rain God* and *Migrant Souls*, is to read the city of his birth: its violent frontier tradition, its isolation from other major cities, its oppressive political history, its *mexicanidad*, and the power of its desert landscape.

The city of El Paso del Río del Norte (Texas) has a unique geographic and historical position in the history of Chicano literature and its antecedents for having produced authors who use the site as content and context. Those who have written specifically about the city, besides Islas, include: Cabeza de Vaca, Pérez de Villagrá, Abelardo Delgado, Ricardo Sánchez, José Antonio Burciaga, Carlos Morton, Dagoberto Gilb, Ray González, Joe Olvera, Juan Contreras, John Rechy, Ricardo Aguilar, Sylvia Chacón, Estela Portillo Trambley, Rafael Jesús González, Alicia Gaspar de Alba, Gloria López Stafford, Pat Mora, and Benjamin Sáenz. Famously, it is also the site of the publication of Mariano Azuela's *Los de abajo* (1915), written in serial form during the Mexican Revolution, a text—fragmented, autobiographical, polemic, proletarian—that prefigures the tone, style, and structure of many future El Paso writers. The El Paso area is in actuality the combined city, historically and culturally, of El Paso/Ciudad Juárez, today with a combined total population of some two million, a dynamic mix of interdependency and density that has produced a unique take on urban life and Chicano/Mexicano culture. Its backdrop is the enigmatic borderlands and its equally hard-to-characterize populations.

On the border of three states, Texas, New Mexico, and Chihuahua, El Paso had the fame as the Pass of the North long before the establishment of the two countries, and has been a major thoroughfare as border trade portal and railway center for Mexico and the United States for some time. This location has created a geopolitical focus that has given rise to Chicana/o writers whose works are embedded in its landscape—imaginative and real; with its multiple cultures—of all classes, genders, races, ethnicities, and sexualities; and with its economic bases—what has been touted as the four Cs of El Paso: cotton, cattle, copper, climate, and a fifth added laconically by Oscar Martínez, Chicanos or cheap labor (*Chicanos* 8). For the Chicana/o writers, El Paso represents and is what Henri Lefebvre describes as a field of encounters and exchanges (*Writings* 122-132) whose landscape is an active mechanism of power that "connotes a contentious, compromised product of society" (Zukin 16).

In critiquing social theory for having emphasized time (history) at the expense of space (geography), such theorists as Henri

LeFebvre, Edward J. Soja, David Harvey, Derek Gregory, and Sharon Zukin, among many others, have posited the significance of *place* as a formative sphere of influence that, along with history, encompasses economic activity, social structure, cultural identity, and symbolic community. Zukin defines place as the expression of "how a spatially connected group of people mediate the demands of cultural identity, state power, and capital accumulation" (12). Soja emphasizes the transdisciplinarity of the social theory he calls "*thirdspace*," which includes the study of the spatial along with the historical and social dimensions in human life and lays its groundwork at the feet of Lefebvre, especially with his publication of *La production de l'espace* in 1974, in which Lefebvre describes three kinds of spaces: the *perceived,* the *conceived,* and the *lived* (Soja, *Thirdspace* 53-82). That is to say, place involves the material form as well as the imagined, and the "lived," as a metaphoric synthesis of the two, in which the representational is simultaneous with the concrete—hence, a third space. In *Writings on Cities*, LeFebvre proposes an initial definition of the city "as a *projection of society on the ground,* that is, not only on the actual site, but at a specific level, perceived and conceived by thought, which determines the city and the urban" (109). Soja compares Lefebvre's lived spaces of representation to Foucault's *heterotopia,* "the space in which we live, which draws us out of ourselves, in which the erosion of our lives, our time and our history occurs." These heterogeneous sites are filled with Foucault's trilogy of "*space, knowledge, and power*" (Soja, *Thirdspace* 15). It is this knowledge set in the context of the material and the representational geopolitics of El Paso that determines how Arturo Islas understands and sets forth the characters and their actions in the two novels set in El Paso, *The Rain God* and *Migrant Souls*. In Islas's works, at least five topoi of geopolitical place constitute the intersections of space, knowledge, and power that have created sites of contestation:

    (1) The mountains as symbol of transition: geographic and historical passage; social barrier, mainly of class segregation in the modern city;

    (2) The desert as symbol of paradox: site of meditation/death; fruitful site of situated knowledge/sterile site of diseased

urbanity; opposition/analogy to the ocean and an image of California (to Islas);

(3) The river as symbol of the liminal: historical ford; bridge/barrier; the border as revelatory of social structure;

(4) The *mexicanidad* of its people, racialized and racially mixed, as symbol of identity: historical origins of El Paso/Juárez racial/ethnic identity construction, class attitudes;

(5) Miguel's body as symbol of desire: diseased, wounded, lame, loved/hated.

Except for the latter, these are topoi that are also found in other Paseño authors in writing about that city. These topoi are the narrative tropes that serve as points of reference in understanding how geography informs power relations in a place marked by race and class struggles since its entrance into the Western imaginary. They are geographies of knowing that the very landscape itself summons up, as material and social structures accrete hierarchical and asymmetrical dimensions in the history of the city. Here spatiality must concede to temporality; while the topos remains the same, its meaning may alter as history changes its characters and its narrative plots. In order to read Islas's novels as articulations of a particular material and representational space, one must understand how the tradition of registering El Paso/Juárez topoi is set out. The history of the representation of the city offers all the socio-geographic topoi of its river valley and mountain pass, the growth of its urbanity, and its peoples. In this essay, for the sake of brevity, I focus on only three of these: the river, the desert, and the *mexicanidad*.

One of the first instances we have of the representation of El Paso is found in Cabeza de Vaca's *Relación* (1542), written as a narrative in the style of heroic romance, which details the journeys of Cabeza de Vaca in the "New World" between 1527 to 1536, the last few years specifically in the southwestern United States. With only three men left from his arduous travel (including Estevanico, a man of Euro-African descent), Cabeza de Vaca gives us a brief description of the area around modern-day El Paso as being "barren and harsh," mountainous with a large river (99). Cabeza de Vaca's group, starving and weary, has the reputation of treating the Indians with tolerance and compassion, but the narratives, including Oviedo's account of it, relate the Spaniards' manipulations and thievery whenever circumstances allow. According to Cabeza de Vaca, the native peoples he meets there are varied in their customs and languages and are almost always welcoming and eager to meet the newcomers. In what scholars have identified as a description of El Paso, the men were led to "a river through some mountains, to a village [with] people's dwellings and permanent settlements" with people who ate beans, squash, and corn. The Indians give the starving men food and blankets and accompany them on their way to the North, after a "great celebration" (101).

Some seventy years later, Gaspar Pérez de Villagrá (1555-1620) publishes his *Historia de la Nueva México 1610*, in which he also describes the El Paso area and calls the Rio Grande "*el río del norte.*" Villagrá was the official chronicler and missionary of the Juan de Oñate expedition (1598-1608) into New Mexico and beyond. While that expedition was responsible for the deaths and mutilations of hundreds of native peoples, Villagrá recounts the journey in verse as an epic event of heroes traversing the far northern regions of New Spain, opening with echoes of the *Aenead*. In a reference to the myth of Aztlán, he says it is from this northern region that the ancient Mexican races originated, laying out the question of who belongs to the land early on. In Cantos 12 and 13, and especially Canto 14, entitled "Come se descubrio el río del norte y Trabajos que hasta descubrirlo padecieron, y de otras cosas que fueron sucediendo hasta ponerse *en punto de tomar posesión de la tierra*," he tells of the "discovery" of the Río del Norte as the expedition seeks the "pass through the mountains" in the land they will soon claim as their own (124-138, my emphasis). After failing to find the place themselves, they are led there, "guided by the barbarians" or "Arabs" (Alárabes); in reality, these are native men, captured after the Spaniards fight and raid the supplies of an Indian settlement (100). Describing perhaps the first known map of the area, Villagrá explains how one of the Indians, "like an excellent geographer," draws on the ground all the features of the surrounding area, including astronomical references, to "the location of the mighty stream" and the "narrow pass" (114). After traveling across parched lands, they find the pass with its swift, deep river so full of fish and game that Villagrá calls the area the "Elysian fields of happiness." The group meets with "friendly" Indians, exchanges gifts, celebrates a mass, and then performs a drama about friars entering New Mexico (122-125).

Thus, the earliest European texts about this area document the perceptions about the landscape and, we should note, its significance for trade, religion, cultural events, and as a meeting ground of diverse peoples. It is obvious that the rich river valley, surrounded by desert and rugged mountains, offers a respite for the native and the foreign alike, and that its geographical features have created a natural corridor that has been in use for centuries. The map drawn by the "guide" clearly shows us the importance this area had for its native populations. We also see with these narratives that the harshness of the environment can be mediated by the generosity of its inhabitants and their knowledge of survival strategies. However, its geography has also created a place of potential conflict, given the scarcity of resources and the eventual commodification of its geographically important trade routes.

The history of El Paso and the border region is replete with the political, racial, social, and cultural violence committed against border Mexicans (equal only to that against the native peoples) as national boundaries and economic rivalries shift, displacing *tejanos* and subjecting them to mistreatment by the U.S. and Anglo-Americans in a protracted series of "armed clashes, raids, thefts, rapes, lynchings, murders, and other outrages" (Martínez, *Troublesome* 80). These and the events of the secession of the republic of Texas, the Mexican-American War, the Mexican Revolution, and other military aggressions, left a legacy of racial enmity between the white and *mexicano* populations that hardened as the whites continued to force their political supremacy far into the twentieth century. Mexico also proved itself ambivalent to these *fronterizos* when their loyalties turned against it. One of the consequences of these events was to crystallize the border communities into self-contained entities, alienated and isolated from the mainstream of the United States and Mexico.

One of the most salient incidents of Mexican border unity is exemplified by the Salt War of 1877-1878, in San Elizario, a nearby settlement of El Paso, in which the native residents of both sides of the border "violently resisted the takeover by Anglo entrepreneurs of the salt beds which had been public property since Spanish days" (Martínez, *Chicanos* 7). Adding to the complexity are the many boundary shifts of the river in the nineteenth and twentieth centuries, which historically have been taken advantage of by the United States. The border as racial and sociocultural boundary clearly lacked definition. Furthermore, as border-related issues, such as immigration policies, nativist language and cultural debates, and severe economic depression continue, the Chicanos of the border remain in a persistent flux of racial and class tensions.

Chicano creative writers have given us their perspectives of these struggles along the border, and in El Paso specifically, exemplifying how they define social structures in terms of place: "Space in itself may be primordially given, but the organization, and meaning of space is a product of social translation, transformation, and experience" (Soja, *Postmodern* 79-80). For example, John Rechy, better known for his queer texts, such as *City of Night* (1963), uses the city as the besieged protagonist in his 1958 short story "El Paso del Norte." In this autobiographical, impressionist piece, Rechy begins a description of the city by invoking the landscape: the desert, the mountains, and the Rio Grande which "only geographically" divides the United States from Mexico, because he says, "the Mexican people of El Paso [. . .] are all and always and completely Mexican, and will be." In his sardonic style, he illustrates his border experiences with the violence committed against those who cross it:

> The Magazine also said, well, wasn't it natural, those wetbacks wanting to come into America?—Christ, they heard about sweet-tasting toothpaste. It really said that. And if sweet-tasting American toothpaste ain't enough to make a man face the Border Patrol (as Bad as L.A. fuzz) and the excellent labor conditions [. . .] well, man, what is? [. . .] (I remember a dead *bracero* near the bank of the Rio Grande. . . .) (129)

Rechy also speaks to the racism endured under the "burden of Big Texas"—its segregation, poverty, and discrimination:

> The hatred in much of Texas for Mexicans. It's fierce. . . . So the Mexicans live concentrated on the Southside of El Paso largely, crowded into tenements, with the walls outside plastered with old Vote-for signs from years back and advertisements of Mexican movies at the Colon. [. . .] So this, the Southside, is of course the area of the Mean gangs. The ones on the other side are not as dangerous, of course, because they are mostly blond. [. . .] El Paso's southside (the Second Ward) gave birth to the internationally famous Pachucos. (Paso—Pacho) (129-130)

(This is one of several variations of how the word pachuco came into being. Since El Paso's Mexican nickname is "El Chuco," folk etymology explains the invention of the term "pachuco" as derivative of it: to go [in the style of or to] El Chuco, or "pa'-chuco.") Moreover, Rechy invests the city with a queer identity: "there was a band of fairies [. . .] and this city became a crossroads between the hot Eastcoast and the cool Westcoast (fuzz-wise, vice-wise)" (131). Most of the text, however, narrates the participation of its residents in Mexican folk, popular, and religious culture: Mexican movies, holiday celebrations, pilgrimages, bullfights, *matachines*. His description of Juárez reeks with its destitution as he discusses gangsters, prostitutes, the mutilated, and its cheap tourist market economy.

He ends the piece with a lyrical description, in a very different tone, again of the landscape of the city in a thunderstorm (here in an abbreviated form):

> The Southwest sky. Beautiful and horrifying. And therefore Wonderful. Because in all the blunder and bluster of Texas about the wrong things, one thing is really so. The sky . . . is depthless blue [. . .] millions and millions of miles deep of blue [. . .] blowing with the wind, the steel clouds cover the sky, and *youre locked down here,* so lonesome suddenly youre cold. The wind comes. The tumbleweeds rush with it. And always there's the fearful wailing. (139-140, my emphasis)

What Rechy stresses in this conclusion and throughout the narrative is the contradiction of the openness of the physical space, the potentiality of freedom, in comparison to the restrictions that race and class have imposed. The immensity of the vistas under Texas skies belies the status of its Mexican communities, imprisoned socially and economically by the strictures set in place against them. Freedom and justice are as illusory as the depthless blue of the sky. Although the river does not divide the inhabitants, class does. The "quaintness" of Mexicano culture on the American side of the city becomes its degradation from border economies on the Mexican side, while the image of Cabeza de Vaca's and Villagrá's river of solace and nourishment is transformed into a river of death and human contraband. The *mexicanidad* of its people, standing against the domination of "Texas," is their cultural resistance against assimilation and homogeneity. What endures are the struggles of its people expressed in the "fearful wailing," which, like the cries of La Llorona, is an enduring traditional and symbolic lament over the reality of their situation. Rechy's lived space speaks to the paradox of Mexicans "locked down" into their social class in a geography of seemingly limitless expanse.

In the poetry of the 1970s, the writers, representing the city by its overpowering natural and urban landscapes, also focus on this problem. In Ricardo Sánchez's dark poem "El Paso," "Death stalks leisurely" through its streets of drug addicts, fast food shops, and poverty. Addressing the city, Sánchez berates it for calling itself an "international city" because it possesses "A taco stand on one side of town / A hamburger haven on the other— / and pancho dealing pot / for a hebe in between." Even its desert landscape where "The river is sand, / the mountains bleak" cannot overcome its malaise: "Yes, desolate, flat-painted el paso / even the thought of mañana tires you, / for bustle could not become you. . . . It is always afternoon siesta time for you / because you are / el paso!" (206).

What Sánchez charts is the pass through the river and the mountains, not as a convenient trade and traveling route, but as an empty and sterile passage. He condemns the City, not its victims, for its situation. Similarly, Rafael Jesús González in his "Sur El

Paso" paints the image of this barrio as drug- and alcohol-infested and in which "aquí no hay obsidiana / y la lengua castiza / está jorobada," but the reference to what he sees as the Chicano's loss of culture, both pre-Hispanic and Spanish, reads less certain of who is to blame (12). Juan A. Contreras draws a more ambivalent picture of the same neighborhood and its government projects in "Así Era Mi Barrio": "Color, Vida, Dolor, y Alegría / Mezclado y revuelto, día tras día; / Mi Barrio de presidios [. . .] Ladrillo frío brotando en el sol" (7); even though there are struggles, hope may still blossom in the sun. The Paseño writers frequently comment on the topos of the river as representative of the city and re-create its image in different guises. José Antonio Burciaga's "Rio Grande, Río Bravo" focuses on the material conditions of the river as a site of both exploitation and unity: "The river now but a stream, a canal of mechanized concrete and the water is hoarded by Gabacho dams up north. Many trips were made across that bridge never losing stride never changing money, language or customs" (*Undocumented Love* 13-14). The white power structure has transformed the once swift river for control of the water, victimizing the river itself, but has not been able to create a viable boundary. Instead, the border residents are reminded of their commonalties even as they cross the border; the city cannot be easily divided. However, when Abelardo Delgado addresses the river in "El Rio Grande," described as "jorobado, arrugado, seco, como viejo mal cuidado," he believes just the opposite: "eres tu la puerta más cruel y la más dura / separas al hombre y haces de su ambición basura / leí que se ahogo un mejicano que te quizo cruzar." Although the river represents and is death for those who cross into the United States seeking their fortune, Delgado predicts the death of the river itself, a future without borders: "un día tus fuerzas como las fronteras se van a acabar [. . .] / hablame pronto Río Grande que el tiempo te va a matar" (21). The 1980s find little change in the perspective on the death-tinged river as illusory promise, as Alicia Gaspar de Alba writes in "La Frontera." With its sides always wet with water or blood, her river is a prostitute and temptress who mocks and kills those who believe her: "En ese cuerpo de sueños nadan los mexicanos / por años la piel tiesa y sofocada / los ojos pardos" (57). The only possible dream for those who consort with her, who believe in her promises, is death. Benjamín Sáenz, in "Juárez: From My Window," offers a meditation on those dreams and aspirations. He studies the iconography offered by both urban and geological structures of the city. From his perspective on the American side, he looks out at the city through his brother and sister's contentious points of view. To his sister, the city towers are "castles," to his brother, "empty temples." The Mexican houses in their bright colors are "grotesque" to his sister "with her North American eyes," but to his brother "with his Chicano accent" they're "like colors on a canvas." His brother speaks of the treasures buried in the Juárez mountains and the beauty of its peaks, while his sister says, "It looks exactly like a poor mountain— / poor as the river." But Sáenz gives us a third perspective: "I should like to step into that scene . . . [of] my brother's dreams, my sister's eyes. And search for my window from the other side" (45-47). Acknowledging the disparate views of the fronterizos, Sáenz reminds us of the "thirdspace" that combines the concrete and the imagined into one space that offers a new vision and possibly a new way of knowing.

In this brief overview of poems and short stories centered on El Paso by Chicana/o El Paso writers, the city is most often represented by the symbol of the river, and its inhabitants by the racialized and segregated Mexicans. The two tropes of river and *mexicanidad* converge in a fractured urban space of violence and poverty. Although the topoi of mountains and desert are also present, the river becomes the most significant trope for the contradictory division/unity of the city. Its representation as border boundary is certainly apparent, but the fragmentation of its populace and the city is more readily seen in the exclusions of class and in the spatial impositions of its economy than in its differing nationalities. While the symbolic landscape of the modern urban city can convey, what Zukin calls "a sense of rupture and discontinuity," representing the destruction "of longevity, of cultural layers, and of vested interest" (27), El Paso/Ciudad Juárez also offers the continuity of its geological formations and the stability of its cultural wealth. These continuities and discontinuities play into the sociopolitical consciousness of its population, especially for those on the lower rungs of the political hierarchy. In this way, our writers symbolically reproduce a physical space of material nature, the river, as a mental sphere for political awareness.

II

For Arturo Islas, embedding El Paso history—the situation of the city and its inhabitants—is primary to his unraveling the nature of his protagonists' dilemmas. The love/hate relationship they have with the city, the push and pull of their cultural loyalties, their defining personal experiences, are all indissoluble from the mystique of its geography. Family relationships are indelibly stamped by the pervasiveness of racial tensions and conflicts, steeped in the continuous political and economic competitions of the city. The obliteration of border history by the dominant population further exacerbates the existential 'contraband' status of its *mexicano* population. Islas recreates the city as a paradox of ambiguities and ambivalences that scars and nurtures the lives of his characters that forms, in Edward Soja's words, a "mix of opposition, unity, and contradiction which defines a sociospatial dialectic" (*Postmodern Geographies* 77). Neither simply Mexican nor American, the city as geopolitical space is innocent and guilty of historical injury, and in this liminal space, its characterizing "border" marks not so much a boundary, as it does a historical and social *memento mori* of U.S. imperialism, exposing the casualties of its power wars.

The city in Islas's novels is concretely represented by the trope of the desert. The desert with its barren and solitary wastes is, perhaps ironically, a fruitful trope to indicate the physical and social alienation of its populace, living on the margins of social justice. His posthumously published novel, *La Mollie and the King of Tears*, offers a clear example of how the desert functions for Islas symbolically and how the city becomes a space to explore the interconnections of his experiences, perceptions, and imagination. It describes one day in the life of Louie Mendoza, former pachuco from El Paso, as he recounts his life to an unnamed researcher in a San Francisco hospital waiting room. While he lives in San Francisco in body, he conceptualizes all he sees and says in scenes from old Hollywood movies and Shakespearean plays, and in much the same way, images of his hometown. The city becomes not only a referential landscape, one of fractured dreams of his youthful forays in school, the barrio, Juárez, alone or with his gang, but also the agent and site of his identity formation. As a fictionalized actor, El Paso joins the cast of Louie's stream of characters that make up his imagined and exaggerated life, including a brief glimpse of Miguel Ángel as a Stanford student, teaching writing at a mental facility. As a sensory experiment, Miguel offers him a smell of sage, which immediately conjures up the city: "the whole desert in bloom came outta nowhere . . . the sage all purple against the wall separating the projects from the Border Highway [. . .]. I wasn't gonna let no Stanford fairy know he could get to me with some spice in a jar. 'I know,' I said, making myself come outta my desert dream. 'It smells like Texas Ranger armpit juice'" (130-31). For Louie, El Chuco is the place of family and culture, but more emphatically, the desert of Texas racism and border poverty, at once a trope of pleasure/pain to which he keeps returning, in memory and imagination if not in deed. The past, held in memory because of its personal significance to the character, explains how the present signifies; it is the knowledge that shapes the moment. Louie's narrative, then, becomes an intensified moment of recognition of his place, dreaming California, but living Texas. "Texas is the strangest state of mind," Louie says (78), one that he cannot escape.

Although it is the desert that filters every scene in *The Rain God*—as emphasized by the subtitle, *A Desert Tale*—the novel opens tellingly with a description of an elliptical urban scene: a photograph "taken in the early years of World War II by an old Mexican photographer who wandered up and down the border town's main street on the American side" (3). It pictures Miguel Chico and his grandmother, Mamá Chona, walking the streets of the city, hand in hand: "Because of the look on his face, the child seems as old as the woman. The camera has captured them in flight from this world to the next" (4). While the border town is a thinly-veiled El Paso, never mentioned by name, this opening focuses on the three figures very central to the novel: the young man, his grandmother, and the border city. The three loom over Miguel Chico's head in his study as a literal and metaphorical reminder of the interconnections of his past, caught in a liminal web of family relationships and situated knowledge. Islas describes the boy and his grandmother in formal dress, separated from the street life around them in a gaze of intense preoccupation, each with a foot off the ground. Each, however, is intertwined with the other and both are seeking escape "in flight." Whatever its truth as representation, the figures as described by Miguel Chico constitute for him both his alienation and his involvement, his struggles to flee from the meaning of that urban scene at the same time that he remains captivated by it. The use of the photograph to open the narrative signifies the importance of the imagined urban landscape and its embeddedness in the lives of its characters, even as its synthesizing eye is an anonymous, nomadic, Mexican one, a characteristic that serves to underscore its historical perspective of United States-Mexico relations. The subtext in the image is the city's urban border experiences. Islas's compression of space-time here is an example of what Lefebvre calls a transfomation of history into representation, "from action to memory, from production to contemplation" (*Production* 21). It is this image of stasis that Miguel Chico, or Mickie, as he is alternately called, hopes to deconstruct and to displace as he contemplates his life under the threat of a deadly illness. He wants to disclose the social processes that have created his family and its "sinners," a category that includes him because, as he says, "he was still not married and seldom visited them in the desert"—an allusion to his homosexuality not revealed directly until the second novel (4). He also, with this sentence, equates the desert with the city.

The desert is not only the literal landscape of his hometown, but also the marker of his estranged and barren relationship to his family. In the "disembodied state of twilight" of the illness he describes early in the novel, the violence of the desert and the pain of his diseased body converge in multiple images: "he longed to return to the desert of his childhood, not to the family but to the *place* [...] the desert was very much in his mouth [...] the fear of being buried in the desert [...] his uncle Felix had been murdered in such a twilight" (5-6, my emphasis). The desert of his childhood is the place that informs his understanding of his people, his family, and himself. This seeming contradiction of the longing for and the rejection of his family occurs because of his compulsion to eke out the secrets of his dead, the innocent and the sinners; in fact, the narrative's most salient motif is death. Each chapter centers around the death of a loved one, as the inscription has forewarned: "I come to speak through your dead mouths." Even from his cool and foggy California garden, Miguel Chico is reminded antithetically of the desert. It is the desert landscape, the natural and the conceived, that he (or Islas) represents as a deathspace in a melding of the concrete and the representational; one of the earliest scenes in the novel that sets up this preoccupation is the memory of visiting the desertlike cemetery after a young friend's death (9-13).

The desert, however, has another equally forceful significance as a site of meditation in the tradition of prophets who wander solitary into the desert to receive visions. From Mickie's perspective, he seems quite aware of the desert's double valence of death/thought because he believes he has survived his illness and colostomy in order to understand and relate the complexities of his family's history. Only then will he be able to "shape himself ... He believed in the power of knowledge" (28). But at the beginning of the narrative, his self-reflexive mode is flawed: "He was still seeing people, including himself, as books. He wanted to edit them, correct them, make them behave differently," and yet, unlike his grandmother, he "wanted to look at motives and at people from an earthly, rather than otherworldly, point of view" (26, 28). The fact that the family is called "Ángel" underlines the significance of this desire since the matriarch of the family values "pure, bodiless intellect" (8). The *earthly* point of view cannot be angelic, however, as Miguel's painful illness reminds him; the earthly in Islas's schema appears to fall squarely on physicality, not only of the body, but also of the desert, yet the body/person, like the desert, is transformed as it is conceptualized "in an altered form, like a plant onto which has been grafted an altogether different strain of which the smelly rose at his side [. . .] was only a symbol" (28).

The desert trope is found in many scenes, but most notably in the presence of the death of one of his relatives: after Tony's drowning, at Félix's murder, upon Tía Cuca's death, and at the deathbed of Mamá Chona. What Islas achieves by conflating the city, the family, death, and the desert, is the spatialization of death. In this manner, the mental space of cognition and representation reproduces the physical space of nature into a symbolic spatiality. When Uncle Ernesto is looking out at the desert after his son Tony's death, he has a vision of desolation: "He thought he had always loved it, but now he understood that he had accepted it as a given fact, like breathing . . . bitterness and despair wrestled with his soul. Both were as dry and timeless as what he was gazing at; only his uncertainty was mortal" (50). His son's death has given him a new understanding of the world, in which the natural is denaturalized, both the desert and death. By this process, he understands his human condition as one of doubt and mortality, as Miguel Chico says elsewhere, "to those who live on earth, humility is a given and not a virtue" (29). From this minor but significant example, we see how Islas incorporates the barrenness of family relations and tragedies into the spatiality of the desert, while at the same time formulating the desert as a vehicle of knowledge. The central focus of the novel, however, the violent murder of Mickie's Uncle Félix, has little to do with family relations, and Islas takes pains to contextualize its setting in the desert, that is, the city. In this nonlinear narrative, the reader has learned about this event earlier, but the murder is fully realized in the chapter entitled "Rain Dancer," which opens with a careful description of the city, coded with natural and political features:

> The border town where Felix spent most of his life is in a valley between two mountain ranges in the middle of the southwestern wastes. A wide river, mostly dry except when thunderstorms create flashfloods, separates it from Mexico. Heavy traffic flows from one side of the river to the other, and from the air, national boundaries and differences are indistinguishable. (113)

But it is just these "boundaries and differences" that are at stake. In the twilight of his study in California, Mickie reminisces about his uncle, and in this way, the reader learns of the details of his life and murder. Félix is a labor contractor, the "loathsome" coyote for Mexican workers, the "middleman between them and the promises of North America" (115). As such, he exists in a liminal place, neither owner nor laborer, in a symbolic domain of transition between fixed social categories, and thus relegated to the margins and rendered ambiguous. The border, like all borders, is a place of ambiguity also peopled by the border-crossers, whose status as "undocumented" or "illegal" reduces their humanity and their rights as well as the possibility of legal retribution for any adversity that may occur.

As a marginal person, defined by Victor Turner as "simultaneously members (by ascription, optation, self-definition, or achievement) of two or more groups whose social definitions and cultural norms are distinct from, and often even opposed to, one another" (233), Félix shares the space with the migrant foreign workers, with his wife of mixed ethnic origin, and by extension, with all his family. This liminality is Islas's root paradigm for Félix, not only in his job, but also in the space in which his sexuality lies, neither conventionally married nor exclusively seeing men, and in the space in which his murder takes place, neither day nor night, but in the twilight of the desert canyon. Even the name "Ángel" connotes a disembodied spirit, neither human nor divine, which can traverse the land of the living and the dead, i.e., the dead Félix's return at his mother's deathbed. The ambiguity of his position falls in all areas. Because of his support for them, in spite of his predatory labor position, the workers, for the most part, like him, and overlook and accept his sexuality. The sexual overtones of Félix's encounter with the eighteen-year-old soldier who kills him leave open the question of whether the young man fully understood Félix's advances, and the ferocity of the murder puts in doubt the soldier's own sexuality. This ambiguity extends into another symbolic device that Islas employs for Félix, the Queztalcoatl myth: "Constantly on the lookout for the shy and fair god who would land safely on the shore at last, Felix searched for his youth in obscure places on both sides of the river" (115). By inhabiting the place of myth, Félix participates in a cosmology that authorizes his actions, and in fact, elevates them to the sacred, that is, the set apart or the liminal. The values and cultural norms of his family and society would then no longer obtain, outranked by the greater force of myth. Within this sphere, his sexuality would not seem to carry the same threat it embodies to the social structure of the staid Ángel family. But it is not only the domain of his Mexican family that Félix operates in, nor is it only his sexuality that puts him at risk. He also inhabits the larger society "whose social definitions and cultural norms" he opposes by representing a people with a long history of resistance against control. Engaging in contraband, he is caught and punished. Even when dying, Félix inhabits a neither/nor place. As Félix lies beaten, "his mouth was full of the desert and then it was not," and as he imagines lying inexplicably "surrounded by water" on the desert floor, "The desert exhaled as he sank into the water" (137-138). Islas demonstrates that the marginalized are not exempt from social strictures, that enforcing boundaries is the work of the elite, and close at hand, differences do matter. We discover that, for someone like Félix, the final resolution of his ambiguity is death.

For Miguel Chico, it becomes increasingly paramount that he find a resolution that embraces life, not death. Even from California, where he sought refuge in distance and in status, he cannot escape the city of death that El Paso has come to signify for him. Because his ambivalent feelings toward his family are analogous to and intertwined with his attitude toward El Paso, it is this place, the desert, where he must search for meaning. The violent death of Félix serves to encapsulate the alienated and tortured relationship that Islas, through Miguel Chico, has with the city. The fact that Félix's murderer is a soldier underlines El Paso's frontier traditions, the militarization of the border, and its displacement into U.S. territory. Fort Bliss, the army base, was established after the Mexican-American War as an outpost for the United States to protect its most recent acquisition and to quell any disturbances that might surface. The fact that the murderer is white fits the image of the returning god and the city's power structure, as does the fact that there is no retribution for his crime. For the most part, Chicanos in El Paso, socially and economically, have remained on the fringes, kept in place by the structural barriers of a hardened, wealthy elite. Félix, like most of the Mexican population, operates on the margins of industry in El Paso; even Miguel Grande's job as a policeman, an arm of the power structure, does not grant him the ability to seek justice for his brother's death. Murder victim or police official, both are Mexican and it is that identity, that contraband, that is foremost in their treatment.

In grief over the death of Félix, Miguel Chico dreams that he wrestles with a death monster on a high bridge, who taunts him with paradoxes: "I am the victim and slayer [. . .] I am what you believe and what you don't believe, I am the loved and the unloved. I approve and turn away, I am judge and advocate" (159). The dream, set significantly in California, ends with Miguel Chico's plunging into the sea with the monster in his arms; by doing so, he cuts the Gordion knot of liminalities—and immediately feels relief. The deadlock of ambivalences and ambiguities that he has created, he also has the power to undo. By the end of the narrative, as we follow Miguel Chico's acquisition of this knowledge, we have accumulated numerous details about the Ángel family in scenes that uncover motives and perhaps explain behaviors and incidents that may mitigate his family's behavior. History, it appears, does have something to teach him; people and events have a context that must be understood. What is most important for his agency is the process of meditation that he underwent: "He needed very much to make peace with his dead, to prepare a feast for them so that they would stop haunting him. He would feed them words and make his candied skulls out of paper" (160). At the end of the novel, set at Mamá Chona's deathbed and from her point of view, the narrator revisits the scene, and Miguel Chico says: "Let go of my hand, Mama Chona. I don't want to die" (180). His grandmother's death is not the event that changes his attitude, for we have learned of it in the first chapter (5); it is the stultifying images of her, his family, and the city, merged and indistinct, that he must unravel and then discard. With this new knowledge, Miguel Chico metaphorically releases himself from the image in the photograph and grants absolution as well to the desert by signifying its potential for growth: "[It] smelled like the desert after a rainstorm." In *Migrant Souls,* Islas's second novel about the Ángel family, one of the characters remarks:

> The truth is [. . .] we don't know what we are because we don't know *where* we are. *And where are we?* [. . .] Just like our souls are between heaven and earth, so are we in between two countries completely different from each other. We are Children of the Border. . . . This was Mexico before it was the land of liberty and equality for some. And before that, it was Indian territory. They knew how to live in it. So where are we? [. . .] We are on the border between a land that has forgotten us and another land that does not understand us. [. . .] So what are we educated wetbacks and migrant souls to do? Let's keep the border and give both lands back to the Indians! (164-165, my emphasis)

Because of the long history of national wars, local political battles, and race and class struggles along the border, the El Paso/Juárez *mexicano* identity cannot be disentangled from the place. The *what* cannot be discerned without the *where* for the "Children of the Border," united by their *mexicanidad* and their oppression. This stance is similar to a position taken by other El Paso writers and also articulated by CASA (the Center for Autonomous Social Action), organized by longtime activist Bert Corona in CASA's newspaper, *Sin Frontera* (1976-1979). The organization rejected the idea of a political border because it believed that what transcended the ethnicity of the border Mexican workers was their class oppression; it believed that the struggles of the Mexicans on both sides of the border could, in time, destroy this artificial creation (García, "La Frontera" 105). This exclamatory speech also reappropriates and realigns the region for its inhabitants by unmarginalizing the border as the peripheries of two nations, and marking the centrality of its place. In this novel, Islas's topos is the what, the *mestizaje* of the Chicano, the place that its mixed racial identity holds in its conceptualization and representation among Chicanas/os and mainstream society in the city. The shifting ethnic and racial loyalties of the Ángel family are as unstable as the border, whose very land changes nationalities with the shifting river channels, not to mention national interests.

The matriarch Mamá Chona, Encarnación Olmeca, whose ironic name is literally the *embodiment* of the ancient origins of the Mexican and the personified actualization, is also the staunchest purveyor of racial hatred against her indigenous heritage. The rest of the family runs the gamut of ignoring, accepting, rejecting, or embracing their *mestizaje*. This theme was also found in *The Rain God*, but in this novel, the Indian/Spaniard opposition is much more apparent as we find it mentioned repeatedly throughout the two books. Josie, Miguel Chico's cousin and comrade in arms against the family, represents the racialized attitude toward those with "Indian" features, and throughout the novel, Islas uses her character to plot the story of the Ángel history of race relations and attitudes: "In their mother's eyes, Josie Salazar knew, she and her sister Serena were more like the Indians than the Spanish ladies they were brought up to be" (3). Another racial opposition, Mexican and white, complicates the picture of cultural identity through the various intermarriages and relations of the Ángel family with Irish, German, and other Euro-Americans. To Mamá Chona, but not for her descendants, the racial lines between Anglos and Mexicans, "an undeclared borderline," were more clearly drawn than her own bloodlines (68). The Ángel family experiences the seemingly contradictory cultural and social heterogeneity of the border: celebrating North American holidays with Mexican foods, growing up on stories of deportations and the deaths of the undocumented, facing racial taunts and exclusions, while enjoying a diverse ethnic mix of friends and in-laws. Islas emphasizes the social contradictions of the city's diversity produced by a predominantly *mexicano* population subjugated by the minority white:

> It was clear [...] that the Mexican and Anglo citizens of Del Sapo remained divided despite all the pretense and effort to make it an "All-American" city proud of its international connections ... As ... the century grew older and the real cowboys

> died out or rode on to wilder frontiers, [they were] replaced by those of the drugstore and bank variety. They took control of the town by making certain the water rights belonged only to a select few among them. For the most part, Mexican Americans . . . were ignored or exploited. When they were educated into the lower middle class, their school lessons contained no mention of their heritage or contributions to history. Those in the working class remained desperate and poor despite their citizenship. (43)

With this novel, Islas seems bent on representing actual El Paso history in his discourse on identity. While *The Rain God* was deliberate in its anonymity of place, *Migrant Souls* is replete with references to actual places, restaurants, shops, churches, schools, hospitals, movie theaters, and neighborhoods in El Paso, affording us fragmentary glimpses of the perceived city and its traditions; even the playful name of its fictional city, Del Sapo, is a close anagram of it.

Islas examines identity by referring to the particular history of a particular place, because as Stuart Hall reminds us, "Representation is possible only because enunciation is always produced within codes which have a history, a position within the discursive formations of a particular space and time" (446). What Islas finds, in keeping with other border Chicana/o writers on El Paso, is that for the Angels, the *mestizaje* of the border population is tied more closely to exploitation and racialization than bloodlines: "'Anglos can do anything they want,' their mother was fond of telling them" (109). The older generation was speaking of social strictures, perhaps those invoked by their own culture, but its generality applies nonetheless. The two groups, Anglo and Mexican, may share a common area but not a common place.

And yet, the Angels persist in seeking a common ground through their love relationships, as Islas continues the spatial metaphors. The only place free of boundaries seemed to be the place of love: "a land where no bridges spanned rivers because no borders existed," thought Josie (190). But the family members like Josie, Armando, Ricardo, Félix, Ofelia, Serena, and Miguel Chico, who cross either racial or sexuality divides, find only a compromised exile or at best, a temporary refuge. Their city can offer them little by way of respite for it is either polluted space—"This is hell and heaven and purgatory right here," or none—"the middle of nowhere is in Del Sapo, Texas" (31, 26). That is, the mixture of religious spatial categories corrupts the distinctiveness or the purity of each space and thus negates their meaning or creates another space of ambiguity. In either case, the city is presented as uninhabitable and has become synonymous with Félix's murder: "this stupid town is narrow-minded, religious in the worst of ways, and condones murder" (121). Miguel Chico, holding close "the gate of his secret territory" (120), cannot seem to find the way out. At one moment, in despair over a failed love affair and his continuing illness, he imagines his family as souls in Dante's Purgatory. "But I'm in the desert," he corrects himself (151). This refrain echoes with a childhood memory of a beloved story: "'Tell us again where we are, Tia Jesus Maria'. . . . 'We are at the bottom of what was once a prehistoric sea. Every day, they find fossils of ancient marine creatures at the very top of these mountains'" (241). Miguel Chico continues to represent his situation in terms of the landscape of the city, until another more encompassing and overwhelming site takes its place. Drunk and lonely at one of their Christmas parties, he perceives his family as "unfamiliar shades in a journey he had begun into an unknown and forbidden land" (242). Only the land of death offers solace. This bleak resolution is mitigated only by the hint of the possibility of transformation, like the ancient seas evolved into desert, and the statue of Santa Lucía dancing out of her bonds at the end of the narrative.

The religious motifs that more significantly extend the spatializations of the novel are found in the titles of its two books, "Flight into Egypt" and "Feliz Navidad." This is Islas's way of parodying the Christian story of birth and flight, here transposed, to highlight the real and metaphoric migrations undertaken by the characters and to delineate the complexities of the border Mexican's "birth" of identity. In the first book, the Angels' journeys cross the borders of nation, race, sexuality, and conformity, while in the second, scenes of the Ángel family gathered at Christmastime over a period of years, presents the heterogeneity of Chicano attitudes and perspectives on religion, love, and politics. Here the city represents both the birth of and journey toward the border Mexican's identity, in which diaspora figures as an unending realm of nomadic subjectivity. Maurice Blanchot explains it thus: "On the one hand, nomadism maintains above what is established the right to put the distribution of space into question by appealing to the initiatives of human movement and human time. And, on the other hand, if to become rooted in a culture and [if] a regard for things does not suffice, it is because the order of the realities in which we become rooted does not hold the key to all the relations to which we must respond" (127). For Islas, the "flight" of the "Children of the Border" comes before the birth because it is the journey that determines identity.

In the light of how Islas presents the perspectives of border Mexicans on their situation, the title "Flight into Egypt" cannot denote simply exile or retreat. When Mamá Chona and her family are forced by the Mexican Revolution to emigrate, like thousands of others, across the "shallow, muddy, ugly" Rio Grande, "hardly a symbol of the promised land," she says, "They were migrant, not immigrant, souls. They simply and naturally went from one bloody side of the river to the other and into a land that just a few decades earlier had been Mexico. They became border Mexicans with American citizenship" (41-42).

For the *mexicano*, American identity is suspect, Mexican identity compromised, and citizenship qualified. Their contraband status persists. The "Children of the Border" may be "the transnational people," as Saldívar writes, "whose lives form the space of a new 'contact zone,' one for which the notion of a singular political, social, or cultural identity may no longer suffice" (*Border Matters*, 229), but what Islas proposes for the city and its inhabitants may in fact be that singularity. For Mexicans in El Paso/Juárez, Islas intimates, the inseparability of history and landscape from the people creates just such a place: a geography of knowing. The commonality of experiences and interests that may bind Chicanas/os throughout the United States does not mitigate particularity, in the same way that "the border," like "the Chicano," is not a monolithic whole. At the same time, Islas posits a paradoxical opposition: the border resident without place, that is, without nation, a geography implying another knowledge. The deliberate use of "migrant" to displace "immigrant" contests the immigrant status of the border Mexican and problematizes the issue of homeland (and therefore, origin, and therefore, traditional identity). The migrant has several "homes" or none; a return may be implicit or not; its domain bound or unbound; journey is the mode of existence and definition. The daily influx of Mexican workers from the interior into the city reinforces and affirms the continuity of Mexican culture, but the contradiction for the "Children of the Border," firm in their *mexicanidad* and their resistance to assimilation, is the contestation of identity they face there. The mainstream, after all, is not their river.

MAKE A RUN FROM THE BORDERLANDS:
Arturo Islas's *The Rain God* and *Migrant Souls* and the Need to Escape from Homophobic Masternarratives

Michael Hardin

I n *Borderlands/La frontera* (1987), Gloria Anzaldúa argues that the borderlands are a kind of plural space, one she makes into a metaphor for plural identity: "From this racial, ideological, cultural and biological cross-pollination, an 'alien' consciousness is presently in the making—a new *mestiza* consciousness, *una conciencia de mujer*. It is a consciousness of the Borderlands" (77). In Latino/a criticism since then, especially Chicano/a criticism, there has been a gravitation toward this metaphor, especially when dealing with writers from the borderlands. The crucial word, however, seems to be "from," since most, if not all, those writers leave the borderlands, especially the gay and lesbian writers. Anzaldúa theorized the border in California and lived there until her death. Richard Rodriguez, who reaches many of the same conclusions, but from a much different political space, resides in San Francisco. Arturo Islas, whom many have associated with border ideologies, lived and taught at Stanford. The obvious connection between these three is their homosexuality; clearly the borderland is a space that represents the physical collision of two cultures/nations, but it also represents a convergence of certain conservative hegemonies, most notably the heterosexist/homophobic nature of Catholic and Protestant, Mexican and American cultures. By moving from the rural areas of the border to the metropolitan areas of San Francisco and Los Angeles, these writers are able to exist in spaces that more adequately represent the confluence of cultures (more than just Mexican and American) *and* are secular enough spaces wherein homosexuality is more accepted and open. This essay will argue that the completed novels of Arturo Islas critique the Texas border metaphor and posit an urban, Californian alternative.

For Gloria Anzaldúa, the border extends beyond the Rio Grande; it is spatial, not linear—the border*lands*. She describes it as "the lifeblood of two worlds merging to form a third country— a border culture" (3). For Anzaldúa, this third space is fed by the lifeblood of both sides; the image is positive, evoking the disembodied but life-giving hearts of Frida Kahlo. Anzaldúa uses her Texas-Mexico border as the model for her metaphor:

> The actual physical border that I am dealing with in this book is the Texas-U.S. Southwest/Mexican border. The psychological borderlands, the sexual borderlands and the spiritual borderlands are not particular to the Southwest. In fact, the Borderlands are physically present wherever two or more cultures edge each other, where people of different races occupy the same territory, where under, lower, middle and upper classes touch, where the space between two individuals shrinks with intimacy. (iii)

From the real, Anzaldúa makes her metaphor and includes in it the sexual; but can she, as a lesbian, find a space in it for herself? When Anzaldúa talks about how she was treated when people found out she was lesbian, she uses the phrase "half and half" in the same way as she talks about the borderlands:

> There is something compelling about being both male and female, about having an entry into both worlds. Contrary to some psychiatric tenets, half and halfs are not suffering from a confusion of sexual identity, or even from a confusion of gender. What we are suffering from is an absolute despot duality that says we are able to be only one or the other. (19)

To be "half and half" is to live in the borderland, to be part of both and yet exclusively neither. In many ways, this definition of the queer space/borderland is one that is potentially most threatening to a heterocentrist society, since it challenges binary identity as well the hetero-/homosexual dichotomy. In positing the borderland as a third state, Anzaldúa challenges the duality of the hetero-/homosexual split; one cannot viably argue for a third state in a dualistic universe. In order for Anzaldúa to make this argument, however, she must rely on the concept of the "third sex," one between male and female; unfortunately, such designations do nothing to describe the reality of gay men or lesbians. A "third sex" merely reinforces stereotypical notions that to be a gay man one must be "effeminate" and to be a lesbian means that one is "butch." It is at this point where Anzaldúa's border metaphor separates from the real. Later, Anzaldúa states, "As a lesbian I have no race, my own people disclaim me; but I am all races because there is the queer of me in all races" (80). If one wants to insist on associating the border metaphor with sexuality, then one would have to define it as some space on the sexual continuum between homosexuality and heterosexuality or as some space that includes both.

When Anzaldúa discusses the border as real, she does so in terms that permit the metaphor to be read in terms of sexuality. She describes it as a "1,950 mile-long open wound / dividing a *pueblo*, a culture, / running down the length of my body, / staking fence rods in my flesh, / splits me splits me / *me raja me raja*" (2). By describing the borderlands as a split pueblo/culture, Anzaldúa forces the reader to see both sides as "same," unjustly kept from each other. As "same," we can read the border as either a homosexual metaphor, or as a borderland, a space where both sides bleed into the other. This "sameness" Anzaldúa defines as feminine inasmuch as she is discussing the land; she talks about "culture," both Mexican and American, as masculine (16). The oversight in this definition is that masculine culture is not separated from the feminine land, and thus at the border any third space is overwritten by the masculine cultures from both sides. A "third space" can represent the coming together of differences, but in the areas where the cultures are similar, the "third space" can amplify the negatives. With Catholicism on one side and Protestantism on the other, the borderland magnifies the homophobia of both sides.

Although not from the Texas border but from California's Central Valley, Richard Rodriguez,[1] in *Days of Obligation: An Argument with My Mexican Father*, discusses his homosexuality and the interaction between Mexico and the United States. (See also Frederick Luis Aldama's essay in this collection, "Ethnoqueer

Re-Archi*text*uring of Metropolitan Space.") By placing his sexuality and the border in one book, Rodriguez makes the connection between these seemingly unrelated topics unavoidable and intentional. At times, Rodriguez's arguments sound as if the border is a line between California and Mexico, and at others, the border seems to encompass most of northwestern Mexico and Southern California; one could even argue that Rodriguez allows the "border" to include all of Mexico and California. One key to Rodriguez's metaphor is semblance: both sides of the border resemble each other. Early in the text, Rodriguez makes a series of rather obvious statements: "the majority of Mexican Americans live, where they have always lived, in the Southwestern United States, one or two hours from Mexico. [. . .] Cities, rivers, mountains retain Spanish names. California was once Mexico" (49). Reminding us that Mexican Americans live near Mexico and that California was once part of Mexico is hardly worth doing unless there is a larger project; Rodriguez is not merely pointing out the arbitrariness of the border, but he is focusing on the sameness of both sides. Although for different reasons, this is also an argument that Anzaldúa makes about the Texas border: "In the 1800s, Anglos migrated illegally into Texas, which was then part of Mexico, in greater and greater numbers and gradually drove the *tejanos* (native Texans of Mexican descent) from their lands" (6).

Rodriguez's argument is furthered by the desire and/or need to make the other side more like one's own. He repeatedly provides examples of how California is becoming more "Mexican" and Mexico is becoming more "Californian." In one passage he writes, "southern California is busy re-creating itself on the far coasts of Baja, building condos [. . .]" (92). In describing the Mexican influence on California, he writes,

> Mexicans have invaded American privacy to babysit or to watch the dying or to wash lipstick off the cocktail glasses. Mexicans have forced Southwestern Americans to speak Spanish whenever they want their eggs fried or their roses pruned. Mexicans have overwhelmed the Church—eleven o'clock masses in most valley towns are Spanish masses. By force of numbers, Mexicans have taken over grammar-school classrooms. (72)

In these observations, Rodriguez reveals the dual migrations and their ironic consequences.

> Children of upper-class Tijuana are crossing into San Diego for school. Mexicans with green cards are heading to their American jobs. From the American side, technicians, engineers, and supervisors are heading for jobs in Tijuana. The thirty-minute delay is in both directions. (93)

The concept of border is not absolute; it is porous. In this section, although Rodriguez does not openly discuss the border as sexual metaphor, he does note that Mexicans refer to "the American side as *el otro cachete*, the other buttock" (85). In the context of a work about male homosexuality and the relationship between Mexico and the United States, this reference allows a reading that identifies the border itself as the crack between buttocks, or more importantly, the anus. At another point, Rodriguez discusses Mexico in terms of drag: "The government of hurt pride is not above political drag. The government of Mexico impersonates the intimate genius of matriarchy in order to justify a political stranglehold. In its male, in its public, in its city aspect, Mexico is an archtransvestite, a tragic buffoon" (61). Mexico is defined in male terms, like the United States, but the difference here is that Mexico is a tragic drag queen; given the association of public drag with homosexuality, Rodriguez is again eroticizing the interaction between countries. Therefore, since the border is penetrated/crossed from both sides, both cultures are defined as male, and the border is referred to as buttocks/anus, the relationship between both sides is depicted in male homoerotic terms. Even in California, the border is more conservative; San Diego is the most conservative major city in the state.

So, despite the metaphorized homoeroticism of the border, gay novelists routinely have their protagonists leave it. One of the first, if not the first, Mexican American novels to advocate leaving the border because of one's sexuality is John Rechy's *City of Night* (1963). Rechy's nameless and pseudo-autobiographical narrator is from El Paso, a city that is described in terms of confinement and separation:

> I felt miraculously separated from the world outside: separated by the pane, the screen, through which, nevertheless—uninvolved—I could see the world. [. . .] I watched other lives, only through a window. Sundays during the summer especially I would hike outside the city, along the usually waterless strait of sand call the Rio Grande, up the mountain of Cristo Rey, dominated at the top by the coarse, weed-surrounded statue of a primitive-faced Christ. (20)

This view of El Paso is one that does not allow the protagonist to interact; it alienates and confines. Overlooking El Paso is the statue of Christ, a panoptic figure representing all of the homophobia of both the Catholic and the Protestant, the Mexican and the American. It is only when the narrator leaves El Paso for the more liberal cities of the North and of California that he can express his sexual self. As he is on his way out of Texas, he refers to the trip in terms of freedom and salvation: "I was on my way now to Chicago, briefly—from where I would go to freedom: New York!—embarking on that journey through nightcities and nightlives—looking for I don't know what—perhaps some substitute for salvation" (22). Although *City of Night* would never be called the feel-good queer novel of the decade, it does reveal the intense repression of the border; Northern and Californian cities are hardly idyllic, but they do provide an environment wherein the protagonist can exist as a gay male.

Islas wrote his first novel twenty years after *City of Night*; however, the geographic dynamics seem equally limiting. Both *The Rain God* (1984) and *Migrant Souls* (1990) are set in the Texas border town of Del Sapo, a simple anagram of El Paso, the city where Islas is from. Since Islas does not change the names of the Californian cities where Miguel Chico and the other characters move, one must ask why he changes the name of the Texan city. In part, this is a joke: he is "from/of the toad." One would hardly refer to a town as "toad" if one were using it as a positive metaphor. According to Manuel de Jesús Vega, fondness is the farthest thing from Islas's desert; he reads "the omnipresence and suffocating reality of the desert" (112) as a space of Biblical punishment. Secondly, given the autobiographic nature of the novels,

Islas may be trying to "protect" some of the characters/people mentioned. However, for this essay, the important element of the name is that it suggests both El Paso and the far smaller border towns along the Rio Grande.

Like Anzaldúa and Rodriguez, Islas presents the borderlands as a potential space for moving beyond simplistic dualities of difference. In his talk, "On the Bridge, At the Border: Migrants and Immigrants," Stanford University's 1990 "Ernesto Galarza Commemorative Lecture," Islas makes use of the metaphors of both the border and the bridge:

> I consider myself, still, a child of the Border, a Border some believe extends all the way to Seattle and includes the northern provinces of Mexico [...]. I often find myself on the bridge between cultures, between languages, between sexes, between nations, between religions [...] between two different and equally compelling ways of looking agape at the world. (Aldama, *Uncollected Works*, 232)

Islas does not define exactly where the border is. If it extends from the northern Mexican provinces to Seattle, then does that not make the entire West Coast (or the entire U.S.) "the borderlands"? And if so, what is accomplished by defining the border so broadly? If Islas is in this borderland, what is it that he is between: Canada and Central Mexico? The other difficulty is that Islas says that he is "between sexes"; this puts him *between* male and female, in that "half and half" space Anzaldúa mentions.

Islas's own use of the border metaphor and its prevalence in Chicano/a criticism explain why so many of the critics of his novels use this imagery. Antonio C. Márquez defines Islas's work as the "bridging of the two literatures" (3). And some of the critics collected here—José David Saldívar, David Rice, and Marta Sánchez—variously describe how Islas's narrative bridges transnational gaps (see Saldívar), his characters see themselves as inhabiting borders between private and public space (see Rice), and ultimately the characters create bridges of understanding (see Sánchez). So long as these writers discuss Islas's bridging of ethnicities and nationalities, the metaphor holds; however, the metaphor slips and becomes problematic when the discussion moves to the issue of Islas's or Miguel Chico's homosexuality. Later in his argument, Rice mentions that "Miguel Chico's hybrid body and marginalized sexuality require alternative models of ethnicity and gender if he is to find a position for himself" (179). A different model—or metaphor—is necessary, but Rice does not provide an alternative to the aforementioned "border." Wilson Neate argues that "Miguel Chico [. . .] effects an ongoing erosion of boundaries, specifically in the context of the family, gender and sexuality" (219). What is the sexual boundary that is being eroded? Miguel Chico is not doing anything that Félix did not do earlier, and he is no more accepted as gay than his uncle was. Miguel Chico has to leave the space of the boundary, leave the border, to exist as a gay man. In Del Sapo, there is no erosion of the (hetero)sexual boundary. Saldívar may provide one possible application of the bridge/ boundary metaphor in terms of sexuality: "Though he did not identify himself as an openly gay Chicano writer, he did not shy away from presenting what we might call the 'spectacle of the closet' as one of the truths of the Chicano homosexual on the bridge of sexuality" (117). If we read Saldívar as defining the closeted gay man as the space between being out and being heterosexual, then there is "border" space, but this still is a negative space, one that leads to Félix's death and Miguel Chico's extreme loneliness.

In *Migrant Souls*, the more theoretically informed of the two novels, Islas plays with the language of the border metaphor, especially through the character of Rudy, Miguel Chico's cousin who attended the University of California at Berkeley and then moved to Washington, D.C.: "Just like our souls are between heaven and earth, so are we in between two countries completely different from each other. We are Children of the Border" (164-65). Rudy maintains his self-definition as a child of the border in the same way that Anzaldúa does and Islas himself does in "On the Bridge, At the Border"; although, as we will see later, Miguel Chico does not. For Rudy, who can fit in with both sides—he can be both Mexican and American (his job in Washington implies being part of the system)—the border represents the coming together of two separate narratives, both of which he can access. Like Anzaldúa, Rudy defines the space of the border as a "third state," an in-between space: "We are on the border between a land that has forgotten us and another land that does not understand us" (165). However, even Rudy has moments of self-reflexivity: "Let's keep the border and give both lands back to the Indians!" (165). To give both sides back and keep the border does not leave a viable space; the space that is left is literally a line, a tightrope. Earlier, in less sophisticated terms, the narrative theorizes the border as a space where one either follows both narratives or is caught between both narratives: "Caught between the future and the past, some of the Angels lived and died for the moment because they had to. The rest led double lives and followed the rules of both cultures as best they could" (42). More than anything else, this tension seems to underlie the metaphor of the border itself: the border doubles identity or negates it.

One of the conventional ways that identity is viewed as double is with regard to ethnic or national identity. Islas begins *Migrant Souls* with direct and indirect references to some of the many ethnic and national identities that are present within Miguel Chico's family and the town of Del Sapo: "When they were children growing up on the 'American' side of the Mexican Texas border, it was, 'Serena, get that braid out of your mouth. Do you want to be taken for an Indian?'" (3). Obviously, this is not a space where all narratives are equal, but they are present. Furthermore, on the other side of the family, the name "Salazar" is significant to this essay for one letter, Z, a linguistic remnant of the Arabic presence in Spain. And the family matriarch, Mamá Chona, represents the indigenous (Olmec) while favoring the conqueror:

> The girls' only surviving grandparent—Encarnacion Olmeca, or Mama Chona as she instructed them to call her—may have had [. . .] Indian origins, but she had married Jesus Angel [. . .]. [who] had more Spanish than Indian blood in his veins. And, the legend continued, if his ancestors had not been in the first army of *conquistadores*, they certainly had sailed in shortly thereafter. (8-9)

These passages destroy the notion of a stable or "pure" identity; each individual represents the American and the Mexican, the *conquistador* and the *indio*, the Spaniard and the Moor.

Despite these attempts to bridge difference, Islas is clear to point out that even though the borderland may be a space of coming together, it is still one of clear hierarchies and binaries. In a telling use of the desert metaphor, Islas uses Mamá Chona to describe its dualistic nature: "'In the desert, there are two seasons,' Mamá Chona told them, 'very hot and very cold'" (*Rain God* 171). There is no idealized border space here, no borderland between hot and cold; it is "very hot" or "very cold," but nothing else. When Eduviges describes the reality of integration between those Americans of Mexican descent and those of Anglo descent, it becomes clear that the climate of the desert is not the only duality:

> [I]t was clear to her that the Mexican and Anglo citizens of Del Sapo remained divided despite all the pretense and effort to make it an "All-American" city proud of its international connections [. . .]. For the most part, Mexican Americans like her and her children were ignored or exploited. When they were educated into the lower middle class, their school lessons contained no mention of their heritage or contributions to history. (*Migrant Souls* 43)

While Anzaldúa herself recognizes the intolerance present on the border, she still insists on the metaphor; Islas's writing seems to challenge the appropriateness of this metaphor. In *The Rain God*, racial intolerance is often associated with Mamá Chona, who taught the family "that only the Spanish side of their heritage was worth honoring and preserving; the Indian in them was pagan, servile, instinctive rather than intellectual, and was to be suppressed, its existence denied" (*Rain God* 142), and who taught Miguel Chico "to avoid the rear [of the bus], which was labeled the 'colored section'" (169). Despite the presence of so many different ethnicities in the borderland, Islas is careful to show that society has prescribed for each one a space within the hierarchy.

Besides the antagonism between ethnicities and nationalities, Islas demonstrates the complete lack of acceptance and even recognition of gays and lesbians. *The Rain God* begins with a veiled reference to Miguel Chico's homosexuality and connects it with his failure to visit Del Sapo: "Miguel Chico knew that Mama Chona's family held contradictory feelings toward him. Because he was still not married and seldom visited them in the desert, they suspected that he, too, belonged on the list of sinners" (*Rain God* 4). The suspicion of sin is based on *both* the lack of a spouse and his absence from the desert; Islas's syntax allows the reader to conclude from the beginning that the border/desert is not a space that permits homosexuality. After hearing about her bisexual brother Félix's murder, Eduviges says, "I don't believe a word of it. There are no homosexuals" (*Migrant Souls* 121). Félix's homosexual desire and encounters are obliterated by the family: Mamá Chona is told that he died in a factory accident (*Rain God* 174), and Miguel Grande would only tell Félix's wife, Angie, that "Felix was dead and that the causes were under investigation" (83). The only gay or lesbian character who exists within the family and town in a relatively healthy relationship is Serena, and her acceptance seems dependent on the family's lack of proof (she is in the closet) *and* her generosity: "Serena's acts of generosity placated her mother's fears and held at bay the judgment of those Angels who were suspicious about the erotic lives of others because their own were so dull" (*Migrant Souls* 106). Although there may be inferences of homosexuality in the desert, Ricardo L. Ortiz points out that "Miguel Chico and Serena's experiences as gay people still remain largely in that marginalizing closet-space of silence" (119).

In contrast to the repression of the desert border, Islas associates urban areas and California specifically with freedom, openness, progress, cleansing, and liberal thought. The one critic to describe Islas's metaphor of California is Paul Skenazy, although he only examines the role of San Francisco. Early in his essay, he defines the role of San Francisco within Islas's works: "San Francisco, by contrast, is seen less as a place than an alternative viewpoint" (200). By defining the city as a "viewpoint" and not a place, Skenazy reads it as a metaphor. Later, he states that "It is the space that provides relief from the enclosures, almost imprisonment, of family" (201). In fact, Skenazy associates everything that is not the desert with San Francisco:

> San Francisco is again the world where the Angel family ways don't rule: where Josie has her affair, where Miguel Chico lives his private sexual life, where Miguel writes his novel [. . .]. San Francisco functions as a place of contemplation and resistance [. . .]. San Francisco is less a beneficent territory that offers its own rewards than a haven that provides a needed indifference to the pressures of the past. (202-03)

Clearly, San Francisco has become metaphor. The only problem with this metaphor is that Islas does not limit it merely to San Francisco, but more often refers to California as a whole.

One of the most telling examples of association with California and the dissociation with Del Sapo occurs near the end of *Migrant Souls*; Miguel Chico has been asked by a Del Sapo waitress, "Are you from here?" and he responds, "No. I'm visiting from California" (207). This exchange is significant because it highlights Miguel Chico's conscious severing of his identity from the border and from his family: he is no longer *from here*. The meaning of California is clearly stated by Josie, Miguel Chico's closest cousin: "Why hadn't she stayed near him [her ex-husband] in California? In some places there at least, the world was not divided into the saints and the sinners" (123). While Josie is in California, she has an affair, during which she says that "she was in a land where no bridges spanned rivers because no borders existed" (190). Admittedly, she is speaking metaphorically, but this is significant because Islas phrases Josie's bliss both in terms of land and border *while she is in California*; and, the metaphors of borders and bridges here are clearly negative. When Josie returns from California, she is able to compare it to her border surroundings: "Josie and her sisters had been born during the Great Depression and as far as she was concerned, Del Sapo, Texas, was still in it when she returned to the desert from California after almost ten years of marriage" (103).

Josie is not the only family member to make similar associations with California. Lena, Félix's daughter, "told Miguel Chico many years later—after she had moved to California and could talk about it—she would have asked two questions" (*Rain God* 88). Lena's questions involve her father's sexuality and the failure of the police, the military, and the town to prosecute his murderer; however, the structure of the sentence combines the movement to California with the ability to talk about Félix. Thus, openness about homosexuality is associated only with leaving the Texas border and being in (urban) California.

While the younger generation defines the movement from the border in liberating terms, the older generation defines California as a state for sinners and "others." Eduviges associates San Francisco with "the end of the world" (*Migrant Souls* 179), a phrase that suggests both an apocalyptic end and that space that is most removed from one's own environment. When Armando, "the black sheep in Mama Chona's family," takes his wife Sally, who is half Irish and half Mexican, and their "two sons away from the desert in 1938, the rest of the family [i]s relieved. 'They belong in California,' Mama Chona said" (79). Again, the "morality" of California is defined in opposition to that of the border.

Miguel Chico, who goes to school and lives in the San Francisco Bay Area, sees the desert/border as reflective of all of the intolerance and turmoil of his family. In fact, each time that he returns from the desert, he has to purge it from his system: "The old childhood feelings were then dredged up and he had to be alone for several days after his return to the West Coast. To recover, to rid himself of the desert, he walked on the beach or in the fog" (*Rain God* 89). What Islas has Miguel Chico rid himself of is "the desert," not the "old childhood feelings." The beach and the fog counteract the arid desert. The fog of San Francisco becomes for Miguel Chico a life-giving and life-affirming force: "He walked out into the garden. The fog was in and thicker than usual in his part of the City. He knew that during the early hours of the day it would moisten and freshen all he had planted there" (28).

Within Islas's borderlands, there are two distinct sources for the cultural homophobia, the Catholic Church and the U. S. military. The same intolerance and homophobia that we find in the Catholic Church we can find in American Protestantism, and since

Islas has María become a Seventh-Day Adventist, we should recognize that the critique is intended to include both branches of Christianity. Within both novels, Islas associates religious holidays with tragedy and despair and also has certain characters openly criticize the church. It is on Easter Sunday that the family is told that Tony is dead (47), and it is also on this day that Ernesto, "Seeing [the desert] at its most beautiful in the sunset of the holy day, [. . .] he felt its desolation for the first time in his life" (50). Ernesto, feeling the loss of Tony, recognizes the desolation of the desert only after he sees it at its most beautiful, on Easter. Islas is consistently using association to tell us things about the desert and, in this case, religion. Later, in *Migrant Souls*, it is Miguel Chico who experiences suicidal despair on Christmas Eve, when his internalized demons speak to him: "they told him he was not a child of the Church or worth of the family name and that Ricardo should have been his father's firstborn son. [. . .] the demons added, he ought to consider destroying himself" (*Migrant Souls* 218). In a rather understated way, Islas writes, "Miguel Chico was thinking how much he did not love Christmas Eve" (240). For Miguel Chico, Christmas Eve represents family, Del Sapo, and the Catholic Church, all three of which are horribly repressive.

Islas uses a number of characters to represent a critique of the church. Josie, who is relegated to the "sinner" category because of her divorce, states outright, "I know that this stupid town is narrow-minded, religious in the worst of ways, and condones murder" (121). The construction here places the responsibility on religion for the town's condoning of Félix's murder. The implicit statement is that homosexuality is a worse sin than murder; one can understand why there would be the need to flee the border if this is the mentality. However, despite Josie's revelation, she returns to Del Sapo and stays, and she becomes entrapped in the social snares of religion. Miguel Chico tells her, "You are just like every smart Mexican Catholic sinner I know. You hate the Church and then you get married and baptize your children in it" (191). Islas makes this point more sinisterly when Josie is responding to a question from her daughters about marriage and answers, "Girls do not marry girls. Girls marry boys" (182-83). Despite being part of Miguel Chico and Serena's generation, Josie repeats and reinforces the cultural and religious taboos even though she knows better; being on the border, surrounded by the Catholic Church, makes it impossible for her and her daughters to think or speak otherwise. Josie's father also presents counter-church arguments: "Sancho Salazar loved telling his wife and her sister Jesus Maria that all religions were the downfall of mankind and had caused the slaughter of untold millions" (48). This furthers Josie's statement that only associated the church with the murder of Félix. The causes for these slaughters include everything from believing in the wrong god to being a non-European to blasphemy to sins such as homosexuality.

The intolerance and hatred of the Catholic Church are part of what pushes Miguel Chico away from it and the desert. Near the beginning of *The Rain God*, Islas identifies Miguel Chico's perspective: "Miguel Chico wanted to look at motives and at people from an earthly, rather than otherworldly, point of view" (*Rain God* 28). What this reveals is a rational point of view, one that is based firmly in earthly reality as opposed to the illogic and eternal condemnation of Catholicism. This rejection of the otherworldly is most succinctly expressed after Miguel Chico has heard his mother repeat the question of one of her dying friends, Herminia: "Why did our Father make me suffer so much at the end?" Miguel Chico answers, "Because 'our Father' is a sadist'" (176). When one looks at those who are the most ardent believers, one can see that they are frequently members of oppressed groups looking for hope in the next world since this world is so bad; Miguel Chico's conclusion is the one that makes sense. However, escape is not easy, especially when it means leaving one's family, one's home, and one's god. Miguel Chico looks at his family and realizes that he is not part of the celebration or the family; "Miguel Chico's throat began to ache. Who are these strangers? What are they celebrating? Who is this God? He could not feel himself breathe or hear the beating of his heart" (*Migrant Souls* 243). This moment even threatens to separate him from himself. Miguel Chico is now alien to this place, but it has cost him. Escape is not without pain.

Of course, the novel is not all painful; Islas does provide an ironic counterpoint for Miguel Chico's loss. After María has joined the Seventh-Day Adventists, she moves to Los Angeles, where she is hit by a drunk driver and killed (*Rain God* 23). The universe is balanced: Miguel Chico leaves the religious intolerance of the border to come to California; María tries to bring her religious intolerance from the border and California kills her.

Besides the church, the U.S. military is the second institution of intolerance on the border. And, just as Catholicism shares many of the same intolerances as other denominations and religions, so does the U.S. military represent the same hyper-masculinity, machismo, and homophobia that can be found in the police, *la migra*, and the Spanish *conquistadores*. The decision to have Félix killed by a soldier on a U.S. military base is not arbitrary. The military is a space where homosexuality is denied; even in the more liberal years of Clinton, "don't ask, don't tell" enforced denial and affirmed the space of the closet. The military's policy on homosexuality is exactly border sexuality: silence. Islas tells us that the person who killed Félix is a southerner, and later adds that he is from Tennessee. Referencing the South forces associations with the lynching of African Americans for their sexuality; some of the most notorious lynchings were sparked by whistles or rumors that an African American male looked at a white female, which inevitably was interpreted as "raped," and then the "honor" of the white woman had to be avenged. The irony with Islas's referring to the soldier as a southerner is that Texas too was part of the South, and geographically, Tennessee is considerably farther north than Del Sapo. The inclusion of the fact that one of Félix's testicles is missing (81) is also reminiscent of lynchings and the Spanish Conquest, in which emasculation was a sign of torture, abuse, and conquest. These associations between the military, the Ku Klux Klan, and Spanish Conquest force the reader to see the border space as unacceptable and unviable, especially for a gay male. The response of the military and the town to Félix's death is equally offensive:

> She [Lena] sat down facing him [attorney] as he explained how the evidence convincingly showed that her father was in fact "excuse me, ma'am" a homosexual and that he had seduced

other men, some of whom were willing to testify during a jury trial. The attorney thought it useless to subject the family to the shame and embarrassment of such an investigation. The young soldier had acted in "self-defense and understandably," given the circumstances, and there was no reason to prosecute him. (87)

The blame is shifted from the soldier to Félix, from the murderer to the victim. While "gay fear" is an excuse used in the metropolitan areas of Northern states and California, in those places there are more liberal and gay and lesbian activist groups that do not stand idly by as such intolerance manifests itself. In Del Sapo, even Félix's family tries to cover it up: "'The family,' as usual—more concerned with its pride than with justice—had begun to lie to itself about the truth" (85).

Related to the military is the concept of machismo, a code of hyper-masculinity exemplified and promulgated by Miguel Chico's father, Miguel Grande. Quite early in *The Rain God*, Miguel Grande finds Miguel Chico playing with paper dolls and dancing the jitterbug with his nanny María; his response is directed at his wife, Juanita: "His father said nothing to him but looked at Juanita and accused her of turning their son into a *joto*. Miguel Chico did not find out until much later that the word meant 'queer'" (16). Crucial to machismo is the *appearance* of heterosexuality; playing with dolls and being a good dancer are not "masculine," and thus are not permitted. Later, we are told why Miguel Grande was so upset about Miguel Chico's dancing: "Miguel shared the macho's distrust of any man who was too handsome or danced too well" (70). Here, "distrust of any man" implies doubt about a man's heterosexuality. Sadly, the insistence on machismo prevents any bond between son and father. Once, when Miguel Chico tried to comfort his father, he said, "Don't do that [. . .] Men don't do that with each other" (*Rain God* 93). Miguel Chico internalizes this rejection: "He had always felt that his father had disliked him for being too delicate, too effeminate" (94). Since he is not macho, Miguel Chico has no space in the borderland or in his family. In fact, his father's rejection of him is so thorough that he devises painful schemes to make his son into a man: "It pained him to see his son walk, and eventually he invented ways to make a man of the adolescent boy. One device had been to ask Miguel Chico's school friends to engage him in fistfights so that he might learn to defend himself" (96). However, the heterosexuality and masculinity espoused by Miguel Grande are a fraud that is exposed at the highly ironic twenty-fifth anniversary of Miguel Grande and Juanita. Félix, the uncle who is cheating on his wife with other men, toasts his brother, who is cheating on his wife with her *comadre*, "paying tribute to the splendid pair whose marriage, he said, was an example to them all, particularly to the younger generation" (54-55). The family and the church promote heterosexuality as necessary to maintain social order, and yet heterosexuality itself actively undermines those structures, leading individuals from their spouses and creating more sins to regulate.

Probably the easiest way to locate a border within sexuality is to define the border as bisexual; however, Félix, the bisexual in the novel, affirms the patriarchal structure and reveals the unattainability of a bisexual or queer border. Wilson Neate sees in Félix a radical space because bisexuality challenges the hetero-/homo- duality: "The case of Felix is significant as his bisexuality collapses and exceeds polarized notions of sexuality derived from a binary conceptualization of gender difference although that experience of 'otherness' is catastrophic as it precipitates his murder" (214). Given the rampant homophobia of the border, it does not make sense that his murder is precipitated by the threat to the binary; more likely, it is caused by the queer "threat" to a heterocentric society. In less specific terms, Manuel de Jesús Vega also posits both halves of the dyad in Félix: "Felix unmistakably embodies two antithetical realities in his person: that of the desert and that of the rain" (114). Although this is phrased in these terms, we cannot help but conclude that Félix's sexuality is part of the equation of encompassed dualities. However, Rosaura Sánchez points out that Félix does not threaten patriarchal hierarchies, but in fact reinforces them: "Felix's homosexual preferences, however, cannot be seen to negate patriarchal structures, for not only is he an authoritarian husband with a wife and four children at home, but in his relations with men he also assumes the position of power and takes advantage of his subordinates" (121).

The best way, it seems, to describe Félix's sexuality is closeted, and it is this insistence in Del Sapo on heterosexuality that forces Félix into the unhealthy manifestations of his sexuality. Not only does he have to sneak around at night, going to "straight" bars to find men (itself a very dangerous act), Félix redirects his attentions to those (heterosexual) males around him, his workers and his son. Before hiring, Félix tells his prospective male employees that a physical is required:

> In those brief morning and afternoon encounters, gazing upon such beauty with the wonder and terror of a bride, his only desire was to touch it and hold it in his hands tenderly. [. . .] In most cases, however, the men submitted to Felix's expert and surprisingly gentle touch, thanked him, and left without seeing the awe and tension in his face. It did not occur to them that another man might take pleasure in touching them so intimately. (116)

Islas is not promoting sexual harassment; instead, he is showing the problems inherent in forcing individuals to repress their natural sexuality. The more worrisome problem comes with Félix's son, JoEl: "As the three of them slept more frequently together, Felix lost his passion for Angie, and he would wake during the night cradling JoEl on his side of the bed. His protective feelings for the child perplexed and disoriented him because they seemed stronger than his desire for his wife" (122). We are probably not meant to assume that Félix had sex with his son, but clearly Félix's "passion" is transferred from his wife to his son. This is further suggested when Angie, Félix's wife, moves out of the bedroom. Islas's criticism, however, does not seem to be directed at Félix; the real critique seems directed at the border's repressive tendencies. At the end, after Félix has died, Islas makes it clear that JoEl does not condemn his father: "I want to see my father [. . .] I want to tell him that I understand and that I love him [. . .] I hate it that Mama Chona is with him. She never understood anything human" (155). JoEl recognizes that Félix's desire was "human," and that it was Mamá Chona's inability to accept all things human that created such problems; repression of natural desire is not natural.

Miguel Chico also experiences the repressive nature of the border, but he is finally able to escape. Despite his "rejection" of machismo, Miguel Chico has difficulty accepting his sexuality while he is in Del Sapo: "he was still denying what he saw in himself" (*Migrant Souls* 52). This denial takes a horrible toll on him, causing Josie to comment on his isolation: "Though she envied his popularity and social grace, Josie thought her cousin one of the loneliest people in the world" (67). Josie eventually figures out the source of Miguel Chico's loneliness, but even then they do not talk openly about it: "It was the first time she had stood in a nonjoking way so near the gate of his secret territory. Years earlier and without having to be told, she had understood that her cousin was a lover of men" (120). The tension and torment of the closet explain the fondness Miguel Chico has for the word *sinvergüenza* ("without shame"); Islas tells us "It was one of Miguel Chico's favorite expressions from childhood" (*Rain God* 56). "*Sinvergüenza*" means "shameless," doing something wrong without feeling bad or without censure; however, the parts of the word themselves can suggest something quite different, an act that does not (or should not) have shame associated with it. Thus, *sinvergüenza* would be the state in which Miguel Chico could exist without shame, and that is not the border, not with his family (other than Josie and Serena), and not with the church.

At the beginning of *The Rain God*, a voice from inside Miguel Chico "kept saying, 'You cannot escape your body, you cannot escape from your body'" (7). At the end of *Migrant Souls*, Miguel Chico thinks to himself, "he was seeing them [his parents] as unfamiliar shades in a journey he had begun into an unknown and forbidden land" (*Migrant Souls* 242). As gay men, Miguel Chico and Arturo Islas could not escape their bodies but they could escape the border and family. At the end of *The Rain God*, Mamá Chona acknowledges and recognizes Félix only after he is dead and she is on her deathbed, not a viable space at all (*Rain

God 179). Miguel Chico cannot live in the borderlands. Josie tells Serena, "You think of love as always being good. Sometimes, it destroys people," but Serena answers, "Not if it's real love" (*Migrant Souls* 108). The "love" in these novels that destroys is from the family, "love" that prevents people from being open about themselves; however, that is not "real love." Real love is unconditional and sometimes one has to leave everything behind to find it.

NOTE

[1] In *Migrant Souls*, Islas describes Miguel Chico's brother Ricardo in a manner that alludes teasingly to Richard Rodriguez's *Hunger of Memory*: "Ricardo brought up his children to ignore their Mexican heritage and to live according to the myths of North America. He was confident that economic, if not social, success awaited them. . . . Ricardo began asking others to call him Richard. Some of his buddies at the YMCA started calling him Dick" (204). In *Hunger of Memory*, Rodriguez adopts the myths of Anglo-America.

Migrant Souls

RACE AND THE BORDERLANDS
in Arturo Islas's *Migrant Souls*

Renato Rosaldo

When decision-making rooms suddenly include people who represent gender and racial diversity, they can produce discomfort for people who once worked in those rooms with a sense of entitlement. In contexts where the opinions of long-term inhabitants of decision-making rooms once went unchallenged, they now find that the new people in the room talk back. Professors, for example, find that new students do not laugh at their old jokes. Where certain individuals once enjoyed a monopoly on authority, they now feel threatened by having to share authority. Even when not recognized as such, privilege quickly becomes so habit-forming, rather like a vested right, that it is (mis)recognized as pure merit or the natural order of things, which must be passionately defended.

Issues at the level of institutional politics derive in certain respects from those of the nation-state in which equality among citizens putatively is based upon their sameness with respect to such attributes as language, culture, and race. Although the nation-state emphasizes its capacity to enfranchise certain citizens, it maintains a discrete silence about how it simultaneously disenfranchises others. Think of the popular slogan of the French Revolution: liberté, égalité, fraternité. Who was not included in the national fraternity? Women, to begin with and, in the United States, non-whites and non-property-holders. The late eighteenth-century egalitarian fraternity probably excluded more people than it included. Although the scope of formal citizenship has expanded, informal matters (often addressed along the spectrum from full to second-class citizenship) remain unresolved. In my view, our national contract is now in a process of renegotiation, with the eventual outcome still uncertain. Will a broader notion of the fully enfranchised citizenry emerge from the current crisis of the national? Can we uncouple the historically forged link between equality and sameness, and thereby find equality and strength, rather than threatening divisiveness, in our differences?

In the context of national debates about diversity, consider the concept of race. Arguably, race is a complex term that appears different from relatively subordinate positions than it does from relatively dominant ones. In considering the dynamics of race from both dominant and subordinate positions, I would like to explore *Migrant Souls* (1990) by the late Chicano novelist Arturo Islas, who died of AIDS on February 15, 1991. Set in Del Sapo, Texas—Del Sapo, which means "from the toad," is a playful anagram that which adds an initial D and transposes the P and S of El Paso—his novel breaks a taboo and addresses matters we as Chicanos are all aware of but do not discuss. It speaks to the dynamics of racial differentiation within the Chicano community as well as between Chicanos and Anglos. In making explicit what is presented somewhat obliquely in Islas's novel, I present selected passages of *Migrant Souls* against a dominant North American notion of race that anchors racial identity in biology or in phenotype. In this version, one that is surely well known to most of us and is too simple, perhaps, for any of us to hold uncritically, race is written definitively, once and for all, on the skin, and it is a binary, as in black versus white or Chicano versus Anglo.

What follows analyzes the dynamics of race in relation to the simultaneous conjuncture of such sources of inequality as class, caste, religion, gender, and sexual orientation. It will contest, first, the phenotypic view that race is written plainly, simply, and only on the skin, and second, the binary view that in all contexts one must be one race or the other, either Chicano or Anglo, and I will argue that social analysis must take into account, in local and specific contexts, a number of competing dominant and subordinate norms to which people adhere in varying degrees. Let me now try to unpack these analytical notions through a closer look at Arturo Islas's novel.

Let us begin at the beginning, with the novel's opening sentence: "In their mother's eyes, Josie Salazar knew, she and her sister Serena were more like the Indians than the Spanish ladies they were brought up to be" (3). This is a curious sentence. The two sisters, Josie and Serena, were brought up to be Spanish, but they have become more like Indians. Although Indian and Spanish are racial categories, they appear to be determined, not only by the seemingly dichotomous choice between heredity (whether biological race or phenotype) and environment (socialization), but also by a third factor. In order to register its presence without defining it prematurely, let us call the third factor something more. In opposing Spanish and Indian ethnicities, the narrator conceives of them along a continuum differentiated by degrees (more or less) rather than as a dichotomous opposition (either/or). The two sisters can be more like one racially encoded heritage than the other, and yet they can partake of both. Such, one supposes, is the nature of mulatto or mestizo notions of race.

Dominant white supremacy rarely bothers with the fine points of *mestizaje*. The narrator describes in the following terms the context of domination, in which crossing racial borders becomes a sign less of their permeability than of their status as a fixed boundary between Anglos and Mexicans: "Crossovers from one group to another were noticed and talked about later, for each race guarded its own and had been taught to fear the consequences of mixing cultures. An undeclared borderline existed between Mexicans and Anglos that only a few dared to cross in the name of love" (67-68). Aside from occasional courtship and marriage, the line between Mexicans and Anglos appears hard and fast. In the most encompassing context of domination, the two races comprise distinct worlds, each bent on maintaining a kind of purity not accidentally reminiscent of a nation-state determined to maintain an equality that derives from a condition of purity—that is, linguistic, cultural, and racial sameness.

Yet the bifurcated vision of Anglos versus Mexicans, each striving for racial and cultural purity, does not exhaust the novel's semiotics and politics of race. The most succinct challenge to the purist phenotypical view of race is voiced by Josie's mother, who, speaking in exasperation, scolds her daughter as follows: " 'She's simply acting like an Indian, that's all,' their mother said. 'Everyone knows they don't talk and can't answer politely when someone asks them a question' " (5). Far from the genetic fatality of being Indian, race in this passage becomes a form of conduct. Such behavior is usually encoded by parents or other adults with Spanish pretensions who reprimand children for failing to conform to the norms of a distinctive set of religious convictions and class aspirations. Consider the mother's admonitions in the following: " 'Serena, get that braid out of your mouth. Do you want to be taken for an Indian?' " (3); or " 'Josie, how many times do I have to tell you that a young lady does cross not her legs like an Indian?' " (3). Indian demeanor in the novel consists of putting a braid in one's mouth, not talking, having stringy hair, not answering questions politely, crossing one's legs indecently, being late, and wearing loud or immodest dress. Such behavior is regarded as Indian (rustic and uncouth), rather than Spanish (polite and refined). Being Indian thus derives as much from behavior as from phenotype.

The analysis just sketched must be located, however, in relation to the position of the speaker. It derives not from the culture in general, but from a particular putatively high-status category of person, *la gente decente*, "the decent people." Late in the novel the narrator describes *gente decente* (or at any rate their class aspirations, though probably not their socioeconomic reality) in the following terms: "Manuel and Ricardo knew that the phrase 'decent people' meant middle-class Catholics" (201). Ascent into the category of decent people in the novel, one should add, often involves the deliberate concealment of personal history and past identity. Concerted efforts to pass as "decent people" (one passes up, not down) reveal both the existence of a social boundary and personal insecurities about a lifetime of negotiating which side of the line one stands on. Even racial identities can be multiple, unstable, and painfully contested.

The mother of the two sisters, Josie and Serena, is described as a woman who once was "a small child with dark eyes, a prominent brow, and cheekbones she learned to powder later on in life so that she might appear as light-skinned as her sisters Jesus Maria and Eufemia Maria" (36). On a daily basis she alters her phenotype (or at any rate, she powders it every morning) because she has inherited the racialized class and religious aspirations of her family, the Angels. In the novel, the Angels epitomize Spanish social and racial pretensions. They set the standards to which the two sisters, Josie and Serena (who are Angels through their mother), fail to conform. The mother's mother is similarly described in the following as having risen through marriage and baptism to her elevated status as a person of Spanish descent, an Ángel (a bilingual pun on the word "angel" in English):

> The girls' only surviving grandparent—Encarnacion Olmeca, or Mama Chona as she instructed them to call her—may have had the Indian origins her maiden name suggested, but she had married Jesus Angel. By this act, as well as by her baptism into the Church of Rome, Mama Chona felt herself and her children to have been elevated into civilization for all time. (8)

The story goes on to describe shifts in racial status, not only for the intermarried women, but also for the male bearers of the Ángel family name who derive more from culture than from phenotype. The family myth long ago elevated her husband, Jesús Ángel, into being more Spanish than Indian in blood. And then, by a few short steps of mythic revisionism, his ancestors were said to have arrived with the first army of Spanish *conquistadores*, or shortly thereafter. A range of strategies, from powdering one's cheeks through intermarriage and baptism to rewriting the past, appear to be the price of admission into the sometimes contested category of *gente decente*.

Passing into a higher-status world can, alternatively, involve efforts to become Anglo rather than Spanish. One character, Ricardo, tried to assimilate and, as the narrator says, "brought up his children to ignore their Mexican heritage and to live according to the myths of North America" (204). His hopes for the next generation were conditioned by Anglo prejudice and efforts to keep Mexicans "in their place" as indicated by the following: "Ricardo's dream was to be a respected member of the middle class on the north side of the river. He was determined to see his children enjoy lives free from the prejudice against Mexican Americans who rose too high above their place in the second largest state of the Union" (202). He appears determined to liberate his children from the effects of prejudice at the same time that he risks the contempt of certain family members who do not approve of his attempts to deny his heritage. The difficulties of Ricardo's position suggest a further complexity.

The world of this novel is governed by multiple and competing norms. By no means do all the characters direct their energies toward the same official version of status mobility. Contrary to many theories that view social norms only from a top-down perspective, not everyone wants to assimilate. The goal of becoming *gente decente*, whether Spanish in conception or Anglo in aspiration, fails to move a number of characters in the novel. The failure to conform to Spanish or Anglo norms of status mobility can be viewed not only from a high-status vantage point as a failure to achieve, but also from a putatively lower-status position, as a positive effort to pursue alternative norms. The father of Josie and Serena, for example, loves to hunt and fish in Mexico where, as the narrator says, "his Indian blood came to life and made him feel at home with the land and sky" (4). This is described in positive rather than in negative terms and the two sisters and their father enjoy a yearning for Indian norms of behavior.

The alternate norms entail race not in isolation, but as it interacts with other dimensions of inequality and identity such as religion, gender, and sexual orientation. For example, Josie, whose behavior is so often coded as Indian, violates gender and status expectations by returning to Del Sapo as a divorced woman with two daughters. Her sister, Serena, who also appears Indian, loves and lives with another woman. Their cousin, Miguel Chico, was once one of Mamá Chona's favorites—that is, he was regarded as Spanish when he was a child—but he becomes socially defined as more Indian in adulthood as it becomes evident to others that he is a man who loves men. Family members know about the sexual orientation of their gay and lesbian kin but, following the code of the public secret, they rarely speak about such matters. Miguel Chico shows, however, that being gay, often recorded as being Indian in Del Sapo, is a game that those subordinated by the local official pecking order can knowingly play back, as suggested by the following: " 'It's our duty to be late,' Miguel Chico said. 'The Angels expect us to be rude and we mustn't let them down. It's all part of the ceremony' " (206). Miguel Chico deliberately delays his arrival for Christmas dinner by taking his cousin Josie and her daughters to a sleazy strip joint. Through his excessive conformity, by seeming to live up to (or, rather, down to) the expectations of his *gente decente* cousins, Miguel Chico flaunts their norms and actively asserts his own. In its own self-conception, the Ángel family sits in judgment of its less than respectable ("sinning") family members, Miguel Chico and Josie, but appears oblivious to how severely it is judged in turn. Miguel Chico sees the *gente decente* of the Ángel family as small-minded, uptight, and pathetic. His canons of pride and respect are at least as fierce and demanding as theirs.

By way of a brief conclusion, I will reflect briefly on the political implications of doing a social analysis of race as a complex category that varies with different positions of dominance and subordination as well as in relation to other sources of inequality. One immediate implication is that it will not do for people in relatively dominant positions to embark on processes of social change by self-righteously engaging in self-criticism. People speaking from positions of privilege often live in socially determined ignorance of how the world looks, feels, and is experienced from subordinate positions. Thus challenging white supremacy and changing the related hierarchical relations that do so much damage in everyday life requires that people in positions of relative privilege behave not unlike ethnographers and listen attentively in order to try to learn the particulars of other people's lives.

Social analysts and other relatively empowered people must recognize that relatively subordinated people's apparent failure to conform to dominant norms may result not from moral turpitude, but from their desire to follow other norms. The code of race may shape and in turn be shaped by other forms of inequality, such as caste, class, religion, gender, or sexual orientation. Thus when it becomes evident that Miguel Chico is gay, homophobia inhibits talk about sexual orientation and becomes recorded as his becoming more Indian and less Spanish than he was as a child. By the end of *Migrant Souls,* being more or less Spanish, Indian, or Anglo involves a complex and painful adjudication of phenotype, behavior, class, religion, being divorced, being gay, and being lesbian. The novel can be read as a parable of variegated Chicano efforts to survive under white supremacy without having to give up being who one is. The characters face pressures to become decent people, both Anglo and Spanish (itself, in this complex social space, often a simultaneous Mexican-style denial of Indian heritage and a determined anti-assimilationist refusal to become Anglo). Some people attempt to rise along the official social scale, while others navigate other trajectories with compromises and resistance born of a conviction that, if the price of admission to higher social status is that one's identity must be left at the door, they will refuse to enter the room; instead they will struggle to create other spaces within which to survive and perhaps thrive.

"THE CREATIVE DEFORMATION THAT IS PLOT":
Arturo Islas, Cultural Authenticity, and Ethno/biography

Rosemary Weatherston

In 1975 everything was, oppressively, Political. By 1985, everything has become, obscurely Cultural.

—Meaghan Morris, *The Pirate's Fiancée: Feminism Reading Postmodernism* (177)

What happens to the literariness of the ethnic works? Think of the numbers of students who read all realistic fiction as a documentary account of real life. When these readers, whom we might designate "naive" since they are relatively less conscious of the functions of literary forms than we are, encounter ethnic literature, they respond to the verisimilitude of the narration so completely that they take the literature as an equivalence of life. [. . .] To be fair it must be acknowledged that more "expert" readers (ourselves) do the same, when, acting upon the assumption that "ethnic" is the operative term in the category of ethnic literature, we seek to recover the raw material of the author's story from the creative deformation it has undergone in becoming plot.

—John M. Reilly, "Criticism of Ethnic Literature: Seeing the Whole Story" (2)

I

In the final section of Arturo Islas's *Migrant Souls* (1990)—the companion volume to his award-winning first novel, *The Rain God: A Desert Tale* (1984)—the characters Josie, her two daughters Hanna and Rebecca, and Miguel Chico (Josie's cousin and a character in *The Rain God*) stop at a Mex-

Tex/strip bar on their way to a family Christmas party. "It's our duty to be late," Miguel Chico tells his nieces, "The Angels expect us to be rude and we mustn't let them down. It's all part of the ceremony" (206). While the group sips margaritas under plastic Christmas wreaths covered with tiny cowboys and cowgirls, Josie begins to needle Miguel Chico about his role as an ethnic writer and his "scandalous" use of Ángel family history in his novel:

> "You have to stop writing about our perfectly happy family," Josie said. "The older generation does not approve. They think you're telling their terrible secrets to the world and they don't like it. And don't call my daughter a snot-nose brat".[1]
>
> "Some of the younger generation don't like it either," Rebecca said. "Grandmother told us that Ricardo [another cousin] read the whole book out loud to Alicia [his wife] and that they both found it very upsetting, especially him." She sipped a pink and green margarita and gave him a beatific smile.
>
> "Well, we knew Ricardo wouldn't like it," Josie said. "It's just envy. I keep telling them all it's fiction and they keep wanting to believe every word. They should be glad I didn't write that book. I'm not as nice as you are, cousin. I would have told the truth."
>
> Miguel Chico's novel had been written during a sabbatical leave when he decided to make fiction instead of criticize it. A modest, semi-autobiographical work, it was published by a small California press that quickly went out of business. *Tlaloc* was an academic, if not a commercial, success and its author became known as an ethnic writer. After seeing what the world did to books, he returned humbly to the classroom and to criticism.
>
> "Maybe I ought to start telling the truth," Miguel Chico said. "Then they would really get mad at me, maybe even get a court order to keep me from coming back to Del Sapo. Sales would go up if I got murdered and cut up by some demented religious fanatic." The cowboys and the cowgirls in the wreath started throwing chili dogs and beer at each other. "I have decided," he said and stopped.
>
> "What? What have you decided?" Josie asked. She was embarrassed for him. Rebecca and Hanna put on their disinterested cat expression.

"What?" Miguel Chico asked. The wreath was perfectly still before him. "Oh. I have decided simply to love them. At least their reaction is honest. The dumb sociologists want only positive images, whatever they are, from fiction writers. As if the whole world, especially their own little one, were one big happy collection of ethnic groups. No one knows how to read anymore." (209-11)

Although ironic in tone, this passage deftly illustrates many of the difficulties faced by U.S. authors who become known as "ethnic writers,"[2] and points to the competing, sometimes mutually exclusive, expectations of the publishers, critics, in-group readers, and out-group readers who comprise their audiences.[3]

Usually, to become known at all, ethnic writers must gain access to a mainstream publishing industry that tends either to ignore or pigeonhole them as spokespersons for the ethnic identity group with which they are associated. In the latter case, their work is more likely to be published if it falls within the industry's narrow parameters of being "about" the experiences and culture of their ethnic group, and if it makes reference to "co-ordinates" of ethnic otherness (Verhoeven 101) with which readers are already familiar, such as geographical and historical events and settings; descriptions and explanations of the customs, foods, folklore, and values of the subject ethnic group; and the use and translation of non-English words and phrases.

Authors whose work falls outside of these conventions are less likely to be published by mainstream presses than those authors who remain within them. Islas, for example, was ignored for years by mainstream publishers who either viewed Chicanos as a people without a literature (Cantú 146) or viewed his work as not being "Chicano" enough. Paul Skenazy, the editor of Islas's posthumous novel, *La Mollie and the King of Tears* (1996), has caustically observed that Islas's rejection letters for *The Rain God* "read like a course in Anglo stereotypes of Mexican Americans: There is not enough barrio life or violence in the novel; there is no reading public to buy the work of a Mexican American; the book lacks the voice of protest and political rage that should be part of any work from a so-called minority population" (Afterword 170).

Sometimes ethnic authors like Islas find warmer receptions at smaller academic or specialty presses—after eight years of rejection by New York publishers, Islas's *The Rain God* was finally printed and released by Alexandrian Press, a small publishing house founded by Stanford University professor Patrick Suppes and his wife, novelist Christine Johnson (Cantú 147-8). However, like Miguel Chico's small California press, such publishers must often struggle to remain financially viable, and frequently lack the marketing resources of the larger, mainstream presses.

Because of the difficulties many ethnic writers face in getting published, once their works enter the public realm, the texts and their authors bear a heavy burden of representation. On one hand, like Islas's Ricardo Ángel or the "dumb sociologists," there can be an expectation on the part of some members of the author's ethnic group and some scholars of ethnicity that such novels should work to avoid, or to counter the negative/false images of the group that circulate within the dominant culture. Regardless of whether the author's text is presented as fiction or nonfiction, these readers believe that the "information" it puts into the public domain should simultaneously be "accurate" and cast the group in a positive light. Authors who veer away from this type of cultural protectionism, either by showing the "terrible secrets" of the group, or by subordinating the demands of cultural veracity to those of literary plot or form are sometimes accused of engaging in "cultural malpractice" (Lott 231).[4]

Consider, for example, the well-documented controversy that arose among Chinese American critics over the publication of Maxine Hong Kingston's *The Woman Warrior: Memoir of a Girlhood Among Ghosts* (1976). Kingston had originally submitted her work as a piece of fiction, but agreed to market it as an autobiography at the request of her publishers.[5] Because *The Woman Warrior* was presented as nonfiction, Kingston's rewriting of traditional Chinese legends and her selective translation of certain Chinese terms in ways that did not always reflect standard Chinese American usage[6] were denounced by some critics as "inauthentic" and damaging to Chinese American communities (especially to Chinese American men), while Kingston herself was accused of lacking personal integrity (Wong 248-252, 255).⁷

The apparent conflation of ethnic author, text, and culture that these sorts of literary consumption and policing represent makes more sense when one takes into account both the widespread expectation of in-group and out-group readers that the author of a novel that engages with ethnic subject matter be a representative member of the particular ethnic group under consideration, and the problematic desire on the part of both readers and critics of ethnic literatures to position and consume "ethno/biographic" novels as indigenous ethnographies.⁸

In the first half of this essay, I discuss the social and academic conditions that provide the context of the consumption of ethnic novels as informant texts. In my examination I pay particular attention to the rise of "culture" as a critical and political distinction, and to the narrowing of Americans' concept of difference from an understanding that includes psychological and ideological components, to an understanding of difference that is primarily demographic or "situational."

As an alternate model of the relations of difference and identity, and of subjective experiences and objective truths, I offer in the second half of the essay a reading of Arturo Islas's *Migrant Souls* (1990), a complex, multi-perspected ethno/biographic novel that strongly resists an ethnographic reading. Rather than subsuming issues of intrapersonal and intragroup variations under a stable, homogenous model of cultural difference, the novel, in fact, formally and thematically depicts culture and difference in terms of contradiction, mediation, and change. Chicano ethnic identity becomes significant in *Migrant Souls* not as inheritable cultural property or descriptive literary content, but as a shifting, mediated process.

II

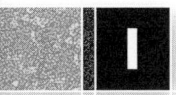n contemporary U.S. society, ethnicity is thought of primarily as a cultural category; indeed, "culture" is what is seen to distinguish categories of ethnicity from those of race

or class. Similarly, the texts produced by members of ethnic groups are defined and read as "cultural artifacts" or "cultural products." The interpretation of ethnicity and ethnic literature as aspects of "cultural" difference conflate anthropological definitions of culture as a system of shared forms of consciousness, values, and patterns of conduct with the definition of culture as "the works and practices of intellectual and especially artistic activity" such as music, literature, painting, theater, film, etc. (Williams 90).

The double identity of ethno/biographic novels as authentic cultural artifacts and artistic cultural products helps explain the odd confounding of aesthetic and political notions of *representation* that surrounds the incorporation of ethnic literatures into U.S. literary canons. Aesthetic or semiotic representation, W. J. T. Mitchell explains, can be thought of as something "standing in for" another thing: a paint stroke stands in for a tree, the word "tree" stands in for a material object or an entire category of material objects. Political representation, on the other hand, involves the act of delegation rather than depiction: someone "acts for" another person—the primary concept behind the ideas of representative government, and of "the accountability of representatives to their constituents" ("Representation" 11-13). As John Guillory observes, the work of ethnic literary incorporation and recovery "has for the most part been undertaken as though the field of writing were a *plenum*, a textual repetition of social diversity" (484-85, emphasis in original), so that "collections" of literature such as syllabi, anthologies, and canons are constructed and evaluated with an eye toward how well they reproduce the demographic diversity of the region or time period from which they are drawn, while the texts themselves are frequently interpreted in terms of how well they mimetically reproduce the cultural beliefs, habits, practices, and products of the particular ethnic identity groups that comprise their subject matter. Once incorporated, these texts are then viewed as if they did, indeed, "act for" those identity groups—either by reinforcing or by countering the negative or false images of the groups that circulate within the dominant culture. Similarly, the authors of those texts are viewed as cultural representatives that "act as" spokespersons for and advocates of group interests. These expectations become the bifurcated "burden of cultural representation" placed on ethnic texts and their authors.

Current U.S. interpretations of ethnicity and ethnic literature as aspects of "cultural" difference rather than of geography, biological/racial diversity, naturalist evolution, or economic class stratification (Domínguez 31-32) have to be understood within the proliferation of the categories and rhetorics of *multiculturalism*, which have significantly displaced earlier, assimilationist models of U.S. political, economic, and social diversity. Building upon the premises of U.S. ethnic and racial nationalist movements of the 1960s and the work done by women's studies and ethnic studies departments in the 1970s and 1980s,[9] the concept of multiculturalism gained widespread social prominence in the U.S. in the late 1980s when it appeared "in connection with demands on behalf of black and other minority groups for separate and equal representation in college curricula and extra-academic cultural programs and events" (Turner, "Anthropology and Multiculturalism" 406). Academic multiculturalism proceeded

> from a critical view of the received curriculum as an instrument for reproducing the hegemony of the dominant social group. This view is specifically grounded in contentions that the canonical humanities curriculum and conventional history-teaching approaches embody notions of "high culture" and social relevance that inculcate and reproduce relations of social inequality by representing the cultural tradition of the dominant social group as being naturally central and preeminent. (412)

Today, anthropologist Terence Turner contends, multiculturalism has assumed "more general connotations as an ideological stance towards participation by such minorities in national cultures and societies and the changing nature of national and transnational cultures themselves." Multiculturalism has become "a code word for minority demands for separate recognition in academic and other cultural institutions" (406-407), and for a variety of forms of identity politics in which the concept of "culture" becomes fused with other aspects of identity.[10]

Multiculturalism, whether in its academic or more general sense, calls for the disassociation of political and social institutions from identification with a single, Anglo-European cultural tradition. It refuses the notion that a common public culture is the indispensable foundation of national politics, insisting instead that political institutions derive their legitimacy "from promoting and coordinating the coexistence of diverse cultural groups, traditions, and identities." Multiculturalism thus replaces the metaphor of the "melting pot"[11] and its emphasis on economic, social, and political assimilation with the metaphor of the "mosaic" and its insistence upon a cultural "equality in difference" (421-22). If the metaphor of the melting pot suggested a utilitarian process of emulation and socialization that occurred over time, and a belief that diversity represented a potential source of conflict, the metaphor of the mosaic suggests a static artifact composed of the synchronic contributions of distinct identity groups and a belief that diversity is an exploitable resource: different cultures can and should coexist side by side, each a unique component in a larger social picture (Hinz vii-xiii).

Such models of the equality of cultural differences can be attractive; however, in the elevation of "culture" as a category and goal of political struggle, there has been a tendency to elide the importance of racial and ethnic exclusion and subordination in U.S. "cultural" life (San Juan 74), and, as Wolfgang Hochbruck so aptly puts it, to forget that the social mosaic of multiculturalism is, in actuality, a relief map "with parts unequal in size, height, and weight" (18). The multiculturalist agendas that have helped establish the importance of cultural identification as an authenticating basis of community for marginalized racial and ethnic groups too frequently have bracketed off culture from the racialized and inequitable structures and relations of political economy (Gordon and Newfield, "Multiculturalism's Unfinished Business" 86), thus obscuring the political and economic origins of those groups' marginalizations (Goldberg 14).

Another important element that the culturalism of multiculturalism frequently obscures is the normative, ideological "grout" that secures relations between and within the cultural tiles of the social mosaic (Gates, "Goodbye" 204). Previous assimilationist models of social diversity insisted that a common public culture was the indispensable foundation of a national politics; newer multicultural models of social diversity refuse the identification of political and social institutions with a single set of cultural traditions, stressing the cultural parity of all groups. However, the majority of multicultural positions maintain—either overtly or covertly—the assertion that there needs to be *some* principle of universality/commonality that will govern the relations between cultural groups and the larger social totality (Gordon and Newfield, "Multiculturalism's Unfinished Business" 92). Depending on what type of multiculturalist agenda is being considered, that principle of commonality or "grout" will most likely be economic competition, democratic politics, the social values of community and tolerance, or some combination thereof. Such principles negate the possibility that cultural differences and/or identities exist in relationships other than those of comparison and contrast, e.g., relationships of juxtaposition, incommensurability, or of unmediated or non-negotiable alterity.[12]

In addition to possessing universal attributes, in order to be compared, cultures and identities must also be seen as coherent and, for the most part, homogenous entities. The multiculturalist model of social diversity considers cultures as distinctive and self-contained, emphasizing shared cultural patterns "at the expense of processes of change and internal inconsistencies, conflicts and contradictions" (Rosaldo 27-8). In these models, Paul Gilroy asserts, "[c]ulture is conceived along ethnically absolute lines, not as something intrinsically fluid, changing, unstable, and dynamic, but as a fixed property of social groups rather than a relational field in which they encounter one another and live out social, historical relationships" (266-7).

This view of ethnic and cultural difference is a highly demographic, or situational one, and places a much greater emphasis on the role of descent than consent in the construction of social identities.[13] In these models the differences that exist between people stem from the different social situations into which they are born, such as their gender, race, ethnicity, culture, nation, and so on. These different social positions, it is assumed, necessarily yield different subjective experiences which, in turn, determine different identities. Most multicultural models find it difficult to accommodate views such as that of "mestiza consciousness" or psychoanalysis that would locate difference within the subject itself, or that views individual subjectivity and experience as inherently hybridized or fragmented. The notion that individuals possess changing, contradictory, or heterogeneous ethnic and/or cultural identities undermines the very idea of coherent identity groups. We see this in the Chicana feminist articulation of a "mestiza consciousness"[14] to theorize and address the multiple and interlocking oppressions (race, class, gender, and nation) to which they are subjected. Such situational models of difference and culture find it difficult to accommodate the idea that cultural identities and differences do not refer to pre-existing, material groups and conditions, but, rather, are products of the contradictory discourses, ideologies, and knowledge constructs through which human beings view themselves, each other, and the world around them.[15] Within the multicultural framework, Joan W. Scott contends,

> "[d]iversity" refers to a plurality of identities, and it is seen as a condition of human existence rather than as the effect of an enunciation of difference that constitutes hierarchies and asymmetries of power. When diversity is seen as a condition of existence, the questions become whether and how much of it is useful to recognize: but the stakes people have in the answers to those questions are obscured, as are the history and politics of difference and identity itself. ("Multiculturalism" 14)

In other words, situational models of difference can interrogate pre-existing categories and manifestations of difference, but have a more difficult time addressing the practices of categorization that result in "ethnicities" and "cultures" in the first place.

Within this context of situational, multicultural difference, the desire of a significant portion of the U.S. reading public to consume ethno/biographic novels as indigenous ethnographies—as objective, transparent sources of information about ethnic and cultural differences—is highly overdetermined. Ethnicity is defined in terms of distinct, homogenous cultural differences; while ethnic novels simultaneously hold the position of authentic cultural artifacts and artistic cultural products, encouraging readers to conflate an ethnic author's narrative strategies, prose style, and plot, with the subjective structures of individual ethnic identities, experiences, and memories, and, subsequently, with the historical and cultural conditions behind those experiences. In this manner, Hazel Carby contends, the consumption of ethnic novels becomes a reliable method "of gaining knowledge of the 'other': a knowledge that appears to satisfy and replace the desire to challenge existing frameworks of segregation" (17).

III

Up to this point, I have been discussing more generally the limitations of the paradigms of multicultural reading and difference that currently dominate the consumption of ethnic literature and the negotiation of diversity in the United States. Now, I would like to turn more specifically to Arturo Islas's 1990 novel, *Migrant Souls,* a text that formally and thematically suggests an alternative to the models of ethnic identity and culture and the relations of subjective experiences and objective truths discussed thus far. Like Islas's other works, *The Rain God: A Desert Tale* (1984) and *La Mollie and the King of Tears* (1996), *Migrant Souls* is a text that deconstructs many of the beliefs underlying ethnographic readings of ethnic literature. It is also a text that emphasizes the contradictions and continuous changes that shape individual Chicano/as' relations to their ethnicities, and thus avoids subsuming the complexity of those relations under a stable, homogenous model of culture. Chicano ethnic identity becomes significant in *Migrant Souls* not as definitive, inheritable content, but as a boundary-drawing and meaning-making process.

I do not wish to imply that *Migrant Souls* is unique in its representation of the complexity of ethnic identity and culture: many of the ethno/biographic novels that are currently consumed as informant texts by U.S. academic and general reading publics also offer sophisticated renderings of the contested and mutable nature of ethnic cultures. However, there are several aspects of Islas's novel and of its reception by critics and readers that make it an especially appropriate vehicle for a discussion of the reading of ethnic novels as ethnographies. The first is the strong autobiographical connection critics and readers consistently draw between Islas and his characters; the second is the novel's intense formal and thematic engagement with the problem of "subjective truth": the problem of determining if and how individual experiences can be used as sources of knowledge about more general psychological, discursive, social, political, economic, and historic conditions.[16] In other words, if and how the lives of individuals can (or should) be used as a means of gaining knowledge about the identity groups to which they are believed to belong.

Migrant Souls is the story of the lives of three generations of the Angels, a Mexican American family that settled in the Texas border town of "Del Sapo" (an anagram of El Paso) after fleeing the Mexican Revolution of 1910. The Angels were also the subject of *The Rain God*, which was awarded the Southwest Book Award for fiction by the Border Regional Library Association in 1986 (Cantú 148). While *The Rain God* focused most of its attention on the first two generations of Angels, *Migrant Souls* concentrates on the lives of two members of the third generation, Josie Salazar and Miguel Chico Ángel. The first section of the novel, "Flight into Egypt" details Josie's struggles as she and her sisters Serena and Ofelia grow into adulthood in a family dominated by the Catholic, patriarchal, and racist worldview of her maternal grandmother, Encarnación Olmeca Ángel, or Mamá Chona. In Book Two of the novel, "Feliz Navidad," Josie and Miguel Chico have grown up to be the family sinners: Josie has had an affair and has divorced her husband, Miguel Chico is a homosexual and has become an alcoholic. Book Two uses the lens of multiple Ángel family Christmas Eve parties (what Miguel Chico deems the family's "annual rite of hypocrisy") to explore the different significances Josie and Miguel Chico, along with several other members of the second and third generations of Angels, attach to their ethnic and familial heritage.

Miguel Chico, who, along with his prominent role in *Migrant Souls*, also serves as one of the main protagonists of *The Rain God*, is the character that shares the most biographical traits with Arturo Islas and is the primary reason Islas's work is frequently read as ethnic autobiography. Among numerous other similarities, both Islas and the character Miguel Chico were raised in multi-generational Mexican American families dwelling in Texas border towns, both received a Ph.D. in English, both became professors of English, both lived as adults in northern California, both were homosexuals, both suffered from childhood illnesses and later from intestinal disease that led eventually to both undergoing colostomies and depending upon external appliances for the rest of their lives, and both became known "ethnic writers."

While it is understandable that these similarities might tempt readers to position and consume *Migrant Souls* as autobiography, doing so requires that readers ignore Islas's own insistence upon the fictional status of his work, that they discount the highly complex and rich formal qualities of the novel, and that they remove the novel from the multitude of literary traditions of which it is a part. In an interview conducted shortly before Islas's death in 1991, José Antonio Burciaga and Islas discuss the tendency of readers to approach Islas's novels as autobiographies. Burciaga asks Islas whether he relates to Miguel Chico as "himself," to which Islas replies, "Oh, of course! He more than any of my other characters. With him I used more of my own experiences in life to make his character." "[B]ut," he continues, "I am all of my characters. I'm Lola, I'm Felix, I'm all those people. They're like dream figures. I use real life people as models and sometimes make composites—like a mural" (163). In the same interview Burciaga asks Islas to distinguish between autobiography and fiction. "Well," Islas replies,

> fiction is lying and I draw—and every fiction writer that I respect draws—shamelessly from their own experience and the experiences of people they know . . . every writer that I have learned from is examining human nature, and one way we can examine human nature is through fiction. To do that, it seems natural to draw from one's experience and what one knows.

> What makes it fiction is that you give it a shape, you know? And you're consciously doing that or unconsciously, depending on the process and depending on the book or the story itself. Life has no shape. We impose shape on it so we can deal with it. It's so scary to think that it's all chaos. And what artists do to the nth degree, what writers do to the nth degree, without seeming to do it—this is the trick, you see—is to give things shape that have no shape . . . the idea of writing a novel today, or a collection of stories, is to make them—at least to me—seem so real that people will be fooled into thinking "Ah, this is real life!" In fact, what one does, at least what I do, is to very, very carefully make it all seem so natural . . . to make it seem lifelike, when in fact it isn't. It's a book—those characters in that book are not real people, but the idea is to make the reader think that they are. (163)

Islas's emphasis on the highly crafted nature of his writing draws attention to the means by which he creates an aesthetic, often ironic disjuncture between himself and his characters that belies a naively autobiographic reading of his work. Perhaps it is, in part, a tribute to Islas's skill as a writer that the formal techniques through which he creates and gives shape to the chaotic experiences and subjectivities of the Ángel family would render them so vivid that readers would want to think of his characters as real people. However, Islas's narrative techniques serve as a means of processing and enunciating rather than transparently describing the anomalous materials of Mexican American/Chicano/a ethnic identity.

Critics of Islas's work such as Roberto Cantú, Antonio C. Márquez, Ricardo L. Ortiz, José David Saldívar, Marta E. Sánchez, and Paul Skenazy consistently emphasize the "literariness" of his novels and the incompleteness of readings that seek to "recover the raw material" of Islas's stories from "the creative deformation" they have undergone in becoming works of fiction. In *Migrant Souls* such literariness includes the disruption of a linear chronology through the use of flashbacks, flash-forwards, and multiple exposures of the same scene from a variety of perspectives; the use of free indirect discourse and interior monologue; scenes of magical realism; the ongoing presence of structuring metaphors such as the colonial Indian/Spanish mestiza heritage of Mexicans and Mexican Americans; extra-literary references to other Chicano critics and writers[17]; and meta-commentary on the nature of discourse, writing, and the consumption of ethnic literature.[18]

In addition to the complexity of Islas's literary techniques, García Márquez, Saldívar, and Skenazy also emphasize the wide variety of literary traditions that inform Islas's scholarship and work, connections that are frequently ignored by publishers and readers who want to view Islas's novels strictly in terms of U.S. ethnic autobiography and/or ethnography. In a letter to his agent about *The Rain God*, Islas discussed the similarities between his approach to character and plot and the approach of William Faulkner. Like Faulkner, Islas wrote, he saw himself as "chronicling the life of a historical creature who happens to live at a time when he was taught to hate what he perceived himself to be." Islas asserted that the character Miguel Chico is "my Quentin Compson; he would say in exactly the same tone Quentin uses at the end of [Faulkner's 1936 *Absalom,*] *Absalom!*: 'I don't hate Mexicans! I don't hate Anglos! I don't hate gays'!" (J. Salvídar 112).[19] In addition to the southern literary tradition of Faulkner, Salvídar locates Islas's work "in the long tradition of psychologically complex novels" such as those of Henry James, in which the consciousness and impressions of characters serve as structuring devices for the narrative (113)[20] and draws comparisons between Islas and other writers of the American west such as Willa Cather and M. Scott Momaday whose work, like Islas's, focuses on migrations through the landscapes of U.S. western territories (117-8).[21]

The literary traditions with which Islas's fiction can most easily be associated, however, are those of Latin America. In an essay entitled "Between Politics and Aesthetics: Problems in Chicano Fiction" Islas describes Chicano fiction as existing in the space between the literatures of Anglo and Latin America (Márquez 5). Certainly, Antonio Márquez asserts, Islas's references to pre-Hispanic mythopoetics, his engagement with three generations of a family dominated by a matriarch, and his use of magical realism suggest a connection between *The Rain God, Migrant Souls,* and Gabriel García Márquez's *One Hundred Years of Solitude* (5-6).

Islas's explorations of the relation between the living and the dead also bring to mind the work of Octavio Paz, Pablo Neruda, and Juan Rulfo. A portion of Pablo Neruda's poem "The Heights of Machu Picchu" served as the epigraph of *The Rain God* (3).

The point of noting affinities between Islas's work and other literary traditions is not to suggest that his novels are derivative; rather, it is to interrupt the relegation of his work to a U.S. ethnic "ghetto" in which ethnic characters are conflated with ethnic authors, and ethnic authors are viewed as indigenous informants who are "less graced with imagination than with recall" (Skenazy, "Borders" 211). Even if, however, one were completely to dismiss Islas's assertions of the fictional nature of his work, and to ignore his literary craftsmanship and his affinities with other literary traditions, it would still be difficult to justify an autobiographic/ethnographic reading of *Migrant Souls*. For, in the course of telling the story of the Ángel family, the novel deconstructs most of the foundational premises of autobiography and ethnography, including the notions of the transparency of experience and the coherency of individual and group identities.

One of the primary ways that Islas negates the notion of an unmediated relation between subjective experiences and objective truths is to detail the myriad of competing and contradictory social discourses that individuals use to impose shape upon the "chaos" of their lives. These discourses, *Migrant Souls* suggests, permeate the world around us and are often absorbed when we are children. The two characters through which this process is depicted in the most detail are Mamá Chona and her granddaughter, Josie Salazar, a doubling that seems highly ironic, for throughout the course of the novel Mamá Chona and Josie are presented as ideological antagonists. Mamá Chona's worldview is dominated by the Catholic upbringing she received as a child in a convent in pre-revolutionary Mexico. In this worldview, which Mamá Chona doggedly attempts to instill in her children and grandchildren, life is something to be endured and the only future that matters is the afterlife (46). All that is good is spiritual, Catholic, Spanish, light, monied, and obedient; conversely, all that is earthly, physical, non-Catholic, Indian, dark, poor, and disobedient is bad. Suffering in this world, especially for women, is a given "and as timeless as the desert around them" (46).

These are the discourses and paradigms through which Mamá Chona gives her experiences shape and meaning, experiences that involve the deaths of five of her ten children, the death of her husband Jesús Ángel as the family fled Mexico, and the racism and prejudice she and her family experience at the hands of Anglos in the border town of Del Sapo. Through Mamá Chona's eyes, theology is much more important than history, and "[t]heir flight northward, Jesus Angel's death, the way she saw her children treated by their Americanized neighbors and bosses were all part of God's plan for the Angels" (42). The extended Ángel family can be divided into those individuals who subscribe to this black-and-white worldview, those who actively resist it, and those, who, caught in between Mamá Chona's certainty and the uncontrollable nature of their own desires and doubts, wander in a perpetual grayness, feeling ashamed for not seeing life as clearly as they believe they should (60).

In this sense, the Ángel family tree becomes a scaffolding that structures the novel's more general exploration of the larger past and present of Mexican Americans along the border. It becomes a heuristic of Mexican American/Chicano/a culture and thus combines an understanding of "family" as an ontological field representing the complexity of relationships of self and other, with that of family as a historical and cultural field. Rather than a complete, linear account of the history of any individual, family, or culture, however, *Migrant Souls* becomes a genealogy that examines a multitude of ethnic and cultural discourses, and that integrates as many aspects of selfhood and culture as are deemed significant by the changing agents of the narrative.[22] The result is a type of genealogical revisionism, a genealogy of perspectives as well as of people.

Josie is the female family member whose perspective most sharply contrasts with the more traditional discourses and ideologies that shape Mamá Chona's and many of her relatives' lives. Since she was a child, she has sensed that her blood "was closer to the earth than an Angel's ought to be" (4). She more readily identifies with the Indian heritage (and with all of its dark, earthly, physical, and disobedient associations) of her father than with the supposedly superior Ángel upbringing of her mother, Eduviges. Yet, while *Migrant Souls* depicts Josie as resisting traditional Mexican/Chicano/a beliefs about the role of women in this world and the next, it does not propose that her subjective experiences of the objective conditions and events of her life are significantly more transparent than Mamá Chona's. Although Josie prides herself on her ability to see the world without sentimentality or exaggeration and repeatedly refers to herself as "the true scientist in this crazy family" (51), the novel depicts her subjectivity, too, as mediated by a myriad of discourses and ideologies which she began absorbing and struggling with as a child.

For example, on a trip across the U.S.-Mexican border to get a Thanksgiving turkey Josie makes the mistake of asking her father, Sancho Salazar, if they are "aliens," a term she has read in newspapers and heard used at school by her Anglo classmates. Sancho is so horrified that he immediately slams on the brakes of his truck and says to Josie, "I do not ever want to hear you use that word in my presence again. About anybody. We are not aliens. We are American citizens of Mexican heritage. We are proud of both countries and have never and will never be that word you just said to me." When Josie protests that she was only telling him what her classmate Kathy Jarvis told her, Sancho entreats her, "Don't you see, Josie. When people call Mexicans those words, it makes it easier for them to deport or kill them. Aliens come from outer space" (29-30).

Much of the novel's depiction of Josie's growth from childhood to adulthood focuses upon just these sorts of epistemological negotiations. In addition to newspapers, classmates, and relatives, we see Josie utilize family epics, fairly tales, urban folklore about the horrors experienced by Mexican American citizens at the hands of the "migra" (U.S. immigration officers), North American Thanksgiving and Christmas traditions, Catholic theology, pop songs, novels by the Brontë sisters, *Modern Romance* magazines, U.S. and Mexican films and television programs, her Anglo public school education, Grateful Dead concerts, and French religious icons to try to make sense of her experiences growing up in the

1950s and 1960s as a Mexican American woman living in a Texas border town. The differences between Mamá Chona's and Josie's worldviews are not strictly generational—Josie's sister Ofelia subscribes wholeheartedly to Mamá Chona's mentality; rather, they represent the multiplicity of ways in which an individual's experiences are constructed by categories of perception and by hierarchies and asymmetries of power. As I will discuss in just a moment, the novel *does* depict some worldviews and cultural discourses as less oppressive and more liberating than others, but it does not assert that individuals can gain unmediated access to the objective truth of the conditions of their lives.[23]

Migrant Souls's rejection of transparent models of experience and its depiction of the multiple, contradictory means by which individuals from the same identity group—from the same *family*—negotiate the same material conditions and ethnic heritage negates the view that "ethnic identity" is a function of the straightforward transmission of a coherent set of cultural values and practices from one generation to another. It suggests instead that ethnicity is something that all generations and individuals must reinvent and reinterpret for themselves (Fischer 173). This process is neither predictable nor painless. In fact, *Migrant Souls* represents the individual negotiation of ethnic identity as being capable of producing a great deal of suffering, a view that refutes more reductive models of multicultural diversity that hold that ethnic identity and culture are necessarily authenticating bases of community or loci of collective rights that, by definition, are superior to the "inauthentic" and repressive normative codes of the dominant culture (T. Turner 420). Instead, as Robert Cantú observes, *Migrant Souls* creates a model of ethnic culture that challenges the reader "to reexamine and distinguish between cultural features which oppress and those which liberate" (151). The fact that the two main protagonists and the most sympathetically drawn characters of *Migrant Souls*, Josie and Miguel Chico, are the characters that find traditional Mexican/Chicano concepts of gender, sexuality, and race the most oppressive tends to reinforce this challenge.

Josie and Miguel Chico are drawn together as children when they discover "that each found the wicked stepmother far more interesting than the boring Snow White, who deserved her even more boring and bland prince" (51). As teenagers they founded "the Order of Saint Wretched" so that "they might laugh at misery. Passion, betrayal, unrequited love were all offered up to Saint Wretched whenever the cousins found themselves or others once again enthralled by the sins of the flesh" (57). Saint Wretched, made manifest by Miguel Chico in the form of a postcard he finds in Paris of a naked flapper with bobbed hair, perfectly shaped breasts, and an ecstatic face "tied to a huge cross by thick and shiny ropes" (115), is mostly a joke, but she is also, in part, an attempt by Josie and Miguel to negotiate the pain they feel due to their refusal or inability to subscribe to their assigned cultural roles.

For Josie, this refusal takes the form of rejecting traditional Mexican/Chicano/a gender roles that define a woman's value primarily in terms of her duties as a wife and mother, and that define proper feminine behavior to be submissive and nonsexual. In Mamá Chona's and most of her daughters' interpretations of these traditional gender roles, female gender perfection includes a guilt-ridden denial of the flesh and a willingness to submit to any type of treatment at the hands of a man in the name of the sanctity of marriage in the Catholic Church. Josie's overt rebellion against their views begins when she is very young. At the age of five, when she and her sisters (like all young Angels) go to Mamá Chona's house to hear the story of their long-dead grandfather, Josie chafes uncomfortably against the family myths that elevate their grandfather to the realm of the divine and denigrate life in this world. Mamá Chona tells her granddaughters they must try to be as much like heavenly angels as they can, but warns that "[i]t's more difficult for girls to be like angels because they are born wicked in a different way from boys" (14). Josie's oldest sister, Ofelia, drinks in every one of Mamá Chona's admonitions; her middle sister, Serena, is distracted by her own thoughts as she looks around the room and tries to stifle her yawns; Josie, however, actively fights against believing what her grandmother says and longs for her father to come and take them away from the over-refined and otherworldly confines of her grandmother's parlor and beliefs.

Josie's awareness as a young child that she does not fulfill her grandmother's and mother's desire for a "delicate and tactful" young woman worthy of her connection to the Ángel family name (4) becomes in high school an open rebellion against their values. On one such occasion Miguel Chico accompanies Josie home after school. Upon their arrival, Eduviges offers him a snack, and at the same time reminds Josie not to eat between meals: "You're a growing boy," she tells Miguel Chico, "You can eat as much as you want. It's only natural" (52). Miguel Chico is well aware of the effect that such blatant gender inequities have on his cousin's state of mind and watches nervously as Josie begins methodically popping one buttered saltine after another into her mouth. Josie fixes Miguel a cracker and says, "Eat, cousin [. . .] You have permission from on high." [. . .] "Josie, I'm warning you," her mother says,

> "If you don't feel like eating your supper later, there won't be any midnight raids on the refrigerator."
> "What are you going to do, Mother? Put a padlock on the door?" Josie laughed.
> "*Malcriada*," her mother said. "Ofelia and Serena know I mean it."
> Josie licked the apple butter on the spoon. "It sure is hard," she said to Miguel Chico, "being the sister of a perfect child and a saint." Then, looking at her mother with even darker eyes, she said, "Leave me alone, Mother. I'm old enough to make my own choices. And anyway, you're never going to approve of anything I do, so why not just give up and be quiet about it? I'll feel your disapproval. How's that? Just don't make me listen to it." (53-4)

It seems that at every significant moment in Josie's life the same sorts of clashes over gender propriety occur. At Josie's wedding she refuses to wear underwear because of the heat and her mother calls her "a little savage." "Thank God," her mother tells her, "I kept Mama Chona from being in here while you changed." "I'm all flesh, Mother," Josie replies, "There aren't going to be any immaculate conceptions in my family" (98). Later, when Josie's marriage dissolves in divorce and she moves back to Del Sapo from northern California, the first words out of her mother's mouth are that, without a father, her two daughters, Hannah and Rebecca, are going "to grow up badly and find themselves on the street." Eduviges utters this dire prediction in "that dead-certain tone that made the rebellious Angels in Josie's generation crazy with rage." Josie controls herself, knowing that "she must not give way to self-pity or anger or she and her girls would be lost and not only to the street" (199), and simply replies in the same tone as her mother that she is saving money to buy a house for herself and her children.

While Islas's narrative presents Josie's struggles sympathetically, it does not demonize Mamá Chona, or Eduviges and her sisters. Using the narrator's omniscient commentary and the perspectives of other characters, *Migrant Souls* provides a historical context for the rigid beliefs held by many members of the Ángel family. In one such passage while Josie and her sister Serena are discussing the beliefs of their relatives, Josie comments, "God, what a world they've invented." Serena replies, "I can see why they did it . . . It keeps them alive and going. Can you imagine what it must have been like for them before we were born? How in the world did they manage?" "Well," Josie retorts, "maybe it worked for them . . . But I'll be damned if I'm going to live that way" (46-47). In the racist environment of the border town of Del Sapo, the Ángel family's and other Mexican Americans' defense of traditional Mexican cultural and religious beliefs enables them to function and to give their life meaning and value in environments in which they are viewed as "aliens," and are economically and politically discriminated against. As one of the black sheep of the Ángel family, Josie has two choices: she either can adhere to those traditional values that she finds oppressive and be accepted into the group, or she can refuse her prescribed familial and cultural roles and risk being "lost."

In this manner, Ángel family dynamics mirror some of the larger dynamics of multicultural politics in the United States in which oppressed minority groups, attempting to establish a collective identity and authority, insist upon homogenous definitions of that particular identity. In this model of group politics the test of membership in an identity group "becomes less one's willingness to endorse certain principles and engage in specific political actions, less one's positioning in specific relationships of power, than one's ability to use the prescribed languages that are taken as signs that one is inherently 'of' the group" (Scott, "Multiculturalism" 18). Individuals who reject the "official" values, beliefs, and behaviors that are the accepted signs of membership in the group are repudiated and excluded. Thus, in the process of establishing a group identity at the margins of U.S. society, members of the group that insist upon the "homogeneity of the self-identical" (Gates, "Ethnic" 296) can end up recreating the marginalizing practices against which they, themselves, are struggling. Similarly, in *Migrant Souls*, the first- and second-generation Angels' insistence that Josie and her sisters and female cousins accept traditional gender roles so that they will be "strong enough to endure the rigorous demands of marriage and motherhood" (4) and the difficulties of life in a country where, for the most part, Mexican Americans are ignored or exploited, becomes the vehicle through which Josie and other rebellious Ángel women are disciplined and marginalized.

While Josie takes the route of open rebellion against those features of her familial and ethnic heritage that she finds oppressive, Miguel Chico is not so overt in his rejection of traditional Mexican gender and sexual mores, choosing for most of his life to keep his homosexuality a secret from all but a few of his family members. Growing up, Josie knows without being told that her cousin is "a lover of men." Their camaraderie as the family "sinners" is born out of "that intuitive and unspoken revelation" (120). For most of the rest of the family, however, homosexuality is viewed either as an abomination against God and man or as something made up by Anglo-run newspapers. When Miguel Chico and Josie's uncle, Félix Ángel, is murdered by a young serviceman who claimed Félix had propositioned him, Eduviges declares, "I don't believe a word of it. There are no homosexuals" (121). Most of the Ángel family follows her example, preferring that Félix's murderer be let free than to have the shame of Félix's "hidden life" continue to be newspaper fodder.

Josie's lesbian sister, Serena, chooses not to disturb their denial. She lives in Del Sapo with Mary Margaret, her "roommate" of twelve years, and attends to the needs of their elderly family and neighbors with "a sincerity of heart that kept anyone from questioning her life too closely" (106). To remain a member of her family and of the Mexican American community of Del Sapo she must subscribe, at least in appearance, to the prescribed values and behaviors that are taken as signs that she is inherently of the Mexican American ethnic group. So, after twelve years, Serena still takes her mother, rather than her lover, to family functions. For many years Miguel Chico also denies his homosexuality, trying to remain the "consummate pleaser" and retain the privileges of being the favorite grandchild (53). As an adult, however, Miguel Chico moves away to San Francisco so he can live an uncloseted life. His struggles with the traditional Mexican definitions of masculinity that praise machismo and male desire but forbid his love of men continue to make him suffer, however. Those cultural discourses occur to him as internal demons who "[i]n matter-of-fact, reasonable voices," tell him he is "not a child of the Church or worthy of the family name and that Ricardo [his cousin] should have been his father's firstborn son," and that "he ought to consider destroying himself" (218). Sometimes the demons drive him to drink, sometimes they drive him to write, but rarely do they allow Miguel Chico to sustain a comfortable balance between his identity as a Mexican American man and his identity as a gay man. In their position on the margins of the margins, family sinners Josie, Serena, and Miguel Chico do not find their ethnic identity and heritage to be an inherently authenticating base of community; instead, they find it a source of contradiction and confusion, at times liberating and empowering, at times a source of great pain.

Migrant Souls's depiction of the contestations that occur within the Ángel family, and, subsequently, within Mexican American/Chicano/a ethnic communities refutes situational and multicultural models of difference that would insist on the stability and homogeneity of ethnic identity. In *Migrant Souls* ethnicity and ethnic culture are defined not in terms of their coherent, homogenous content, but as boundary constructing *processes*, which, Frederik

Barth explains, function as categorical separations between groups: "It is the ethnic *boundary* that defines the group," he asserts, "not the cultural stuff that it encloses" (15, emphasis in original).

Approaching ethnic cultures as boundary projects and practices of categorization rather than as aggregations of "cultural stuff" allows Islas's readers to make sense of an apparent paradox in *Migrant Soul's* depiction of life in a "Mex/Tex" border town. On one hand, the novel depicts life in Del Sapo as a constant exchange across national and ethnic borders of consumer goods, languages, ideas, traditions, populations, and medias. Josie's epistemic repertoire of Anglo, Indian, Spanish, Chicano, and French social discourses, and her marriage to a half-Anglo, half-Mexican military man are only two examples of the ongoing cultural hybridization that occurs every day in Del Sapo. On the other hand, however, the novel also spends a great deal of time delineating the problems that arise due to the sharp divisions that exist between the Mexican and Anglo cultural communities of Del Sapo.

A good example of this seeming paradox is found in a scene in *Migrant Souls* in which Josie and Miguel Chico attend a school dance. When they arrive at the gymnasium, all the Chicano and Anglo girls are wearing the same crinolines and rolled bobby socks, all the boys are in similar suits, and everyone is listening to the same music and dancing the same dances. The scene would appear to be one of assimilation and/or hybridization. Yet, through Josie's observations the reader learns that "[c]rossovers from one group to another were noticed and talked about later, for each race guarded its own and had been taught to fear the consequences of mixing cultures. An undeclared borderline existed between Mexicans and Anglos that only a few dared to cross in the name of love" (67-8). In fact, the "cultural stuff" of the two groups *is* mixed; what determines the ethnic identities of the two groups is the borderline, the importance that both Anglos and Chicano/as attribute to the racial component of their ethnic identities, and that both use to determine economic, political, and social boundaries. In this version of the multicultural mosaic, the cultural "colors" of the tiles intermix and shift. The larger social picture is determined solely by the outline of the ideological "grid" through which those colors flow and pool.

An even more striking example of ethnicity as a boundary-making process can be seen in the way in which the colonial categories of Indian and Spanish ethnicity are used *within* the Ángel family and Chicano communities to establish hierarchies and power relations. Contemporary Mexican/Chicano/a peoples are mestiza descendants of both the indigenous inhabitants of the Americas and the Spanish soldiers who conquered their civilizations in the sixteenth and seventeenth centuries. Ángel family mythology holds that Mamá Chona's venerable husband and family patriarch, Jesús Ángel, "had more Spanish than Indian blood in his veins . . . if his ancestors had not been in the first army of *conquistadores*, they certainly had sailed in shortly thereafter" (8-9). Mamá Chona and her sister (Tía Cuca) had been raised in a Catholic convent and were taught to speak Spanish with a Castilian accent. Despite both women's dark skin and high cheekbones that strongly suggest an Indian heritage, they see themselves as Spanish ladies and try to raise their children and grandchildren to revere their Spanish heritage and disparage their Indian background.

Within the Ángel family, the colonial Indian/Spanish ethnic binary is used as a Manichean metaphor that both structures, and is conflated with, a number of other binary relations such as bad/good, damned/saved, dark/light, ignorance/wisdom, savage/civilized, poor/monied, physical/spiritual, and so forth. Josie's rebellion against traditional gender roles is attributed by both her family and herself to her "Indian blood": when Josie refuses to act as if she is enjoying herself at an Ángel family function, her mother announces, "She's simply acting like an Indian, that's all . . . Everyone knows they don't talk and can't answer politely when someone asks them a question" (5); and upon her return to Del Sapo, Josie calls her children her beautiful little Indians to antagonize her mother. On another occasion, when the Ángel family attends Christmas Eve mass at St. Lucía's in the poorer part of town, Eduviges's sister, Jesús María, complains that "It will be like going to church in a wigwam. I am not an Indian" (143). In her mind, poverty and Indian ethnicity are one and the same state.

These are just a few of the many scenes in *Migrant Souls* in which ethnic heritage is used as a means of drawing distinctions between members of the Ángel family. The rebels of the family choose to identify with the "Indianness" of their mestiza ancestry while the more tradition-oriented members of the family associate themselves with the Spanish part of their cultural heritage. In situational models of difference these distinctions would make no sense: the Ángels descended from the same ancestors and are members of the same ethnic group; therefore, they necessarily share the same ethnic identity. However, in models of ethnic identity that view "ethnicity" as a practice of categorization rather than as a pre-existing category, the Angels' use of ethnicity as a metaphorical construct that enables them to establish hierarchical boundaries makes perfect sense. Indeed, the ideological function of ethnicity within the Ángel family underscores the ideological functions of the categories of Anglo and Chicano ethnicity within the town of Del Sapo, and in the United States at large. In the model of multicultural diversity offered by *Migrant Souls,* ethnic identity is always a "difference-in-relation" (McLaren 58) rather than a pre-existing state of separate being.

IV

If individual experience is so highly mediated, if different individuals can find the same aspects of their ethnic heritage either liberating or oppressive, if ethnicity and ethnic culture are better defined as boundary-making processes than as pre-existing, homogenous conditions, how likely is it that single individuals or single texts could offer a definitive, objective account of an ethnic culture? By focusing on the "microdifferences" within Mexican American/Chicano/a cultures and on the political, economic, and social macrostructures that comprise the context within which ethnicity becomes meaningful as a category of identity (59), Islas's *Migrant Souls* moves away from contemporary U.S. models of multiculturalism in which ethnic diversity is seen as "a condition of human existence" rather than as the effect of "an enunciation of difference that constitutes hierarchies and asymmetries of power" (Scott, "Multiculturalism" 14). Instead, Islas's narrative offers an exploration of the different stakes different individuals and groups have in recognizing the discourses of "ethnicity" and "culture" as "meaningful way[s] to confront American experience" (Reilly 7). What is of interest in *Migrant Souls* is not so much the problem of subjective truth—how the subjective experience of individual ethnic subjects can yield objective knowledge about their ethnic culture—but the question of how material conditions in the United States are both produced and mediated by social and subjective discourses of ethnicity, race, and culture.

In this sense, Islas's narrative does address the issue of whether there is a relation between the subjective structures of literature, the subjective structures of individual experiences, and objective, material conditions of existence. However, the model of that relation it depicts seems to be the exact opposite of the model held by readers who wish to read ethnic novels as ethnographies. Rather than objectively and mimetically reproducing the transparent material experiences of a distinct ethnic identity group, the text of *Migrant Souls* represents those experiences as inescapably enmeshed in competing social fictions, recalling Islas's assertion that, in creating their fiction, writers simply do what all people do: they give shape to lives and experiences that have no intrinsic shape or meaning.

Perhaps the most fruitful way to think about U.S. ethnic literatures has little to do with questions of objectivity and authenticity at all. Perhaps what is of most interest in the novels of individuals who become known as U.S. ethnic writers is not the ways in which they describe the ethnic "content" of the identity groups with which they are associated, but the different ways in which they "imaginatively render the significance" (Reilly 3), or lack of significance, of the category of ethnicity in the United States. In Islas's *Migrant Souls* the significance different characters place on Chicano ethnicity varies as widely as do their personalities. For Mamá Chona issues of ethnicity are subsumed by issues of religion: theology is more important than history. For Josie and Miguel Chico, ethnicity is inescapably enmeshed in categories of gender and sexuality; for their cousin Ricardo, Mexican American/Chicano/a ethnicity is something to be ignored. He wants to live solely according to the myths of North America. For his Anglo bosses, that same ethnicity and ethnic heritage represents a burden that "those from Ricardo's background" can overcome "if they set their minds to it" (203). From their position of economic, political, and social privilege, Ricardo's bosses see ethnicity as something possessed by others and something that should be discarded in the pursuit of assimilation. Cousin Rudy, the immigration lawyer, has an entirely different understanding of Chicano/a identity. He views Chicano/as as a group of people, much like African Americans, who are economically and politically exploited and, thus, sees his ethnic heritage both as a source of oppression and as a potential source of political activism and coalition (165). While Islas's narrative suggests that some of these views are more empowering than others, and have a greater potential to challenge existing frameworks of oppression, none of them is represented as objectively correct or incorrect.

Approaching ethno/biographic novels in terms of significance rather than in terms of the veracity of their content not only interrupts readings by out-group readers who would seek to consume such novels as reliable methods of gaining knowledge of the 'other' (Carby 17); it also provides a way to acknowledge and accommodate the very real desire on the part of in-group readers to find images of their own experiences in literature. But, rather than depending on essentialized, homogenized, and mosaic models of ethnic culture to provide those images, an emphasis on the significance of ethnicity allows both out-group and in-group readers to engage in the processes of categorization that define for whom and with what material effects "ethnicity" is a relevant concept—both on the page and in their own lives.

NOTES

[1] Islas's working title for *Migrant Souls* was "A Perfectly Happy Family."

[2] One of the factors that contribute to the difficulties faced by U.S. "ethnic writers" is the ambiguity that surrounds the term "ethnicity" itself. Usually thought of as a sociological concept that positions itself against the categories of race and class, ethnicity is commonly defined as "a collectivity within a larger society having real or putative common ancestry, memories of a shared past, and cultural focus on one or more symbolic elements which define the group's identity, such as kinship, religion, language, shared territory, nationality, or physical appearance" (Gilman 19). As professor of human biology and Germanic studies Sander L. Gilman points out, however, this definition of ethnicity, put forth by sociologist M. Bulmer in the essay "Race and Ethnicity," contains elements that could just as easily apply to the categories of race and class against which it defines itself and so, like most encyclopedic definitions of the term, proves less definitive than it at first might appear.

Another element adding to the confusion surrounding ethnicity is the question of who exactly possesses the attribute. In *Beyond Ethnicity: Consent and Descent in American Culture,* Werner Sollors explains that there is an inherent conflict between universalist/inclusive uses of ethnicity and other uses of the word that omit dominant groups, thus establishing what Sollors describes as "ethnicity minus one" (24-5). Sollors identifies this conflict as intrinsic to the etymological roots of the term:

> To say it in the simplest and clearest terms, an ethnic, etymologically speaking, is a *goy*. The Greek word *ethnikos* from which the English "ethnic" and "ethnicity" are derived, meant "gentile," "heathen." Going back to the noun *ethnos*, the word was used to refer not just to people in general but also to "others" ... In the Christianized context the word "ethnic" (sometimes spelled "hethnic") recurred, from the fourteenth to the nineteenth century, in the sense of "heathen." Only in the mid-nineteenth century did the more familiar meaning of "ethnic" as "peculiar to a race or nation" reemerge. (25)

In this essay, I follow the example of both Sollors and Frederick Barth in approaching ethnicity less as a definitive category of identity than as "boundary-constructing processes which function as cultural markers between groups" (Sollors, summarizing Barth 27). In this sense, what may be of most interest in the novels of individuals who become known as ethnic writers are not the ways in which they describe the ethnic "content" of the identity groups with which they are associated, but the different ways in which such authors "imaginatively render the significance [or lack thereof] of ethnic experience in the United States" (Reilly 3).

[3] By "in-group readers" I mean readers who are considered by others or who consider themselves members of the ethnic group that is depicted in the work of fiction under consideration. "Out-group readers" refers to individuals who are not considered by others or who do not consider themselves to belong to that group.

[4] In an interview published in *Body Politics and the Fictional Double*, cultural critic and performance artist Coco Fusco addresses some of the motivations and limitations of this type of cultural protectionism, especially among minority intellectuals:

> There is this sense of "The main stream culture fucks us over, so we have to take care of our icons. We have to take care of our cultural symbols, we have to take care of our culture, we only can show the good." That doesn't convince *anybody!* It doesn't begin to address just how complex the cultural dynamics that we're dealing with are! And it's *boring* for one as an artist to be limited to only telling happy stories. Happy stories are not interesting. I really cannot insist on that enough because it comes up every single time I perform or do a presentation. I did a video tape a few years ago, *Pochonovela* (1995), that makes fun of *telenovelas*, and I got responses like, "Oh my god, you are making fun of our culture, we shouldn't make fun—" I say "why *not*?" you know? If we don't, who will? Isn't it better to understand your foibles? Isn't it better to understand your weaknesses than to pretend that everything is fantastic? (126)

[5] Arturo Islas was also encouraged to alter *The Rain God* and publish it as an autobiography in order to make it more "believable" (Skenazy, "Borders" 211).

[6] Sau-ling Cynthia Wong identifies Kingston's translation of the Cantonese word *kuei* as "ghost" as a primary example of this. While *kuei* can be translated as "ghost," as Wong points out, it is more often

used in the sense of "demon," "devil," or "asshole" in Chinese American communities, causing critics such as Jefferey Paul Chan and Benjamin R. Tong to deem Kingston's translation as inaccurate and as "pandering to white taste" (252).

[7] In the essay "Autobiography as Guided Chinatown Tour? Maxine Hong Kingston's *Woman Warrior* and the Chinese-American Autobiographical Controversy," literary critic Sau-ling Wong points out that the Chinese American critics who condemned the "fictional" or "negative" aspects of Kingston's "autobiography" were doing so not simply out of a concern for generic integrity, but out of "a keen awareness of the sociopolitical context of minority literary creation" (250). Cognizant of the tendency of publishers, of critics, and of much of the reading public to consume ethnic works as documentary accounts of ethnic culture, the critics saw the problem with Kingston's novel/autobiography not so much in the stories themselves, but in her failure to take into account readers' desire to consume *Warrior Woman* as an indigenous ethnography: "to make story into guidebook, turn artist into anthropological source, and distort personal experience into cultural generalization" (Skenazy, "Borders" 210). As one critic, Katheryn Fong, wrote in an open letter to Kingston, "Your fantasy stories are embellished versions of your mother's embellished versions of stories. As fiction, these stories are creatively written with graphic imagery and emotion. The problem is that non-Chinese are reading your fiction as true accounts of Chinese and Chinese American history" (67).

[8] By "ethno/biographic novel" I am referring to novels that thematically are "about" the lived experiences of ethnic subjects and of ethnic identity groups. Simply by definition this term could refer to texts ranging from James Joyce's *Ulysses* to Louise Erdrich's *Tracks* to Michael Ondaatje's *The English Patient* to John Howard Griffin's *Black Like Me*. In this chapter, however, I am limiting my discussion to texts written by U.S. authors who either identify themselves or are identified by others as being a member of a U.S. ethnic group.

[9] For more extended discussions of these development paths see Barbara Christian, "A Rough Terrain: The Case of Shaping an Anthology of Caribbean Women Writers" 241-59; Henry Louis Gates Jr.'s "'Ethnic and Minority' Studies," 288-302; Ramón A. Gutiérrez's "Ethnic Studies: Its Evolution in American Colleges and Universities" 157-67; and Avery F. Gordon and Christopher Newfield, "Multiculturalism's Unfinished Business" 76-115.

[10] The identity groups for which the domain of cultural representation and the use of cultural affiliation serve as means of social resistance include sexual and gender minorities as well as racial and ethnic minority groups. However, most uses of the term "multiculturalism" in the United States are made in specific reference to the latter.

[11] First coined in 1908 by playwright Israel Zangwill, the phrase "melting-pot" quickly became the shaping metaphor of U.S. discourses of immigration and ethnicity (Sollors, *Beyond Ethnicity* 66). To become a U.S. citizen and a fully functioning member of U.S. society, immigrants/ethnic minorities were expected to assimilate fully: to renounce their cultural and linguistic particularities and adopt the language and political, moral, and social values of the U.S. "common" (read Anglo-European) culture. In exchange, they would enjoy the political freedoms and economic opportunities that came with being an American. Through the 1940s and 1950s most ethnic and minority civil rights sought peaceful change through assimilation by means of "petitions for governmental beneficence and through appeals to white liberal guilt" (Gutiérrez 158).

Although Zangwill coined the phrase "melting pot," the drive toward assimilation and fusion it describes was not unique to the twentieth century. Werner Sollors traces its crucible or alchemic symbolism from Biblical images of melting into or merging with Christ, through, among other things, the poetry of Edward Taylor in the early 1700s; Michel-Guillaume-Jean de Crèvecoeur's discussion of what is "American" about Americans in *Letters from an American Farmer* (1782) in which he describes the individuals of all nations being "melted into a new race of men" (39); Ralph Waldo Emerson's 1845 notebook entry on "the smelting pot of the dark ages" (*Journals* 9:299-300); and assimilation cartoons in the 1880s and 1890s in which Lady Liberty tries to use the mortar of equal rights to mix a multitude of ethnic and racial groups in the pot of citizenship (Sollors, *Beyond Ethnicity* 75-96).

[12] These limitations do not apply only to multicultural comparisons; rather, as W. J. T. Mitchell observes, they are the limitations of the comparative *method* itself. For an extended discussion of the comparative method and its elimination of the possibility of relationships of juxtaposition, incommensurability, or of unmediated or non-negotiable alterity see "Beyond Comparison: Picture, Text, and Method" 83-110. See esp. p. 87.

[13] In *Beyond Ethnicity: Consent and Descent in American Culture*, Werner Sollors offers an in-depth examination of the ideologies of descent and consent. By "descent" Sollors refers to ideologies based on notions of ancestry and filial connections such as biological definitions of race, and hereditary old-world hierarchies (embodied, Sollors asserts, in European lines of nobility) (4-6). In contrast, "consent" ideologies refer to affilial connections such as orders of law and conduct, the metaphor of the melting pot, and unions of love and marriage (6-8).

[14] "Mestiza consciousness" is a term utilized by many Chicana feminists in their efforts to theorize and address the multiple and interlocking oppressions (race and class and gender and nation) to which they are subjected. Maria Lugones defines mestiza consciousness as a praxis that "defies control through simultaneously asserting the impure, curdled multiple state and rejecting fragmentation into pure parts. In this play of assertion and rejection, the mestiza is unclassifiable, unmanageable. She has no pure parts to be 'had,' controlled" (460).

[15] For an illuminating comparison of these three types of theories of difference, see Lawrence Grossberg, "The Context of Audiences and the Politics of Difference" 320-42.

[16] Gayatri Spivak has labeled the question of if and how "subjective structures can, in fact, give objective truth" as "the problem of autobiography," and considers it to be the primary question facing all post-Enlightenment theory ("Questions of Multi-Culturalism," 66).

[17] Roberto Cantú identifies two such references in *Migrant Souls*: the "Don Luis Leal's Famous Tex-Mex Diner" at which Josie and her family stop and have dinner (36) refers to Luis Leal the critic; "Tano Hinojosa," the guest at Josie's wedding who almost goes out of his mind because he cannot determine which of the Portillo twins he desires more (93) refers to novelist Rolando Hinojosa (153).

[18] My recognition of these formal techniques owes much to Roberto Cantú, who identifies many of the same techniques in his discussion of *The Rain God* in his biographical entry on Islas in the *Dictionary of Literary Biography*, volume 122 (150).

[19] In addition to identifying many of the literary traditions and individual writers and critics that had an influence on Islas's writing, in the essay "The Hybridity of Culture in Arturo Islas's *The Rain God*" José David Saldívar also presents an astute analysis of mainstream editors' and reviewers' ethnocentric readings of *The Rain God*. Like the fiction of other Chicano/a writers, Saldívar claims, Islas's novel was

read by New York publishers strictly in terms of its "cultural message." Such readings, he asserts, draw "simplistic attention" to such texts' "otherness" and undervalue their authors' place in U.S. society and "the relation of their work to global literature" (107).

[20] In *Migrant Souls*, Miguel Chico completes a dissertation on the work of Henry James.

[21] José David Saldívar points out that Islas's dissertation advisor at Stanford, Wallace Stegner, also wrote about the American West, and about the work of Willa Cather. In an essay on Cather, Stegner asserted that Cather found her voice when she began writing about the people and places with which she was most familiar. Presumably, Saldívar posits, Islas read his mentor's essay. Even if he did not, he shares with Stegner and Cather "the use of narrative masks" in the form of characters such as Jim Burden, Lyman Ward, and Miguel Chico, which enable the authors to exercise their sensibilities "without obvious self-indulgence" (118).

[22] For a discussion of this type of genealogy see Chapter Three of Françoise Lionnet's *Autobiographical Voices: Race, Gender, Self Portraiture*. See esp. p. 98.

[23] While *Migrant Souls* does emphasize the constructed nature of experience, it does not assert that there is no reality outside of discourse or that reality *is* a linguistic fiction: the narratives of all three of Islas's novels are largely driven by the conflicts that occur when the beliefs that individuals, families, cultures, and nations use to make meaning of experience fail to account for, or to accommodate, the material, socioeconomic conditions in which they exist. Mamá Chona may have chosen not to believe any of the outrages that were occurring during the Mexican Revolution and to lecture her maid that "There has only been one real revolution in the history of this dismal world . . . [t]hey nailed Him to a cross" (38-39), but she still loses her son and her husband to those outrages. Ricardo Ángel may want to reject his Chicano heritage and ask his coworkers to call him "Dick," but he is still held up by his employers "as an example of what those from Richard's background could accomplish if they set their mind to it" (203). The underlying premise of *Migrant Souls* is not that there are no objective truths, but that an individual's subjective experiences of them are inescapably and unpredictably enmeshed in a multitude of social discourses that organize how they and others view, and, hence, interact with the material world.

La Mollie and the King of Tears

ETHNOQUEER RE-ARCHI*TEX*TURING
of Metropolitan Space

Frederick Luis Aldama

I n *La Mollie and the King of Tears* and *Days of Obligation* respectively, novelist Arturo Islas and journalist Richard Rodriguez pen homographic texts that queer the contemporary Chicano/a and mainstream U.S. textual landscape. Islas and Rodriguez create first-person narrating subjects—a smooth-talking *pachuco* straight Louie Mendoza for Islas and a hesitantly vulnerable yet penetratingly bold self-as-narrator for Rodriguez—who journey through world cityscapes to destabilize zones of hegemonic control, then re-inhabit and reinscribe such zones *sans* a North versus South, straight versus bent oppositionality. The authors thus invent "autoethnographic" texts (see Mary Pratt and José Saldívar) that sidestep old-school us/them models for understanding the formation of the subaltern self, re-placing their protagonists within a metrotextual space that allows for a panoply of selves to coexist within oneself.[1] To this end, Rodriguez and Islas soften time, and disemplot character to shift their ga(y)ze to subjectivity as informed by its various spatializations. Their multispatialized texts spin Chicano/a literature into, as Ramón Saldívar writes, the "heterotopian social spaces of the imaginary [. . .] within the real conditions of existence" (R. Saldívar, *Chicano Narrative* 65).

This move to locate Chicano/a subaltern subjectivities in the contemporary U.S. metroplex does not originate with Islas and Rodriguez. Speaking to the rise of urban Chicano novels generally, critic Juan Bruce-Novoa claimed,

> if the novel gives us an accurate reading of the Chicano community [. . .] we can say that our community is less sexually

repressive than we might expect. [. . .] This makes the Chicano [urban] novel a progressive space for dialogue, an appropriate space in and through which a more androgynous and humane Chicano identity may be forged. (Bruce-Novoa, "Homosexuality and the Chicano Novel" 105)

Since the early 1970s, Chicano/a textscapes have looked increasingly to the formation of the Chicano/a in the city.[2] Nonetheless, these early cityscape texts mostly turned to urban centers to foreground an us/them struggle between the brown characters and the Euro-Anglo powers that be. Chicano writers like Rudolfo Anaya and Ron Arias painted cities heavily scratched with the grit and grime of racial oppression while thickening the sepia-toned layers that describe Chicanos in the Aztlanified countryside—a space that sanctions the hardened Chicano phallus while denigrating the Chicana *panocha*. And when writers complicated the characters' sense of self/other in the city—as with Oscar Zeta Acosta's massively ingestive narrator-as-self, who metastasizes all of mainstream and marginal culture—they often reproduced restrictive heteronormative paradigms: Chicanas are either virgins or whores (*Chingadalupes/malinchistes*); queers are either invisible or hypergenitalized half-men. As more Chicana-authored texts made it to print—Isabella Ríos, Lucha Corpi, Cherríe Moraga, Gloria Anzaldúa, Alma Luz Villanueva, to name a few—the cityscaped text (Tijuana, San Francisco, or Los Angeles, for example) was radically revised and constructed as a space to disrupt age-old heteronormative, masculinist master narratives.

Writers Arturo Islas in *La Mollie and the King of Tears*[3] and Rodriguez in *Days of Obligation* turn to the metropolis to invent coexisting subjects that inhabit palimpsestic city spaces that enfold race, sexuality, class, and gender.[4] For example, while Rodriguez-as-narrator *comes out* in the telling of his life in San Francisco's Castro, he inhabits a simultaneously soft/hard queerness that destabilizes heteronormative constructions of the masculine and feminine. And while Islas invents a straight protagonist to narrate the *La Mollie*, Louie comes into a *bent* revisioning of straight/queer self and city. Both authors re-archi*tex*turize queer and straight spaces, constructing selves that float somewhere in a tangible in-between space that de-differentiates Chicano subjectivity.

Not surprisingly, the texts that Arturo Islas and Richard Rodriguez build to house their multiply coexisting metroplexed subjects destabilize conventional genre and storytelling technique. For example, in *La Mollie* Islas shifts gears from his other mythopoetically narrated, pastorally set dynastic novels—*The Rain God* and its sequel *Migrant Souls*—and uses the narrative technique and fast-paced tempo that readers associate with noir; there is a mystery to solve, and Islas's Louie uses short, quick Dashiell Hammett-styled sentences to unfurl it. And in *Days of Obligation*, Rodriguez's narrator uses an investigative journalist voice—snappy openers, short and to the point paragraphs, and an in-the-crack probing eye/I—to describe Mexico City, San Diego, Tijuana, and the reconstructed California missions. However, neither author uses conventional forms simply to house a narrating subject. Each de-forms a genre. Islas's noir is revised as the storytelling frame shifts from the white, hetero-masculine subject *à la* Chandler to the *pachuco*, *caló* speaking and troping Louie Mendoza. Likewise, Rodriguez's narrator does not simply factualize to provide an entry into the national journal of record (*Los Angeles Times* for example); his narrator's detailed offerings of the sociomaterial reveal often contradictory narrating selves. *Days of Obligation* turns out to be not exactly objective. His writing often makes visible personal issues like AIDS, for example.

Rodriguez and Islas (con)fuse narrative form as their narrating subjects move through the metroplex. For example, Rodriguez's narrator employs quick-tempo journalese and the autobiographic confession to detail his alienation as a Chicano who cannot speak Spanish in Mexico City. He opens the first chapter, "I am on my knees, my mouth over the mouth of the toilet, waiting to heave" (Rodriguez, *Days* xv). Islas's Louie begins, "I shoulda told La Mollie I'd be back to her place right after the gig" (Islas, *La Mollie* 3). As the narrative progresses, the hip, noir slang moves increasingly to the background as Louie's Chicanismos emerge. Louie's hybrid Chicano *caló* and noir-speak thus re-situate the narrative frame.

Hybridizing form for Islas and Rodriguez is not just about performing Euro-canonically high/low coded genres (pulp fiction and autobiography, objective journalism and the subjective essay). Their confused narratives work also to displace expected moments of heteronormative textual *jouissance*. *La Mollie* (manuscript and published novel) ends *sans* conclusion; the reader never discovers whether or not the hospitalized and near-death La Mollie will live. In *Days of Obligation* the narrator's voice—a style *Kirkus Reviews* identifies as "disarmingly baroque" (Anonymous, Rev. of *Days* 1115)—consistently inverts and collapses back on itself through a series of syntactic and word-play acrobatics. For all of Louie's hard-edged noir/*pachuco* stylization, the novel's *coming* denouement finally hangs limp; and Rodriguez's narrator's inverting sentences cruise forward through a paradoxical series of double takes. Both open up the textual space Roland Barthes calls a "site of bliss" (18) either by defying the coming expectation (adding a softness to Louie's hardness) or by syntactic double takes that engage the reader's cruising gaze just long enough to delight in "the perverse bliss of words" (35).

Both Islas and Rodriguez create urban-based narrators that confuse forms as they inhabit various cityspaces that allow them to manifest melancholia and/or ecstasy as racially, nationally, and sexually inscribed desiring subjects. Namely, both authors abuse city-associated genres to underscore the plurality of ethnoqueer subjectivity. For both writers, then, subjectivity shapes and is shaped by the city and its consequent genre. Now for some urban-embodying specifics.

Rodriguez's Hol(e)y Logos

As mentioned already, in *Days of Obligation* Rodriguez-as-narrator (distinct from the textualized, arguably fictionalized Rodriguez and the biographical Rodriguez) first cruises, then forces a double-take to make the reader "see" such metropolises as Mexico City, Tijuana, and San Francisco. While his cruising deterritorializes otherwise tightly surveilled geocultural spaces—turning upside down the U.S. popular imagining that restricts San Francisco's Castro district to queers and Mexico City to the hypergenitalized, uncivil Other—he does so while he himself is located in both the metropolis and the familial home. The narrator comes out while a writer living in San Francisco, and such a coming out is still, he reminds, "predicated upon family laundry, dirty linen, skeletons" (Richard Rodriguez, *Days* 30). Indeed, "to grow up homosexual is to live with secrets and within secrets. In no other place are those secrets more closely guarded than within the family home" (*Days* 30). Yet the home's urban location allows him to gain the requisite distance to remember the hetero-familial space. He can then reinhabit his past domestic space, and newly inhabit the present, tangible space of the Castro's erstwhile hetero-occupied Victorian houses. Such houses were traditionally, writes Rodriguez caustically, "the reward for heterosexuality, with all its selfless tasks and burdens" (*Days* 35). The hetero-inscribed homes of the present and past coexist with his present queer subjectivity and inform his homographesis.

Indeed, Rodriguez-as-narrator's simultaneous present/past, straight/bent self-locating allow him to turn topsy-turvy the master narratives that have aligned Mexican and U.S. national identity with masculine and feminine constructs. Namely, as the narrator moves through his homes (the Castro and the Sacramento of his childhood) and various cities north and south of the "tortilla curtain," he confuses and realigns the masculine/feminine heteronormative nationalizing matrix. Senses of home and nation go hand in hand, but in the case of Rodriguez-as-narrator, the mother (traditionally coded as passive, soft) and the father (traditionally coded as macho, active, hard) switch places to reveal the constructed nature of gendered home/nation spaces. For Rodriguez the mother is the figure who is hard and assertive in the public domain; she learns and uses English to earn higher wages and fight for her family's rights, concluding, "because of my mother there is movement" (*Days* 203). Rodriguez locates the mother's ability to come into a hardness with her non-nostalgic approach to life; she doesn't position the lost homeland— Mexico—in a glorified, static past. Conversely, the father becomes paralyzed north of the "tortilla curtain." He fails to conceive of himself within non-binary oppositioned gender roles vis-à-vis nationality, losing himself to images of a romanticized, macho-spirited Mexican never-never land.

Rodriguez-as-narrator not only begins to show how gendered identity is linked with sense of national belonging, but he also redraws the blueprint for gender hierarchies (feminine = soft and masculine = hard) naturalized within the home. As he deconstructs his familial space from a new queer Castro perspective, he announces, "I was born at the destination" and that destination, as he identifies earlier, is indeed San Francisco (208; 202). The process of selecting information to present as he sits and writes from within a queer space, allows his life story to appear to come full circle: he is back where he began. However, this time he emerges with a *bent* writerly voice that penetrates and destabilizes the narrating of the self as a whole. To this end, Randy A. Rodríguez identifies Rodriguez's style as a "double-voiced, ironic writing" that lacks "narrative integration and resolution [to resist] the ideological progressive, linear, and aesthetic demands of a strong (masculine), resistant, and representative minority voice" (Randy Rodríguez, "Richard Rodriguez Reconsidered" 397). The text taken as a whole, then, envelops Rodriguez within the core of the story and creates a line of angled penetration that rubs in and out of the reader's sense of self as whole. So, while the narrator packages himself and his text to be consumed as a whole by the reader, his coming into a sense of a penetrative vulnerability—an influxing (w)hole—resists the reader's attempt to fully penetrate, control, and contain the Rodriguez-as-narrator while he recreates a sense himself within a home.

The Impure Within the Pure

Rodriguez-as-narrator's simultaneous holer/holed penetrative/vulnerable narration splits open and interrogates his *activo/pasivo* coded Euro-colonial legacy. Here, the traditional Euro-hetero-macho construction of self-as-*activo* (the holer) and *indio*-as-*pasivo* (the holed) is revised while in Mexico City. Coming into contact with his *mestizaje* replays through inversion (he is invested with the power to move and penetrate spaces) the conquistador's forced penetration of the New World subject:

> I am on my knees, my mouth over the mouth of the toilet, waiting to heave. It comes up with a bark. All the badly pronounced Spanish words I have forced myself to sound during the day, bits and pieces of Mexico spew from my mouth, warm, half-understood, nostalgic reds and greens dangle from long strands of saliva. (Richard Rodriguez, *Days* xv)

As Spanish (the language of the Euro-father) forces its way inside, he bends over and performs the Euro-*hispano* father's construction of the *indio*-as-*pasivo* (subordinate). Here, the Euro-father-as-bully sissifies Rodriguez, forcing him to react by spewing his "warm" pieces from his mouth. However, subordination swiftly turns into resistance as Rodriguez actively locates himself within a history of an *indio* subjectivity that can penetrate back. He comes to inhabit a contradictory space of simultaneously being sissy and bully to perform a Chicano identity that is not quite macho *hispano* (his Euro-Spaniard bloodline coded as *activo*) and not quite Mexican (his mestizo bloodline coded as *pasivo*). On another occasion, he writes, "I had a dream about Mexico City, a conquistador's dream. I was lost and late and twisted in my sheet. [. . .] I dreamed sheets, entanglements, bunting, hanging *larvaelike* from open windows, *distended* from balconies and from lines thrown over the stress" (21; emphasis mine). Here, he is both conquistador (*activo* and penetrating) and the *indio* (*pasivo*) who dreams. Rodriguez is both the one impregnated (*pasivo*) and the one about to give birth (*activo*); he is both the circularity of the flowing dream and the hard-strung lines that hold the linen. Rodriguez envisions himself neither simply as *activo* nor *pasivo*, *gringo* nor *hispano*, Chicano nor *indio*—but as a confluence of coexisting subjectivities.

Rodriguez-as-narrator's re-visioning of binary-essentialized epistemological and ontological spaces reveals the clashes and confusions (*indio*-as-sissy versus Euro-father-as-bully) that continue to inform the contemporary Mexico City metroplex. Ironically, for Rodriguez it is the very exaggerated belief in the colonial sissy/bully model that leads this city into a space of *indio*/queer emancipation. Indeed, because of Mexico City's extreme need to separate bully from sissy and *indio* from *hispano*, it has become "centuries more modern than racially pure, provincial Tokyo" (*Days* 87). Namely, in its excessiveness Mexico City cannot help itself; it will spill over into impurity where the *activo* and *pasivo* invert and coexist as holer and holed. He continues to refine his definition of Mexico City, writing, "in its male, in its public, in its city aspect, Mexico is an archtransvestite [that] doesn't even bother to shave her mustachios. Swords and rifles and spurs and bags of money clink and clatter beneath her skirts" (61–62). The narrator's city becomes such an exaggerated society of the spectacle that it spectacularizes and denaturalizes the scaffolding that holds in place racial, gender, and sexual hierarchies. In Mexico City the Euro-gazing and light-skinned *hispano* becomes so hyperbolically macho that he becomes a parody of himself, exposing (unwittingly) the fragility of the sissy/bully relational paradigm. Finally, however, Rodriguez does not uncritically represent his desire to inhabit such an unbounded space. He still "fears being lost" (96) in the impure womb-space of the city where the traditionally hard, Euro-Western epistemes soften and enfold.

It is the narrator's slanted vision that lets him see Mexico City as looking simultaneously forward (post-modern) and backward (colonial legacy), allowing the "impure" and "pure" to coexist and, in their frictitious rubbing up and down, constantly re-invent themselves. Yet, while he wants to inhabit such a space, he also "fears being lost" in it. It reflects too accurately his own sense of co-being, threatening to swallow him up and not provide an outside anchor to his consciousness. Rather, it is the hetero/imperial-gazed "pure" space of the U.S. that offers up just such an anchor: an antithetical position that allows him to maintain an identity that is brown and Mexican and that co-exists with, yet isn't synthesized by, such a chaotic surrounding nation-state space. For example, he identifies the Anglo-American space as pure and oriented toward individuation and self-creation, writing that it functions as the site "long imagined [as] clean, crew-cut, ingenious" (91). Moreover, he settles into an age-old Manichean duality, opposing the space of Mexico with that of the U.S.—he identifies himself as *gringo*, writing, "*we* are an odorless, colorless, accentless, orderly people"—with the space of the Mexicans, who are "carriers of chaos [with] diarrhea, leprosy, brown water" (91).

Rodriguez does not keep clear the lines between United States-as-individualizing center and Mexico-as-miscegenating chaos. Just when Rodriguez seems to be pinpointable—appearing to celebrate the assimilatory, individualist space of the United States—he (con)fuses U.S. and Mexican (North/South, macho/sissy) epistemic spaces. We see this in the aforementioned dreamscape sequence and in his celebration of Mexico City as a multiply layered ethnosocial space. Later he comes to celebrate such "impure" spaces as Tijuana not as a chaotic dystopia that threatens to swallow his identity, but rather as a city that exists in a fully miscegenating present—a space that is already "here" (*Days* 106). (Conversely, in this reformulation nearby San Diego is a place never present, always future-oriented and ephemeral.) Rodriguez seeks to empresence himself in the counterhegemonic space of Tijuana, allowing him to trace, as Homi Bhabha theorizes generally of the third-space inhabiting subaltern subject, "two original moments from which the third emerges, [but also that] which enables other positions to emerge" (Bhabha 211). Rodriguez's active inhabiting of a dislocated, world-city position allows him to come into a third-space self that fluidly contests both Mexican and U.S. nationalisms.

Church as Homotopia

Rodriguez's third-space subjectivity not only destabilizes traditionally restrictive nation spaces, but also that of the church. Unlike his asexualized construction of self in *Hunger of Memory* (1982), *Days of Obligation* locates specific sites of spatialized pleasure. Architexturized spaces of the Catholic church, perhaps oddly, become sites of an eroticized memory for Rodriguez. On one occasion, as the adult narrator enters into a California mission, he remembers Brother Michael from his parochial school days: "passionate, athletic, sarcastic, the stuff of crushes" (Richard Rodriguez, *Days* 178–179). Not only does Rodriguez come to see Brother Michael through a third-space inhabiting ethnoqueer lens, but he realizes that Brother Michael first awakened his same-sex desire and inspired him to become a writer. The queer erotic and his double-voiced writing (the soft/hard style I discuss earlier) conflate in Rodriguez's mind as he stands physically within the walls of the mission church. The church, then, acts as the glue that holds the two identities—public writer and private queer—together.

Yet, while Catholic space opens up an ecstatic same-sex desiring space for Rodriguez—he eroticizes both Brother Michael and Larry Faherty, whose hair, he recalls with delight, descended like a woman's "over his collar"—it also acts as the space coded as *pasivo* and feminine. He rejects the Catholic church because of its association with the passive and feminine, turning to Protestant spaces where "in its purest mold [the episteme] is male" (181). Rodriguez is not so much interested in the Protestant doctrine here, however. Rather he is drawn to its "call to manhood, a call to responsibility" (182). For Rodriguez it represents that space he identifies with the U.S. generally as *activo* and where, he writes, "I feel a masculine call to action" (Rodriguez, *Days* 188). However, as in his third-space gaze's destabilizing of U.S. and Mexican nation (genderized) spaces, here too he emplaces himself in an in-between zone. He remarks with an ambiguity that blurs the boundary between his choice of desired object (men, especially Larry Faherty) and his choice of religious faith, "I will always be attracted [to men and both faiths], for the same reason I will never become" (179). Rodriguez inhabits a space in between the two circumscribed faiths—both feminine and masculine coded—that allow him to exist in a constant state of non-normative erotic becoming.

San Francisco as Homotopia

Rodriguez-as-narrator's third-space/queer point of view not only destabilizes restrictive national and theological epistemic spaces that traditionally encode hetero-gazed race and gender hierarchies of difference, but his acts of narration re-envision a traditionally white/brown, queer/straight panoptically surveyed San Francisco city space. Here Rodriguez-as-narrator's cut voice (soft/hard) seeks to complicate queer spaces, setting the Castro up, for example, not as de facto resistant to, but rather as coexistent with mainstream hetero-erect spaces. Notably, queer- and straight-coded places are separated in a time/space palimpsest. Typically straight- and queer-identified spaces crisscross and overlay one another through time. For example, the Miesian-heteroerect phallus of today—found in Market Street's financial district and Union Square's department store monoliths—was the seminal space for al fresco cruising and bath house transgression during San Francisco's Gilded Age.

In Rodriguez's most homographic chapter, "Late Victorians" (first published in the conservative and hard-edged hetero-Anglo journal *Harper's*), he superimposes constructions of what he defines as the "human infused," "playful," and "carnivalesque" Castro with the white, hetero-moneyed "interests of downtown" (37). Here, within the lived space of the spectacle—defined by Guy Debord as "*capital* accumulated to the point where it becomes image" (Debord 12)—queer neighborhoods and straight, hetero-identified spaces exist side by side in a late-capitalist society. For Rodriguez-as-narrator the queer subject—himself especially—does not necessarily inhabit a bent space of capitalist resistance. Indeed, the celebration of his queer home space spins out of the middle-class process of gentrifying unwanted (mostly) ethnic enclaves. He lives in a revisioned Victorian—a structure that he emphasizes was symbolic of the hetero-erect, middle-class gender divided household of yesteryear. So while he identifies the queer reclaiming of heterospace—transforming the Victorian's vertically hard, hetero space into a set of free-floating apartments co-existing horizontally and housing "four single men" (Richard Rodriguez, *Days* 30)—his inhabitation and re-territorialization are middle-class dependent. Those without the means—racialized others without the dollar incomes to rise up to the Twin Peaks heights—were swallowed up by middle-class *activos*. For example, when Rodriguez locates this queer transformation of space with details of his hallway's various disguises—it was "repainted to resemble an eighteenth-century French foyer" then later transformed by a "baroque mirror" and the laying of a "black-and-white marble" floor and painting of "faux masonry" walls—he describes participating within the faux-making enterprise of the society of the spectacle (31). His metaphoric "glory hole" where single men could float in and out of horizontally coded communal spaces is swept into the commodity machine and becomes a decadent reconstruction of an eighteenth-century foyer (33).

This spectacle-making process extends beyond the domestic and into Rodriguez's sense of queer public spaces. For example, he describes the local gym's mirrored interior and its all-glass walls that separate the street from the bodies inside as both "a closet of privacy and an exhibition gallery" (39). The gym, like his gloryhole-cum-decadent French foyer, enacts a politics of socioeconomic privilege. It exists as a queer space, and is therefore marginalized in the heterosexual scheme of things, yet it also acts as a place for privileged bodies who have the power to put on an exhibit and make public a commodity-culture-oriented, "aestheticized" look. Of course, Rodriguez-as-narrator's cut revisioning of queer space leads to his critique of a hetero-inscribing queer subject that in its "architectural preoccupation" demonstrates "a parody of labor, a useless accumulation of the laborer's build and strength" (39). For Rodriguez, the built queer body does not so much make visible a subject traditionally invisible in heterospaces, but refashions the body into an armored object that only desires to consume. Rodriguez concludes, "The effect of the overdeveloped body is the miniaturization of the sexual organs—of no function beyond wit" (39). Finally, while queer and mainstream spaces are traditionally surveyed by a hetero-controlled panoptic public policy-making apparatus, Rodriguez de-essentializes both spaces—straight spills into queer and queer into straight—by setting them up within a society of the spectacle. Rodriguez's Castro with, as he defines, its "human infused," "playful," and "carnivalesque" spirit (37), is overlaid by the urban grid of hetero spectacle making. However, there is room for critique and resistance here. As he explains of his own redecorating impulse, it "is not to create but to re-create, to sham, to convert, to sauce, to rouge, to fragrance, to prettify. No effect is too small or too ephemeral to be snatched away from nature, to be ushered toward the perfection of artificiality" (33). He works within the frame that governs the hetero-spectacle, but from an ethnosexually queer angle that stylizes and parodies archi*text*ured bodies—straight and bent—that continue to control and contain subjectivity generally.

Islas's Queering of Straight World-City Spaces

In *La Mollie and the King of Tears,* Arturo Islas's first-person narrator and protagonist, Louie Mendoza, coexists with other sociosexually emplaced subjects while physically traveling *across* a 1973 San Francisco metroplex. (To reiterate, while I will be quoting from Islas's posthumously published novel edited by Paul Skenazy, the plot and style differ little from Islas's June 1987 manuscript. Where significant changes were made, I will identify them in endnotes.) We first meet Louie telling an unnamed academic with a tape recorder in hand his experiences during the last twelve-plus hours. It is here, in the absolute present tense of the story while Louie sits in the hospital, that he remembers the immediate past of his journey through San Francisco's ex-centric spaces: Haight/Ashbury, Castro, South of Market Tenderloin, and the Mission. The act of telling provides the fluid container for him to re-experience the many spatialized selves that co-exist palimpsestically and come to inform the Louie-as-narrating-subject. Louie does not experience the sort of epiphany that traditionally identifies a character's dialectical synthesis of the encountered other, but rather he comes to coexist as a straight, thirty-something *pachuco*[5] with a vision that queers binary oppositioned world-city spaces. For queer author Arturo Islas, then, straight Louie's *queer* re-territorializing of traditionally white, hetero-controlled ethnosexualized ex-centric spaces builds a politics of resistance that expands beyond sexual-object choice (male-male, female-female, female-male) to make room for a straight-inclusive queerspace imaginary.

As mentioned above, *La Mollie* is a text that does not so much fuse different genres as allow them to speak in and through one another. The testimonial-like novel speaks through 1950s noir through the loose-ended, episodic picaresque; genres traditionally coded masculine and hard, like grittily realist detective fiction, coexist with those coded feminine and soft such as romance. For example, Louie's storytelling technique is simultaneously hard, as with tough-guy, *pachuco* slang and "take-no-shit" posturing; and soft, as he aches for that sappy, *telenovela*-styled romance. Louie's act of narrating through multiple generic registers takes place as he moves through San Francisco's ex-centric spaces. As the story unfolds, Louie's hybridizing of narrative style crystallizes into a counterdiscourse that both spatializes local knowledge within a world-city space and foregrounds the formation of a despatialized global city that only allows those deemed racially and sexually "pure" to transcend the local while limiting the mobility of the "impure" others. Louie's speech act and the novel as text act displace, as Mary Louise Pratt writes, the "normative vision of a unified and homogeneous social world" and accentuate instead "the relationality of social differentiation" (Pratt 1989, 59). Louie's multiple-voiced speech act and the narratives deforming of genre foreground an interstitial Chicano subjectivity that reveals the hegemonic substructures of a world-city space where archi*tex*-*t*ured geopolitical structures naturalize hierarchies of difference.

Louie learns from an early age that multiple speech acts can permeate and therefore threaten racially inscribed border zones. He grows up in El Paso, Texas, a place that constructs borders between subjects according to skin color and sociolect. For example, Louie recalls attempting the crossover as a multiply speaking *caló* subject into an English-inscribed school space. However, when Louie's Euro-Anglo school teacher overhears his codeswitch into Spanish, he is punished and locked in a closet. So when the adult-narrator Louie uses the multiply voiced *caló*, he dares to cross a border. He also dares to come out of the closet.

Much like his linguistic codeswitches that destabilize dominant/subordinate linguistic hierarchies, Louie confuses the traditional borders between high- and lowbrow aesthetic culture. For example, he recalls reading *Hamlet* in high school not as a great European tragedy, but as "Shakespeare's version of *High*

Noon with a big swordout instead of a shootout at the end" (*La Mollie* 9). He mingles the high and low aesthetic in a mode typical of Chicano *rascuachismo*. To be *rascuache*, Tomás Ybarra-Frausto writes, "is to posit a bawdy, spunky consciousness, to seek to subvert and turn ruling paradigms upside down." (Ybarra-Frausto 155). Louie is a self-described "eclectic man" who takes "from here and from there whatever works" (Islas, *La Mollie* 45), turning the "ruling paradigms" that naturalize linguistic, racial, and aesthetic difference "upside down." As Peter Stallybrass and Allon White write generally, "the most powerful ruses of the dominant [group are] to pretend that critique can only exist in the language of 'reason,' 'pure knowledge' and 'seriousness'" (43). The logic that underlies certain forms of subculture can, they continue, "unsettle 'given' social positions and interrogate the rules of inclusion, exclusion and domination which [structure] the social ensemble" (43). So Louie's resignifying *rascuache* sensibility and slanted vision congeal, as Dick Hebdige argues of British subaltern subjects, "in the space between surveillance and the evasion of surveillance, [translating] the fact of being under scrutiny into the pleasure of being watched. It is hiding in the light" (Hebdige, *Hiding* 35).

Louie's multiple inhabitation of speech-act spaces is informed by his movement into and out of hegemonically bounded marginal city spaces. For example, when he enters the Latino enclave of the Mission district, he transforms the urban barrio space, coded in the white imaginary as dangerous and savage, into a place of quiet refuge. This is the place that Louie associates with his Latin jazz/salsa playing and where he resignifies temporality. Time, he informs, becomes "nothing to me except a beat for my sax" (*La Mollie* 45). As he enters into a space traditionally controlled by residuals of the brown-as-savage/white-as-civilizer colonial narrative, he emplaces the Chicano-as-subject.

Yet, even Louie does not slip into a *raza* romanticism that ends up containing the brown subject. Rather, his place of refuge (utopia) exists within a larger, more omnipresent space of white, moneyed hetero-hegemony that objectifies and oppresses women of color. He describes, for example, how the brown women walk "up and down the street in crotch-length miniskirts, their tits playing peekaboo with the dudes driving by in their limos and giving em the once over" (82). Louie does not sepia-hue his reinhabitations of space. Rather, he reveals how ethnosocial subjects can create a small corner of stillness within white, heterosexist hegemonic urban griddings of marginal space. Louie coexists within spaces that oppress/repress and those that emancipate. For example, he is an underclass El Paso born Chicano living with a white, upper-middle-class, self-assured cosmopolite, La Mollie. Louie reveals La Mollie to be oppressive—even, in her P.C. way, a racist and homophobe—and her apartment suffocating. La Mollie tells him on more than one occasion that he's "a dumb Mexican" (25), for example. The street, on the other hand, provides Louie with a cure-all to the hetero-middle-class space of the apartment. When he leaves the apartment at two o'clock in the afternoon—fed up with her manipulations of his emotion and desire—he delights in the carnivalizing of space and desire that the street offers.

An Erotics of Remembered Space

Louie's "pure San Francisco" (37) revolves around his transformation of space into place—the city's abstract white gridded spaces becoming the place of ethnosocial infused memory. Yi-Fu Tuan defines the process of transforming space into place as the following: "The ideas 'space' and 'place' require each other for definition. [. . .] Furthermore, if we think of space as that which allows movement, then place is pause; each pause in movement makes it possible for location to be transformed into place (Tuan 6). For example, as Louie passes children playing in the Hayes Valley low-income projects, he recalls being a kid in El Paso afraid of *cucuys*—Mexican bogeymen. The movement in space triggers a memory that anchors Louie within his Chicano imaginary. Louie transforms abstract space into the place of felt ethnic heritage.[6] And, when he moves through the Mission district's streets, he remembers his first love-interest, Sonia, who "was pure Chicana" (*La Mollie* 47). Sonia triggers memories of her parents—who make him "thinka my own parents. They have that Indian way, man—silent, proud, all-knowing [. . .]" (27)—firmly anchoring him (albeit to a clichéd degree) within his *mestizo* heritage.

Space is not only transformed into a variety of racialized zones (hetero-romancings with Sonia and the *cucuy*s of his El Paso childhood), but also into the place of macho hetero-romance. As Louie walks through Golden Gate Park he pauses at the arboretum, a place that triggers memories of the first time he met the white, middle-class anthropology Ph.D. student La Mollie "during a love-in while the Dead were wailing away [. . .]" (46). Also from this stretch of grass, he sees the Kezar Stadium, reminding him that all stadiums, from the moment he met La Mollie forward, make him "think of one thing and one thing only. Vaginas" (59). The racial and heterosexual remembering of space are not so unconnected. La Mollie, he recalls, expressed interest in him only because he proved a good ethnic-object specimen of study. As he walks the undifferentiated street spaces, then, certain built objects and/or bodies in space (brown and black children playing) trigger a recall process that transforms spaces into, at this point, simultaneously heterosexualized and positively racialized places.

This is not to say that Louie uncritically reproduces delimiting heterosexist, racialized paradigms. His exaggeration of such Chicano phallic transformations of these spaces—the stadium as vagina, for example—into differentiated racial/sexual places de-differentiates such ideologically infused built spaces. For example, during his walk he recalls the father of his best friend, Virgil Spears. He was a "Jack Daniels poppa did all kindsa things to make a man outta him and make sure he wasn't no momma's boy on his way to being queer" (73). After Louie describes with horror the father's forcing Virgil (arguably his long unrequited love) to shoot some puppies to make a man out of him, we begin to see how Louie further de-naturalizes heterosexualized spaces, here demonstrating the hetero-fascist fear of dissolution into a female subject constructed as the dark abyss.

While Louie identifies as straight, he goes to great lengths to spectacularize that heterosexualized identity. For example, when he travels through street-spaces and a memory of La Mollie is triggered, it is often filtered through an exaggerated silver-screened imagination. On one occasion he recalls how he keeps his "Bogart cool" (24) when she glares at him "like Bette Davis at Joseph Cotten" (24). Katherine Hepburn, Olivia de Havilland, Rita Hayworth, Rock Hudson, Spencer Tracey, Montgomery Clift, James Dean, and Marlon Brando, to name a few, all stand in at different moments to describe his interaction with La Mollie (all mentioned and more in the manuscript). Jack Babuscio identifies such a reimagination of Hollywood icons as the main ingredient of the camp aesthetic. Babuscio writes that the focus "on the outward appearances of role, implies that roles, and, in particular sex roles, are superficial—a matter of style. Indeed, life itself is role and theater, appearance, and impersonation" (Babuscio 24). Of course camp isn't about mere imitation, it's about exaggerating the imitation: super red-lipsticked mouths that gape and caked-on facial powder that accentuates facial hair to exaggerate the feminine look. While Louie does not put on the red lipstick when he filters his relationship with La Mollie through the Hollywood silver screen, he recycles an otherwise wasted mode of white, heterosexual cultural production to denaturalize hegemonic Euro-Anglo, hetero-cultural icons and meaning. As a Chicano (albeit straight) subject, Louie is also denied access to traditional "masculine" and "feminine" positionalities. Andrew Ross's definition of camp in "Uses of Camp" also applies to the mestizo subject. Like Ross's camp performers, Louie is "excluded by conventional representations of male-as-hero or narrative agent, and female-as-image or object of the spectacle, the gay male and lesbian subcultures express their lived spectatorship largely through imaginary or displaced relations to the images and discourses of a straight 'parent' culture" (Ross 70).

As Louie spectacularizes "masculinity" and "femininity" as roles performed, he sidesteps a heterosexual descriptive authority that assumes all places he inhabits are heterosexual. For example, even when he fleetingly mentions meeting his first partner, Sonia, he identifies the locale as a "unisex bar on the edge of Pacific Heights" (*La Mollie* 27). And when he stumbles on a homeless person while walking in the Haight, he thinks of the progenitor of homogenic love, the poet Walt Whitman, whom Islas quotes in the novel's epigraph: "Who goes there? hankering, gross, mystical, nude . . ." (2). Not only do the multiple references to Whitman resonate loudly with his homographesis, but they anchor the reference to Gold Rush San Francisco—an era when male-male relations and desire dominated this city space. Les Wright comments on Gold-Rush crazed San Francisco (circa 1848–9):

> The first Anglo-American migrants, predominantly from Puritan New England, engaged in homosexual activity and created homosocial spaces within the liminal moral and social spaces crated by San Francisco's vast geographic remove from the structured moral spaces of the urban and even rural communities of mid-nineteenth-century America. (Wright 164)

Often, too, Louie mentions rainbows, Judy Garland singing *Over the Rainbow*, and Dorothy and the yellow brick road (same in manuscript). During 1950s conservative era, when many queers were forced into the proverbial closet and used coded language to communicate, "Are you a friend of Dorothy's?" became a universally recognized code. As Les Wright comments, "Garland became the most beloved camp idol to several postwar generations of homosexual men. San Francisco became the land of Oz, the Technicolor world over the rainbow where gays would finally find a home" (173). Louie's space/place memory teeters between the straight and queer, taking neither as natural fact.

If Louie's choice of references betrays a homographic sensibility, then his admiration and hero making of queer characters runs this home. Indeed, not only does Louie admire Virgil Spears (Islas's partner who died of AIDS was named Jay Spears) for his pool game and his take-no-shit butch-daddy attitude, but he also sees him as a masterful guide into San Francisco's infernoesque other worlds. For Louie, Virgil is the holder of alternate epistemologies. He recalls, "It was Virgil Spears taught me about queers, man, I ain't ashamed to tell you" (*La Mollie* 72). For example, it is Louie is boyhood friendship with Virgil that stands in as an alternate possibility of desiring in the world. After Louie is made to feel abnormal by his peers for masturbating *en masse* with other boys in a basement, it is Virgil who depathologizes these formative experiences. On another occasion, when Louie slips into a heteronormative mindset, asking Virgil if he is queer because of his abusive upbringing, Virgil responds matter-of-factly,

> look at me and tell me exactly when you decided to be straight. I wanna know the moment you looked down at your crotch and your brain told your dick it was only gonna be interested in pussy for the rest of its life. [. . .] You see. You can't tell me . . . Cause it's not something you decide with your head. Hell, if that was how it worked, I'd decide to be straight in a second. You sons-of-bitches have the whole world at your fucking feet and nobody minds you screwing as long as you keep away from the real little girls. (75-76)

Thanks to Virgil, Louie comes to understand that the straight-as-normal versus queer-as-perverse oppositionality is a heteronaturalized construct that contains both sexualized subjectivities. (To really drive home the point, Islas expands this Virgil-educating-Louie scene in the manuscript.) Moreover, in depathologizing queer desire, Virgil makes it clear that this isn't simply a fashionable *look* ("Hell, if that was how it worked, I'd *decide* to be straight in a second"), but rather a permanent reality with very real consequences.

As Louie moves back and forth through present (San Francisco) and past (El Paso) time/places, he floats into an in-between straight/queer space. Ironically, it is when Louie is most assaulted by the queer gaze that he slips most into a queer sensibility. For example, while looking for his brother Tomás at an S & M club called The Mind Shaft he is quick to remind his interviewer, "Like I told you, man, I can't even think about sex without tits around. Real soft ones" (138). Yet, it is right after his entering into this place of male-male erotica that he comments, "I still don't know what it was that got in my skin about that place, but it had me stuck there in the alley so's I couldn't of moved if Sherman's army'd showed up" (146).[7] On occasion, however, this amorphous something under his skin gels into a tangible quantity. For example, in the same bar where he spots Sonia, his attention shifts away from hetero-gendered love object to "the cute little waiter

[...]" (48). And while Louie doesn't slip entirely into a male-male desiring libidinal economy, he does edge up against a semi-formed bisexuality.

Indeed, Louie's abrupt moving in and out of queer spaces happens during the night—that time most associated with the transgressive and with subconscious desire. For example, when Louie arrives in the Castro he recalls, "When I got there, all them guys were flexing their pecs on their fire escapes like they were putting the make on the sun, which was setting behind them buildings. It's the saddest part of the day for me, man, when the light's starting to change from day to night and the dark's coming on like a big wet heavy wool blanket all smothering" (69). Then later, he informs, "I can't figure out why, man, but it's the getting dark that gets me" (69).[8] Of course, it is not that Louie comes into a straight/queer identity at night, but that this is when the struggle manifests itself. So even when the hetero-panic snaps into place—"I try not to pay no attention to the way the guys walking up to Castro Street keep looking first at my crotch and then at my face the way straight dudes look at girls' asses and legs behind their backs" (72)—it is expressed in such a way that Louie actually reveals why heterosexuals fear the queer gaze—not because of the man who stands in for the woman as object ("the way straight dudes look at girls' asses"), but because his role as active penetrator is subverted. As Susan Bordo writes, "orthodox masculinity dreads being 'stripped' of whatever armor it has constructed for itself, dreads being surveyed and determined from without" (Bordo 717). But there is more to Louie's "looking away" from the queer gaze. He looks away, yet knows he is being objectified like a woman. He fears and desires the male-male encounter as a point of reordering heteromasculinity-as-active (one that gazes, shapes, and evaluates reality) to open up the space for his own desire to *actively receive* the sexual Other.

Finally, Arturo Islas reterritorializes San Francisco as a palimpsest queer/straight space through Louie's nondialectical, coexistent relationship to straight/queer, *activo/pasivo* paradigms. Louie's journey through San Francisco's cityspace, then, moves away from straight/queer oppositionalities, moving into a more fluid, multilocal understanding of coexistent spaces that de-essentialize constructions of desiring subaltern subjectivities.

Conclusion

Queer Chicano writers Richard Rodriguez and Arturo Islas (in manuscript and published form) thus invent speaking subjects who *emplace* subjectivity within an in-between, borderland space where essentializing sexual/racial ontologies—straight vs. queer, soft versus hard, white versus brown, self versus other—are denaturalized and revealed to be constructs of a Euro-patrilineal colonial legacy that continues to control subaltern, sexual, and gendered space from within and without. Islas and Rodriguez seek, then, to embody not one self but many selves within the interstitial spaces of nationally, sexually, and racially constructed difference. Homi Bhabha discusses just such a subaltern inhabitation of space as counterhegemonic, allowing the subaltern not only to "trace two original moments from which the third emerges," but also to enable "other positions to emerge" (211). However, where Bhabha's model of what he calls a "third space" is effectively a synthetic dialectic that, he writes, "displaces the histories that constitute it, and sets up new structures of authority [and] new political initiative" (211), Islas and Rodriguez present a model in which the world-city subaltern self coexists with and does not displace other positionalities. Rather, their narrating subjects' reterritorializing of world-city spaces is more fluid and coexistent with the many selves—white, brown, black, queer/lesbian/straight, sissy/bully—that define collective space.

Islas and Rodriguez's subaltern world-city subjects "queer" the sociometroplex experience to reveal how ideology works to survey and create hierarchies of identities in space. Such restrictive us/them models continue to delimit sexual orientation, gender, and racial/ethnic places in the discourse of the "authentic" that many Chicano/a writers continue to employ. Much work still needs to be done to *architexturize* and build relational paradigms—such as Islas's and Rodriguez's world-city co-existing subjects—that open up a transecting space where race, gender, and sexuality produce—and not in that poststructuralist in-fluxity that leads to inaction and political deferral—a civic body politic filled with new relational possibilities.

NOTES

¹ In *Border Matters* José David Saldívar applies the term "autoethnography" to borderland-authored texts—modern-day incarnations of Mary Louise Pratt's identified post-conquest "autoethnographic texts" that refashioned genres through cross-cultural contact—and to Chicano/a texts generally that align, he writes, "with the deterritorializing gestures of borderland social science theorists such as Rosaldo, Sánchez, García Canclini, and Ruiz, who see in their postmodern ethnographies and in feminist theories of *la frontera* a representative liminal site for the postmodern condition" (13).

² Exceptionally, there was the Chicano writer John Rechy, who published his urban-focused, young hipster novel *City of Night* in 1963. Here Rechy's Chicano-identified, El Paso-raised protagonist discovers a counter-heteronormative space at the city's dark edges. However, Rechy plays down the "Chicano-ness" of his protagonist to amplify his "queerness." Furthermore, *City of Night* was not marketed as a Chicano text. The first Grove Press 1963 hardcover and 1964 paperback were marketed as an expression of a new generation of young, hip writers. Later it was marketed not as Chicano but as queer: "The Great Novel of the Gay World" splashes across the 1973 Ballantine paperback edition.

³ Islas wrote *La Mollie and the King of Tears* in a flurry between October 1986 and January 1987. However, the text remained unpublished until 1996—five years after Islas's death from AIDS—after the University of New Mexico picked it up. His own attempts to publish the novel met with a series of rejections, including one from University of New Mexico Press itself. In a letter dated October 30, 1990, the editor, Elizabeth C. Hadas, wrote:

> Dear Arturo Islas. Thanks for letting us read LA MOLLIE AND THE KING OF TEARS. As you know, we have not traditionally published original fiction and are extremely nervous about taking this plunge. We are still too nervous to take the plunge with this novel. Rest assured that I did not send the manuscript out of the house. I read part of it and then gave it to our editorial

intern, a young Mexican-American woman with a special interest in Chicano literature. We don't feel that it's right for us. Probably if we ever do publish an original novel it will have a New Mexico setting." (Letter from Elizabeth C. Hadas)

According to friend and self-described "stand-in" writer for Islas, Paul Skenazy, who helped publish the novel after Islas's death, "the novel that you have in your hands is the novel Arturo wrote" (Afterword 196). However, as Skenazy goes on to point out in the afterword to *La Mollie*, "on almost every page it differs slightly from the manuscript I picked up from him" (Afterword 196). Skenazy determined that there were "imbalances apparent in the novel that had to be rectified: scenes needed to be shortened, sometimes shifted in relation to each other. Certain characters were undeveloped, certain references were inconsistent" (Afterword 197). Surprisingly, however, there is little difference between the manuscript Islas intended to publish—dated June 1987 by Islas and housed in Stanford's Special Collections Library—and the published version. Certain scenes are trimmed down—less characterization of La Mollie, for example—but minimally; and, oddly, the manuscript's chronologically coherent plot is made less coherent in the published version. However, the text itself (style, technique, genre, and mode), especially the moments in the novel that reveal the tropes or ideas of queerness I analyze in this essay, remain unchanged from the June 1987 dated manuscript to 1996 published version.

[4] The pairing of Islas and Rodriguez might seem a little odd, considering that they were not exactly ideologically on par when they were both coming into their careers as writers. Islas was outraged not just with the conservative voice in Rodriguez's *Hunger of Memory* ("a well written description of how someone can paralyze himself with an intellectual dichotomy" he writes in an early review), but with the fact that Rodriguez is the first Chicano writer to be published by a New York house since 1959 (qtd. in Aldama). *Days of Obligation* radically turns away from *Hunger of Memory*'s conservative voice, allowing the earlier ideological rift, at least textually, to come closer together.

[5] The pachuco figure fuses time/space intra-textually, too. In *Days of Obligation* Richard Rodriguez celebrates the pachuco's urban toughness in contradistinction to Octavio Paz's figuration in 1959. He quotes Paz: "The pachuco does not want to become Mexican again; at the same time he does not want to blend into the life of

North America. His whole being is sheer negative impulse, a tangle of contradictions, an enigma" (58).

⁶ At a certain point in the translation from manuscript to published novel, the line "sneaky like the border patrol, waiting to pull you in just when you think you're free" (69) was added to Louie's sense of remembering his past in El Paso. The line is not in the June 1987 manuscript. Yet the published version similarly projects the sense that Louie's memory is strongly racialized and in constant threat of being policed by characters like la Mollie, who threaten to deny him an affirming sense of a Chicano-infused self-knowledge.

⁷ Louie's reaction to the male-male erotica differs in the June 1987 manuscript. Here Louie remarks, "It was eerie, man, and I reconnized the old demon lust winking in the background of all them pictures I couldn't erase from my head. [. . .] Maybe the whole thing felt strange to me cause there wasn't no women in that room and women always bring something mysterious into any room" ("La Mollie" ms. 198-199). While the sentence differs from that of the 1996 novel, both reveal Louie's exaggerated ("strange cause there wasn't no women") heterosexual role play. Moreover, like the novel, the manuscript includes Louie's frequent slips—such as the comment about the "cute little waiter" (58)—that suggest a hesitating desire to move into a male-male libidinal economy.

⁸ Louie also walks through the Castro at dusk in the June 1987 manuscript. However, the manuscript adds to Louie's struggle with his sexuality a sense of his troubled history with alcohol: "In my heavy drinking and drugging days, I couldn't ever figure out how come they called that time of day the Happy Hour. It was anything but happy for me and all I wanted to do was drink away my fear of the dark that was coming on like a big, wet and heavy wool blanket all smothering and dark and scarier than a pillow Othello uses to snuff out his darling Desdemona" (93).

FROM EL PASO TO DEL SAPO:
Intersections of Biography and Fiction

Mimi Gladstein

A photograph of Mama Chona and her grandson Miguel Angel—Miguel Chico or Mickie to his family—hovers above his head on the study wall beside the glass doors that open out into the garden. (*Rain God* 3)

Not one, but two photographs of Arturo Islas, both facing front, staring into the camera, penetrate my imagination and stir my memory as I sit in my study, remembering the man, admiring the writer. One is of a skinny, gawky kid with prominent ears, in a plaid shirt and jeans, his hand holding open the door from the school auditorium. It is in the 1953 *Spur*, El Paso High School's annual publication, and he is smiling, as well he should, being one of the rare freshmen selected to "Who's Who." Being chosen was an indication of major status; qualifications called for combining academic accomplishment, popularity, and extracurricular achievement. Another key indicator of status in the world of high school annuals is the number and size of one's pictures. In the "Who's Who" section that year, each 8½" x 11" page contains only three pictures. On the page opposite Islas, Rosa Ramírez, already a senior, poses seductively, leaning against a tree. Perhaps it is some indication of the quality of our high school student body that two who would make such indelible marks in the world were recognized and appreciated so early.[1]

The second photograph, taken more than three decades later, is of a beautiful, doomed man. It is the picture chosen for the bookplate, designed by Ben Alire Sáenz, that adorns each book in the Arturo Islas Memorial Collection, part of the Chicano Studies Special Collection in the library at the University of Texas at El

Paso, where Arturo spent what he described as one of the happiest years of his life as a visiting distinguished writer in the English Department. Cynthia Farah, the photographer, captured both the beauty and sensitivity in his face. His eyes stare directly at you and a smile plays around his mouth as he leans his cheek on the fingers of his left hand. The look is perceptive, saying to the reader, "Yes, I know you." A hint of gray in his hair gives him a distinguished look. The opening lines of *The Rain God*—"A photograph of Mama Chona and her grandson, Miguel Chico"—are imprinted below his chin.[2] This particular bookplate is pasted in my copy of the uncorrected bound galleys of *Migrant Souls*. Stirring the sands of time and memory, these photographs provoke thoughts of Arturo Islas's El Paso, Miguel Chico's Del Sapo, and the methodologies that mediate their interconnections.

The correlations between Islas and his narrators/protagonists and between his fictional Del Sapo and the real El Paso situate *The Rain God* and *Migrant Souls* clearly in the category Marta E. Sánchez identifies as "a contemporary tradition of autobiographical fiction by Latino men and women" (284). Though it is not a part of the Ángel family saga, and does not share the autobiographical point-of-view character, this reading will argue that *La Mollie and the King of Tears* is undoubtedly another example of Arturo Islas's adept mining of his life and experiences to create fiction, his projection of self in a number of characters. Paul Skenazy, who edited the work, has also noted the "dense autobiographical underpinning" of the Islas oeuvre (Afterword 177). What distinguishes this exploration of the blurred boundaries between reality and its re-creation in Arturo's fiction is its perspective—that of a privileged reader. I knew Arturo Islas and many of the models, both family and friends, for the characters in his novels. We also shared many of the times described and inhabited, as it were, parallel adolescent universes. Therefore, I hope to contribute a unique viewpoint to the growing number of critical essays inspired by Arturo Islas's too-slender body of work, to shed more light on the intersections of biography and fiction.[3] The amalgam of self-knowledge and technical skill that inform these seminal works of contemporary Chicano fiction is striking; the interweaving of fact and fiction can be studied by creative writing students as a textbook example of how it is done. In Islas's Del Sapo, my El Paso comes alive; his Miguel Chico evokes my friend "Turo." And more than that, the resonance of forgiveness and love that permeates his works, provide a positive lesson in life, a model of transcendence.

Like his fictional counterpart in *The Rain God* and *Migrant Souls*, Miguel Ángel, who is called Miguel Chico or Mickie, to distinguish him from his father, Arturo Islas was also a junior. Arturo Islas, Sr., was called "Art" by his large group of male friends, some of them Anglo. None of his friends at El Paso High called the son anything akin to Art, Little Art, or Art, Jr. He most often signed himself Arturo, particularly on the title pages of his novels; many of us called him "Turo" and, in high school, he alternated between "Turo" and "Arturo" at each place in the annual where he was pictured. Occasionally, in his characteristic self-deprecating way, he might sign himself "burro." Thus, though he was his class's most popular boy, he would, in one and the same text, cast himself in the various roles of school beast of burden on one page or school role model on another. It foreshadows future narrative techniques of multiple perspectives and self-ironic tone. Marta Sánchez writes appreciatively of the "device of creating a gap between narrator and character and yet having them be one and the same" that Islas employs. She calls this technique the novel's most important formal feature (286). These texto-biographical gaps are prefigured in his adolescent presentations of self.

Frederick Luis Aldama is another who has written perceptively about Islas's narrative techniques. His focus is on Louie Mendoza, the protagonist of the posthumously published *La Mollie and the King of Tears*. Aldama explicates Louie as the first-person narrating subject and subaltern self who destabilizes metropolitan hegemonies in the novel. In Aldama's reading, Islas creates, with this narrator, a significant "autoethnographic" space and "allows for a panoply of selves to coexist within one self" ("Ethnoqueer" 581). Aldama's identification of the number of selves that he detects as coexisting in the one character Louie Mendoza is instructive. Further exploration, however, argues for an expansion of the many selves to include not just those coexisting in Louie as an Islas alter ego, but also for the Islas selves who exist in a number of other characters in the novel.

Louie Mendoza is Arturo Islas, but Louie is not Arturo. Some parts of his biography and sexual preference are decidedly different from those of his creator; some are quite similar. Both are El Pasoans, though Islas gives Louie a south El Paso barrio home in El Chuco, rather than his own middle-class background. Louie's education is limited; Islas had as elite an educational pedigree as the U.S. education system provides, a Stanford Ph.D. Louie is a musician, whereas Islas was an academic, although Islas was a member of the All-State Orchestra during high school. Louie is heterosexual; Arturo was homosexual, albeit as Frederick Aldama notes, Louie "betrays a homographic sensibility" (596). At one point in the text, Louie is invested with a "gimpy" leg like Arturo, and he does share that beautiful, "sandblasted," clear Yaqui skin of his creator. But, if they are different in terms of class, education, and sexual preference, there are marked similarities in their memories of their hometown and youth.

There is nothing remarkable about that. It is standard fictional technique, and as Arturo noted in his interview with José Antonio Burciaga, "I draw—and every fiction writer that I respect draws—shamelessly from their own experience and the experiences of people they know" (163). Also, in terms of imagery and narrative technique, the blurring and transcending of borders between self and characters is quintessential Islas. Thus, it is not unusual that biographical boundaries between Islas and Mendoza often disappear. Boundaries between texts are also crossed as, at one time, Louie Mendoza is mentioned in *Migrant Souls* and Miguel Chico appears as Mr. Ángel in the V.A. sections of *La Mollie*. This may be explained, in part, because it is my recollection that Arturo originally planned to make Louie's story an element in the *Migrant Souls* manuscript. It certainly got a positive reception when he first read it, identifying it as part of his current novel at one of the events that marked his tenure as a distinguished visiting writer in El Paso. The audience at the reading was falling on the floor laughing at the whole movie allusion conceit and the Pachuco character. El Chuco prides itself on having been the birthplace of el pachuco, the cool dude in slacks with a reet pleat, pegged at the cuff, small porkpie hat, and long watch fob, who often had a cigarette dangling from his lip. The "Louie" reading in El Paso was helped by Arturo's theatrical flair and experience in public performances. He won many an oratory or interpretation contest in high school. Everyone appreciated the reading, but we "homeys" were especially amused because we recognized the characters and places. For us, he was invoking shared high school memories. I was astounded when Arturo told me later that an early editor recommended excising the Mendoza portion because it detracted from the story of the Ángel family.

Louie's culinary memories are another instance of autobiography superimposed on fiction. Mendoza drinks at the Kentucky Club and Curley's, two Juárez, Mexico, bar/nightclubs where generations of El Paso youngsters used to hang out in high school and college. They were both sites for the teen rites of passage in the region. The Kentucky Club, in particular, was a big draw for its amazingly cheap drinks and the fact that age was no barrier to getting served. If you were big enough to put your quarter on the bar, you were big enough to drink. Much of the attraction, of course, was that at that time, Texas was still a dry state. Restaurants in El Paso did not serve drinks. One had to belong to a private club to have wine or cocktails with dinner. It is fitting that Louie would remember good and inexpensive food as coming from Juárez, not El Paso.

The border, in reality and in our experience was permeable and of no great consequence. Juárez was our after-hours habitat. Teenagers had but to park their cars in any of the many parking lots north of the Rio Grande and walk over the bridge. Adults were more likely to drive over, giving a "watchiecaro" a tip to see that the car was safe or to be sure that the meter did not run out. Visitors from out of town were almost always wined and dined in Juárez. Not only were the restaurants better, but they were also incredibly inexpensive compared to equivalent fare in the United States. Therefore, blurred borders, migrations to and fro, and unstable boundaries are endemic El Paso experiences.[4] When Louie makes a comparison between his recollections of the good food he got at those Juárez establishments and his current culinary fare, he refers to the only food in San Francisco that he claims can equal it. The reference is to the Tadich Grill, which was always an Islas favorite. It is where he insisted we eat during one of my visits to him at Stanford on the day we drove up to San Francisco.

Great parts of the humor of the novel as well as its title derive from Louie's readings of Shakespeare. "The King of Tears," of course, refers to King Lear and Islas, like some five generations of El Paso High School students, before and after him, was introduced to *King Lear* by the indomitable Miss Fanny Foster. All El Paso High School alumni of her period recognize her immediately.[5] The descriptions of her class and teaching techniques are another of the Islas realities that is furnished to Mendoza's memory. Of course, Louie Mendoza would have gone to Bowie High School, called La Bowie or La High by its students, not El Paso High where Fanny Foster taught. The major fictional component of this memory occurs in the wonderful irony of transposing the school memories of an exceptional student into the mind of one who has difficulty "getting" Shakespeare. Or perhaps Louie is one who really "gets" Shakespeare, and that is part of the novel's message. Rather than identifying Miss Foster by name, Islas creates an amalgam of the names of two of our other teachers. Perhaps in this way Islas could immortalize more than one of his favorite teachers. He took the first name of our chemistry teacher Miss Leila Oliver and the last name of our Latin teacher, Miss Annie Harper, thus creating Miss Leila Harper. But in all other aspects, Louie's Miss Leila P. Harper is none other than Miss Fanny Foster.

Miss Fanny, as we affectionately dubbed Ms. Foster, was a school legend, and quite a character. She ruled her classroom seated behind her desk, with all the students arranged in two semicircles around her, none out of reach of her punishing cane. This was because of a crippled leg; she wore a brace and I wonder if Islas felt an affinity there. And, just as Louie remembers, she had to be able to see each face clearly. You could not hide. Throwing things was another of her habits. Arturo has Leila P. throw a paperweight at Louie that he claims almost robs him of his manhood (*La Mollie* 157). She may well have thrown any number of things at Arturo, although I doubt it. He was a favorite, being as bright and well-mannered as he was. Perhaps he saw her throw a paperweight at someone else in his class. I remember her throwing a glass of water at a poor girl who inadvertently interrupted her class. Fanny Foster was, as Louie describes her, "pretty wrinkled up and her hair was snow white" (156). Our mothers and grandmothers remember when her hair was red. And her eyes were blue—as Louie remembers, "so blue they poke holes right through you." Leila P. Harper differs hardly at all from her real-life inspiration.

Louie's hilarious readings of Shakespeare are not totally unlike some of the in-group joking we did about the lines we had to memorize in those days before education reformers decided that memorization was an oppressive pedagogical technique. Islas invents a black student, Dolores Conrad, who antagonizes Miss Harper by walking up to her desk and doing a black-speak version of the announcement that Lady Macbeth is dead: "Mizz Macbeth, she dead" (12). The story is another instance of Islas's skillful weaving of fact and fiction. In reality, there were no black students at El Paso High School in those days. Nor were there "cholas" to appreciate such antics. The term is anachronistic in this context, although Louie may be using a term of his times to describe an earlier era. There is little doubt that the story about having to memorize the "tomorrow and tomorrow and tomorrow" speech from Macbeth is pure fact.

The story about the fun derived from the Texas twang reading of *Macbeth* is also probably based in reality. Our high school group had a penchant for taking a funny reading and endlessly signifying on it. On one occasion we laughed for weeks over a student's misreading of a line in *Treasure Island*. The line is "Pugh, they've been here before us." We, of course, turned it into "Phew, they've been here before us," giggling and holding our noses. We would take any occasion to enter a room, flare our nostrils, and remark: "Phew, they've been here before us." Years later, if someone inadvertently passed gas in our presence, I could look at Arturo or anyone of our classmates and we would immediately intone, "Pugh, they've been here before us."

Louie is not the only character in *La Mollie* that Islas invests with bits and pieces of his personality and experiences. Islas inhabits a variety of characters and is textualized in bits and pieces of a multiplicity of selves. He also shares characteristics with Louie's younger brother Tomás who, like Arturo, was the first in his family to move to the San Francisco area. Tomás is gay and Louie goes looking for him in the gay establishments that Arturo was familiar with. Islas does an interesting autobiographical reversal by giving Tomás an older brother Louie, who is straight, whereas Arturo has a younger brother named Luis, who is straight. Luis Islas is married to a blonde woman—perhaps a model, physically, for La Mollie? Arturo's re-creation of Louie's passion for La Mollie could be projections not that distant from his creator's own early experiences of attraction to women. In high school, Arturo dated a lot and was "in love" with Harriet Reisel. During one of our conversations, Arturo told me that the one woman he could have seen himself married to was Harriet.[6] On the other hand, the problematic nature of Louie and La Mollie's relationship may be a reflection not just of their distance in terms of class and education, but also of their author's unconscious projection of his own sexual preference.

A number of critics have analyzed the biographical implications in the characterization of Virgil Spears.[7] Most note the similarity between his name and Jay Spears, a noted lawyer with whom Arturo had a love affair. Like Jay Spears, Virgil Spears is Anglo and gay. However, it has also been suggested that there is much of his creator subsumed in the character of Virgil Spears, whom Louie credits with teaching him about homosexuality. Virgil is obviously Islas's mouthpiece in the speech about whether or not he chose to be queer and in his depathologizing of queer desire. Moreover, Virgil's actions while he responds to Louie's question about whether it was his father's brutality that made him "decide" to be queer are redolent with Islas-inspired imagery. Louie describing Virgil while he is shooting pool is like Islas looking in the mirror. As Virgil makes one difficult shot after another, Louie thinks, "Man, that gay boy could sure play pool." It is an evaluation that could have been made about Arturo.

Louie's travels around Castro Street, Haight-Ashbury, the Tenderloin, and other districts evoke memories of an evening when Arturo took me to see "his" San Francisco. We visited Golden Gate State Park and the church he called "St. Mary Maytag," ate at Tadich Grill, and then spent the whole night wandering through the gay bar scene, from the mauve velvet, glass, and chrome of one place to the leather and spikes of another. Wherever he could, Arturo stopped to play pool and he was good at it. The evening was a memorable one for me, stimulating and surreal, capturing what Frederick Luis Aldama describes in his essay collected here as the rearchitexturing of San Francisco and the "carnivalizing of space and desire."

While much of Arturo is perceptibly subsumed in the characterization of Virgil, there is also a sardonic joke embodied in his naming. Spears is obviously a tribute to Jay Spears, but his choice of Virgil for a first name provokes other connotations. Virgil was Dante's guide through hell and, in creating the character who is partially modeled on his lost love, Islas also evokes memories of how the loss of that love inspired a journey through his own private hell. Sometimes one does not fully grasp the implications of a situation while experiencing it. Though I did not know many of the details when we made our San Francisco pilgrimage, I knew that Arturo was going through the pain of the breakup. Like Louie in his tortured wanderings in the novel, we made our peregrinations through the variety of establishments and identities that were Arturo's San Francisco and I sensed they were memory-laden. As we walked and talked, we alternately dredged up reminiscences of El Paso, enjoyed the moment, and spoke of present problems. The past, present, and future we surveyed could be likened to the rings of hell, each holding its own category of sinner. Drinking and dancing our way through the streets, we aped Tina Turner, howling, "What's love got to do with, got to do with it? What's love, but a second-hand emotion?" Arturo loudly hollering, "Who needs a heart, if a heart can be broken?" He, of course, was going through the hell of a broken heart. Reflecting on that night, I realize how our experience was replicated and transformed in the fiction. Of course, that experience was but a droplet in a flood of such San Francisco experiences that furnished Islas's paradigm for Louie's sojourn. I imagine he made this tour often.

One can even argue that Islas invests La Mollie with bits and pieces of himself. Through her he is able to articulate some of his own ambivalences about his hometown, to express political views more consonant with his than those espoused by Louie. For example, La Mollie taunts Louie about his lack of sophistication and cynicism when he cites newspapers as a source for his opinions. She asks, "How can you possibly believe what the press in this country says about anything? There are even more lies in the newspaper than there are in the history books" (28). Such views are clearly those of the author. About El Paso, she asks, "Were you drugged into happy obedience by lithium in the water or did they just choke every molecule of oxygen out of your brain with all that junk they spew into the air out of the world's tallest smokestack?" (28) Politically active El Pasoans have often theorized about the complacency of the populace in the face of incredible stupidity and abuse of power by our so-called leaders. An EPA study once found that our water is naturally richer in lithium than the waters of most other American cities. It is an issue that Arturo brings up in two of his three novels. His concern that the lithium in the water was making the populace apathetic and content with a less than satisfactory situation was such that he also made it part of a conversation in *Migrant Souls*. In this case he puts it in the mouth of Aunt Sally, who like himself is a member of the family who has moved to California. After Trinidad describes Del Sapo as a "wonderful town," Sally comments: "I wonder how wonderful it would be if the guys who control the water department stopped putting lithium in it." She explains that it is "so that you'll all stay nice and happy and obedient" (*Migrant Souls* 82).

Arturo would also have been especially sensitive to the pollution spewed from ASARCO's huge smokestack. It is located not far from his family home and all of us growing up on the West side of El Paso experienced its suffocating fumes. Giving Mollie those lines allows Islas to express his concerns about the quality of life in his hometown. When she talks about "the scum that runs down the sewers and ends up polluting the Rio Grande" and declares, "They're poisoning everybody with lead," she is speaking not only for herself, but also for Arturo.[8]

The intersections of biography and fiction are more opaque in *La Mollie and the King of Tears* than in the two earlier works, *The Rain God* and *Migrant Souls*, where the transparency of the identification of author and narrator is more obvious. In the posthumous work, as illustrated, Islas's autobiographical projections are transmuted and diverse. One almost needs to have been an El Pasoan who went to El Paso High School to recognize some of the source material. On the other hand, El Paso is presented as itself, not as the pseudonymous Del Sapo and locations are accurately named, although people are disguised. In the first two novels, almost the only attempt, and that at a minimal level, Islas makes to camouflage the autobiographical aspects of his presentation of the Ángel/Islas family saga is by calling his hometown Del Sapo.[9]

The Rain God plot develops the stories of various members of the family of the narrator, Miguel Chico, as much or more than his own. Parts of his story are told, specifically remembrances of his early childhood and then bits and pieces of his adult years after his move to California. Left out are the adolescent years and college, as well as any sense of his personal life in California. The high school experiences do not make their appearances until *Migrant Souls* and *La Mollie and the King of Tears*. College and his professional life may have been projected for the third in the unfinished trilogy of the Ángel family saga. In the first book, the reader is helped to understand the development and identity formation of the narrator/author through his recounting of stories of the early battles between his mother and father about how he was to be raised, as well as the narrative technique of self-analysis whereby the course of his growing self-knowledge is charted. A key example of this is the passage in which the older narrator describes his younger self: "he was still seeing people, including himself, as books. He wanted to edit them, correct them, make them behave differently" (*Rain God* 26). The author, in his loving yet critical depiction of self and family demonstrates the evolution of his identity and differential consciousness. In presenting the Ángel family "sinners" with none of their flaws or foibles "edited" or "corrected," he evidences what Chela Sandoval calls "a neorhetoric of love in the Postmodern world" (129), part of her "methodology of the oppressed," which I will discuss later.

The distinct quality of *The Rain God,* a quality that distinguishes it from similar works of "genealogical imperative" in Chicano writing, is identified by Wilson Neate as its "foregrounding and examination of certain considerations which have remained conspicuously absent from or at least unproblematized in many male Chicano narratives of family" (211). This he identifies as "body and affect." Furthermore, Neate calls into question the tendency to essentialize and fix Chicano identity as determined only by race and ethnicity. By analyzing how Miguel Chico uses the novel to minimize his repression by the "Law of the Father" as instilled by Mamá Chona to create his own individualized textualization of experience, Neate defines Miguel's self as a "product of multiple and ongoing grafting" (229). His focus is Miguel Chico's experience of and presentation of body. On a more superficial level, this exploration of the intersections of biography and fiction, of the realities of growing up on a permeable border in one of the few islands of "happy days" high school experience is also one of the "grafts" of the many branches of Arturo Islas's unique identity, the junction of author and narrator as character.

Marta Sánchez argues that Islas uses "narrative strategies that highlight the 'minority' writer's role of mediator between cultures" (285). She explains that he "writes in a mode that reflects his own bilingual, bicultural heritage," building bridges of understanding between Anglophonic and bilingual readers. It is another example of his replicating through his fiction what he did in his life. Our high school context was one in which we often used bilingual humor, anglicizing Spanish, and Spanifying English. It is a characteristic of the border culture; linguists call it code switching. In *The Rain God*, the narrator tells of his aunt saying to his mother, "That's my herman." He explains "They had Anglicized the word for sister [hermana] and used it as a term of endearment with each other" (74). In English, of course, it sounds funny to call someone your "herman." Our Mex-Tex code switching was part of the identification and affection we felt with and for each other. For example, we would routinely anglicize Spanish phrases, substituting "much grass" for "muchas gracias" or "es verdaddy" for "es verdad."* This language use was a means

---

* When we ran into each other in the hall, we would shout, "Que dites?" [¿qué dices?—what do you say?], more often than not affecting a distinctly Texas twang. The response was "Que dites uts?" or "No dites natz." The words were not always used in place of their original meaning. For example, in my sister's *Spur*, Arturo begins one of his inscriptions to her by addressing her as "Que dites."

of identification—a signal of affinity with the other "border babies," bilingual speakers.

Another instance in the novel that illustrates the humor that can derive from code switching is when the narrator is describing his early memories of being taken to the cemetery. His grandmother calls it "Campo Santo," and so the narrator explains, "for a long time Miguel Chico thought it was a place for the saints to go camping" (9). Sometimes the code switching is inadvertent, as when Angie, who speaks little English, confuses slang and crepe suzettes and comes up with the expression "the suzie creeps."

José David Saldívar, remonstrating against the Anglocentric monocultural bias of the New York editors who initially rejected *The Rain God*, sees Miguel Chico, Arturo's fictional alter-ego as a Henry James-type character "affected with certain high lucidity" ("Hybridity" 114). Arturo would have chortled with glee at the comparison. Those who knew him at Stanford know that one of his most popular courses was on Henry James and that James was a writer whose excellence he vociferously defended. That comparison also provokes my memories of Arturo. My thoughts go back to the mid-eighties and a treasured time when four old El Paso High School chums gathered for a dinner party in my home.* All went well until the men turned to the subject of literature. At that point

---

* I was the only one of the group who had stayed in El Paso. Norma Levine Trusch is a respected lawyer in Houston, a fellow of the American Academy of Matrimonial Lawyers, specializing in family law, about which she gives seminars in cities all over the country. When she left El Paso she worked on several Emmy-Award winning programs for NBC and ABC in New York City before returning to Texas. She thought it strange when I called her, out of the blue, and invited her to Friday night dinner. Her question was: "Why should I fly 850 miles for dinner?" My response: "I think you'll like my guest list." She made arrangements to come. Rafael Jesús Gonzales is a professor, poet, visual artist and anti-nuclear activist. For many years he taught at Laney College in San Francisco. Arturo was in town for one of his regular home visits and had promised to come over and make his fabulous leg of lamb recipe. None knew who the other dinner guests would be, so each ring of the doorbell offered a new surprise. The evening was magic. We had all been Masque and Gavel club members and laughed till we cried remembering high school speech tournaments and high jinks.

I thought I had fallen into the alternative universe of a Woody Allen movie. The argument between Rafael Jesús González and Arturo over the merits of Henry James could not have been more hilarious. González sneered at the effete snobbery of James. Islas defended the complex and psychologically astute writing. It was all too surreal. Thinking about that evening in terms of the questions of biographical and cultural context, there are several observations that can be made. One is about the singular quality of our high school experience. Whatever the other realities about growing up ethnic in Texas and the pre-Civil Rights Movement United States, El Paso High School was an island of multicultural sanity. Every school generation had its newest member of the Schwartz clan, a Haddad or Abraham, a Yip or a Yee, a Ruiz, a Chávez, or a Salazar. And the friendships were long-lasting, not just factors of a high school experience. Rosa Ramírez recalls El Paso High as special; she calls it a "familia," remembering: "We had a wonderful understanding, respect for each other."[10] Rafael Jesús González refers to El Paso High as a "blessed place" during the years that we attended.[11]

Although Islas pointedly draws attention to the divisions between groups in *Migrant Souls*, in particular the "undeclared borderline [that] existed between Mexicans and Anglos" (68), he also presents evidence of the blurring and crossing of that line. Josie marries Harold Newman, who has a Mexican mother and Anglo father, thus showing that love had crossed the line in the previous generation also. In *The Rain God* El Compa takes the surname of his Anglo stepfather. Something indicative of what Rosa Ramírez remembers as "familia" and what I have described as the ecumenical character of our high school is substantiated in Islas's peopling of the attendees at Josie's wedding: "Several of her Syrian and Jewish friends from high school came to her wedding" (*Migrant Souls* 95). Islas uses the real names of our high school Syrian friends, the Haddads, the Abrahams, and the Ekerys; he also uses the actual names of two prominent Jewish families, Schwartzes and Shapiros. Aunt Sally is one of the surprise guests at the wedding, a member of the family by marriage who is described as "half Irish and half Mexican" (79). It is a combination that is quite common in our area. John Rechy is perhaps the most famous example, acknowledged for his breakthrough as a gay writer, but not uniformly accepted in the earlier days of the Chicano movement as a Chicano writer. He is still largely absent from anthologies and excluded from lists of pioneering Chicano writers. Borders were obviously permeable.

This is not to say that prejudice was not rampant. It was. We were all cognizant of it. But, wherever else Arturo may have felt its sting, it was not a constricting factor in either the author's or his fictional counterpart's experience in high school. In *Migrant Souls* the narrator acknowledges Miguel Chico's popularity in high school, introduced in the context of Josie's rebellion. Josie realizes that she is not kind or charitable, "nor was she popular like her cousin Miguel Chico, two years younger than she and already a class favorite" (51). She intuitively grasps the split between his public and private selves as she "watched him charm his life away through high school, where, with little effort, he carried off all the prizes" (52). Indeed, in those benighted days of the early fifties, when racist behaviors were rampant in most parts of Texas, El Paso High School, generally considered the most elite public high school in town at that time, was markedly ahead of its time in terms of the integration of not only Hispanics and Anglos, but other religious and ethnic groups.

In the early fifties, Hispanics were still in the minority in the school and in the community. Nonetheless, both Arturo Islas and Rafael Jesús González were student senate officers, named to Who's Who, and winners of many other accolades both on the basis of academics and popularity.* Nor were Arturo and Rafael tokens or the exception. My yearbooks provide the evidence. Rafael Chávez was elected president of the student body in 1954; Sam Meraz, Ben Endlich, and Blanca Guzmán are three of the five cheerleaders, a position of much popularity; Mary Helen Márquez

---

* The same is not true for the Anglo attendees at my dinner party. Though both of us were high achievers academically and in extra-curricular activities, we did not garner the same awards and recognition they did, nor get named to Who's Who or Student Council. If one wants to argue the presence of oppression as opposed to the vagaries of popularity, we could consider that sexism trumped Anglocentrism in our case.

is program manager; Martha Ruiz, Cecilia Quiñones, Celia González and Blanca Guzmán are football princesses; Oscar Pando is junior favorite and Guillermo Ruiz is freshman favorite.

The ecumenical nature of the El Paso experience is also explored by José Antonio Burciaga in many of his works. Of course, his was a special case, as his father was the custodian of a Jewish synagogue. In *Drink Cultura* he writes that his father's death as well as his life were ecumenical: "The funeral was held at Our Lady of Peace, where a priest said the mass in English. My cousins played mandolin and sang in Spanish. The president of B'nai Zion Congregation said a prayer in Hebrew" (117).[12]

When Arturo returned home after the publication of *The Rain God* to spend a year as a visiting professor at UTEP, I was at first surprised that he chose to live at home with his parents. Some family members—not in the immediate family—had expressed anger at the revelations in the novel. I wondered how his father would feel, having been portrayed as a rejected adulterer. I had not reckoned with the power of love.

The transcendent tone of *The Rain God* is at once one of empathetic, yet objective forgiveness. Although the Ángel family's "sinners" are unveiled, with many of their racist, sexist, and exploitive characteristics highlighted, it is their humanity that shines through. The process by which the author deals with his family ghosts and the skeletons in their closets, is not unlike the procedure Chela Sandoval identifies as the "methodology of the oppressed" (69). Certainly Arturo Islas, Jr., belonged to many "oppressed" groups. He was Chicano in a city, state, and country dominated by Anglos; he grew up disabled before the culture took notice of the need to provide access for all its citizens; he was gay in a time when most gays were still closeted. Sandoval defines this methodology of the oppressed as a differential consciousness working in resistance to dominant social hierarchies. Hers is a call for love as a social movement of revolutionary citizen-activists, allied through the apparatus of emancipation, and her study charts the various strategies used to develop this differential consciousness, such as "*mestizaje*," a consciousness developed "on borders and in margins" that keeps "intact shifting and multiple identities with integrity and love" (168). Arturo demonstrated his differential consciousness in fiction; he lived many of the strategies.

One such strategy is the technique of wearing the "mask," the kind of masking defined in Frantz Fanon's *Black Skin, White Masks*, producing what some writers have defined as a "split consciousness." Citing such third-world thinkers as W. E. B. Du Bois, Audre Lorde, Gloria Anzaldúa, and Paula Gunn Allen, Sandoval writes: "These theorists see what they do as they do it from the dominant viewpoint as well as from their own, shuttling between realities, their identities reformatting out of another third site" (84). Islas functioned similarly. As narrator/protagonist, Miguel Chico is both observer and observed, an actor in, but distanced from much of the action of the novel. The distance between the surface privileges of Miguel Chico and the narrator's presentation of them represent the space between the skin and the mask. Noting the separate groups formed by the Mexicans and the Anglos at a school dance, the narrator, from Josie's perspective observes, "Her cousin bounced with ease from one group to another and was friendly to everyone, sometimes insincerely, Josie knew." The insincerity is tantamount to the mask. "His smile and wit opened doors that warned others to stay out" (*Migrant Souls* 67). Friendliness and wit were two other "masks" that maintained the success of Arturo's persona. The space between, or the "gap" is underlined by Josie's observation that she thought "her cousin one of the loneliest people in the world" (67).

Another description of "masking" occurs when Josie expresses the idea that she is unpopular because she is honest, whereas Miguel Chico's way of being popular comes from not being honest. Josie responds to a story of a mixed couple that leave town by saying they are better off than in a town full of hypocrites: "Her honesty made her unpopular and she knew it. When Miguel Chico was told about the doomed couple, he looked very concerned and then smiled without saying a word. Later that year, he was elected class favorite." The narrator/author implies that Miguel is able to negotiate the undeclared borderline because of his dishonesty, a mask for his true feelings. However, many popular people, particularly those who achieve political success, do so by not being honest, by wearing the mask of caring and concern. It is not just the tool of the oppressed.

A third masking feature for Arturo was his limp. Part of the fear of otherness is muted when the other is perceived as nonthreatening. Because of his slight stature and limp, Arturo could be discounted in a Texan culture where the athletic hero is king in high school. In fact, Arturo's great spirit could be celebrated because he did not let the limp inhibit his mobility in other ways. If he was not athletic, he did develop into a good dancer, one all the girls wanted as a partner at the school sock hop or homeroom dance.

"Love . . . is an important source of empowerment when we struggle to confront issues of sex, race, and class," writes bell hooks, and in *The Rain God*, the narrator's overarching love for his family, even as he exhibits their flaws and imperfections, empowers him to transcend, to pull the loathsome monster that killed Mamá Chona into the fog with him, feeling the pleasure of the avenged, to feel the rain god in the room, and yet remove his hand from the touch of his dying grandmother in a choice to live. *The Rain God* is the narrative of a man who has broken through, one who finds understanding and community. In writing the book, Arturo Islas and his fictional self Miguel Chico are engaging in an act of purgation and propitiation. He describes it as his need to "make peace with his dead" (*Rain God* 160). He characterizes the act as "feed[ing] them words" and making them "candied skulls out of paper." In many ways, although it came first, it is a work of greater maturity than the subsequent works. From its presentation of murder, death, and medical problems to its elegiac tone, it embodies a calmer and more accepting moment in its author's life.

NOTES

[1] Rosa Ramírez gained fame as a teacher of dance. She founded a folkloric dance company that was featured nationwide during Sun Bowl halftime shows. More than just a dance teacher, Ramírez has used dance to teach tolerance and harmony and to transcend cultural boundaries. She has won numerous awards and been selected to the Texas Women's Hall of Fame. Rosa Guerrero is the only living

woman in El Paso to have a public school named after her. She married Sergio Guerrero, another of our high school's popular students, who became a coach in a local high school. Rosa continues to give motivational and inspirational speeches at schools and conferences.

[2] Farah took the picture in March of 1986. It was first printed as part of her book *Literature and Landscape*, a book of photographs of writers of the southwest. Each full-page photograph is faced with a statement by the writer about how the landscape has influenced his or her work. Rudolfo Anaya, Tom Lea, Denise Chávez, Rolando Hinojosa-Smith, and Scott Momaday are also among those featured.

[3] The inscription in my copy of *Migrant Souls* reads, "for my dear Mimi—friend, fellow teacher *and* a character in this book. Love, Arturo." He drew a little red heart in the margin of the pages at the two places where I appear. Arturo and I were good friends in high school. We reestablished our friendship as colleagues and saw each other often whenever he visited El Paso. I went to visit him in Stanford on three different occasions, staying with him in his apartment when he was a faculty fellow in a dormitory, at his condominium in Peter Couts Village, and staying with Steven Orgel once because Arturo was in the hospital during one of my visits. When I was chair of the English Department at the University of Texas at El Paso, I invited Arturo to spend a year in the department as distinguished visiting writer. Sadly, during my second term as chair, we had the occasion to establish a memorial book collection.

[4] It is not so anymore. Border traffic has become so difficult that trips back and forth are less frequent; much of the traffic is business-related because of NAFTA and the *maquiladores*. When I was first teaching at UTEP, we would often go to Juárez for lunch and be back in time for afternoon classes and meetings. We always took candidates across the border for sightseeing and often for dinner. These days, when the return trip might include a 45-minute wait on the bridge, there is no longer that easy interchange. Still, some 1,500 students from Juárez make the trip each day to attend UTEP.

[5] Paul Skenazy writes in his afterword to the novel that "In a note to himself on the back of a page of manuscript, for example, Arturo says that Leila P. Harper is based on two teachers from his high school in El Paso" (175). Since I have not seen the note, I cannot tell how much of this is Skenazy's interpretation or how specific Arturo was about exactly what was based on them.

⁶ Harriet Reisel is my sister. We are referred to in *Migrant Souls* as the Reigel sisters. Arturo changed only one letter in our last name. He even mentions our father, who was very active in resettling Holocaust victims. Arturo came to our home often for Friday night dinners and would have long conversations with our father, whom all our friends adored. When Harriet went to college, friends began to call her Holli, a name that has stuck. In response to some questions by Frederick Luis Aldama, Arturo's biographer, I asked her about the nature of her relationship with Arturo. She recounted for me a very romantic memory. At the time, she was attending UC Berkeley and Arturo was rooming with Alan Kahn at Stanford. Both boys had dated her in high school. She had a date with Alan, and when it got too late to return to Berkeley, she spent the night in their rooms. On awakening the next morning, she found a rose on her chest and Arturo sitting on the floor by the bed. Alan was not awake yet, so she and Arturo took off and spent the whole day at the beach and generally having a wonderful time. She remembers their kisses as warm and loving, though not passionate. During his year in residence here and on trips to El Paso before and after that time, Arturo maintained a strong friendship with Holli and her husband Bill Berry.

⁷ Skenazy writes of the journal entry in which Arturo noted that he was incorporating Jay's name into the figure of Virgil Spears. He is also pleased that he incorporates Jay's favorite line: "And yet I wish but for the thing I have." Skenazy likens the love of Louie for La Mollie to Arturo's with Jay: "the adoration of a blond, blue-eyed person from another class and ethnicity, raised in privilege" (*La Mollie* 173).

⁸ Toxic levels of lead have been found in all areas close to the smelter, including UTEP. What once was Smeltertown is now deserted; ASARCO (American Smelting and Refining Company) ceased smelting several years ago. The smokestack still looms above the cityscape, an eyesore from any vantage point.

⁹ When I objected to his choice of pseudonym for our hometown, arguing that it evoked the idea of a place of saps, he insisted that had not been his intention. He explained that a *sapo* is a toad in Spanish and that the mountain sitting in the middle of the city looked like a squatting toad. I think the choice has unconscious connotations—"echar sapos y culebras" means to pour forth abuse. The novels are infused with a combination of attraction and revulsion for his hometown.

[10] Telephone interview, June 29, 2001. I wanted to check my remembrances, to make sure time had not rose-colored my backward vision, so I interviewed a number of both Hispanic and Anglo students who attended during the period Arturo describes. Rosa said that if she experienced prejudice, it was from the teachers, not other students. It was not so when she went to study dance in Denton, Texas. There she was told, "you've got to stay in your place."

[11] E-mail to Mimi R. Gladstein, July 5, 2001. Rafael, too, remembers the prejudice of the teachers, especially one English teacher who would not accept him in Kalevala because she did not believe he wrote the essay he submitted. He grants, however, that she changed her attitude toward him later. He, too, loved Miss Fanny, playing hooky to spend the day at the library writing a paper for her class. Rafael lists the high school friends with whom he still maintains strong relationships. It is quite a multiethnic list: Chávez, Levine, Sherman, Sotelo, Engle, Kranzthor, González, Harmon, and of course, Gladstein.

[12] Burciaga and Islas were friends at Stanford. Burciaga did not go to El Paso High School and so was not part of our group during that period of our lives. Antonio "Tony" Burciaga and his wife Cecilia were faculty fellows at the Zapata dormitory, where Tony painted a mural, *Last Supper of Chicano Heroes*, on the wall. Tony is among the writers quoted in the jacket blurbs for *The Rain God*.

Interview

FACTS AND FICTIONS:
A Last Interview with Arturo Islas

Héctor Torres

Héctor Torres: Let's begin with your talking a little about your early background: family, schooling, and so on.

Arturo Islas: I was born and raised in El Paso in 1938. I was the first of three sons. My father is the last of ten children, so on that side of the family I have a lot of relatives, including three of his older sisters that are still living; his brothers have died. I have lots of first cousins and we all went to public schools in El Paso. In fact, a lot of us went to the same high school where my parents went: El Paso High, where my parents met. I was the first in my generation to go away to college straight out of high school. I mention this fact not to brag, but to give you a sense of what education was like for Chicanos in the 1940s and 1950s. It was even more of an oddity that someone of my generation would go away to college on a scholarship; I was lucky in this regard. You had to do really, really well to even be noticed.

H.T.: Tell me more about your early family life.

A.I.: Well, we were from a lower middle-class Mexican family, growing up in the Five Points Area of El Paso, populated mostly by other lower to middle-class Mexican families and about twenty or so black families. (I think you could buy a house in those years for three thousand dollars.) But that was the hardship of my parents. Both my parents worked all their lives. My mother was a secretary for various companies in El Paso and my father was a policeman. Starting out as a rookie in the late 1930s, early

1940s, my father was one of three of the first Mexican policemen on the force. I grew up with my brothers, Mario and Louis; both are younger than me, Mario is six years and Louis is ten years younger. We all went to the same public schools.

The prejudice against Mexicans was still very, very strong in the 1940s and 1950s. Even though 40 percent of El Paso's population were those with a Mexican heritage, they weren't allowed to hire my father, when it became his turn to become chief of police, they wouldn't let him be chief of police. It wasn't because he lacked experience, it was clearly a case of racism. He was passed over for the Anglos again and again.

H.T.: Were there signs that you could read that showed that there was a systematic exclusion?

A.I.: The signs were more than visible. Even in grade school, the Anglo and the Mexican kids were segregated. It was always there throughout my schooling in one form or another. I always walked the line in between, partly because I always occupied a kind of privileged position. I was a very good student and was thought to be somewhat precocious. I surprised a lot of my teachers who, as a result, treated me in a special way.

I remember when a friend of mine, I was like around eight years old and he wanted me to join the Cub Scouts with him. I went to one meeting with him, but wasn't invited back. I never heard again why I wasn't invited back; he quit the Cub Scouts because they wouldn't let me as a Mexican be a Cub Scout. There was a lot of this insidious prejudice everywhere.

Much of the racism was never up front. Anglos could be awfully nice to you, but they wanted to keep Mexican people in their place. They didn't know what to do with people who did well in school because we weren't supposed to do well in school. We weren't supposed to know how to read. Along with my cousins, I had been taught

	that by my grandmother—who had been a teacher—how to read and write in Spanish.
H.T.:	What was your experience with language?
A.I.:	My experience with language. I am so glad that I was brought up speaking Spanish.
H.T.:	You said your grandmother taught you in Spanish?
A.I.:	I grew up in a bilingual, bicultural atmosphere. To speak both Spanish and English was natural for me; it was no big deal for us. I don't understand all this anti-bilingual education to-do today. I think anybody and everybody should know more than one language fluently. It can only make you a richer person. Being able to speak both English and Spanish so naturally is largely why I was so happy with school and in life later. At the time, of course, at school you couldn't speak Spanish at school or on the school grounds. Most of us followed the rules because otherwise we would be punished.
H.T.:	Were you ever punished?
A.I.:	Even though we were told that this was not the thing to do, I would just slip into Spanish. Often, the teacher would overhear and knock me down—not physically or directly, but in subtle ways. So, even though I was a straight-A student, instead of getting an A, I'd get a B, for example. There were these subtle forms of racism operating then and that continue to operate today. The racism doesn't just come from the Anglo people in El Paso. It is a big military town, so a lot of the soldiers and military personnel are from outside of El Paso; they are mostly xenophobic and bigots, treating Mexicans like dirt. This has always been a source of disturbance for me.
H.T.:	How did you and your parents communicate?
A.I.:	We communicated in Spanish and English, screaming and yelling just like a normal family. Chicano *caló*—slang—filled our household, especially coming out of my father's

mouth. My father doesn't speak English or Spanish perfectly, so he speaks this wonderful admixture of both.

Many of the Chicanos of my father's generation that grew up in the Five Points barrio in El Paso speak *caló* to communicate with one another. It's a wonderfully alive and vibrant language all of its own.

H.T.: Where did you go for your undergraduate?

A.I.: Stanford University. From my B.A., M.A., to the Ph.D., all my education has been at Stanford. To give you a sense of how different it was back then, as far as representation of ethnic minorities, in my graduating class here in 1960, there was one black woman and one with a Spanish surname—myself.

H.T.: Even as late as 1960?

A.I.: Even as late as 1960, because you know it was the end of the Eisenhower era. Kennedy was elected in the fall of 1960 and that was the beginning of the sixties revolution and all of that, the civil rights; however, you didn't really see the changes at Stanford in any dramatic way until the late 1960s.

H.T.: What was that like for you being on the Stanford campus?

A.I.: Well, the first two years were very alienating and very lonely; it took awhile, but I finally began to get used to the place. And after that it was okay. I started out as a pre-med. because I always thought I wanted to be a doctor. Unfortunately, the kind of training in math—no calculus—I had at El Paso High didn't prepare me well enough for the chemistry and biology courses at Stanford. I didn't do as well as I'd have liked in these courses.

I also had the added pressure of having to maintain a very high grade point to keep my scholarship. I was doing very well in literature, so I switched. Then, I received another scholarship to stay on for graduate school. I began the Ph.D. program, then left for five years. When I returned, I finished my degree in 1970-71, and the

	English department hired me on first as an adjunct then as a tenure track professor.
H.T.:	Where did you go for those five years?
A.I.:	Well, I'd been a student all my life. And I wanted to see the world. I wanted to live. More than anything, then, I just wanted to get out of the academy. I didn't want to read a book, take exams, or anything. And I had five part-time jobs, including working as a cashier and as a deliveryman. One of my jobs was a teaching job at the VA hospital in Menlo Park where they sent the hopeless cases. The patients were all zonked out on Thorazine and I was supposed to teach them public speaking. Actually, they taught me how to speak. They taught me how to communicate to people. They were wonderful and pathetically sad men and women; their lives were essentially governed by medication. Once you're on Thorazine for that long you become an institutionalized personality. Working as a speech therapist, if I could get some of them to put two sentences together and understand what they were saying, that was a triumph. I learned much from their lives and the stories they shared. I saved enough money to go to Europe for the first time as well as to travel to Mexico. It was also during this period—the Haight-Ashbury era—that I moved to San Francisco.
H.T.:	This was clearly part of your education too?
A.I.:	You bet it was. During this period, I learned to see myself as somebody in the world and not just as somebody in an academic community. This was very good for my overall education as a human being. When I returned to the academic setting, my education was enriched by my experiences in the bigger world. In 1969, I returned to the academy, accepting a job offer from San Jose State. Unfortunately, in a sudden turn of events, I almost died in June of that same year. I had an ulcerated colon. After nearly dying, I had to have an ileostomy and a colectomy. Needless to say, I couldn't take

the job in the fall. So Stanford kept me on just teaching freshman English so that I'd draw a check while I was recovering. And then the following year they hired me as a regular faculty member. I draw from that experience in my portrayal of Miguel Chico in *The Rain God*. He himself goes through a life-threatening series of operations and I use my own experience in order to draw his character. And then in 1976 I was given tenure and I've been at Stanford ever since.

H.T.: To return to your bilingual/bicultural upbringing, do you draw on this experience of linguistic code shifting in your creative work?

A.I.: Yes, I do. However, I had problems with this bilingualism when trying to get published; Northeastern established presses simply will not publish you unless you write completely in English. The smaller California presses and some of the Chicano presses will do it, but you're not going to get the same kind of distribution or backing that you get out of New York. So, in my books *The Rain God* and *Migrant Souls*, I give the flavor of the Spanish language in my use of English—this is especially the case for the members of the older generation in the books. So while in reality all these older characters speak Spanish, in the book they speak English—but an English that really captures the sense of them speaking Spanish. This was a real challenge: to get these characters to sound like they were speaking Spanish but who were speaking in English. I couldn't use the Spanish because nobody would publish it that way.

H.T.: What other kinds of strategies do you find yourself using to connote the flavor of the Spanish language?

A.I.: Well, like when there were words that you can't really translate them completely, I just went ahead and used them like *sinvergüenza*, *malcriado*, or words for foods. So the trick became how to explain them in English without seeming to be explaining it. This was both a challenge and fun. The main task is to communicate the atmosphere of that culture; sometimes you're successful and sometimes you're not, but the thing is to try it. A lot of us are faced with this challenge and deal with it differently. I think of Denise Chávez, Ben Sáenz, Ana Castillo, Sandra Cisneros, as well as Rolando Hinojosa and Tomás Rivera, who all faced this problem of how to write in Spanish/English that wouldn't alienate the reader. Tomás, for example, resolved it by having Spanish and English page to page, back to back so that you could do either.

The ideal way to publish the kind of work that I do and that a lot of writers from my background do would be to do it in Spanish and in English and a mixture of the two, but this would mean not publishing with the New York publishing houses. As such, we only end up talking and reading to each other. That's fine, but we need to get out there in the imaginations of the rest of the country.?

H.T.: Any other strategies that you can think of?

A.I.: I've written another novel, "La Mollie and the King of Tears," that I'm having a hard time getting published because it's in barrio dialect. While there is the small El Paso-based Cinco Puntos Press that wants to publish it, I keep holding out, hoping that a larger press will do it because the imagination of this character needs to reach a larger audience. Maybe that audience will eventually arrive, but for now, the challenges of writing bilingual fiction in mainstream publishing continues.

More and more Anglos in California have a familiarity with the Spanish language. They're not like the Anglos of the Northeast that should have some familiarity because of the large Puerto Rican and Cuban populations in New York, but that don't. And here at Stanford, I urge all of my students—minority, non-minority—to learn more than one language; it seems to me perfectly natural that the language they ought to learn is Spanish, because that's the language that's spoken most in the Western hemisphere. It's Spanish so they could get jobs. It seems a practical suggestion. But the minute you say that, all of a sudden it turns into this big political issue and I'm labeled a revolutionary radical and a this and a that. For me, it should simply be natural for people to speak and think in two languages.

H.T.: Changing the topic, just a little bit. What in your mind is the relationship between Chicano literature and American literature?

A.I.: I think there's a strong relationship. In the case of Tomás Rivera's . . . *y no se lo tragó la tierra*, where he uses a form and organization modeled after Hemingway's *In Our Time*; Hemingway himself was enamored of the Latin and Spanish culture and literature—its spirit/soul. Rolando Hinojosa has the same links to American literature. After all, many of us writers have passed through the American learning institution, so writers like Rivera and others have read the literature of Britain and America. So, when it comes to writing their own novels and poetry, and so on, they transform all the information they've learned into their own. Whether you acknowledge it or not, whether you want to admit to it or not, American, British, you name it, it all gets incorporated into your imagination.

More so than twenty years ago when I first began writing, writers today like Denise Chávez and Ben Sáenz are giving voice to the Chicano/a experience that's been a central part of North American life for centuries even that people are opening up and listening to.

H.T.: When does Chicano literature begin for you?

A.I.: Well, some people date it back to the Treaty of Guadalupe Hidalgo in 1848, with scholars uncovering mostly Spanish-language documents such as newspapers from this period; there's even creative writers that are beginning to surface from this period. This is all very exciting and interesting. I mean that's what scholars do. They uncover all that material and then make it available to us.

However, some will say that that is too far back to go to date the beginning of Chicano literature. That it really starts in the 1960s with the Chicano political and aesthetic movement; that moment when we began to look at literature through political and historical perspectives. This perspective is fine, too. As long as Chicanos keep writing and recovering, I don't care when you want to date the origins of Chicano literature.

H.T.: Is that tantamount to saying that Chicano literature doesn't have an identity?

A.I.: No, I don't think so at all. I mean to me it has very much its own multiple identity. It's not just one identity. It isn't fair to get a writer to speak for an entire concept or mythical concept. It doesn't work that way. Some guy or woman writing in the barrio of East L.A. is going to have her or his own voice. Some guy or woman writing from the migrant experience in *Tejas* is going to have his or her own voice. And yet they both come from the same history: They're Mexican. To me, that's all part of the same thing. It's just like a cut crystal with lots of different edges and reflective surfaces. It's the same crystal, but with many different lights reflecting off it.

A culture that is static is dead. Chicano culture is far from dead. It is this definite, distinct, and unique voice of the multiply-layered and variously articulated Chicano experience that informs Chicano literature and that forms part of what we call American literature. Here, I define "American" broadly as not only the United States, but Canada, Mexico, Latin America, and South America. That's all America. I've always had a problem with the definition of "American" literature; it's not as narrow a concept as people conceive it to be. When most professors teach American literature here at Stanford, what they mean is the literature of the United States. So, when I begin my Masterpieces of American Literature class, I always remind my students that we are looking at only a narrow slice of a larger literature that extends North and South of our borders.

As a writer myself I don't even like to think in terms of nationalisms or traditions because all of that seems ridiculous to me. The plain fact of the matter is that a lot of the most exciting writing that's being done is in the United States, is being done by so-called minority groups—people from those groups who have systematically been excluded from the canon. Afro-American authors have made great strides into American literature. I mean now they are taught in the canon. And that's bound to happen with Chicano writers because our voices are exciting, interesting—and new. They're keeping the tradition alive. If you stay within one little tradition, it's going to remain static and die. No matter how good the writing is.

H.T.: As a writer, what kind of categories do you feel comfortable with?

A.I.: None. I don't like the labels and the categories. In my role as a professor, I use them to say these are labels and categories and they're arbitrary. They were chosen by a committee deciding that this is what we were going to teach in an American literature course or in a French literature course or in a whatever the literature.

H.T.: Are your students distressed when they find out that these are social constructions? These categories are socially constructed?

A.I.: At least in my classes, they're usually very open-minded. There are some narrow-minded students. Students who want to have those demarcations, those boundaries because they feel more secure having them. But there are pedagogical ways to deal with that and to talk about that.

H.T.: What are some of the ways that you use to begin to dismantle some of those arbitrary categories?

A.I.: Well, I always start my introductory lectures in every class that I teach stating that I'm looking at these works from a writer's point of view—and not from the point of view of the critic, sociologist, anthropologist, linguist. I focus on delineating what have I learned from my fellow writers about writing. As such, fiction is my interest.

In everything that's written by the writers that we read or talk about we should ask, What is distinctively American about this? Why do we identify it as European, Mexican, or Latin American literature? What is so distinctive about a given literary text that makes it such? You see, I don't like to do a reading of literature that is based on nationalism. That to me is wrong. Writers cross borders constantly in their imaginations. The best writers from any country are usually pretty critical of the countries that they're writing in. It's one reason that makes them good writers because most of them see what a sham nationalism is. That doesn't mean they don't have pride in their countries, or have visions about their countries like the Russians, for example, Tolstoy, Dostoyevsky in the 19th century, but it means that they're also critical. They're not nationalistic—they're creative writers.

H.T.: When did you first begin to realize that you wanted to be a writer?

A.I.: Well, I think people are writers when they're writing. You can't want to be a writer. You're either writing or you're not writing and when you're not writing you're not a writer. I tell my students this. Because I always have students coming in and say, "I want to be a writer." And I'll say, "Well, what have you written? Show me what you've written." And they'll say, "Oh, I haven't done anything yet, but I want to be a writer." I say, "Well, go write. Then you're a writer while you're writing. Then we can talk about what you've done." I've been writing all my life. As a student in one way or another, I always wrote—fiction and nonfiction.

However, I never imagined I'd become a novelist until my year leave as an assistant professor at Stanford. Instead of writing literary criticism during that year off—for tenure, this is what one is supposed to do—I took the plunge into creative writing, beginning with several short stories that then grew into the novel "Día de los Muertos," that later became *The Rain God*.

H.T.: Did you have a design in mind when writing *The Rain God*?

A.I.: To answer that question I can tell you how the structure changed over time. Right from the beginning, it had the bilingual title: "Día de los Muertos/Day of the Dead" and was only three long chapters. After a process of writing and revising, it turned into six chapters. The central organizing principle was the family—the Ángel family. I didn't want there to be a central character or a central voice. I wanted the family—it the idea of the family—to be the hero of the novel. However, to have the family as the central hero—among other things like the bilingual element—also meant that I would have difficulty publishing the novel. I would send it off to New York, where they would respond negatively because they couldn't find a central, focalizing intelligence that they could identify with.

H.T.: How did that make you feel?

A.I.: Horrible. I didn't like rejection; nobody likes rejection. So, finally I just gave up. They're not going to do it. They'll do it after I die. Then the small California press Alexandria Press published it. We changed the title to *The Rain God*, as well as the organization of the book. So it grew over time. It took about three years to write it—and it took about ten years to publish it.

H.T.: *Migrant Souls*?

A.I.: Well, *Migrant Souls* took about two and a half years, but I was lucky with that one. It's getting published right away out of New York, which is a first.

H.T.: What was the design behind *Migrant Souls*?

A.I.: Well, I had established the Ángel family as a group of characters in *The Rain God*, and so I stuck with this in the two-part *Migrant Souls*. Both novels are really like one big novel they're so interrelated and their stories of the Ángel family set in a border town are so interwoven. However, the two central characters that appear hadn't been mentioned at all in *The Rain God*; the one that I had mentioned in *The Rain God* came off as a religious fanatic—and this wasn't very fair to the character so I bring her back as a more complex character in *Migrant Souls*. It's filled with a lot of surprises and characters you never dreamed would show up. It's in two parts.

H.T.: Would you say that the spiritual/religious dimension plays an important role in those two works?

A.I.: Yeah, because the Ángel family is Catholic and the minute you bring the Church as a force into the lives of the characters it's bound to determine character. I mean I have my own quarrels with the Church and what I see the Church to be doing in real life, but in my fiction I can really use it. I can use all of these dimensions and watch how people have fun with the way people are given their religious leanings away or toward the Church and that's a lot of fun.

H.T.: Can you talk about those quarrels?

A.I.: Oh, I do. I portray them. I constantly have characters who are arguing with each other about religion—mainly the Catholic Church. I grew up with those discussions. All of it is very rich, rich material for fiction. In this new book, one of the strong supporting characters is the priest, Gabriel, who ends the novel with a long meditation. There are many key scenes in *Migrant Souls* where the Church figures as a point of departure for the characters to come into some form of self-realization.

H.T.: Are there any writers that have influenced you especially?

A.I.: Everybody I've ever read has influenced me. Everybody. Even the bad writers because they teach me what not to do. I mean I have my favorites, and they're my favorites for various reasons, but I couldn't tell you from this person I learned this and from that person I learned that. It's sort of a mixture of things. They opened doors for me. That's what good writers and good writing can do, is open doors to your imagination so then your imagination is larger.

I love the nineteenth-century Russian writers like Dostoyevsky and Tolstoy, Turgenev, and Chekhov. Great writers. In the twentieth century, some of my favorite writers are the French like Collette and Proust. Also in the twentieth century, the Latin Americans like García Márquez, Juan Rulfo, Vargas Llosa, and Borges—though often his writing is too abstract and too intellectualized. I enjoy reading these writers and I learn from them.

H.T.: What kinds of doors has García Márquez opened for you?

A.I.: García Márquez's way of dealing with everyday reality and turning it into the magic of miracle every time. It's terrific. And he does it better than anybody. I also like the way that he incorporates historical, or social or political movements into his fictions without giving up the beauty of the writing. Like other Latin Americanist writers, they do so without becoming ideologues. They don't start writing propaganda.

H.T.: How would you like your readers to interpret your work?

A.I.: I'd like to think that my characters are so alive and interesting that the reader, after finishing the book, will be thinking about them, and wondering about them as if they were real people. And if I can bring them to life, or if they can be brought to life like that on the page, then I've succeeded as a writer. I also draw and discuss controversial things in my books, and I'd like people to look at these things with compassion rather than having to take sides. It's more complex than that. It's much more complex than life is and that's what I would like. I'd also like my readers to enjoy reading my work. To laugh and to cry and to think,

"Oh, that character is acting so stupid and why doesn't she do this? Or why doesn't he do that?" And yet still feel sympathy because they would understand from their own experience in life that that's the way it is sometimes.

H.T.: Are you working on other projects?

A.I.: I have one more book about the Ángel family that I want to write, with several scenes floating in my head. And, there's "La Mollie and the King of Tears" that I told you about that has nothing to do with the Ángel family. It's a first-person narrator. His name is Louie Mendoza and he's a musician from the barrio in El Paso who lives in San Francisco. It takes place in the early 1970s. His buddies in the gang that he belongs to call him Chakespeare Louie because he knows Shakespeare; it's really the story of a guy who's had quite a tragic life.

H.T.: Is Louie drawn from someone you knew?

A.I.: Well, various people, you know. All my characters are composites of people and fictional characters I've encountered. I never draw from one single person to characterize.

H.T.: So you write mainly in the genre of the novel. Do you write in other genres like poetry?

A.I.: Well, I have written some poetry. And I've had some of it published. But poetry's always a surprise for me because I never think of myself as a poet. To me, poetry is the hardest of all of the genres. It requires the most self-discipline so you don't get self-indulgent and wacky—though several poets do. I don't think of myself as a poet, but I have written poems, and they have been published, and that's nice. I like that, but whether there's enough for a book, I don't know. I have a book of poems in a drawer somewhere that I've never published. I don't know if I'd be embarrassed reading them.

H.T.: In teaching Chicano/a literature, there's the question of gender.

A.I.: Well, we were talking about gender in an interdisciplinary seminar that Tomás Ybarra and I offer this quarter on Chicano culture. In this class—that includes a number of feminists, lesbian, and gay students—a man gave a presentation on John Rechy's *City of Night*, *The Rain God*, and on the Mexican novelist Luis Zapata's *Adonis García*. It was very interesting how that opened up the whole question of gender. If you look at the Chicano literature that's available right now, you see the different roles gender plays in the characters' lives. In *Migrant Souls*, I include a woman character who some people read as a lesbian. She may or may not be, but that's not important to me in her characterization or the way that people read her, and I like leaving it a mystery because within the culture, that's how it's done, that's how it's looked at. At least the culture that I'm writing about. In *Migrant Souls*, I include characters that are "out" as divorced women and as gay men; each explores and questions the otherwise restrictive roles available to them within the Chicano/a community. I call all of the myths that operate in Chicano/a culture about masculinity and femininity into question in my work. At least that is my hope: that my work open up the reader's eyes and compassion to other gender relational possibilities.

CHRONOLOGY OF MAJOR EVENTS

1938 On May 25, Arturo Islas La Farga is born in El Paso, Texas; he spends his early childhood in the Five Points barrio of El Paso.

1946 In late September, Islas contracts polio, paralyzing his left leg and stunting its growth.

1951-56 Islas attends El Paso High School—the school where his parents and *tías* and *tíos* went—and graduates as valedictorian. With a limp from polio, Islas takes to the books with the idea of studying to become a neurosurgeon.

1956 Islas enters Stanford as an undergraduate with an Alfred P. Sloan scholarship.

1957 In the fall, Islas's craft as a short story writer wins him acceptance into a graduate creative writing class with Hortense Calisher.

1958 Islas writes the essay "An Existential Documentation," which explores Chicano identity as a subject formed in between U.S./Mexican cultural and national boundaries. The same year John Rechy publishes in *Evergreen Review* a similar bicultural experience in the piece "El Paso del Norte."

1959 José Antonio Villarreal breaks new ground, publishing *Pocho* with New York's Doubleday. Islas later critiques *Pocho* for being an overly sentimental, essentializing portrait of Chicano subjectivity.

1960 Islas graduates with a B.A. in English (minor in religious studies) in June, then enters the Stanford English Department as a Ph.D. candidate in the fall. Times are shifting: John F. Kennedy takes the high office and is young and Catholic. Islas is the first Chicano in the country to enter into Stanford's English department for a Ph.D.

1960 One of the first courses Islas takes—and one of the most influential when it comes to his development of a belletristic scholarly approach to Chicano/a literature—is "Chief American Poets" with Yvor Winters.

1962 In the spring quarter, Islas takes an influential course, the "Development of the Short Story" with Wallace Stegner.

1964 Disenchanted with academics, Islas drops out before writing his dissertation. He is unhappy with the campus's "provinciality and homogeneity."

1964 One of Islas's many jobs is that of a "public speaking" teacher at the V.A. hospital in Menlo Park—the same hospital that employed Ken Kesey, who refashioned his experience into the novel *One Flew over the Cuckoo's Nest* (1973). He meets Mr. Martínez, who becomes the inspiration for Louie Mendoza in *La Mollie and the King of Tears*.

1964 Islas moves to San Francisco and shares an apartment with three others. He begins to explore with more freedom his gay sexuality.

1967 Richard Rodriguez graduates with a B.A. in English from Stanford; Islas is his graduate student instructor. Islas comes to resent his ex-student Rodriguez for selling out—and not coming out—in his 1982 publication *Hunger of Memory*.

1967 The night of February 19, Islas's Uncle Carlos is murdered for making a pass at an 18-year-old Anglo soldier he picked up at bar on the south side of El Paso. His beloved uncle's murder leads to Islas's feelings of extreme bitterness and anger toward the world; he is forced to question his own sexual identity vis-à-vis the homophobic world he inhabits.

1967 Berkeley-based *El Grito* evolves into the Chicano/a-focused publishing house Tonatiuh Quinto Sol. Quinto Sol goes on to publish in 1969 the first Chicano anthology of writing, titled *El Espejo* (*The mirror*). By 1971, Quinto Sol has published over sixty writers.

1968 On January 25, one of Islas's most influential mentors during his student days at Stanford, the poet and critic Yvor Winters, dies at 67 from cancer.

1968 School walkouts in East L.A. by Chicanos over educational and political issues; 15,000 walk out and stage "blowouts" in high schools, demanding transfers of racist teachers, revised curricula to show Chicano contributions to "our country," no punishment for speaking Spanish, unlocked toilets, unfenced campuses. Walkouts lead to curriculum reform. By the end of the 1960s, Claude Brown's *Manchild in the Promised Land*, Eldridge Cleaver's *Soul on Ice*, Graham Greene's *The Quiet American*, and the *Autobiography of Malcolm X* are required reading for freshmen entering Stanford.

1969 Stanford professor Ian Watt gets in touch with Arturo Islas and insists that he finish his Ph.D. Before other English departments in the country, Ian Watt recognizes that future shifts in college demographics will require more Chicano faculty. Islas returns to finish dissertation, "The Work of Hortense Calisher: On Middle Ground" and teach freshman English.

1969 June: Islas almost dies. Undergoes three surgical procedures—an ileostomy—at Stanford Medical. Islas must learn to live with a colostomy bag.

1971 With some difficulty as a result of the surgery, Islas manages to complete his dissertation on Hortense Calisher and is rehired by Stanford as a tenure-track professor. Islas becomes the first Chicano Ph.D. to be hired to a tenure-track job in Stanford's English department.

1971 Islas, Renato Rosaldo, Jerry Porras, and Jim Leckie establish the groundbreaking Chicano Fellows Program that recognizes Chicano/a faculty and curriculum needs of incoming Chicano/a students.

1971 Islas teaches one of the first Chicano literature courses ("Chicano Themes") offered by an English department at a private university. Twenty-four Chicano students enroll.

1971 Tomás Rivera publishes . . . *y no se lo tragó la tierra* with Berkeley's Chicano press, *Quinto Sol*.

1972 Islas becomes involved with Jay Spears, who becomes an inspiring force behind his fiction writing and appears as the character Virgil in *La Mollie and the King of Tears* and Sam Godwin in *Migrant Souls*.

1973 Islas begins living with Jay Spears and explores the S&M and San Francisco bathhouse scene.

1976 In March, Islas is promoted to associate professor based on a draft of his novel, "Día de los muertos/Day of the Dead" (an early version of *The Rain God*). The decision is unanimous and the first time a professor in the English department is promoted to tenure without an academic book.

1977 In the autumn, Islas begins his medical year off. During this period, Islas reworks "Día de los muertos," works on "American Dreams and Fantasies," and writes a collection of poems.

1980 In the spring, Islas team teaches the course "Chicano Culture" with the Chicano faculty at Stanford: Professor Al Camarillo, Professor Renato Rosaldo, and Tomás Ybarra-Frausto.

1982 Islas begins to write book reviews for the *San Francisco Chronicle*: Carlos Fuentes, Mario Vargas Llosa, Richard Rodriguez, Danny Santiago, Ricardo Romo.

1984-85 The culture wars heat up across the country: Western canons are being revamped; ethnic-themed houses sprout up on campuses across the nation. At Stanford, while the Anglo conservatives attack the ethnic theme houses on campus for encouraging segregation, Islas helps to engineer the radical reformation of Stanford's Western Culture Program, forcing the curriculum committee to include works by women and minority writers.

1984 The same year Chicano novelist and academic Tomás Rivera dies, Islas's novel *The Rain God* is published by the Palo-Alto based Alexandrian Press on October 28.

1985 While Islas takes a leave of absence from teaching in the fall, *L.A. Times Book Review* nominates *The Rain God* for a prize and Islas receives the department's unanimous vote of promotion to full professor.

1986 On January 25, *The Rain God* wins the Southwest Book Award for its literary excellence and enrichment of the cultural heritage of the Southwest. Islas is awarded along with Tony Hillerman for his detective stories.

1986 While a visiting professor at the University of El Paso, Texas, Islas teaches "Creative Writing for Bilingual Students" in the fall and writes a draft of his novel, *La Mollie and the King of Tears*.

1986 In December, Stanford University gives its seal of approval to Islas's promotion to full professor. He also publishes a short story, "The Blind" (the seed of what would become *Migrant Souls*) in the San Francisco-based literary journal *Zyzzyva*. However, Islas's recent successes do not help cushion the devastating blow Islas feels when his ex-partner, Jay Spears, dies of AIDS-related pneumonia on December 6.

1987 On the weekend of May 28-30, Stanford puts on the groundbreaking Chicano Literary Criticism in a Social Context national conference. Islas reads his poem "Between the Sheets [Chits] for Lorna Dee Cervantes with a nod toward T.S. Eliot."

1988 On January 14, Islas receives news from his doctor that he has tested positive for HIV antigens. His greatest fear becomes a reality and he worries that he will not be able to finish *Migrant Souls* before his body gives out.

1988 After receiving rejection upon rejection of his manuscript "La Mollie and the King of Tears," Islas finally has a section of the novel published as the short story "Chakespeare Louie" in *Zyzzyva*.

1990 Islas worries about getting a New York publisher to issue a contract for *The Rain God*. The anxiety dissipates as soon as Avon sends him a contract and a $7,500 advance.

1991 On February 15, Arturo Islas dies of AIDS-related pneumonia in bed at home in Palo Alto. Just before his death, University of Texas, El Paso elects him to their Writers Hall of Fame.

WORKS CITED

Aldama, Frederick Luis. *Arturo Islas: The Uncollected Works*. Houston: Arte Público P, 2003.

———. *Dancing with Ghosts: A Critical Biography of Arturo Islas*. Berkeley: U of California P, 2004.

———. "Ethnoqueer Re-Architexturing of Metropolitan Space." *Nepantla* 1.3 (2000): 581–604.

Althusser, Louis. *Lenin and Philosophy, and Other Essays*. Trans. Ben Brewster. London: New Left Books, 1971.

Anaya, Rudolfo A. *Bless Me, Ultima*. New York: Warner Books, 1972.

Anzaldúa, Gloria. "Matriz sin tumba o 'el baño de la basura ajena.'" *Borderlands/La Frontera: The New Mestiza*. San Francisco: Spinster/Aunt Lute, 1987.

Arias, Ron. *The Road to Tamazunchale*. Tempe: Bilingual P, 1987.

Armstrong, Tim. *Modernism, Technology, and the Body: A Cultural Study*. Cambridge: Cambridge UP, 1998.

Babuscio, Jack. "Camp and the Gay Sensibility." *Camp Grounds: Style and Homosexuality*. Ed. David Bergman. Amherst: U of Massachusetts P, 1993. 19–38.

Bakhtin, M. M. *The Dialogic Imagination: Four Essays*. Ed. Michael Holquist. Trans. Caryl Emerson and Michael Holquist. Austin: U of Texas P, 1981.

Baldwin, Neil. *Legends of the Plumed Serpent: Biography of a Mexican God*. New York: Public Affairs, 1998.

Barth, Fredrik. *Ethnic Groups and Boundaries: The Social Organization of Cultural Difference*. Boston: Little, Brown, 1969.

Barthes, Roland. *The Pleasure of the Text*. Trans. Richard Miller. New York: Hill and Wang, 1975.

Benjamin, Walter. "The Storyteller." *Illuminations*. Ed. Hannah Arendt. Trans. Harry Zohn. New York: Harcourt, Brace & World, 1968.

Bercovitch, Sacvan. "The Rites of Assent: Rhetoric, Ritual, and the Ideology of American Consensus." *The American Self: Myth, Ideology, and Popular Culture*. Ed. Sam B. Girgus. Albuquerque: U of New Mexico P, 1981. 5–42.

Bhabha, Homi K. "The Third Space." *Identity: Community, Culture, Difference*. Ed. Jonathan Rutherford. London: Lawrence & Wishart, 1990. 207–21.

Birken, Lawrence. *Consuming Desire: Sexual Science and the Emergence of a Culture of Abundance, 1871–1914*. Ithaca: Cornell UP, 1988.

Blanchot, Maurice. "The Indestructible." *The Infinite Conversation*. Trans. Susan Hanson. Minneapolis: U of Minnesota P, 1993. 123–35.

Boelhower, William. *Through a Glass Darkly: Ethnic Semiosis in American Literature*. New York: Oxford UP, 1987.

Bordo, Susan. "Reading the Male Body." *Michigan Quarterly Review* 32 (1993): 696–737.

Bourdieu, Pierre. *Distinction: A Social Critique of the Judgement of Taste*. Trans. Richard Nice. Cambridge: Harvard UP, 1984.

Bradford, Richard. "Non Racial, Non Regional . . . Bless Me, Ultima." *Santa Fe Reporter* 29 June 1974.

Bruce-Novoa, Juan. "Canonical and Noncanonical Texts: A Chicano Case Study." *Redefining American Literary History*. Ed. A. LaVonne Brown Ruoff and Jerry W. Ward Jr. New York: MLA, 1990. 196–209.

———. "Homosexuality and the Chicano Novel." *European Perspectives on Hispanic Literature of the United States*. Ed. Geneviève Fabre. Houston: Arte Público P, 1988. 98–106.

Bulmer, M. "Race and Ethnicity." *Key Variables in Sociological Investigation*. Ed. R. G. Burgess. London: Routledge & Kegan Paul, 1986. 54–75.

Burciaga, José Antonio. "A Conversation with Arturo Islas." *Stanford Humanities Review* (1992): 158–66.

———. *Drink Cultura: Chicanismo*. Santa Barbara: Joshua Odell Editions/ Capra Press, 1993. 117.

———. *Undocumented Love/Amor indocumentado: A Personal Anthology of Poetry*. San Jose, CA: Chusma House Publications, 1992.

Burgess, Clarissa. "Tlaloc-Rain God." Ramírez home page. 30 Oct. 2001; site now discontinued <http://www.cwrl.utexas.edu/~ramirez/clarissa/tlaloc.html>.

Cabeza de Vaca, Alvar Núñez. *The Account: Alvar Núñez Cabeza de Vaca's Relación*. Trans. Martin A. Favata and José B. Fernández. Houston: Arte Público P, 1993.

Calderón, Héctor, and José David Saldívar. *Criticism in the Borderlands: Studies in Chicano Literature, Culture, and Ideology*. Durham: Duke UP, 1991.

Calleros, Cleofás. *El Paso, Then and Now*. El Paso: American Printing Co., 1954.

Callinicos, Alex. *Marxism and Philosophy.* Oxford: Oxford UP, 1985.

Cantú, Roberto. "Arturo Islas." *Dictionary of Literary Biography.* Vol. 122. *Chicano Writers, Second Series.* Ed. Francisco A. Lomelí and Carl R. Shirley. Detroit: Gale Research, 1992. 146–54.

Carby, Hazel V. "The Multicultural Wars." *Radical History Review* 54 (1992): 7–18.

Carrillo, Leonardo, et al., eds. *Canto al Pueblo: An Anthology of Experiences.* San Antonio: Penca Books, 1978.

Cash, W. J. *The Mind of the South.* New York: Alfred A. Knopf, 1941.

Castillo, Ana. *Massacre of the Dreamers.* New York: Plume, 1996.

Chávez, Armando B. *Historia de Ciudad Juárez, Chihuahua.* Mexico City: Editorial Pax, 1991.

Christian, Barbara. "A Rough Terrain: The Case of Shaping an Anthology of Caribbean Women Writers." *The Ethnic Canon: Histories, Institutions, and Interventions.* Ed. David Palumbo-Liu. Minneapolis: U of Minnesota P, 1995. 241–59.

Clifford, James, and George Marcus, eds. *Writing Culture: The Poetics and Politics of Ethnography.* Berkeley: U of California P, 1986.

Comito, Terry. *In Defense of Winters: The Poetry and Prose of Yvor Winters.* Madison: U of Wisconsin P, 1986.

Contreras, Juan A. *Blessed with Bilingual Brains.* El Paso: Solitos, 1998.

Cornfield, Robert. Letter to Arturo Islas. 31 Dec. 1978. Arturo Islas Papers. Box 5, folder 1. Stanford U Special Collections, Green Library, Palo Alto.

Cosgrove, Denis E. *Social Formation and Symbolic Landscape.* London: Croom Helm, 1984.

Crafts, Hannah. *The Bondwoman's Narrative.* Ed. Henry Louis Gates Jr. New York: Warner Books, 2002.

Dasenbrock, Reed Way. "Intelligibility and Meaningfulness in Multicultural Literature," *PMLA* 102.1: 10–19.

Rev. of *Days of Obligation*, by Richard Rodriguez. *Kirkus Reviews* 60 (1992): 1115.

Debord, Guy. *The Society of the Spectacle.* Trans. Donald Nicholson-Smith. New York: Zone Books, 1994.

de Jesús Vega, Manuel. "Chicano, Gay, and Doomed: AIDS in Arturo Islas' *The Rain God.*" *Confluencia: Revista Hispánica de Cultura y Literatura* 11.2 (1996): 112–18.

Delgado, Abelardo. *Chicano: 25 Pieces of a Chicano Mind.* El Paso: Barrio, 1972.

Domínguez, Virginia R. "Invoking Culture: The Messy Side of 'Cultural Politics.'" *The South Atlantic Quarterly* 91.1 (1992): 19–42.

Donadio, Stephen. *Nietzsche, Henry James and the Artistic Will*. New York: Oxford UP, 1978.

Doriani, Beth Maclay. "Black Womanhood in Nineteenth-Century America: Subversion and Self-Construction in Two Women's Autobiographies." *American Quarterly* 43.2 (1991): 199–222.

Douglas, Mary. *Purity and Danger: An Analysis of the Concepts of Pollution and Taboo*. London: Routledge & Kegan Paul, 1966.

Douglass, Fredrick. *My Bondage and My Freedom*. 1855. Urbana: U of Illinois P, 1987.

———. *Narrative of the Life of Frederick Douglass, an American Slave, Written by Himself*. New York: Signet, 1997.

Doyle, Laura. *Bordering on the Body: The Racial Matrix of Modern Fiction and Culture*. Oxford: Oxford UP, 1994.

DuBois, W. E. B. *The Souls of Black Folk*. New York: Vintage Books/ Library of America, 1990.

Edwards, Richard. *Contested Terrain: The Transformation of the Workplace in the Twentieth Century*. New York: Basic Books, 1979.

Fanon, Frantz. *Black Skin, White Masks*. Trans. Charles Lam Markmann. New York: Grove Press, 1967.

Fischer, Michael M. J. "Ethnicity and the Post-Modern Arts of Memory." *Writing Culture: The Poetics and Politics of Ethnography*. Ed. James Clifford and George E. Marcus. Berkeley: U of California P, 1986. 194–233.

Fischer, Michael M. J., and George Marcus, eds. *Anthropology as Cultural Critique: An Experimental Moment in the Human Sciences*. Chicago: U of Chicago P, 1986.

Fong, Katheryn M. "To Maxine Hong Kingston: A Letter." *Bulletin for Concerned Asian Scholars* 9.4 (1977): 67–69.

Foreman, P. Gabrielle. "The Spoken and the Silenced in *Incidents in the Life of a Slave Girl* and *Our Nig*." *Callaloo* 13.2 (1990): 313–24.

Foucault, Michel. *The History of Sexuality, Volume 1: An Introduction*. Trans. Robert Hurley. New York: Vintage, 1980.

Fowler, Carol. "Death and Family Dominate Novel. Rev. of *The Rain God*." *Contra Costa Times* 26 Jan. 1985.

Frederiksen, Thomas H. "Tlaloc: 'He who makes things grow.'" *Phenomenon: The Civilization Page*. 10 Oct. 2001 <http://www.stateoftheart.nl/phenomenon/frames/subjects/mythology/aztec/gods/tlaloc.htm>.

———. "The Rain of the Earth." AOL Members Information Database. 30 Oct. 2001 <http://members.aol.com/xiuhcoatl/tlaloc.htm>.

Fusco, Coco. "Performing Bodies, Performing Culture: Interview with Rosemary Weatherston." *Body Politics and the Fictional Double*. Ed. Debra Walker King. Bloomington: Indiana UP, 2000. 105–30.

García, Mario T. *Desert Immigrants: The Mexicans of El Paso, 1980–1920*. New Haven: Yale UP, 1981.

———. "La Frontera: The Border As Symbol and Reality in Mexican American Thought." *Between Two Worlds: Mexican Immigrants in the United States*. Ed. David G. Gutiérrez. Wilmington: Scholarly Resources, 1996. 89–117.

Gardner, Eric. "'This Attempt of Their Sister': Harriet Wilson's *Our Nig* from Printers to Readers." *New England Quarterly* 66.2 (1993): 226–46.

Gaspar de Alba, Alicia. "El domingo es día de tallar." *Palabra Nueva, Poesía Chicana*. Ed. Ricardo Aguilar, Armando Armengol, and Sergio D. Elizondo. El Paso: Dos Pasos Editores, 1985. 53–54.

Gates, Henry Louis, Jr. "'Ethnic and Minority' Studies." *Introduction to Scholarship in Modern Languages and Literatures*. Ed. Joseph Gibaldi. New York: MLA, 1992. 288–302.

———. *Figures in Black: Words, Signs, and the "Racial" Self*. Oxford: Oxford UP, 1987.

———. "Good-Bye, Columbus? Notes on the Culture of Criticism." *Anatomy of Racism*. Ed. David Goldberg. Minneapolis: U of Minnesota P, 1990. 203–17.

———. Introduction. *The Bondwoman's Narrative*. By Hannah Crafts. New York: Warner Books, 2002. ix–lxxiv.

———. Introduction. *Our Nig*. By Harriet E. Wilson. New York: Vintage Books, 1983. xi–lv.

———. "Introduction: Writing 'Race' and the Difference It Makes." *"Race," Writing, and Difference*. Ed. Henry Louis Gates Jr. Chicago: U of Chicago P, 1986.

Gilman, Sander L. "Ethnicity-Ethnicities-Literature-Literatures." *PMLA* 113.1 (1999): 19–27.

Gilroy, Paul. "One Nation Under a Groove: The Cultural Politics of 'Race' and Racism in Britain." *Anatomy of Racism*. Ed. David Goldberg. Minneapolis: U of Minnesota P, 1990. 263–82.

Girard, René. *Violence and the Sacred*. Trans. Patrick Gregory. Baltimore: Johns Hopkins UP, 1977.

Gladstein, Mimi. Rev. of *Migrant Souls*, by Arturo Islas. *El Paso Times* 11 March 1990: 2D.

Goldberg, David Theo, ed. *Multiculturalism: A Critical Reader*. Oxford: Blackwell P, 1994.

Gonzales-Berry, Erlinda. "Sensuality, Repression, and Death in Arturo Islas's *The Rain God*." *Bilingual Review* 12.3 (1985): 258–61.

González, Rafael Jesús. *El Espejo/The Mirror: Selected Chicano Literature*. Berkeley: Quinto Sol, 1972.

Gordon, Avery F., and Christopher Newfield. Introduction. *Mapping Multiculturalism*. Ed. Avery F. Gordon and Christopher Newfield. Minneapolis: U of Minnesota P, 1996. 1–18.

Gregory, Derek. *Postmodern Imaginations*. Oxford: Blackwell, 1994.

Griffin, Henry William. Letter to Robert Cornfield. 5 April 1976. Arturo Islas Papers. Folder 1, "Correspondence, 1974–1975." Stanford U Special Collections, Green Library, Palo Alto.

Grossberg, Lawrence. *Bringing It All Back Home: Essays on Cultural Studies*. Durham: Duke UP, 1997.

———. "The Context of Audiences and the Politics of Difference." *Bringing It All Back Home: Essays on Cultural Studies*. Durham: Duke UP, 1997. 320–42.

Guillory, John. "Canonical and Non-canonical: A Critique of the Current Debate." *ELH* 54.3 (1987): 483–527.

Gutiérrez, Ramón A. "Ethnic Studies: Its Evolution in American Colleges and Universities." *Multiculturalism: A Critical Reader*. Ed. D. T. Goldberg. Cambridge, MA: Blackwell, 1994. 157–67.

———. "Hispanic Diaspora and Chicano Identity." *The South Atlantic Quarterly* 98.1-2 (1999): 203–15.

Hadas, Elizabeth C. Letter from Elizabeth C. Hadas. 30 October 1990. Arturo Islas Papers. Box 8, folder 1. Stanford U Special Collections, Green Library, Palo Alto.

Hall, Stuart. "Culture, the Media and the 'Ideological Effect.'" *Mass Communication and Society*. Ed. J. Curran, et al. London: Arnold, 1977. 315–48.

———. "New Ethnicities." *Critical Dialogues in Cultural Studies*. Ed. David Morley and Kuan-Hsing Chen. London: Routledge, 1996. 441–49.

Haraway, Donna. "A Manifesto for Cyborgs: Science, Technology and Socialist Feminism in the 1980s." *Feminism/Postmodernism*. Ed. Linda J. Nicholson. New York: Routledge, 1990. 191–233.

Harvey, David. *The Condition of Postmodernity*. Oxford: Blackwell, 1989.

Hebdige, Dick. *Hiding in the Light: On Images and Things*. New York: Routledge, 1988.

———. *Subculture: The Meaning of Style*. London: Methuen, 1979.

Hinz, Evelyn J. "What Is Multiculturalism? A 'Cognitive' Introduction." *Mosaic* 29.3 (1996): vii–xii.

Hochbruck, Wolfgang. "Cultural Authenticity and the Construction of Pan-American Metanarrative." *Cultural Difference and the Literary Text: Pluralism and the Limits of Authenticity in North American Literatures*. Ed. Winfried Siemerling and Katrin Schwenk. Iowa City: U of Iowa P, 1996. 18–28.

Hoffman, Daniel. "Poetry: After Modernism." *Harvard Guide to Contemporary American Writing*. Cambridge: Harvard UP, 1979. 439–95.

Hollinger, David A. *Postethnic America: Beyond Multiculturalism*. New York: Basic Books, 1995.

Islas, Arturo. "American Dreams and Fantasies." Unpublished ms. Arturo Islas Papers. Box 9, folder 1. Stanford U Special Collections, Green Library, Palo Alto.

———. "Día de los Muertos." Arturo Islas Papers. Box 5, folder 4. Stanford U Special Collections, Green Library, Palo Alto.

———. "Felix." Arturo Islas Papers. Box 12, folders 1–8. Stanford U Special Collections, Green Library, Palo Alto.

———. Journal. Arturo Islas Papers. Box 55, folder 1. Stanford U Special Collections, Green Library, Palo Alto.

———. Lecture on Rudolfo Anaya. 21 October 1974. Arturo Islas Papers. Box 32, folder 3. Stanford U Special Collections, Green Library, Palo Alto.

———. Letter to Robert Cornfield. 8 January 1979. Arturo Islas Papers. Box 5, folder 1. Stanford U Special Collections, Green Library, Palo Alto.

———. Letter to Ron Arias. Arturo Islas Papers. Box 22, folder 5. Stanford U Special Collections, Green Library, Palo Alto.

———. *Migrant Souls*. New York: William Morrow, 1990.

———. *La Mollie and the King of Tears*. Albuquerque: U of New Mexico P, 1996.

———. "La Mollie and the King of Tears." Ms. Arturo Islas Papers. M618, box 8, folder 1. Stanford U Special Collections, Green Library, Palo Alto.

———. "On the Bridge, at the Border: Migrants and Immigrants." Ernesto Galarza Commemorative Lecture Series. Palo Alto. Stanford U. 1990.

———. *The Rain God: A Desert Tale*. New York: Avon, 1991.

———. "The Rain God." Ms. Arturo Islas Papers. Box 2, folder 1. Stanford U Special Collections, Green Library, Palo Alto.

Jackson, John B. *Discovering the Vernacular Landscape*. New Haven: Yale UP, 1984.

Jacobs, Harriet. *Incidents in the Life of a Slave Girl*. Ed. Jean Fagan Yellin. Cambridge: Harvard UP, 1987.

James, Henry. "The Beast in the Jungle." *The Heath Anthology of American Literature*. Vol. 2. Ed. Paul Lanter et al. Lexington, MA: D.C. Heath, 1994. 597–625.

Jameson, Frederic. Foreword. *The Postmodern Condition: A Report on Knowledge*. Jean-François Lyotard. Minneapolis: U of Minnesota P, 1984. vii–xxi.

———. *The Political Unconscious: Narrative as a Socially Symbolic Act*. Ithaca: Cornell UP, 1981.

———. "Postmodernism and Consumer Society." *The Anti-Aesthetic: Essays on Postmodern Culture*. Ed. Hal Foster. Port Townsend: Bay P, 1983. 111–25.

JanMohamed, Abdul R., and David Lloyd. Introduction. *The Nature and Context of Minority Discourse*. Ed. Abdul R. JanMohamed and David Lloyd. New York: Oxford UP, 1990.

Kaup, Monika. "The Architecture of Ethnicity in Chicano Literature." *American Literature* 69 (1997): 13–18, 361–97.

Klein, Marcus. *Foreigners: The Making of American Literature, 1900–1949*. Chicago: U of Chicago P, 1981.

Krupat, Arnold. *The Voice in the Margin: Native American Literature and the Canon*. Berkeley: U of California P, 1989.

Leal, Luis, and Pepe Barrón. "Chicano Literature: An Overview." *Three American Literatures: Essays in Chicano, Native American, and Asian-American Literature for Teachers of American Literature*. Ed. Houston A. Baker Jr. New York: MLA, 1982. 9–32.

LeFebvre, Henri. *The Production of Space*. Oxford: Blackwell, 1991.

———. *Writings on Cities*. Oxford: Blackwell, 1996.

Lenin, Vladimir I. *La literatura y el arte*. Moscow: Editorial Progreso, 1968.

Lentricchia, Frank. "Writing after Hours." *Ariel and the Police: Michel Foucault, William James, Wallace Stevens*. Madison: U of Wisconsin P, 1988. 135–244.

León-Portilla, Miguel. *Aztec Thought and Culture: A Study of the Ancient Nahuatl Mind*. Trans. Jack Emory Davis. Norman: U of Oklahoma P, 1963.

Limón, José. *American Encounters: Greater Mexico, the United States, and the Erotics of Culture*. Boston: Beacon Press, 1998.

Lincoln, Abraham. "The Gettysburg Address." Gettysburg, 19 Nov. 1863. Library of Congress Exhibits <http://www.loc.gov/exhibits/gadd/gadrft.html>.

Lionnet, Françoise. *Autobiographical Voices: Race, Gender, Self Portraiture.* Ithaca: Cornell UP, 1986.

Lotman, Jurii M., and Boris A. Uspenskii. "Binary Models in the Dynamics of Russian Culture." *Semiotics of Russian Cultural History.* Ed. Alexander D. Nakhimosvsky and Alice Stone Nakhimosvsky. Ithaca: Cornell UP, 1985. 30–66.

Lott, Tommy L. "Black Vernacular Representation and Cultural Malpractice." *Anatomy of Racism.* Ed. David Goldberg. Minneapolis: U of Minnesota P, 1990. 230–58.

Lugones, María. "Purity, Impurity and Separation." *Signs* 19.2 (1994): 458–79.

MacAdam, Alfred J. "Carlos Fuentes: The Burden of History." *World Literature Today* 57 (1983): 558–63.

Márquez, Antonio C. "The Historical Imagination in Arturo Islas's *The Rain God* and *Migrant Souls*." *MELUS* 19.2 (1994): 3–16.

Martínez, Oscar J. *Border Boom Town: Ciudad Juárez Since 1848.* Austin: U of Texas P, 1978.

———. *The Chicanos of El Paso: An Assessment of Progress.* El Paso: Texas Western, 1980.

———. *Troublesome Border.* Tucson: U of Arizona P, 1988.

Marx, Karl. *Capital.* Vol. 1. New York: International Publishers, 1967.

———. *Grundrisse. Foundations of the Critique of Political Economy.* Trans. Martin Nicolaus. New York: Random House, 1973.

McLaren, Peter. "White Terror and Oppositional Agency: Towards a Critical Multiculturalism." *Anatomy of Racism.* Ed. David Goldberg. Minneapolis: U of Minnesota P, 1990. 45–74.

McCullough, Frances. Letter from Frances McCullough. 30 December 1975. Arturo Islas Papers, folder 1, "Correspondence, 1974–1975." Stanford U Special Collections, Green Library, Palo Alto.

Meinig, E. W., ed. *The Interpretation of Ordinary Landscapes.* New York: Oxford UP, 1979.

Miller, Mary, and Karl Taube. *The Gods and Symbols of Ancient Mexico and the Maya: An Illustrated Dictionary of Mesoamerican Religion.* London: Thames and Hudson, 1993.

Mirandé, Alfredo, and Evangelina Enríquez, eds. *La Chicana: The Mexican-American Woman.* Chicago: U of Chicago P, 1979.

Mitchell, W. J. T. "Beyond Comparison: Picture, Text, and Method." *Picture Theory: Essays on Verbal and Visual Representation.* Chicago: U of Chicago P, 1994. 83–110.

———. "Representation." *Ariel and the Police: Michel Foucault, William James, Wallace Stevens.* Ed. Frank Lentricchia. Madison: U of Wisconsin P, 1988. 11–22.

Morris, Meaghan. *The Pirate's Fiancée: Feminism Reading Postmodernism.* London: Verso P, 1988.

Mungo, Raymond. "Strange Murder in the Desert." Rev. of *The Rain God*, by Arturo Islas. *San Francisco Chronicle* 4 Nov. 1984: 5.

Neate, Wilson. "Repression and the Abject Body: Writing the Family History in Arturo Islas's *The Rain God.*" *Revista Canario de Estudios Ingleses* 35 (1997): 311–32.

Newfield, Christopher, and Avery F. Gordon. "Multiculturalism's Unfinished Business." *Mapping Multiculturalism.* Ed. Avery F. Gordon and Christopher Newfield. Minneapolis: U of Minnesota P, 1996. 76–115.

Newman, Charles. *The Post-Modern Aura: The Act of Fiction in an Age of Inflation.* Evanston: Northwestern UP, 1985.

Nietzsche, Friedrich. *The Genealogy of Morals.* Trans. Walter Kaufmann and R. J. Hollingdale. New York: Vintage, 1969.

Ohmann, Richard. "The Shaping of a Canon: U.S. Fiction, 1860–1975." *Critical Inquiry* 10.1 (1983): 199–223.

Ortiz, Ricardo L. "Sexuality Degree Zero: Pleasure and Power in the Novels of John Rechy, Arturo Islas, and Michael Nava." *Journal of Homosexuality* 26.2–3 (1993): 111–26.

Palumbo-Liu, David. Introduction. *The Ethnic Canon: Histories, Institutions, and Interventions.* Minneapolis: U of Minnesota P, 1995. 1–27.

Paredes, Américo. *A Texas-Mexican Cancionero: Folksongs of the Lower Border.* Austin: U of Texas P, 1976.

Paredes, Raymund A. "The Evolution of Chicano Literature." *Three American Literatures: Essays in Chicano, Native American, and Asian-American Literature for Teachers of American Literature.* Ed. Houston A. Baker Jr. New York: MLA, 1982. 33–79.

———. "The Promise of Chicano Literature." *Minority Language and Literature.* Ed. Dexter Fisher. New York: MLA, 1977. 29–41.

Payne, James Robert, ed. *Multicultural Autobiography: American Lives.* Knoxville: U of Tennessee P, 1992.

Pearce, Richard. "Chicano Myth, Chicana Tactics." Wheaton College, Richard Pearce home page. 18 Dec. 2001 <http://acunix.wheatoncollege.edu/rpearce/MultiC_Web/Culture/Tactics/body_chicana_tactics.htm>.

Pérez de Villagrá, Gaspar. *Historia de la Nueva Mexico 1610.* Ed. Miguel Encinias, Alfred Rodríguez, and Joseph P. Sánchez. Albuquerque: U of New Mexico P, 1992.

Pratt, Mary Louise. "Linguistic Utopias." *The Linguistics of Writing*. New York: Methuen, 1989.

Radway, Janice. "The Book of the Month Club and the General Reader: On the Uses of Serious Fiction." *Critical Inquiry* 14.3 (1988): 516–38.

Rain of the Earth. AOL Members Information Database. 30 Oct. 2001 <http://members.aol.com/xiuhcoatl/tlaloc.htm>.

Rechy, John. *City of Night*. New York: Grove P, 1984.

———. "El Paso del Norte." *Evergreen Review* 2.6 (1958): 127–40.

Reilly, John M. "Criticism of Ethnic Literature: Seeing the Whole Story." *MELUS* 5.1 (1978): 2–13.

Rice, David. "Sinners Among Angels, or Family History and the Ethnic Narrator in Arturo Islas's *The Rain God* and *Migrant Souls*." *LIT: Literature Interpretation Theory* 11.2 (2000): 169–97.

Rivera, Tomás. "... *y no se lo tragó la tierra*/. . . *And the Earth Did Not Part*." Berkeley: Quinto Sol Publications, 1971.

———. "... *y no se lo tragó la tierra*/. . . *And the Earth Did Not Devour Him*." Trans. Evangelina Vigil-Piñón. Houston: Arte Público P, 1987.

Rodríguez, Randy A. "The Promise of Chicano Literature." *Minority Language and Literature*. Ed. Dexter Fisher. New York: MLA, 1977. 29–41.

———. "Richard Rodriguez Reconsidered: Queering the Sissy (Ethnic) Subject." *Texas Studies in Literature and Language* 40 (1998): 396–423.

Rodriguez, Richard. *Days of Obligation: An Argument with My Mexican Father*. New York: Viking, 1992.

———. *Hunger of Memory: The Education of Richard Rodriguez*. New York: Bantam, 1982.

Rosaldo, Renato. *Culture and Truth: The Remaking of Social Analysis*. Boston: Beacon P, 1989.

Ross, Andrew. "Uses of Camp." *Camp Grounds: Style and Homosexuality*. Ed. David Bergman. Amherst: U of Massachusetts P, 1993. 54–77.

Rushdie, Salman. "Censorship." *Imaginary Homelands: Essays and Criticism 1981–1991*. New York: Penguin, 1992.

Sáenz, Benjamín. "Juárez from My Window." *Rio Grande Review* 6.1 (1986).

Said, Edward. *The World, the Text, and the Critic*. Cambridge: Harvard UP, 1983.

Saldívar, José David. *Border Matters: Remapping American Cultural Studies*. Berkeley: U of California P, 1997.

———. *The Dialectics of Our America: Genealogy, Cultural Critique, and Literary History*. Durham: Duke UP, 1991.

———. "The Hybridity of Culture in Arturo Islas's *The Rain God.*" *Disposito: Revista Americana de Estudios Comparados y Culturales* 16.41 (1991): 109–19. Reprinted in *Cohesion and Dissent in America.* Ed. Carol Colatrella and Joseph Alkaua. Albany: SUNY P, 1994. 159–73.

Saldívar, Ramón. *Chicano Narrative: Dialectics of Difference.* Madison: U of Wisconsin P, 1990.

———. "Transnational Migrations and Border Identities: Immigration and Postmodern Culture." *The South Atlantic Quarterly* 98.1-2 (1999): 217–30.

Sánchez, Marta E. "Arturo Islas' *The Rain God*: An Alternative Tradition." *American Literature* 62.2 (1990): 284–304.

Sánchez, Ricardo. *We Are Chicanos: An Anthology of Mexican-American Literature.* Ed. Philip D. Ortego. New York: Washington Square, 1973.

Sánchez, Rosaura. "Ideological Discourses in Arturo Islas' *The Rain God.*" *Criticism in the Borderlands: Studies in Chicano Literature, Culture, and Ideology.* Ed. Héctor Calderón and José David Saldívar. Durham: Duke UP, 1991. 114–26.

Sandoval, Chela. *Methodology of the Oppressed.* Minneapolis: U of Minnesota P, 2000.

San Juan, E., Jr. "Problematizing Multiculturalism and the 'Common Culture'." *MELUS* 19.2 (1994): 59–84.

Santiago, Danny. *Famous All Over Town.* New York: Simon and Schuster, 1983.

Scott, Joan W. "The Campaign Against Political Correctness: What's Really at Stake." *Radical History Review* 54 (1992): 59–79.

———. "Multiculturalism and the Politics of Identity." *October* 61 (1992): 12–19.

———. "The Evidence of Experience." *Critical Inquiry* 17.4 (1991): 773–97.

Sedore, Timothy S. "Violating the Boundaries: An Interview with Richard Rodriguez." *Michigan Quarterly Review* 38.3 (1999): 424–46.

Skenazy, Paul. Afterword. *La Mollie and the King of Tears.* Albuquerque: U of New Mexico P, 1996. 167–98.

———. "Borders and Bridges, Doors and Drugstores: Toward a Geography of Time." *San Francisco in Fiction: Essays in a Regional Literature.* Ed. David Fine and Paul Skenazy. Albuquerque: U of New Mexico P, 1995. 198–216.

Soja, Edward W. *Postmodern Geographies: The Reassertion of Space in Critical Social Theory.* London: Verso, 1989.

———. *Thirdspace: Journeys to Los Angeles and Other Real-and-Imagined Places*. Cambridge: Blackwell, 1996.

Sollors, Werner. *Beyond Ethnicity: Consent and Descent in American Culture*. New York: Oxford UP, 1986.

Sonnichsen, C. L. *The El Paso Salt War*. El Paso: Texas Western, 1961.

———. *Pass of the North: Four Centuries on the Rio Grande*. 2 vols. El Paso: Texas Western, 1968.

Spivak, Gayatri Chakravorty. "Questions of Multi-Culturalism." *The Post-Colonial Critic: Interviews, Strategies, Dialogues*. New York: Routledge, 1990. 59–66.

Stallybrass, Peter, and Allon White. *The Politics and Poetics of Transgression*. Ithaca: Cornell UP, 1986.

Stegner, Wallace. "The New Literary Frontier." *San Francisco Examiner* 5 Aug. 1990: E3.

———. "Willa Cather, *My Antonia*." *The American Novel: From James Fenimore Cooper to William Faulkner*. Ed. Wallace Stegner. New York: Basic Books, 1965.

Stowe, Harriet Beecher. *Uncle Tom's Cabin, or, Life Among the Lowly*. 1852. New York: Penguin, 1981.

Strauss, Roger. Letter from Roger Strauss. 29 January 1975. Arturo Islas Papers. Box 5, folder 3. Stanford U Special Collections, Green Library, Palo Alto.

Tatum, Charles. *Chicano Literature*. Boston: Twayne, 1982. 135.

Taylor, Howard J. "Chicano Writers Can't Crack Prejudice of New York Publishers." *San Francisco Sunday Examiner & Chronicle* 5 Aug. 1984: E2.

Tuan, Yi-Fu. *Space and Place: The Perspectives of Experience*. Minneapolis: U of Minnesota P, 1977.

Turner, Terence. "Anthropology and Multiculturalism: What is Anthropology that Multiculturalists Should Be Mindful of It?" *Anatomy of Racism*. Ed. David Goldberg. Minneapolis: U of Minnesota P, 1990. 406–25.

Turner, Victor. *Dramas, Fields, and Metaphors: Symbolic Action in Human Society*. Ithaca: Cornell UP, 1974.

Verhoeven, V. M. "How Hyphenated Can You Get? A Critique of Pure Ethnicity." *Mosaic* 29.3 (1996): 97–116.

Villa, Raúl. *Barrio Logos: Space and Place in Urban Chicano Literature and Culture*. Austin: U of Texas P, 2000.

Villarreal, José Antonio. *Pocho*. New York: Anchor-Dell, 1989.

Villaseñor, Victor. *Macho!* New York: Bantam Books, 1973.

Vološinov, V. N. *Marxism and the Philosophy of Language.* Trans. L. Matejka and I. R. Titunik. New York: Seminar Press, 1973. Cambridge: Harvard UP, 1986.

Vygotsky, L. S. *Mind in Society: The Development of Higher Psychological Processes.* Cambridge: Cambridge UP, 1978.

Wald, Priscilla. *Constituting Americans: Cultural Anxiety and Narrative Form.* Durham and London: Duke UP, 1995.

Walsh, Eileen. "The Book Report." *Campus Report* [Stanford U] 16 Jan. 1985.

White, Barbara A. "'Our Nig' and the She-Devil: New Information about Harriet Wilson and the 'Bellmont' Family." *American Literature* 65.1 (1993): 19–52.

Williams, Raymond. *Keywords: A Vocabulary of Culture and Society.* New York: Oxford UP, 1983.

Wilson, Harriet E. *Our Nig, or, Sketches from the Life of a Free Black, in a Two-Story White House, North, Showing that Slavery's Shadows Fall Even There.* 1859. New York: Vintage Books, 1983.

Winters, Yvor. "Poetic Styles, Old and New." *Four Poets on Poetry.* Ed. Don Cameron Allen. Baltimore: Johns Hopkins UP, 1958.

Wong, Sau-Ling Cynthia. "Autobiography as Guided Chinatown Tour? Maxine Hong Kingston's Woman Warrior and the Chinese-American Autobiographical Controversy." *Multicultural Autobiography: American Lives.* Ed. James Robert Payne. Knoxville: U of Tennessee P, 1992. 248–79.

Wright, Les. "San Francisco." *Queer Sites: Gay Urban Histories Since 1960.* Ed. David Higgis. London: Routledge, 1999. 164–89.

Ybarra-Frausto, Tomás. "Rasquachismo: A Chicano Sensibility." *Chicano Art: Resistance and Affirmation, 1965–1985.* Ed. Richard Griswold del Castillo, Teresa McKenna, and Yvonne Yarbro-Bejarano. Los Angeles: Wight Art Gallery, 1991. 155–63.

Zukin, Sharon. *Landscapes of Power: From Detroit to Disney World.* Berkeley: U of California P, 1991.

CONTRIBUTORS

Frederick Luis Aldama is an associate professor of English and comparative studies at Ohio State University. He teaches U.S. Latino and British postcolonial literature and film. He is the author of several books, including *Postethnic Narrative Criticism*; *Dancing With Ghosts: A Critical Biography of Arturo Islas*; *Arturo Islas: The Uncollected Works*; and *Mapping Contemporary Chicano/a Letters by Interview*. He has published articles that explore a variety of topics such as music and culture as well as the works of authors such as Charles Dickens, Arundhati Roy, and Richard Rodriguez. He serves on several editorial boards for journals such as the *Journal of Narrative Technique*, *Aztlán*, and *English Language Notes*. He has recently published the book *Brown on Brown: Chicano/a Representations of Gender, Sexuality, and Ethnicity* with the University of Texas Press.

Mimi Gladstein and Arturo Islas were high school friends who continued their close personal relationship professionally. As chair of the English Department at the University of Texas at El Paso (UTEP), Gladstein invited Islas to be a distinguished visiting writer in the department. She and her sister are characters in "Migrant Souls." Currently, Gladstein is the chair of the Department of Theatre, Dance, and Film at UTEP. Previously, she has served as associate dean for the humanities, director of the Western Cultural Heritage Program, director of women's studies, and as the executive director for the university's diamond jubilee celebration. Gladstein has won international awards for her research and teaching on John Steinbeck. She has been a Fulbright professor in Venezuela and Spain. Her publications include five books, numerous articles, and chapters in scholarly anthologies, some of which have been translated into Spanish and Japanese. She is also a member of the Chicano studies faculty at UTEP.

Erlinda Gonzales-Berry is chair of the Department of Ethnic Studies at Oregon State University and professor of Chicana/o and Latina/o studies. She has published extensively on Chicana/o literature and culture and is editor or coeditor of the following: *The Contested Homeland: A Chicano History of New Mexico*; *La Herencia: The Anthology of Hispanic Literature of the United States*; *En otra voz: Antología de la literatura hispana en los Estados Unidos*; and *Pasó por aquí: Critical Essays on the New Mexican Literary Tradition 1452-1988*.

Michael Hardin is a visiting assistant professor at Susquehanna University. He is the author of *Playing the Reader: The Homoerotics of Self-Reflexive Fiction* (Lang, 2000) and has edited a collection of critical essays on Kathy Acker, *Devouring Institutions* (San Diego State University Press, 2004). He has also published critical articles and poetry in many national and international journals.

Vivian Nun Halloran is an assistant professor of comparative literature at Indiana University. Her research interests include Caribbean literature and theory, Chicano/a and Latino/a literature, and the role of the memoir in ethnic American literature.

John Honerkamp is currently finishing his Ph.D. at New York University and has been a visiting scholar at Duke University. His dissertation is entitled "Inside Out: Negotiations of Domesticity and Captivity in African American Women's Literature." His study interests are American literature and culture, with an emphasis on African American literature, minority discourse, modernism, and cultural studies. He recently organized a panel for the 2003 Modern Language Association Convention in December 2003, "Close Encounters: The Captivity Narratives of Octavia E. Butler."

Theresa Meléndez is director of Chicano/Latino studies and associate professor in English at Michigan State University. Her latest coedited book is *Racial Liberalism and the Politics of Urban America*. Her current work is collecting oral histories of Michigan Chicanos, including those repatriated during the Depression. She teaches Chicana/o literature, film, folklore, and medieval literature.

David Rice is an assistant professor of English at the College of Saint Rose. He teaches American and Native American literature and is presently writing on urban Native Americans in the twentieth-century Native American novel.

Renato Rosaldo is a professor of anthropology at New York University. He is the author of *Ilongot Headhunting, 1883-1974* and *Culture and Truth* as well as a bilingual collection of poems, *Prayer to Spider Woman/Rezo a la mujer araña*, which won an American Book Award in 2004. He is a member of the American Academy of Arts and Sciences.

José David Saldívar is a professor of English and ethnic studies at the University of California, Berkeley. He teaches literary and cultural studies, the history of the ethnic novel, inter-American subaltern studies, and Chicano/a studies. His articles have appeared in a number of journals, including *ALH* (American Literary History), *Daedalus: Journal of the Arts & Sciences*, *Nepantla*, and *Revista Casa de las Américas*. He serves on editorial boards of the University of California Press and *Revista Chicano-Riqueña* and the scholarly journals *ALH* and *Nepantla*. He has published several books, including *The Dialectics of Our America: Genealogy, Cultural Critique, and Literary History* (1991) and *Border Matters: Remapping American Cultural Studies* (1997), edited *The Rolando Hinojosa Reader* (1985), and coedited *Criticism in the Borderlands: Studies in Chicano Literature, Culture, and Ideology* (1991). He is currently working on a book on the War of 1898 and United States empire.

Marta E. Sánchez is a professor of literature at Arizona State University and professor emerita of the University of California San Diego where she taught Chicano, Latin American, and U.S. ethnic literatures from 1977 to 2004. She is the author of *Contemporary Chicana Poetry: A Critical Analysis of an Emerging Literature* (University of California Press, 1985), the first critical analysis of poetry by Chicanas. She has published articles in *Diacritics*, *MELUS*, *SigloXX/20th Century*, *American Literary History*, *American Literature*, *Genders*, and *PMLA*. Her new book, *"Shakin' Up" Race and Gender: Intercultural Connections in Puerto Rican, African*

American, and Chicano Narratives and Culture (1965-1995), was published by the University of Texas Press in 2005.

Rosaura Sánchez is a professor in the Department of Literature at UCSD. Her recent work is on California *testimonios* and, with Beatrice Pita, on María Amparo Ruiz de Burton. She also works on twentieth-century Chicano/a literature and Latin American literature.

Karen E. H. Skinazi teaches American literature at New York University, where she is currently finishing her Ph.D. Her dissertation, "Canadianation: Remapping the Popular Literature of the United States of North America" examines the significance of border-crossing and dual-national objectives in twentieth-century Canadian American writing.

Héctor Torres is an associate professor at the University of New Mexico in Albuquerque. He teaches courses on Chicana/o narrative, postmodern and poststructuralist theory, literary criticism, and linguistics. Currently, he is working on two manuscripts. They are "Temas y Discursos: Interviews with Chicana/o Writers of the Postmodern, 1990-2003" and "Writing Under Empire: Erasure, Postmodernism and Contemporary Chicana/o Literary Discourse."

Rosemary Weatherston is a professor of English and the director of the Dudley Randall Center for Print Culture at the University of Detroit Mercy, where she teaches in the fields of U.S. literature, critical theory, and cultural studies, and is the coeditor of the interdisciplinary journal *Post Identity*. Her essays, interviews, and reviews have appeared in *AUMLA, Discourse,* and *Theatre Journal,* and in the anthologies *Body Politics and the Fictional Double; Queer Frontiers: Millennial Geographies, Genders, and Generations;* and *A Different Image: The Legacy of Broadside Press*, which she coedited. She is currently completing a book-length project titled *Turning the Informant: The Making of Difference in Contemporary U.S. Literature and Culture.*

David N. Ybarra graduated with a degree in Chicano and Latino studies from Portland State University.